· M O S I M A N N'S ·

· W O R L D ·

MOSIMANN'S WORLD

B☐XTREE

First published in Great Britain in 1996 by Boxtree Limited,
Broadwall House, 21 Broadwall, London SE1 9PL

Text © Anton Mosimann 1996
Food photography © James Murphy 1996

The right of Anton Mosimann to be identifed as Author of this
work has been asserted by him in accordance with the
Copyright, Designs and patents Act 1988

1 3 5 7 9 10 8 6 4 2

ISBN 0 7522 0511 0

Designed by Hammond Hammond
Stylist – Roison Nield
Home economist – Kit Chan

Typeset by SX Composing DTP, Rayleigh, Essex
Printed and bound by Lego, Italy

A CIP catalogue entry for this book is available from the
British Library

CONTENTS

MOSIMANN'S WORLD

THE RECIPES

INTRODUCTION

One of the principal pleasures of my job is that I am enabled to travel. In fact, ever since I started my training as a chef, I have been lucky enough to work around the world, learning new aspects of my art as interpreted by different cuisines on different continents. I have lived and cooked in eight countries, but visited many, many more, and in each I have experienced new approaches, new combinations and new inspirations which have contributed to what I am and what I do today. I think a chef needs to be the eternal apprentice, for-

ever discovering, experimenting, questioning and adapting, and this is a quality I believe I still possess. May I never be too old to learn something new!

The reason I travelled so much in the past was not just to find out more about the food, the markets or the local produce, but to learn about the culture of individual peoples. I always like to discover as much as I can about people, and to understand them. I find it fascinating, for instance, that the Italians, who so love their food, talk passionately at high volume, using their hands all the time. The Japanese, however, although equally passionate about food, are quiet and

calm in temperament, and don't use their hands at all in conversation, in fact they don't even shake hands. Such differences in national character enthral me still, and one of the best ways of getting to the heart of a nation or culture is to watch the people cooking and eating. I still travel to all parts of the world to do just that, and I virtually plan what and where I am going to eat before I plan where I'm going to stay!

Most of my travels involve work in some way. I may be travelling to Thailand or India to cook for a night or a week in a hotel, or to South Africa to promote a new product, or to Germany or Switzerland to accept an award or to teach or demonstrate. Since 1992 I have been World President of Les Toques Blanches, a society whose membership is composed of chefs from all around the world. Wherever I go, therefore, I always meet fellow chefs, and we exchange ideas, take each other to the latest 'in' restaurant, or to the unassuming restaurant off the tourist track which serves the most authentic national or regional dish. My memories of countries I've visited, as might be expected, are mainly culinary ones, and even twenty years afterwards I can still call up the tastes and aromas of a particularly memorable dish or meal.

This book is a collection of recipes I have gathered over the years, many of which I have adapted from basic ideas, and some of which I have learned from colleagues all over the world. They should give a good overview of the diversity of tastes, textures and ingredients in the cooking of the five continents. I have also briefly explored aspects of the culinary fusions that historically have taken place all over the world, and which are still in train even today, most excitingly in Australia and New Zealand.

Mosimann's World is a celebration of the food of the world. I would also like to see it as a homage to all those who have worked with me over the years – the mentors in kitchens in Europe and Canada, foreign colleagues who have introduced me to their styles, techniques and ingredients, and friends and family who have indulged me in these passions.

SOUTHERN EUROPE

Southern Europe encompasses the countries which cluster along the north of the Mediterranean – Turkey, Greece, Italy, France and Spain – as well as Portugal which, like western Spain, has a long coastline on the Atlantic.

All of these countries are different in a cultural sense – with differing languages and differing customs – but they also share aspects of their history. Many great civilisations have dominated the region over the years, and this, as well as wars, migrations and trade (in goods, foods and people) has led to a certain blurring of geographical, political and cultural boundaries. At the same time, the countries have remained uniquely individual.

The cuisines rely on home or locally produced vegetables and fruit, and foods such as pasta, grains and pulses supplement small amounts of protein. Largely temperate, but with extremes of heat in summer, southern Europe has crops of wheat, olives and a rich variety of vegetables and fruit. The latter include, after the great explorations of the sixteenth century, introductions from the New World of plants such as tomatoes, sweet and chilli peppers, potatoes, corn, avocados, and kidney beans.

Onions and garlic are important basics in southern European cooking, and indeed garlic is synonymous in many peoples' minds with the cuisines of southern France and Spain. But it is the olive above all that characterises southern European food and cooking.

Herbs form another distinguishing characteristic, for it was in this part of the world that a large number of our present-day herbs originated – among them bay laurel, borage, coriander, fennel, hyssop, mint, parsley, rosemary, sage, savory and thyme. The Romans during their centuries of empire building were responsible for the spread of herbs from the Mediterranean throughout Europe.

SPAIN

The Iberian peninsula, composed of both Spain and Portugal, is the most westerly major land mass of Europe, with a long coastline on the Atlantic.

Spain has been a prize for many conquerors over the centuries. It was, however, Muslim Arabs, the Maures or Moors from Mauretania, the Roman province in North Africa, who were to have the most significant and lasting effect on Spain. They invaded across the Strait of Gibraltar in AD 711, and were to rule over most of the country for the next seven centuries. They introduced rice, aubergines, nuts, spinach, artichokes, sugarcane, figs, quinces, citrus fruits, peaches and many spices which are used a great deal in the cooking of Iberia still, as are almonds: many sauces for meat and poultry are thickened with almonds, a direct legacy of the Arabs, as are the many types of almond-based cakes and sweetmeats.

The Moors were not finally expelled from Spain until 1492, the year in which Christopher Columbus first set foot in the New World. This latter discovery led to immense wealth for Spain, and to the introduction to Europe of many new and significant foods – the tomato, sweet and hot peppers, turkey, kidney beans, potatoes and chocolate, all of which feature in the cooking of Iberia.

Spain today is a country with a characterful and strong culinary tradition, but one which is still regional in essence. I have visited Spain several times, and I have wonderful memories of paella with seafood and rabbit, and of the very freshest fish, simply grilled.

Geography plays a major part in Spain's regionality because, like Italy, the southern parts are more Mediterranean in feel. There, where olives and almonds grow in profusion, the influence of the Arabs still lingers. Andalucia is best known for fish dishes, and most of these are fried in olive oil. As a result the area is known as *zona de los fritos*, the 'zone of fried food'. Gazpacho originated here, as did many almond sweetmeats. Many egg yolk desserts all over Iberia were, historically, made in convents, the nuns having acquired surplus egg yolks from wine-makers using the whites for clarifying purposes. Andalucia is also the home of Jerez, or sherry, and of *jamón serrano*, the best of Spanish hams.

The coastal region of the Mediterranean known as the Levante comprises Murcia and Valencia, and is a fertile, semi-tropical plain. Here rice is cultivated as well as sugarcane, oranges and a variety of exotic fruits, many of them cropping twice a year.

The capital city of Spain sits in the centre of the land mass of Iberia, in New Castile, north of La Mancha. Here regional specialities include *manchego*, a hard cheese made from ewe's milk, and a three-course stew or *cocido* (*castellano* or *madrileno*), very like the *bollito misto* of Italy. The Spanish version of ratatouille, *pisto*, uses the prolific garlic and vegetables of La Mancha, and often has eggs scrambled into it. These same eggs appear in the famous tortillas, which are often a feature of the tapas (see box) served in bars in Madrid.

Old Castile and Rioja lie north of Madrid, in the heart of Spain, and here the influence of the Moors was less felt. The cooking relies primarily on meats – lamb, kid and suckling pig, plus game – and these are often roasted, thus the region is known as *zona de los asados*, 'zone of the roast foods'. Pork is more popular here, introduced by the Celts, and was welcomed after the centuries of Muslim rule when pork was proscribed. Vegetables grow in lush profusion as do grape vines, resulting in the wonderful wines of Rioja.

Aragon and Navarre sit on the border with France, where many vegetables and fruit are grown. *Bacalão* (dried salt cod) and eels are eaten, as are pork, lamb, trout and snails. Because of the popularity of chilindron sauce, made with tomatoes, red peppers, onion and garlic, and served with lamb or chicken, the area is often called *zona de los chilindrones*.

Catalonia is the region of Spain which has absorbed most influence from the rest of Europe, because of its common border with France, and Catalonia's gastronomy is revered by the rest of Spain. A particular feature of the cooking here is the number

---

TAPAS

I ate many tapas when I was in Spain, and they are a good casual way of eating. These highly spiced and delicious little snacks or dishes are served in advance or instead of a meal and they can consist of virtually anything – meatballs, small pies, fried aubergine slices, mushrooms in garlic, pepper and other vegetable salads, and a legion of fish dishes such as mussels, clams, prawns in garlic or prawn fritters, clams, and fresh anchovies. Tapas can be found in bars at any time of the day, and once were served free with a drink. The word *tapa* means cover or lid, from the habit of putting a slice of bread or cheese over a glass of wine or sherry to keep the flies away.

The 11th-century Castillo de Milmanda, Catalonia, set amongst rows of Chardonnay grapevines.

of basic sauces. These include *alioli*, *picada*, *chanfaina* and *romesco*.

There are a number of fish soups, including *zarzuela* and a *bullabesa* which is very like the French *bouillabaisse*, both in content and name. *Olla podrida*, the forerunner of the *cocidos* of elsewhere in Spain and the *cuzidos* of Portugal, are popular here, and there is a great charcuterie tradition. Flan, a caramel custard, is perhaps the most common dessert of Spain (as it is in Mexico, a former Spanish colony).

The Basque provinces are perhaps even more famous than Catalonia for their good food, and particularly for one aspect of their culinary culture. In the cities of San Sebastian and Bilbao, *cofradias* or gastronomic dining societies flourish. The Basques also established a new or nouvelle cuisine, La Nueva Cocina Vasca, in the early 1970s, and this has rekindled an interest in Spanish traditional foods all over Spain.

In Asturias and Galicia, regions to the far west and north, the fare is hearty, to match the cold weather. There are traditional bean stews, cabbage soups, pasta dishes, corn breads and dishes cooked with the local shellfish and cider.

Extremadura is the region which borders with Portugal to the west, and is rich in ingredients, particularly game, lamb, red peppers, wheat and charcuterie.

PORTUGAL

Portugal lies to the extreme west of the Iberian peninsula. Like Spain, it was overrun and ruled by the Moors until their expulsion, and the cuisine has also been influenced by Moorish and Arab introductions, ingredients and techniques, among them rice, quinces, oranges, olives, almonds and many spices. The cooking of Portugal makes a bold use of spices and herbs, and displays some startling combinations (pork with clams, for instance). Most of these exotic touches are a legacy of the colonial ambitions of the nation in the fifteenth and sixteenth centuries. Fresh leaf coriander is a native Mediterranean herb, for instance, but nowhere else in Europe is it used to such an extent as in Portugal, probably an influence from the East. Curry powder, too, is quite common in many Portuguese dishes.

These famous voyages of exploration were mainly in search of spices. Other ingredients were introduced as a result of the Spanish discovery of the New World. Portugal was one of the first countries to adopt the potato enthusiastically; potatoes still play an important part in the cooking. Chilli peppers are also a New World ingredient of significance; *piri-piri*, an extremely hot chilli sauce, is used as a spicy condiment with pasta, fish or meat, to flavour stews, and as an on-table sauce. (The peppers used in *piri-piri* originated in Mexico, were transplanted to Brazil, then to Africa, to Angola, where the name was acquired.)

Portugal divides roughly into north and south, as do Spain and Italy. In the colder northern regions, warming soups are common, among them the famous *caldo verde*, made with *couve*, a kale-like cabbage, and potato. All over Portugal, and Spain as well, roast suckling pig is a dish for celebrations, and especially famous are the pigs of Coimbra. Pig's kidneys are cooked in (white) port, the famous fortified wine made from grapes grown in the Douro valley, and which is shipped from Oporto, at the mouth of the river. I once visited this port-producing area, and had some memorable meals – and some memorable port! Here too the grapes are grown for vinhos verdes, 'green' or young, slightly *pétillant* red and white wines.

Bacalhao or dried salt cod is one of the most famous ingredients of Portuguese cooking. The passion for this arose, it is thought, when fishing boats sailing to Newfoundland (possibly before Columbus), salted and dried the cod for the long journey back. The Portuguese claim to have a *bacalhao* recipe for every day of the year, including leap years, and most dishes are served with potatoes.

SOUTHERN FRANCE

Southern France encompasses the Basque country, the Pyrenees and Gascony, the Languedoc, and Provence.

Here, because of climate, the agriculture and the cooking are typically Mediterranean, and the crops include olives, grapes, fruits and flowers, rice and many vegetables. Garlic and olive oil are early introductions, and they are dominant ingredients; the many pungent flavours of the region are possibly the legacy of the Romans and Greeks – tapenade and anchoiade, for instance.

Spain has influenced the cooking of these parts of France, and there are many similarities in dishes and ingredients, particularly in the Basque country, and where the Roussillon and Catalonia meet. Further east, many Provençal dishes tend towards the Italian with ravioli, cannelloni and gnocchi (the latter's name coming from a Provençal rather than Italian word). *Pissaladière* is virtually indistinguishable from pizza, and *pistou* is the Italian pesto minus the pine kernels.

Here, too, the influence of the New World is felt. Tomatoes and peppers, both from the Americas, are used a great deal in the cooking, as they are just across the Spanish and Italian borders.

Basque cooking in France is not dissimilar to the Basque cooking of Spain. Red peppers, sweet and piquant, are the dominant vegetable, and a dish christened *à la basquaise* usually contains peppers. *Piment d'Espelette*, a small hot pepper, is widely used. *Pipérade*, sautéed sweet peppers with eggs scrambled into them, is virtually the same as the Spanish *piperrada*. Tuna, sardines and anchovies are the principal fish, but salt cod, salted anchovies and salted pork are popular too; the ham of Bayonne is cured with salt and dried Espelette peppers. Bayonne also makes a nougat, *touron* (like Spanish *turron*), and chocolate (thought to have been brought from Spain by Jews fleeing the Spanish Inquisition).

The country of the Béarn, north of the Pyrenees, is the birth place of *poule au pot*, the variant of pot-au-feu that uses chicken, and there are many warming *garbures* or vegetable soups. Sometimes these latter can be enriched by pieces of duck or goose *confit*, for this and the neighbouring Gascony are the home of *foie gras* and thus *confit*. Many local dishes also use goose or duck fat for cooking in preference to the omnipresent olive oil. And the pride of the region is Armagnac, the first brandy of France, in which many fruits are bottled.

The Roussillon, the area on the Spanish border, is very Catalonian in feel, featuring peppers and olives, and there is some Arab spicing. Further inland from the Mediterranean, in the Languedoc, the flavourings are more traditionally French, with olive oil, much garlic, and many wild herbs from the *garrigue* (Mediterranean scrubland), such as thyme, rosemary, savory and fennel. Cassoulet is the most famous dish of the Languedoc, and each town has its own version; that of Toulouse is reckoned to be the richest of all. The hills of the Languedoc provide grazing for sheep, whose milk is made into Roquefort cheese; this is cured in limestone caves, the only environment in which the penicillin mould specific to Roquefort will grow.

On the Mediterranean coast, the lagoons stretching from south to north and round to the Camargue, are rich in fish and shellfish, such as mussels and clams, and all of these can form part of *bourride*, the fish soup which is cousin to the Provençal *bouillabaisse*. Salt cod and hake are popular here as well. In the marshy Camargue, where the Rhône delta meets the Mediterranean, there are salt pans and green paddy fields – the only place in France that has the right conditions for rice cultivation.

The Rhône marks the border between the Languedoc and Provence, and east of the river, the cooking becomes truly Mediterranean in style. Dishes styled Provençal are usually cooked with olive oil and garlic, but many other dishes sing with flavours thought to typify Provence. Ratatouille is probably the most famous and is closely related to similar dishes all round the Mediterranean.

Nice has named the salad which uses tuna, tomatoes, anchovies, lettuce, beans, olives and hard-boiled eggs, *salade Niçoise*.

Wild and aromatic herbs symbolise Provence for many, for they perfume the air in the countryside, and are used to make essential oils for perfumes at Grasse. Perhaps the most interesting feature of Provençal cooking is the number of pungent, thick, olive oil-based sauces, which are generally served with bread or crudités, and olives, salt cod, hard-boiled eggs and other accompaniments. Anchoiade is made with anchovies, one of the principal Provençal flavours, and these pungent fish are also used in the olive purée, tapenade, along with capers. The other three sauces are *aïoli*, *rouille* and *pistou*, all served as above, or with soups – bouillabaisse, bourride, *soupe de poissons* and *soupe au pistou*. Bouillabaisse is the primary fish soup of the region and is traditionally made with Mediterranean fish only.

I have very fond memories of Provence, primarily because I worked for a while with Roger Vergé at Le Moulin des Mougins in Cannes. I also loved Corsica, the French island south-east of Provence. It is Italian in influence primarily, with interesting charcuterie (prisutto, raw ham, and coppa).

ITALY

Italy's cuisine is very regional, and utilises good, fresh ingredients, preparing and cooking them carefully and in simple ways.

It remains intensely regional – the city states which formed the country did not become unified until as late as 1861 – but it is often divided into two basic threads: in the north of the country the basic ingredients are rice, polenta, meat, butter and cheese, while pasta, fish, vegetables and olive oil dominate in the south.

The differences are becoming blurred though. Pasta has always been more associated with the south. It is now popular all

The ingredients for a typical bouillabaisse.

Making pasta and ravioli in a Tuscan kitchen.

over the country, although it didn't become so universal an Italian dish until the turn of the century. One commentator has recorded no less than 650 basic shapes of dried pasta. However, regional differences still exist; generally speaking, the pasta of the north is of the flat ribbon type, while that of the south is rounder, larger and more robust in shape.

Another famous dish known all over the country is minestrone. As Marcella Hazan says, 'a vegetable soup will tell you where you are in Italy almost as precisely as a map', and she cites the tomato, garlic and olive oil of southern soups, the dried beans in the soups of the centre, and the rice of the north. Virtually any vegetable, though, can be cooked in a minestrone, and the soups are very seasonal.

Although pasta is eaten in the north of Italy, rice grown in the valley of the Po River, introduced in the mid fifteenth century, is just as significant. This is used in *risotto primavera* (young spring vegetables) and *risi e bisi* (rice and peas, a soup) of Venice, the saffron and marrow

risotto of Milan, and the *risotto nero* (black with squid or cuttlefish ink) of Florence. Another speciality of the north is a wild mushroom risotto topped, in the season, with shavings of white truffle. Gnocchi or dumplings also originated in the north, in Piedmont, but are now popular all over Italy.

Polenta too is more northern, and this basic 'porridge' would once have been made with millet before maize was introduced in the sixteenth century. It is cooked to be served wet, or left to go cold, cut into shapes, and then fried or grilled.

Because of the climate, cattle can be bred in the north, and thus beef, veal and dairy produce are more readily available. Beef is a major constituent of the famous *bollito misto*, mixed boiled meats, of the northern regions. Most of the famous Italian veal dishes come from the north as well, the best *osso buco* from Milan, and the best calves' liver dish from Venice.

The milk from the cows of the north is used in some of Italy's famous cheeses, most notably Parmesan, Fontina,

Gorgonzola, Bel Paese and mascarpone. The same regions produce the pigs for *prosciutto di Parma*, or Parma ham. The pig is also responsible for a legion of preserved meats and sausages.

Fish from the northern Adriatic are plentiful and include spider crabs, soft-shell crabs, sardines, scampi, monkfish and sole. On the Mediterranean side, there is a multitude of fish and shellfish, including the *vongole* or clams which ally so magically with pasta.

In the south of Italy, the emphasis is more on pasta, fish and vegetables than on meat. The vegetables which grow so prolifically in the southern sun are eaten raw, cooked by themselves, used in pasta sauces, preserved in olive oil or dried in the sun. Broad beans and artichokes are particular specialities of Rome, the latter being stuffed with a mixture of finely cut mint, parsley and garlic. Aubergines are cooked in a huge variety of recipes in Calabria (the toe of Italy) – stuffed, marinated, layered with Parmesan, fried and preserved.

The sun-ripened tomatoes of the south

are made into sauces for pasta (the shapes including cannelloni, macaroni, penne and rigatoni), or for the base of a pizza, which originated in Naples, a city famous for its pastry cooks. I remember going to a pizzeria in Naples where the oven was bigger than the restaurant. The pizza also uses another of the south's principal products, mozzarella cheese.

Roman dishes are a combination of ideas unique to the ancient city, and borrowings from other regions. Great Roman seasonal favourites are *abbachio al forno*, roast milk-fed lamb, and roast kid and suckling pigs. I worked one summer in Rome, as a young chef, at the Cavalieri Hilton. It was my first job away from Switzerland, and tastes, aromas and lessons learned at that time are still with me. I would visit my colleagues' families at weekends, and their mothers always seemed to have been working all day to produce a wonderful Sunday lunch, starting with perfect home-made pasta, and I will never forget a truly memorable dish I had on the island of Capri: ravioli of goat's cheese and spinach, served simply with melted butter infused with sage.

Every town and village on the southern Adriatic coastline has a sea or freshwater fish dish, and many recipes involve anchovies. In Naples, though, seafood is a way of life, and octopus, cuttlefish, sardines, eels and clams are all used, often together in a marine *fritto misto*.

GREECE

Greece is situated in the eastern Mediterranean, a mainland land mass with a plethora of archipelagos and islands to the south. I have never visited Greece, but I had a Greek girlfriend when I lived and worked in Montreal. She would cook Greek dishes for me, and I love Greek food to this day.

Ancient Greece was famed for good food, and it is said that every rich Roman wanted to have a Greek chef. However, after many invasions and occupations, the civilisation declined, and the style of cooking inevitably changed, influenced by those of the invaders. The Venetians brought pasta dishes to Greece, but perhaps the most significant occupation – it lasted for four centuries – was that of the Ottoman Turks. They brought with them a style of cooking that was more Arab in influence, but which bore traces of many of the other countries over which they held sway. This explains why many dishes in Greece and Turkey today, and all over the Middle East, are so similar in concept and in name.

Waterside restaurants in Chania old harbour, Crete.

The most obvious characteristic of Greek food now, however, is the freshness of the ingredients and the simplicity of the preparation: some *mezze* (see box), a plain grilled fish or meat on skewers, a Greek salad, and perhaps a sweet pastry.

Beef pasture is rare, so lamb is very much the principal meat, although some pork is eaten. Meat usually features in *souvlaki* kebabs, very much a Turkish influence, stews such as *kleftiko* (very slow roasted lamb on the bone), and composite dishes such as moussaka. Fish and seafood are popular, and are cooked plainly, on a charcoal grill seasoned with the local herb, *rigani* (wild oregano).

Lemons and olive oil are perhaps the two principal flavours of Greece. Both are important in the two savoury dips popular as a first course or as part of a *mezze*: hummus, which is made from chickpeas and tahina (sesame seed paste) and taramasalata, made from grey mullet roe (or, more usually, smoked cod's roe).

Aubergines are a major vegetable in Greece as they are all over the Balkans and the Middle East. They are puréed for a cold dip, *melitzanosalata* (very similar to many other Middle Eastern purées), and they are an ingredient for moussaka. The ubiquitous Greek salad is spiked with black olives and cubes of feta, the local salty and tangy ewe's milk cheese. Halloumi, another sheep cheese, is usually grilled in slices as part of a *mezze*. Sheep's milk is also made into a gloriously creamy yoghurt, another leaning towards the Middle East.

Pitta bread – a flattened, oval, slightly leavened bread – is common to most Middle Eastern countries; it has a hollow running through it which can be stuffed with a variety of ingredients from salads and cheese to kebabs. Vegetables are stuffed too, as they are in Turkey and elsewhere. Filo pastry, another ingredient shared with Turkey, is used in baklava.

MEZZE

It is through Greek restaurants that most of us have become acquainted with *mezze*, but it is a style of eating, a way of life almost, that is common to the whole of the Middle East and parts of North Africa. This selection of hot and cold appetisers can include cubes of feta, bowls of taramasalata, hummus and tzatziki served with pitta bread, some plump green pickled chilli peppers and gleaming black olives, *dolmades*, *börek* (both more Turkish in style) or some slices of hot, charcoal-browned halloumi. In restaurants, these starters would be followed by a selection of small fish dishes – prawns, red mullet fillets, circles of deep-fried squid – and then by meat, a *souvlaki* kebab, a *sheftalia* (a caul-wrapped sausage), and perhaps a lamb cutlet.

TURKEY

Turkey lies in the eastern Mediterranean, acting as a bridge between Europe and Asia. The great empire once enjoyed by the Ottoman Turks enriched Turkish cooking enormously, and the style absorbed many influences throughout the centuries – those of Greece, Venice, the Arab world, and further afield, even those as far away as India. Turkish cooking today is thus very varied and exotic. It is very similar to Greek cooking (because of the Turkish occupation of Greece for around four centuries). Turkish cooking is somewhat spicier and fruitier, though, an influence from the Arabs and the East. Another Middle Eastern ingredient is yoghurt, used in soups, dressings and sauces for fish, meat and vegetables. Ewes' milk also makes cheeses very similar to those of Greece, which are used in *börek*.

Another principal influence is that of religion, for in Muslim Turkey certain foods are proscribed, among them pork. Lamb, as in the whole of the Middle Eastern area, is the principal meat, and shish kebab is probably Turkey's most famous dish. It is said to have been invented during the Ottoman Turk campaigns, when soldiers were obliged to cook on open fires, skewering their meat with their swords ('sis' means sword). Lamb is also stewed, with tomatoes and beans, and when minced, is used as a stuffing for vine leaves.

Turkey shares the Middle Eastern passion for stuffed vegetables, among them tomatoes, aubergines, peppers and courgettes. Aubergines are a particular favourite and they are cooked to flavourful purées which can form part of a *mezze*. As in Greece, rice often forms part of vegetable stuffings, and rice is very significant in Turkish cooking. The *pilavs* served as side dishes or cooked with meats and vegetables are very similar to the *pullaos* of India, and the *polos* of Iran.

The long coastlines of Turkey produce an abundance of fish and shellfish, most of which are cooked and served fairly simply as in Greece. I visited Istanbul some years ago for a food promotion, and had some wonderful swordfish.

Turkey has a number of very sweet desserts, including baklava and kadaif (shredded wheat pastry) and other syrup drenched pastries which glory in names like 'ladies navels'. The most famous sweetmeat, however, must be *rahat lokum* or Turkish delight; a jelly paste containing green pistachios and coated with icing sugar.

NORTHERN EUROPE

As in southern Europe, all the northern countries are different, with differing languages, climates and cultures, but they too, to a certain extent, share a history. Many of them were invaded by or invaded other countries in the area, and Britain for instance has seen incursions of many peoples, including the Saxons, Angles, Jutes and, later, the Vikings and Normans. It was the Romans, though, who carved out the greatest empire, one which stretched from North Africa to the borders of England and Scotland, encompassing the bulk of the countries of continental Europe. In a culinary sense, the Roman occupation meant an introduction to northern Europe of many fruit and nut trees, and herbs, and the cultivation and use of these in cooking would undoubtedly have become familiar to the native peoples.

The moderate to cold climate and fertile lands has meant a shared cultivation of many hardier vegetables and fruits – potatoes and other root vegetables, cabbages and apples. There is also a shared tendency towards heavier foods, a characteristic of colder countries. Lush pastures have made possible the rearing of beef and dairy cattle, as well as sheep and pigs, and thus the diet of northern Europe is largely meat based, and the principal cooking fats come from animals – butter, lard, dripping, with some duck and goose fat in parts of France. Very few of these meats, because of their quality, have needed elaborate cooking, and a lot of meat cookery in northern Europe is historically rather plain. The abundance of meats, and the weather conditions – long snow-bound winters when food gathering is impossible – have led to many techniques of preservation of meats, particularly pork, such as salting, drying and smoking. Many northern European countries have wonderful hams and sausages.

These preservation methods are applied to fish as well, and fish and shellfish, abundant in the cold waters around northern Europe, are an important part of the diet, particularly in Scandinavia.

NORTHERN FRANCE

Northern France includes the whole of the country apart from the southern departments which are more Mediterranean in influence (see Southern Europe). Northern France has been less affected by outside influence than the south, but the Romans were still important, bringing with them their herbs and fruit and nut trees.

There are two faces to Brittany in a culinary sense – its long deeply indented coastline, and its agricultural interior. All around the coast, fish and seafood are of necessity major ingredients, and the *cotriades* or fish stews, and dishes of mussels cooked *à la marinière*, are justly famous. Fishing remains a major occupation, as it has been for centuries. Breton fisherman sailed as far as Newfoundland and Iceland in search of cod in the seventeenth and eighteenth centuries. It was they, in fact, who are said to have introduced the idea of fish chowders to the eastern coast of America. Another speciality of the coastal area is *pré-salé* lamb, the young lamb fed on land reclaimed from the salt marshes near St Malo (engineered by the Dutch, experts in keeping the sea at bay). The famous Breton crêpes and galettes which can act as wrappers for so many foods, savoury and sweet, are made from buckwheat. There are also a number of traditional batter puddings, known as *fars*.

Brittany's neighbour to the east, Normandy, has a long coastline, too. A dish that is offered in restaurants all along the coast is *plateau de fruits de mer*, a seafood platter. The fish that reigns supreme, though, is the Dover sole, and it is cooked in innumerable ways, most famously *à la normande*, with local cider and cream, and garnished with the Norman 'grey' shrimps and mussels.

The apples grown for that cider are another characteristic ingredient of Normandy, the sweetness being used in many superb apple pies and distilled into Calvados (apple brandy).

Much cream is eaten in Normandy, for the black and white dairy cattle produce hundreds of gallons of milk per day; fine butter makes for many pastries and biscuits. Normandy lays claim to brioche, the name perhaps coming from an Old Norman word for kneading.

Pigs are widely bred in Normandy, and their meat is made into *boudin noir*, blood sausage, and *andouilles*. The latter are thought to be the origin of similar sausages in the American Cajun south, as many of the original inhabitants of Acadia came from Normandy and Brittany.

Champagne and the North includes Paris, Flanders, Picardy and the wooded hills of the Ardennes and, as the area borders on Belgium, it shares many culinary characteristics with Belgian cuisine. Pork offal goes into the making of many pâtés, *andouillettes* and other sausages, and many meat dishes are enclosed in pastry. Along the coast a particular speciality is herring, lightly salted as *harengs saurs*, and served with vinaigrette and hot potato salad.

Vegetables are very northern: cabbage is cooked with juniper berries, leeks are baked in a tart, and onions are cooked to a purée for a *sauce picarde*, or baked in the oven for the famous onion soup of Les Halles market.

The eastern departments of Alsace and Lorraine, bordering on Germany and Switzerland, only became part of France in the seventeenth and eighteenth centuries, and their cooking very much shows the influences of their neighbours. The Germanic one is particularly strong in Alsace, with the locals cooking *choucroûte* (*sauerkraut*), *spätzli*, noodles, potato and other dumplings and many excellent German-style fresh and smoked pork sausages. Strasbourg is actually known as the sausage capital of France.

Freshwater fish from the lakes of the region and the three major rivers – the Rhine, Moselle and Meuse – are cooked simply; truite '*au bleu*', for instance. Poultry is a major industry, with goose the most valued. This appears as the famous Michaelmas goose in both Alsace and Lorraine, stuffed with apples or chestnuts, but it is its liver which is most valued. The *foie gras* of Alsace is thought to be as good as, if not better than, that of the Périgord.

Lorraine specialises in egg dishes, not least the quiches which have become so famous, and in many sweet cakes and biscuits. But the best known product of all is Alsace wine, in style like those from across the Rhine.

Franche Comté is above all dairy country. The cheeses are made on the Swiss model, with Gruyère and Emmenthal as well as the local Comté, and dishes such as *fondue savoyard* and cheese croûtes and chicken or veal cooked in cheese sauces. Beef is air-dried like that of Grisons in Switzerland.

With Lake Geneva marking the border between France and Switzerland, many Savoyard specialities are similar to those of the Swiss; both cook the *féra* and *omble chevalier* or char found in the deep cold waters of the lake, as well as eels, pike, trout and perch.

Further south, where Savoie and the Dauphiné mark France's border with Italy, long-time Italian influence is apparent. Walnuts are made into oil, and walnuts and apricots appear in rich dessert tarts. Pasta and noodles are not uncommon.

Dairy produce is important in Savoie and the Dauphiné, and both milk and cream and cheese are used in the famous potato gratins of the area.

Burgundy is said to be the centre of gastronomic France, and has been since the fourteenth century. In an area blessed by some of the great rivers of the country grow the grapes for many of the most famous wines of France. The best beef and chickens in the country come from Burgundy: Charolais cattle in one of the slow-cooked stews of the area, such as *boeuf à la bourguignonne*, and Bresse chickens, seen at their best in something like *coq au vin*.

Lyons to the south is the city in which the restaurant tradition is said to have begun, with the rise of '*les mères*', the women cooks of the city. Burgundy and the Lyonnais are still home to many of the best chefs in France. Lyons is famous for its charcuterie, with fresh pork and garlic sausages, *andouillettes*, and types of salami.

Along its length, particularly in Aragon and Touraine, the valley is rich in fruit, including the grapes for the many wines of the Loire, and vegetables. Pears are poached in red wine, apricots, greengages and apples are made into many wonderful and unique fruit tarts, among them the original *tarte tatin*, and plums are dried for prunes to be cooked in white wine or to accompany pork. The grapes themselves are often used to accompany game birds such as partridge. Another speciality of the Loire valley and Tours is pork *rillettes*.

In the centre of France rises a great volcanic plateau which stretches into the Bourbonnais, the Limousin, the Auvergne and the Berry. The peaks of the Auvergne are a range of extinct volcanoes, and here green-blue lentils – *lentilles du Puy* – take their colour from the volcanic soil. They are cooked with salt pork and some of the many game birds of the area.

The volcanic soil of the Massif Central is also a good medium for wild mushrooms, and these are layered with potatoes into a gratin; potatoes are also baked with cream inside puff pastry for a rich pie.

In the Limousin, beef and veal are bred, and the local speciality is *clafoutis*, a batter pudding made with tart black cherries – which are also cooked with duck.

A flock of free-range *foie gras* geese.

Stretching from its northern border with Brittany, the area designated the South-West encompasses Poitou, the Vendée, Charentes, Guyenne and the Landes, and includes Quercy, Périgord and the Dordogne. Bordeaux dominates the area, both because of its size, and because of the wines which have brought it its prosperity. It is a gastronomic city which can call upon the riches of the Atlantic, and those of the rich agricultural land surrounding it. Beef from Charentes is cut into steaks for a Bordeaux speciality, *entrecôte à la bordelaise* (with wine and bone marrow). Cognac and Armagnac, both specialities of the region, are used in much of the meat cookery, as are truffles, the black truffles of Périgord and Quercy. The other famous product of Périgord is *foie gras*, the fatty livers of force-fed geese. Of the geese themselves (and duck as well) nothing is wasted; the carcasses and other offal are used for soup or in pâtés, the limbs and flesh in *confits*, preserved in the natural rendered fat of the bird.

GREAT BRITAIN AND IRELAND

Most cuisines borrow from others, and do not stay permanently immune to infiltration from outside, but the cooking of Britain has perhaps been more open to this than others because of its geography – two main islands tucked into the lee of a great continental land mass – which made it subject from the earliest times to invasion and occupation.

The culinary basis on which these influences were to have their effect was one of seasonal food, plainly cooked. The Romans were probably the first to influence British cooking, during their 400 or so years' occupation. Invasions from Angles, Saxons and Scandinavians had an effect too. The Saxons introduced good farming practice, and the Scandinavians brought methods of preservation such as smoking and drying, of fish in particular. The famous Aberdeen Angus beef cattle are thought to have developed from Scandinavian stock.

The Norman Conquest of 1066 introduced the cooking styles of France. These Gallic refinements, however, were confined to the court and the homes of wealthier Britons. The poor, those who lived far from the trading centres (in Scotland, Wales, Ireland and the north of England), remained to a large extent unaffected by culinary change. Theirs remained a plainer and simpler tradition and this was to form the bases of regional British cooking.

Tiers of herring in a Scottish smokehouse.

In the Middle Ages, many exotic ingredients were imported and used in British cooking, particularly spices, and the foods of the wealthy were heavily flavoured by cloves, mace, nutmeg, galingale, cubeb and grains of paradise. Pepper was considered so valuable that it was used as money or tribute.

Much later, during the sixteenth and seventeenth centuries, a significant introduction to British cooking was that of the potato. By 1650 it had become the staple food of Ireland, which was to lead to the tragic devastation caused by the potato blight in 1845; in that one-crop country, it is estimated that up to a million died of starvation.

The British Empire was to add more threads to the already polyglot patchwork of British cooking. The medieval passion for spices was rekindled by the foods encountered in India during the years of the Raj – mulligatawny soup, chutneys and ketchups among them. Kedgeree, a rice and lentil

dish originally, now fish and rice, is truly representative of what became known as Anglo-Indian cooking, for it exists properly in neither British nor Indian cuisine.

The essential 'plainness' of British cooking is most evident in poultry, meat and game recipes. The renowned roast beef of England was originally cooked on a spit over or beside the fire, the fat dripping into a tray below, in which the equally famous Yorkshire pudding would be cooked.

In casserole and stew dishes, the emphasis once again is on a basic simplicity. I must admit to a weakness for boiled silverside, boiled beef with carrots, and a slowly braised oxtail. Lancashire hotpot is lamb topped with potatoes in a tall pot, and variants of this one-pot, whole-meal stew are found all over Great Britain. Irish stew is perhaps the most famous, and it would originally have been made with the dispensable young male kid or lamb, not mutton. There is a strong tradition of pork and bacon cookery all over Great Britain.

Chicken was a special treat for many British families until well into the twentieth century, because good egg-layers were far too valuable to eat until they became tough and old. Boiling fowl is used in the elegant combination of leeks, chicken and prunes of the Scottish cock-a-leekie, perhaps the nearest idea in British cookery to a *bollito misto* or *cocido*.

Pastry pies seem to be a British speciality. They probably evolved because foods inside a casing were easier to transport and eat before the fork came into general use. The tradition continues today, whether savoury (steak and kidney or pork pies, and the humbler Cornish pasty and Forfar bridie) or sweet (made with fruits such as apple, still spiced with its medieval clove). Many of these pies, even the savoury ones, were very sweet at one time, and one such was the forerunner of the modern Christmas 'mince' pie, now without meat.

The concept of savoury puddings echoes that of the pastry pie – a mixture of ingredients contained and cooked in a casing. The rich would cook steak and kidney in suet pastry and often oysters would be slipped under the crust at the last moment. (Mushrooms are used nowadays, instead of expensive oysters, but 150 years or so ago, mushrooms would have been much rarer, whereas oysters were commonplace and cheap.) Poorer households would use fillings of a cereal such as oats with some flavouring (blood, offal or onion). Some of these puddings were enclosed in the stomach bag or intestines of animals. The Scottish haggis, black and white puddings, and sausages are relics of this.

Wonderful game is found in Britain – venison, hare, rabbit, partridge, wild duck, woodcock, pigeon and pheasant and the unique grouse.

No part of Britain is further than 60 miles from the sea, so there is plentiful seafood. Atlantic salmon, caught in Scottish and Irish rivers, fresh or smoked over oak, are unique British delicacies.

In Scotland there are mussel stew-soups and smoked fish soups; herrings or river trout are coated in oatmeal and fried in bacon fat, or simply grilled. From Cornwall, Norfolk and Scotland come fresh crabs, which are simply dressed, or potted with butter. Deep-fried whitebait are another speciality, as are Dover sole and eels.

Some of the vegetables grown in Britain, such as English asparagus, are very special. The tiny Jersey new potatoes which appear briefly in the spring taste sweet and of the volcanic soil in which they grow. I love them. Peas are another traditional British vegetable, and I almost caused a revolution at The Dorchester, when I replaced them on the daily menu with mangetouts!

Many wonderful fruits are grown in Britain, among them many varieties of apples, pears and members of the plum family such as greengages and damsons. There are a multitude of soft fruits and berries used in many jams, jellies and chutneys, and in the famous British desserts, particularly summer puddings.

It was these that most intrigued me when I first encountered them. Many of the hot puddings were rather heavy. All of them taste wonderful though, especially when accompanied by a well-made custard. This sauce in itself is the basis of many characteristic British puddings, among them custard tarts and pies, trifle, bread and butter pudding, and the famous burnt cream (the British equivalent of *crème brûlée*). Bread and butter pudding has virtually become my 'signature' dish, and I recently cooked it in Atlanta for 500 people, at the request of ex-president, Jimmy Carter. Fruit pies as opposed to tarts seem to be uniquely British, as do many other fruit desserts such as crumbles or fools. In early 1996 I won an award in Germany (presented by the wife of Chancellor Kohl), and I served a traditional blackberry and apple crumble as thanks.

Many of these desserts are based on, or use, milk or cream, for the climate of Britain is perfect for dairy as well as beef cattle. Butter is the principal fat, used in baking and cooking, and as a preservative in potted foods (as goose or duck fat would be in France, or olive oil in Italy). There are many milk puddings such as junket, and cream-based puddings such as syllabub and the Scottish *cranachan*.

And as for baking, there is such a strong regional tradition of cakes, teacakes, scones, pancakes and breads that an entire new meal, that of afternoon tea, had to be invented in Britain to do justice to them.

THE NETHERLANDS

Eponymously low-lying, much of The Netherlands has been reclaimed from the sea, and there is a precarious balance between land and sea, held in check by a system of canals and dykes, and by constant vigilance.

Germany is a major influence on the cooking of Holland, and the Dutch are as fond of hearty wholesome eating as the Germans. Dairy products are a major feature of Dutch cooking – cheeses such as Edam and Gouda, and butter, which is used in a rich tradition of butter pastries, cakes and biscuits. *Speculaas*, for instance, are spiced biscuits very akin to many others baked throughout Europe at Christmas time. They come in the shape of windmills or of St Nicholas himself.

With the long coastline and inland waters, the Dutch enjoy many fish and shellfish, including eel, oysters and mussels. They like salt cod too. The favourite fish, though, is herring (as it is all along this northern mainland European coast), and it is sold raw from street stalls, and eaten in the hand as a street snack.

The Netherlands once had a huge empire in the east, and perhaps the most surprising element of Dutch cuisine is the *Rijstaffel* or 'rice table', which is a direct importation from the former Indonesian colonies. The Dutch have also exported *Rijstaffel* to Surinam, their colony in the north of South America.

BELGIUM

Belgium, with a short coastline on the North Sea, consists of a geographical region much fought over throughout its history, and only became an independent kingdom in 1830. The country is culturally divided still, one part of the population in Flanders to the north speaking a dialect of Dutch or Flemish, the remainder in the south, the Walloons, speaking French.

The Belgians like to eat, and they have large appetites. The cooking is not dissimilar to that of The Netherlands and Germany, but it is more delicate. It is essentially provincial, but there are common features: pork is the favourite meat, cooked all over the country and made into wonderful hams in Flanders and the Ardennes in the south; vegetables are of supreme importance, most of them grown in the country itself; and many dishes are cooked with beer, the national drink of the country. Another thread has survived since medieval times, as it does in other countries, notably Belgium's neighbour Germany: the combination of sweet and sour in one dish.

The Belgian dishes that have become famous were regional specialities before they became 'national'. These include *Waterzooi*, a fragrant fish soup which originated in Ghent in the north. This soup can in fact be made with rabbit and chicken as well. With access to many rivers, eels are a seasonal speciality, and these are eaten with a green herb sauce. Mussels are a national passion, even in regions far from the sea; they are cooked with onion, celery, parsley and white wine, and eaten with *frites* or thin chips; essential accompaniments are mustard or mayonnaise for the *frites*, and black pepper for the mussels.

Carbonnade à la Flamande or, in Flemish, *Vlaamse Karbonaden*, must be one of the most famous of Belgian dishes. It is local beef braised in local beer, and it is cooked all over the country. *Carbonnade* should be made with a traditional *gueuze*, a very special beer which comes from the region around Brussels.

Trout dishes and game stews are a speciality of the Ardennes in the south, a region of hills, moors, rivers and forests, and many of these stews are cooked with dark sauces spiked with juniper, one of the principal spices of Belgian cooking. The aromatic ham of the Ardennes is smoked over juniper wood, and juniper is the flavouring of *genever* or gin, which is said to have been first produced in Belgium.

I worked in Brussels for a while before I started at The Dorchester, first at the famous Villa Lorraine in Brussels, the only restaurant outside France to have been awarded three stars by the Guide Michelin. I learned a lot from the chef, Camille Lurkin, a small man who smoked cigars nearly as big as himself! I also spent some time in another Brussels restaurant, L'Ecailler du Palais Royal, which specialised in fish. It was owned by M. Kreusch, who had got the idea from visits to restaurants like Bentley's and Wheeler's in London. I still love Brussels; it's a foodie city, one which is very close to my heart.

GERMANY

Germany has a short 500-mile coastline on the North Sea and the Baltic Sea, divided by the peninsula that is Denmark. Many frontier changes and political and social upheavals, particularly those of the last 100 years, have all had a considerable effect on the cooking and eating habits of Germany.

In northern Germany, a number of dishes have been influenced by the proximity of Scandinavia, Poland and Russia. The food here tends to be heavier than in other regions, and considerable amounts of potatoes and other root vegetables are eaten. Vegetables such as cabbage and broad beans are grown as well.

Pork is the most popular meat in Germany, and Westphalia to the north-west is famous for hams, speciality meats and sausages, traditionally eaten with dark, aro-

An open-air *Wurst* or sausage stall in Berlin.

matic pumpernickel bread (which originated there as well); these are washed down with Steinhager, a clear schnapps made from juniper berries. This is a classic combination, because Germany is famous for the almost infinite variety of sausages, of breads (at least 200), and of schnapps and other flavoured spirits.

The cooking of the north has many fish dishes, and herring takes pride of place: the types available include *matjes* herring fillets, rollmops, and buckling. Smoked fish are common and they include sprats and eel. Eel is the major ingredient in a Hamburg speciality soup. This displays a characteristic northern German combination of sweet and sour, or bitter, flavours: and this is also seen in many other generally northern dishes. Fruits, often dried, are cooked with or served as a sauce for pork, venison, tongue and goose dishes. Fresh apples, for instance, are added also to beef dishes, to a potato purée (known as *Himmel und Erde*, heaven and earth, and served with blood sausages), to cabbage salads and to *sauerkraut*, perhaps the most famous, and one of the oldest, of German dishes.

In the Rhineland to the west, the confluence of so many great rivers means that freshwater fish are available, among them

carp, pike and trout. Carp is traditionally served on Christmas Eve when it is simmered in a beer-flavoured stock, and served with a sauce thickened with gingerbread or *Lebkuchen* crumbs.

Frankfurt stands on the river Main, and lays claim to a famous German export, the definitive Frankfurter sausage. Another speciality is a green sauce which contains up to eight different herbs. The Main divides Germany in half in a culinary sense, and even culinary terms change: dumplings called *Klosse* in the north become *Knödel* in the south. Here potatoes are eaten more in the form of dumplings, and various types of pasta noodles are also used as an accompaniment to meats. *Spätzle*, 'little sparrows', are from Swabia to the south-west, close to Switzerland, where such small pasta shapes are familiar as well. The meats they accompany are hearty and generous – Black Forest venison, and pot-roasts such as *Sauerbraten*. Interestingly, versions of *Sauerbraten* were taken from Germany to the USA where they feature in Pennsylvania Dutch country; these were probably the origin of the famous American pot-roasts. Perhaps the best-known creation of the Black Forest is its *Kirschtorte*, a chocolate sponge cake with cherries and a Kirsch-flavoured cream. The

A selection of cakes on offer in a German pastry shop.

area is rich in fruit orchards, and some of these fruit are eaten in pancakes, layered in strudel pastry, or tucked into dumplings.

The Alpine borders with Switzerland and Austria produce many fine cheeses, and beer is a major product of the south – in a country which produces more than 5,000 varieties! In Munich the autumn *Oktoberfest* is the world's largest beer festival, and many dishes of the area are cooked with beer. The Bavarians are great meat-eaters, and *Gebratene Kalbshaxe*, knuckle of veal, is the national dish of Bavaria.

The *Konditorei* or pastry chefs of Germany are justly famous. All over the country, there are bakers, cake and biscuit makers who produce local or national specialities. Nuremberg, a centre for the spice trade since the Middle Ages, produces *Lebkuchen*, spiced honey biscuits which are particularly popular at Christmas time. Stollen, a traditional Christmas cake, origi-

nated in Nuremberg as well, although it is now most associated with Dresden.

I'm a regular visitor to Germany, through both pleasure and business. In April of 1996 I went there to receive an award for excellence of cuisine, presented by the wife of Chancellor Kohl.

AUSTRIA

Austria is a country partially composed of mountains, the Alps marking the boundary where the Austrian Tyrol meets Switzerland.

At the end of the nineteenth century, Vienna was the capital of the Austro-Hungarian Empire, and was one of the most sophisticated cities in the whole of Europe, with a cuisine to match. The latter was very largely influenced by France at that time, but there are also influences from Austria's other neighbours.

Austria is German-speaking, and for that reason, the culinary associations are prob-

ably strongest with Germany. Vegetable soups similar to those of Germany and meat broths are garnished with a variety of potato, breadcrumb and other dumplings, with *nockerln*, a light pasta made from semolina, and with shredded strips of pancakes, all to German taste as well. *Tafelspitz*, the most famous of Viennese lunchtime meat dishes, is boiled beef, usually topside, which is not dissimilar to the pot-roasted beef of Germany. I flew to Austria in 1995 to collect an award, and as soon as I landed, I went straight to my favourite *Tafelspitz* restaurant!

Veal cutlets are popular in both Germany and Austria, but it is the Viennese recipe, *Wiener Schnitzel*, that has become most famous. Both countries also share a love for sausages of all kinds, for asparagus, for potatoes, for cabbage salted as *sauerkraut,* and for sweet fruit dumplings.

Hungary has been influential too, and the Austrians eat several types of goulash.

Hungary also shares a love for desserts and pastries made with the thinnest possible pastry, strudel (very similar to the filo of Greece and Turkey). But it is probably in the quality of her pâtisserie that Austria is supreme. Viennese pastries and cakes include *Gugelhopf*, *Dobostorte* and the famous *Sachertorte*, a rich chocolate cake covered with chocolate. *Linzertorte* is a speciality of Linz, made with a crumbly nut pastry or shortcake, jam and a traditional lattice topping.

Desserts too are a feature of almost every meal in Austria. The dumplings from Salzburg, *Salzburger Nockerln*, are similar to the French *oeufs à la neige*. There are steamed puddings too, some made with walnuts, some with chocolate, and all are enjoyed with another Austrian speciality, whipped cream.

SWITZERLAND

Switzerland has absorbed many influences from the countries surrounding her. The first was probably that of the Romans who conquered the indigenous Celtic inhabitants (the Helvetii) in the first century BC. A very small proportion of Swiss, some 40,000 people, speak Romansch, said to be a dialect of Ancient Roman. The principal language of Switzerland is German but there are also French and Italian speaking minorities.

The linguistic borders of Switzerland also form culinary borders. In Ticino, which lies south of the Alps and borders on Italy, they speak Italian, and the canton draws its culinary inspirations from Lombardy. Graubünden, in the east, also known as Grisons, is where Romansch is spoken, and there is an amalgam of many culinary influences from north, south and east. In the west, French is spoken, and the cooking is very much influenced by France. The German-speaking part of Switzerland – which runs roughly from the Austrian and German borders in the east across to Berne, and which includes Zurich and Lucerne – has hints of Germanic in its cooking. The famous Rösti is a speciality of German-speaking Switzerland, and was the origin of a phrase, the 'Rösti barrier', which is said to divide the French and German-speaking regions. At a recent talk by my good friend and colleague, Jean Pierre Corpaatoo (a one-time butcher, turned painter), he said he could not now find this barrier – there was no more 'them' and 'us'!

Many people think Swiss food heavy, and of course it can be, but this is not unexpected in a country that is mountainous and cold for a major part of the year. The farmhouse cooking of the centre consists of thick vegetable soups such as the one found in the market at Berne, and vegetable stews or hotpots which are often so lengthily and slowly cooked that the vegetables dissolve to a virtual purée. This is echoed by the *Papet Vaudois*, the potato and leek stew of the western canton. In the northern cantons there is a fondness for other Germanic tastes such as beer and cabbage. A *Berner Platte* – a mixture of boiled meats and sausages – is just as often served with *sauerkraut* as it is with French beans, fresh or dried. Another Berne treat is the onion market held every year on the first Monday of November. Afterwards everyone eats onions with everything – in soups, in tarts, in dishes with meats.

One of the most famous of Swiss dishes is Zurich's *Emincé de Veau Zurichoise*. The Lucerne version of *Emincé* includes marinated raisins and shelled peeled walnuts. This sweet accent is a theme that recurs in much northern Swiss cooking. Pears, for instance, fresh, poached or dried are a common accompaniment to meats such as lamb, and sausages, and are baked into an aromatic *Birnbrot*, pear bread, along with nuts, raisins, spices and Kirsch, the famous Swiss cherry *eau de vie*.

In the French-speaking parts of Switzerland, lie the great lakes which produce another speciality unique to Switzerland – freshwater fish. Fish cookery is one of my passions and has been ever since I was a child and fished in the nearby Lake Bienne, in the foothills of the Jura. There I would catch perch and dace, but there are also *omble chevalier* (a char, from Lake Geneva), *féra*, *rötel*, trout, salmon and *bondelle*, a type of salmon trout.

Cheeses are another unique product of Switzerland, and they vary from the hard such as Gruyère, Emmenthal and Sbrinz, to the semi-soft such as Appenzell, and soft goat Tommes from the Alpine areas. Fondue, the most famous Swiss cheese dish, originated in the French-speaking parts of Switzerland (as did the more modern dish, *fondue bourguignonne*, using meat and oil or *bouillon* rather than cheese). Raclette, another cheese speciality, comes from the Valais in the southwest; a large circular cheese is halved and heated, then the melted cheese is scraped on to a plate to be eaten with boiled potatoes, baby gherkins and pickled onions.

In the southern cantons which border with Italy, the Italian-speaking Swiss eat pasta, gnocchi, polenta and risotto. In Graubünden, or Grisons, one of the major specialities is *Bündnerfleisch*, an air-dried beef (which is also produced in the Valais).

Graubünden boasts many expert bakers and pâtissiers, perhaps reflecting the proximity of Vienna to the east, and one of their wares is the delicious Engadine walnut tart. Every canton throughout the country has its own sweet speciality, however. Carrot cake comes from Aargau in the north, and a famous cherry tart comes from Zug, the *Zuger Kirsch Torte*. *Lebkuchen* and ginger-

A still-life of Swiss specialities, including air-dried ham and Tommes cheese.

breads are popular in the north, and the Bernese are proud of their meringues (which are thought to have originated in the health resort of Meiringen).

I cannot resist another uniquely Swiss speciality, chocolate. Apparently we Swiss are the champion chocolate eaters, consuming nearly 10 kg or 22 lb each per year!

SCANDINAVIA

Geographically, Scandinavia is the peninsula formed by Norway and Sweden, but culturally and historically, it also includes Denmark and Finland, and by association, Greenland, the Faroe Islands, and Iceland.

The history of all the Scandinavian countries has long been linked, with one of the countries laying claim to the others throughout the centuries. The cultures and cuisines are very closely related as a result.

Because of the climate in the furthest northern islands – long freezing winters when seas, inland waters and ground are frozen – seasonality is a significant characteristic of Scandinavian eating. And with their long coastlines, it is not surprising that fish and shellfish are major ingredients, which are enjoyed fresh in the spring and summer.

Fish soups are made in all the countries, the best and most famous perhaps being that of Bergen, the major port of western Norway; this has small fish balls as a garnish. When on a Norwegian cruise, we stopped off in Bergen, and I visited the fish market. I have never seen so many varieties of fish, familiar and unfamiliar, in one place. Fresh cod is much appreciated, particularly in Norway, as are salmon, trout and eel.

But again, because of the climate, these fish need to be preserved throughout the winter, so catches from the North Sea, Atlantic and Baltic are salted, dried or fermented, and this type of fish characterises Scandinavian cuisine perhaps more than anything else. In all of the countries, Baltic or Atlantic herring are a major ingredient, preserved with sugar and vinegar, flavoured with onion, mustard and dill (the prime Scandinavian herb).

Before coming to live and work in London I spent some time working with a colleague at the Grand Hotel in Stockholm. There I fully learned to appreciate the many varieties of herring, and the many ways of preparation. Pickled herrings form the first course of the famous Swedish *smörgåsbord* (see right), and are a frequent topping of the Danish *smørrebrød*, an open sandwich which is also popular in Norway.

SMØRGÅSBORD

It is said that Scandinavian countries were the first to devise a formal assortment of little eating dishes to accompany pre-prandial drinks. This, a form of 'aquavit table', migrated to Russia, where it became *zakuski* (little bits) to accompany shots of the local vodka. From there the idea developed to become *Vorspeisen* in Germany, *antipasti* in Italy, *mezze* in the Middle East, *tapas* in Spain and *merienda* in the Philippines.

The most famous and original *smørgåsbord* is that of Sweden, and it is formally presented in large hotels and restaurants, less so now in private houses. The first course – or the first trip to the buffet table – always consists of pickled or marinated herring or *bockling* (smoked Baltic herring). You might eat this with a boiled potato, soured cream and chives. On the next trip to the table, you might try some salmon, boiled, smoked or marinated, or eel. Cold meats – sausages, pâté, smoked reindeer – and salads, eaten with pickles of beetroot and gherkins, might be next, on a clean plate, and cheese could very well be on offer too. Finally there are some small hot dishes, usually including small meatballs, various types of egg dishes, and *Jansson's Frestelse*. Aquavit and beer are traditional accompaniments.

An autumn delicacy in Sweden is *surstrømming*, young herrings which were salted in barrels in the spring, and which are famously pungent. Salmon (and trout and mackerel) are 'graved' or 'buried' in Sweden, Norway and Finland with sugar, salt and plenty of fresh dill for gravlax or gravadlax. In Sweden, *lutfisk*, dried ling, is soaked in lye to soften it and make it palatable. In Norway, *lutefisk* is stock fish or dried cod softened with caustic soda in much the same way.

Meat is popular in Scandinavia as well, ranging from reindeer in the far north, to the perennially popular meatballs, the roast geese and cured ham of celebrations, and the pork dishes of the most southerly country, Denmark. Reindeer is eaten fresh, dried and smoked in Finland, Lapland and Norway; the Finns serve it with cranberries and the Norwegians add *Gjetost* goat cheese to the accompanying rich sauce. Lamb and mutton is the most popular meat in the more northerly countries.

In Denmark, the pig reigns supreme, and *hamburgerryg*, boned smoked loin, is very popular, as is fresh pork with the same sweet and sour flavours Norway likes, often supplied by dried fruit such as prunes (very definitely a Germanic influence).

Dairy produce features throughout all the countries of Scandinavia. Butter, cream, soured cream and yoghurts are eaten enthusiastically, thick yoghurt for lunch in Sweden, a soured cream porridge for breakfast in Norway. They are also used in cooking, and are made into some wonderful cheeses.

The traditional vegetables of Scandinavian cooking are like the rest of northern Europe, potatoes, other root vegetables (swedes particularly) and pulses. Potatoes are as omnipresent as preserved fish, and no main course lacks its boiled or fried potato (the latter in Denmark).

Pulses, which once would have been virtually the only vegetable available during the winter, are cooked with meats in stews and soups.

Dark, mainly rye breads are characteristic of most northern European countries, and feature in Scandinavia, most notably in the Danish *smørrebrød*, literally buttered bread, or open sandwiches.

All the Scandinavian countries like sweet things, particularly Denmark. Interestingly the yeast dough used in the famous Danish pastries came originally from Vienna (the Danes call them *Wienerbrod*). Ginger biscuits (*pepperkakor* in Sweden) and various celebratory cakes and breads are baked, especially around Christmas, and they contain spices, some of which are traditionally associated with Scandinavia, such as caraway.

Iceland lies in the North Atlantic, just south of the Arctic Circle. The rich fishing grounds around Iceland dictate the country's most valuable natural resource, that of sea fish and shellfish, and these are the mainstay of the Icelandic diet. Because of the long winters, preservation is a major consideration, and many varieties of fish are dried (haddock, cod and catfish), smoked (trout, salmon) and pickled (salmon and shark).

The pickling medium is often whey (*mysa*) which is a by-product of a fresh cheese (*skyr*) made from skimmed milk (and not dissimilar to yoghurt). Whey pickling of foods, *surmatur*, is unique to Iceland, and meats are also treated and 'soured' in this way, among them breast of lamb, ram testicles and seal flippers.

The culmination of my Scandinavian cruise was a very brief visit to Iceland. I had the most unexpectedly delicious meal – some smoked lamb and some locally caught prawns which were so delicately cooked. I wish I'd been able to stay longer!

EASTERN EUROPE

Eastern Europe consists of the countries which lie to the east and south-east of Austria and Germany, and which were allied until fairly recently with the communist USSR – including Poland, Hungary, the former Czechoslovakia and Yugoslavia and Romania and Bulgaria. The countries which once formed the USSR must be included, although strictly speaking the land mass east of the Urals is considered to be part of the continent of Asia.

Many soups and stews of Eastern Europe consist primarily of vegetables, although they may be given added flavour and interest by the addition of a little meat protein. When filming in Budapest for one of my television series, we visited the vegetable market – it was one of the most exciting markets I have ever seen.

If one vegetable were to be said to define the area, it would have to be the cabbage, and this is closely followed by beetroot, potato and other root vegetables. Cabbage is eaten fresh and salted (*sauerkraut*) in many countries. Poland's national dish, *Bigos*, is a *sauerkraut*-based stew with sausages, a little meat (usually venison) and some fresh white cabbage. Cabbage, fresh or salted, is also used in much the same way as vine leaves are in Turkey and Greece, to wrap around a filling; these cabbage rolls are common in Poland, Hungary, the former Yugoslavia and Romania. Cabbage is used in salads too.

Potatoes appear in soups, stews, and accompaniments, some of which are surprisingly like the Swiss Rösti and other potato cakes of northern Europe. Potatoes are also made into dumplings.

Beetroot is another popular eastern European root vegetable, and its sweet and earthy flavour and bright colour feature in many soups and salads. The most famous usage must be in *borscht*, the Russian soup. *Barszcz* is the Polish version, said by some to be the original.

Other vegetables which feature in the cooking of eastern Europe include mushrooms and marrow. Vegetables are cooked together in ratatouille-type dishes: the Hungarian *lecso* is a colourful mix of sweet peppers, tomatoes, onion, bacon and paprika; *ghivetch*, a baked vegetable stew, is the national dish of Romania.

An unusual vegetable for this part of the world is the capsicum pepper, which appeared in the Old World only after the sixteenth century, but, as in Greece and Turkey, it is cooked with a stuffing in the former Yugoslavia, Poland, Romania, Hungary and Bulgaria. The most surprising manifestation of capsicum pepper, though, is in a dried form, as paprika. Hungary is alone in this usage. The hot seeds are processed separately from the flesh, and then the two are mixed in different proportions to create different grades of heat.

Paprika is used primarily in three basic Hungarian stews: *Bogracsgulyas* (named after the *bogracs*, the stew pot which is suspended over the fire, and the *gulya*, the traditional herders of the Hungarian plains), *Paprikas* and *Porkolt*. *Tokany* is similar to *Porkolt*, but is made with little or no paprika. Paprika is also used in some egg dishes, soups, in pastas, pancakes and a fiery fish stew containing carp and other freshwater fish.

Skewered spicy sausages are common, and are reminiscent of *kofta*, as are rissoles and meatballs; ground meat is also layered with filo pastry for a meat pie in Yugoslavia. Sausages are smoked, and in Bulgaria, with its Greek border, there are composite dishes like moussaka. Magnificent hams are produced in the former Czechoslavakia. Prime beef is momentarily sautéed for Beef Stroganov, a dish which is always considered to be Russian, but which was probably invented by a French chef to the Russian noble whose name adorns the dish. Russian cooking is a blend of many styles, and there was a time when that of the French was to the fore at court.

Coulibiac is one example of the pastry and dough 'pies' of which the eastern Europeans, particularly the Russians, are so fond, and these include *pirogi* and *pirozhki* (respectively, large and small individual meat pies using a yeast-based dough). The Polish *pierogi* can contain cheese, vegetables or meat. A pasta-like dough is also used to enclose fillings in *pelmeni* (meat-filled dough envelopes similar to ravioli or won-ton) and *vareniki* (like *pelmeni*, but often containing fruit or curd cheese). Pastas are eaten in the east,

A paprika stall in Budapest Market.

particularly the *tarhonya* of Hungary. Noodlesand pastas are common in the former Yugoslavia.

Other staple foods are the Romanian *mamaliga* (a cornmeal paste, similar to polenta and to the *coocoo* of Africa and the West Indies), and buckwheat, wheat and rice. Breads are the principal staple, though, ranging from white sourdoughs to virtually black rye breads; flavourings are added to these, often poppy or caraway seeds, which are particularly characteristic of eastern Europe. Buckwheat flour is used in the making of blinis, yeasted pancakes.

As the majority of eastern European countries are land-locked, most of the fish eaten are freshwater. With its coastline on the Adriatic, the former Yugoslavia can boast a greater variety. The Danube has many fish which are cooked in fish soup-stews, but the most common fish is the herring, salted or smoked, which is eaten with blini, in salads, or as a *zakuska* in Russia (see below). Perhaps the most famous fish is the sturgeon, principally valued for its roe, as caviar.

Desserts in eastern Europe largely consist of sweet dumplings and pancakes, filled with curd or cottage cheese or fruit, and doughnut-like cakes. *Kulitsch* is a Russian cake similar to *Stollen* and *panettone* and other celebratory bread-cakes around the world; it is baked in tall moulds and served with *paskha*, a sweetened cream cheese pudding, at Easter time. Fruits are made into soups in Hungary – a sour cherry one is particularly interesting – and rolled into layers of filo pastry in strudels.

ZAKUSKI

The Russian tradition of *zakuski* was brought from Scandinavia by the first Viking Prince of Kiev, its ancestor the Scandinavian *smörgåsbord*. The first *zakuski* were something to bite into while having a glass of vodka (rather as a tapa is eaten), but now *zakuski* are eaten as the first course of a meal, still with plenty of vodka (which can be plain or flavoured with pepper, lemon or caraway seeds). A beer flavoured with fruit might be drunk instead. Usually two or three *zakuski* are served – something tart or salty like herring or marinated mushrooms – but for a special occasion, a whole buffet table may be laid out with a selection of salads (beetroot, cucumber, cabbage, *sauerkraut*, mushrooms, a Russian salad, and some aubergine caviar), perhaps along with hard-boiled eggs topped with sturgeon caviar, and little *pirozhki*, or pies, with meat or cheese fillings.

THE AMERICAS

Together the two major parts of America approach Asia in continental size. They are, however, much less populated than Asia: vast tracts of northern Canada are uninhabitable, as are many peaks of the Andes in South America. From north to south, the Americas stretch some 9,500 miles, many more degrees of latitude than in any other continent, so the botanical, climatic and cultural zones involved – from the polar wastes of Canada to the tip of South America, virtually on the opposite pole – make it difficult to generalise in any culinary sense.

What is indisputable, though, is that with the discovery of the New World of the Americas, and with the great ingredient exchanges of the sixteenth century, the whole culinary map of the world was to change irrevocably.

USA

When the Pilgrim Fathers arrived on the shores of New England in 1620, they could hardly have been more ill-prepared to tackle the rigours of a hostile environment. Among their luggage were candle snuffers and a sundial, and one man even packed 126 pairs of shoes, but between them they failed to bring anything of real value, such as a horse, a cow, a fishing line or plough. This might not have mattered, as the woods abounded with wild duck, turkey, venison, mushrooms and countless berries, and the coastal waters teemed with fish, lobsters, oysters and scallops. But the settlers ate nothing but their dwindling supplies of salted pork, salted beef, salted fish and hard tack.

Their saviours were the native American Indians. They introduced the sceptical settlers to such unique New World delicacies as corn or maize, the white and sweet potato, the peanut, the pumpkin and other squashes, the maple tree and its syrup, the cranberry and blueberry, and the pecan nut to name but a few, and told them how to prepare and cook them.

Corn was to be the most significant introduction, as European wheat did not flourish at first in the cold windswept soil of New England. Recipes like cornbread, corn muffins, hoe cakes, johnny (or journey) cakes, hush puppies, corn fritters, corn chowder, dried corn casserole and, of course, popcorn gradually became commonplace, recipes brought by English, Dutch and other settlers, being adapted to use this new grain.

From these humble beginnings a great food culture was to grow, a culture which is arguably one of the most cosmopolitan in the world. For North America is a melting-pot of world foods and world cooking styles. After that first blending of English and native Indian, other influences were assimilated from later settlers, as a result of which pastrami today is as American as clam chowder, yet neither truly originated in the land with which they are so closely associated.

It was New England and the East Coast that saw the arrival of the Pilgrim Fathers in 1620, and America's culinary patchwork began with the adoption of native Indian dishes into the fairly bland English diet. Perhaps the first new speciality was the Indian succotash (from a Narragansett word meaning 'something broken in pieces'). Succotash was included in the first Thanksgiving feast in celebration of the harvest, and eaten alongside turkey, sweet potatoes and pumpkin pie. Roast turkey and those same trimmings are still the centre-piece of Thanksgiving dinners today. The pumpkin pie with which they finished their feast was a combination of the English pie-making tradition, and a local ingredient, the pumpkin. Pies are still a major feature in American cooking, especially the famous American apple pie.

Dutch settlers were to be influential. They were forced to leave New Amsterdam (which became New York under the British), but introduced their sweet biscuits, *koekje*, which became cookie, and the *wafel* made in a special press which became the waffle. The Pennsylvania Dutch were not Dutch but Swiss-German (the Dutch is a corruption of Deutsch, or German), and were probably the next grouping to make their mark on American cuisine. They brought with them reminders of the old country: good farming techniques, a love of dumplings and noodles, and a fine sausage and ham tradition. It was they who introduced slow-cooked meats such as *Sauerbraten* (possibly the origin of the famous American pot-roasts), and pickling with sugar (the Germanic affection for sweet and sour tastes which is

Pumpkins for sale in a field south of San Francisco.

still a characteristic of American cooking). German settlers were later responsible for such American specialities as the frankfurter, the hamburger and the doughnut.

All the settlers, of whatever nationality, enjoyed the bounty of the sea on that east coast. Cod was a staple, eaten fresh and salted, and clams or cod were used in chowders. The clambake is perhaps the best known use of seafood. Crab cakes are also a speciality of the region, particularly in Maryland.

One-pot cookery was prevalent, related to the British tradition, and the New England boiled dinner, an amalgam of beef or chicken with vegetables, is similar to other European dishes as well – *pot au feu, cocido, bollito misto, Berner Platte* etc. Boston baked beans has its roots this early, the long and slow cooked beans (instead of European peas) stewed with pork for flavour, and molasses or maple syrup for sweetness.

Throughout the years immigrants from all points of the globe massed into America via New York, and it is here that the melting pot of American cuisine is most palpable. Jews and settlers from eastern and northern Europe brought with them the deli

tradition, and many of their specialities such as salt beef, pastrami, lox and bagels, kugele and blintzes. Italians introduced their pastas and pizzas, and pizza now is almost more American than Neapolitan.

The Mid-West of America is America's breadbasket, with its rich fertile soil and its high agricultural yield. These immense tracts of land are peopled by a hospitable farming population whose simple, unadorned, home-cooked food epitomises the Middle American mentality. Corn cakes and puddings of all types are typical of Mid-Western fare, but so are many other dishes which are considered to be quintessentially American – fried chicken, hot biscuits, steaks with hash browns, spare ribs, potato salad, shortcakes, apple pie, cherry cobbler, chocolate brownies, pancakes with eggs and bacon, scalloped potatoes.

The American West is cattle country, home of the cowboy. The people who settled here, of European origin, are hardy and resourceful, and their food is straightforward, much as it is in the Mid-West.

Food is taken rather more seriously in the South than anywhere else in America. Pigs are bred in preference to cattle or sheep, and there are many pork dishes

such as spare ribs, crackling, fatback, and chitterlings. Hickory-smoked Smithfield ham is a speciality of Virginia, made from pigs fattened on peanuts, and ham is served with such evocatively named dishes as collard greens, red-eye gravy and candied sweet potatoes. Bacon and ham feature large in southern breakfasts, served with grits (dried processed corn) and hash browns.

Corn is as ubiquitous in the South as elsewhere, and it is made into innumerable biscuits, breads and cakes as well as grits. Chickens are very popular, and are fried, stewed, baked and barbecued. Often fried chicken is served with a cream sauce, and a favourite accompaniment is fried green tomatoes. Shellfish abound in the coastal waters, and oysters, for instance, are used in many dishes, raw or cooked, with a variety of toppings or accompaniments.

The southern states along the Atlantic were first populated in the colonial period between the sixteenth and eighteenth centuries, and were occupied at first by the Spanish and later by the French. Eventually these territories were given back to the United States, in 1803, but by then influences from both countries and from the thousands of slaves brought over from Africa and the Caribbean during the years of the slave trade, had infused not only the southern culture, but also the cuisine. Creole cookery had been born.

New Orleans, the centre of the hybrid Creole tradition, reveals its history in the subtle French flavourings, the stronger Spanish seasonings, the presence of indigenous herbs such as *filé* (a powder ground from the dried sassafras leaf), and the culinary ingenuity of the African cooks. Jambalaya is one of the most famous Creole dishes, and its name is a combination of '*jambon*', ham, 'ala' from French '*à la*', and '*ya*', an African word for rice. It is very similar to the Spanish paella. Other specialities include the distinctive Creole gumbo, a highly seasoned dish of fish or meat thickened with okra. (Gumbo is the Bantu word for okra, and the dish is very closely related to the okra soups and stews of Nigeria.)

Cajun is another strand of southern cooking. Acadia was a French-Canadian colony in what is now Nova Scotia, and its Catholic inhabitants were deported by the British in the early seventeenth century and resettled by the Spanish in Catholic Louisiana. The present-day Cajuns have a distinct culture and language, as well as cuisine, and although the ingredients are similar to those of Creole, the spicing and heat are very much more robust. Crawfish, oysters, crabs and prawns are prolific in the Mississippi delta that is the Cajun heartland, and they are the prime ingredients; mixtures of hot spices are sprinkled on to fish such as catfish and grilled to 'blacken' them. Spicy sausages known as *andouillettes* bear witness to their French ancestry.

Desserts in the South include ambrosia (layers of fruit sprinkled with coconut), a sweet potato pudding/soufflé, and the achingly sweet, much-loved American classic, pecan pie, made with nuts indigenous to the South. Native blueberries are eaten raw, or cooked into pies or sauces. In the sun-drenched state of Florida, citrus fruits flourish, resulting in lemon and lime tarts and pies such as Key Lime Pie.

The South-West is, like the South, another culinary hotchpotch. On the Gulf of Mexico, it can show French, Spanish and black influences – the Creole of further east – and many southern accents brought in by those who fled west after the Civil War. The huge tracts of land which are Texan cattle ranches have given rise to a strong tradition of barbecue cookery, with fiery sauces to accompany the steaks. But the strongest

Crawfish are the speciality of a typical New Orleans restaurant.

and most pervasive influence is that of Mexico, as parts of the southern states once belonged to Mexico. The melding of Spanish, Mexican and Indian ingredients and flavours is known as Tex-Mex or Mexamerican, and is an important and strong thread in America's culinary consciousness.

The topography of the west coast of America is diverse and complex, and these contrasts are replicated by a population who enjoy a culinary fusion, combining the unusual and seemingly incompatible: this is where surf 'n' turf or ranch 'n' reef predominate, and where you can find chicken with anchovies, turkey with cheese, a cassoulet of shellfish, and pizza topped with smoked salmon or goat cheese.

The area was colonised mainly in the nineteenth century, and became so popular that the Great Transcontinental Railway was built to make it more accessible. Chinese labourers were shipped in in their thousands to help with its construction, and settled there after its completion, a legacy still seen in San Francisco, which has become home to the second largest Chinese community outside Asia.

Other influences which pervade the cuisine of California come from Thailand, Japan (sushi bars are big business now), Vietnam, Italy and Mexico. The Caesar salad, for instance, which originated in Tijuana (devised by a restaurateur named Caesar Cardini), *chilli con carne* and a host of other Mexican ideas, were probably brought across the border by migrant Mexican workers. The Italians, who form the largest foreign-born group in the United States, imported their pasta as well as their vegetables.

The constant supply of sunshine and the mineral-rich earth make possible the cultivation of a huge variety of fruits and vegetables, many of which are combined in the fresh and healthy salads which characterise Californian cuisine almost as much as its eclecticism and love of novelty.

The waters of the Pacific are rich in good ingredients. The early settlers discovered abalone, salmon, tuna, lobsters, enormous crabs and many beds of oysters. It was during Gold Rush days that recipes such as hangtown fry, fried eggs, oysters and bacon, and San Francisco oyster loaf, a hollow loaf filled with oysters (based on La

Médiatrice of New Orleans) became popular. Oysters are also stuffed into sirloin steaks for carpetbag steak (later exported to Australia), and added to the omnipresent *cioppino*, an Italian inspired seafood stew made in every port and harbour along the whole of that western coast.

CANADA

Canada's cuisine in many ways is very similar to that of the United States; it too has chowders, fried scallops, baked lobsters and a myriad varieties of fish (the British Columbian coast is home to six types of salmon), as well as its stews, pies and puddings. As in the West and Mid-West of America, the original farmers (mostly of northern European stock) ate simply and heartily of what they could pick, grow, catch and shoot, and ingredients include moose, wild duck and geese, river and lake trout, berries and – a particular delicacy of New Brunswick – shoots of the fiddlehead fern.

Canada was known as New France until 1763 (when it was ceded to the British), and the oldest and most evocative dishes are those of the early French settlers of Quebec and elsewhere. A yellow pea soup named for the 'habitants', French-Canadian farmers, is very similar to the many dried pea soups flavoured with ham that exist in the European tradition (and most Canadians originated in Europe). There are many unusual pies in the French rather than the British mould.

There are also original native influences, and a major one involves the wild rice indigenous to Canada. This is in fact an aquatic grass, and it was once harvested in canoes by the local Indians (now done by machinery). I first encountered wild rice when I worked in the Elizabeth Hotel in Montreal: I went a year early, in June 1966, to prepare for the 1967 Expo, but stayed until the beginning of 1969! My mentor in the kitchen, Albert Schnell, used to stuff Rock Cornish hens with wild rice, and it is a recipe I have used and adapted many times since. I shall never forget those years in Canada. Coming from a land-locked country, I was particularly astounded by the variety of seafood available. We were also cooking some less familiar dishes in order to win support for the Inuit, North American Eskimos, whose way of life was under threat. One of my jobs was to boil whale skin (for about five hours) to be used in salads. I also learned how to make beaver-tail soup! It was an exciting time for me, and I have been back to Canada many times since.

THE CARIBBEAN

In October 1492, Christopher Columbus, sailing from and under the flag of Spain, proclaimed his first landfall – actually one of the Bahamas – to be the West Indies. It wasn't until a few months later that the scale of his navigational blunder became apparent. Spice-laden India, the object of his voyage, was still half a world away. Undeterred, he claimed as many other Caribbean islands for Spain as he could.

The archipelago that forms the islands of the Caribbean lies in the Caribbean Sea, and stretches for 2,500 miles from Florida in the north to Venezuela in the south.

Before the arrival of Columbus, these islands were all inhabited by Amerindian peoples from South America, who were divided into two groups, the Arawaks and the Caribs. The Europeans transformed the lives of these indigenous peoples on their arrival, stamping out their customs and enslaving them. The settlers imported such staples and exotics as cows, pigs, mangoes, coconuts, bananas and sugarcane, many of which were to become important cash crops for the islands. Sugar mills were established, and slaves from Africa were shipped in to work them. When the Abolition Act of 1834 finally brought an end to slavery, migrant labourers from India and other parts of Asia were called upon to work the land, and all of these influences combined to enrich the cuisine of the

Flying fish in a Barbados market.

islands of the Caribbean.

Part of the culinary legacy left by the Caribs included the flavouring allspice, or Jamaica pepper, the dried berry of an evergreen tree, which has the combined flavours of cinnamon, nutmeg and clove. It is added to many dishes, but most notably to pepperpot, an Amerindian meat stew from Trinidad, Barbados and St Kitts, into which meats and other ingredients are constantly thrown, fuelling rumours that some pepperpots are over 100 years old.

The British introduced breadfruit to the West Indies in 1792; it was brought from Tahiti by Captain Bligh; he is also credited with the transposition of the ackee from West Africa. It is most famously incorporated into the Jamaican national dish, saltfish and ackee.

The flavours of Africa dominate the Caribbean islands, and native African dishes are common, due to the successful transplantation of many of the African slaves' favourite ingredients. Okra is added to *coocoo*, a dish of steamed cornmeal derived from the Ghanaian *banku*. Taro, which is common in West Africa, is now widely eaten in the West Indies, prized for its versatility and taste, which is similar to that of yam or sweet potato. Its leaves are called 'elephant ears', and are cooked in the most famous of island soups, *callaloo*. The plantain is a member of the banana family which also originated in Africa, and is eaten in the Caribbean as fried 'crisps', baked into breads, cooked and mashed for the dish *foo foo*, or used in chutneys.

Other obvious colonial influences are those of France, Spain and Britain. Martinique and Guadeloupe are the principal French islands, and the food combines French techniques and seasoning with Caribbean ingredients and flavours. Later Indian influences have resulted in curries which are unique to the islands, called 'colombos', and which are served with rice prepared in a creole style.

Criolla means much the same as creole, but is the term used in the Spanish speaking islands (and in Latin America). Rice or arroz is cooked with prawns and meats in Dominica and Latin America – a simplified form of paella – and meats are cooked in one-dish meals – *sancochos* – which are directly comparable to the *cocido* of Spain. Kidneys are cooked with sherry almost exactly as they would be in Spain, and *Moros y Christianos*, an amalgam of black beans and rice, is a direct reference to the Christian Reconquest of Spain. Salt codfish fritters can be served as a *tapa* in Spain and Portugal, but appear in many of the Spanish islands and Latin America as well as the French islands: they are variously known as stamp and go (Jamaica), *acrats de morue* (Martinique and Guadeloupe) and *bacalão* (in the Spanish islands).

The British culinary influence has been small. Even in Bermuda, the British islands some 1,000 miles north of the West Indies, and 600 miles off the North Carolina coast, the cuisine is more Caribbean in flavour, using the plethora of seafood in many recipes, some with accents of France and the US (a fish chowder) and some of Japan (a raw fish with a sashimi dressing). I am most fortunate in that I visit Bermuda four times a year, to cook a gala dinner using local ingredients.

The Hindu Indian influence on the cooking of the Caribbean has been significant, and masalas and curry powders are common on all the islands, especially on Trinidad. Dhals and flat Indian breads are eaten there too, and ghee or clarified butter is the cooking medium.

However, despite the cultural and linguistic differences between many of the islands, there are remarkable similarities in many of the dishes, whether they appear on French, Spanish or British tables. These can be attributed to the nomadic nature of the Caribbean cooks – who 'island-hop' – and to the proliferation of the same natural ingredients on every island.

MEXICO

Mexico was the birthplace of some of the world's greatest civilisations, among them the Toltecs, the Mayans and the Aztecs. It was the latter who were to be conquered and destroyed by Cortes when he invaded in around 1520. Thereafter Mexico became part of the Viceroyalty of Spain for some 300 years, achieving independence only in 1810.

The civilisation that Cortes encountered was a rich, peaceful and agricultural one, with a highly developed social structure. It was this conquest, and the discovery by Columbus of the 'West Indies' and America to the north, that led to the importation of many new foods to the Old World – tomatoes, peppers, avocados, beans, corn, turkey, chocolate, vanilla etc, all of which were to change the taste of foods eaten throughout the whole of the rest of the world. But the Spanish *conquistadores* also brought foods to the New World from the Old, which were to be assimilated into the basic Mexican cuisine. These Spanish influences were imbued with memories of

Plaited bread from Central America.

the 700-year rule by the Moors, so Mexico encountered not only ingredients which were from Europe (livestock such as cattle, pigs and poultry, thus milk, cheese and eggs), but those which originated from further south and east (such as sugarcane, lentils, chickpeas, citrus fruit and rice).

Pig meat rapidly became popular, and rendered pork fat introduced new techniques to a cuisine that had hitherto been basically fat-free: grilling, poaching and steaming were now augmented by frying and roasting. The rich sauces of Moorish Spain and Spain itself were influential – the use of marinades, of ground nuts as sauce thickener, the inclusion of dried fruit in slow-cooked dishes of beans or lentils – and the sweet, vanilla-flavoured milk pudding known as *flan* is now as popular in Mexico as it is in the Iberian peninsula.

A Spanish aristocracy was to rule in Mexico for those 300 years, and the Catholic religion they brought with them became heavily influential in culinary as well as social terms. Just as convent nuns developed many of the sweet desserts of Spain, so convent nuns in Mexico were to be as involved in a food sense. The nuns of Puebla are thought to have invented the famous *mole* dishes (from an Aztec word meaning sauce or concoction). *Mole poblano de guajalote*, a *mole* of the indigenous turkey, with poblano chillies, is said by many to be the national dish of Mexico, and it also includes some chocolate.

Missionaries operating in areas of Mexico now belonging to the USA, were said to have invented *chilli con carne*, a combination of local beans with the imported beef.

Another influence on Mexican cooking has been that of the Caribbean and thus of Africa. There are many shared recipes and ingredients, as there are further south in Latin America where black slaves were transported. The bananas introduced from Asia to the Caribbean are flamed with rum in Mexico just as they might be in Antigua, and black bean soups are as popular all over Mexico as they are in Cuba or Puerto Rico (both islands, of course, also ruled by Spain at one time).

The principal staple of Mexican cuisine, however, is one of its most ancient indigenous ingredients, maize. The ears of corn are boiled with lime or charcoal to soften the skins, then crushed to a paste, kneaded and formed into flat pancakes to be baked on a griddle. These tortillas are the basic bread of Mexico and are eaten at every meal and in a variety of ways. *Tamales* is a traditional festive dish of the Mexican Indians; it consists of raw cornmeal dough, topped with a savoury or sweet mixture, wrapped in banana leaves and steamed.

The second most important ingredient in Mexican cooking is the chilli pepper, and there are said to be over 100 varieties available. Chillies, whether fresh or dried, influence almost every dish in Mexico, particularly the fresh sauces that accompany every meal, such as *salsa verde* and *salsa cruda*. Another accompaniment to grilled meats (or tortillas) would be guacamole, the now famous avocado purée, used as a dip, sauce, garnish and relish.

I have only visited Mexico once, after I had finished my years in Montreal. I went during the Summer Olympics of 1968, and loved every minute. I took a bus from Mexico City to Acapulco, and tasted tortillas, very hot chillies, and tequila with salt and lime for the first time.

CENTRAL AND SOUTH AMERICA

North America and Mexico are connected to South America by a narrow land bridge with the Pacific on one side, the Caribbean on the other; this bridge is divided between seven small countries – Guatemala, Belize, Honduras, San Salvador, Nicaragua, Costa Rica and Panama. Where Panama meets Colombia, the longest mountain range in the world begins. The Andes run for over 4,000 miles down the west coast of the continent to Argentina's southernmost tip.

The Incas of Peru were sun-worshippers, and it is possibly because of this that food in Peru is generally quite yellow in colour. Much of this yellow coloration comes from a yellow herb and from annatto, a dye and flavouring obtained from the seeds of a small flowering tree. Aztec and Carib warriors also used annatto's red-gold colour in their warpaint, and annatto is still used a great deal in both Caribbean and South American cooking. Food played a highly important part in Inca culture. It was they who brought maize from Mexico and who discovered the peanut. They also cultivated the potato, a plant known nowhere else in the world, and they had developed some 100 varieties by as early as 2,500 BC. Thousands of years before the advent of freeze-drying, the Peruvians were preserving potatoes for times of crop failure or hardship. The potatoes were pounded to a pulp which was frozen in the Andean night air, then thawed in the tropical sun; the moisture was squeezed out until the potato was dehydrated and hard – called *chuño*.

Apart from the potato, other ingredients encountered by early explorers and colonists were similar to those met in Mexico to the north – maize, chilli peppers (which are used in many highly seasoned dishes throughout the continent, and in table-top pepper sauces), tomatoes, avocados (stuffed in many cuisines) and nuts (peanuts, Brazil nuts and cashew nuts). They also discovered guinea pigs, or *cuys*,

which are still roasted and eaten as the Ecuadorian national dish. Because of the long coastlines, there was an abundance of seafood, especially on the Pacific side, including abalone, clams, conch and lobster, as well as two Chilean favourites, a variety of conger eel and a giant sea urchin.

To this diversity, as they had in Mexico, the Europeans contributed cattle (thus beef, milk, cheese and butter), pigs, citrus fruits, wheat, rice and sugarcane, all of which were incorporated into the cooking of the continent. Beef has since become the staple meat of South America, and is held in high regard, particularly in Argentina. Cheese is now an important ingredient, the technique taught to the Indians by the Iberians; a cheese sauce coats boiled potatoes in several cuisines or, as in Ecuador, cheese is added to mashed potato and made into cakes to be sautéed and served with a peanut sauce (and often sprinkled thereafter with fresh coriander, a favourite South American herb).

In Central America and the countries to the north of the continent, the influences on the cuisines are mainly Spanish, but there are distinct Mexican accents, as well as West Indian, thus African, borrowings. In Dutch Surinam, the Dutch have introduced curries and *Rijstaffel*, the rice table they encountered in Indonesia. Another curious influence involves the seviche so well known throughout South America, but

considered to be at its best in Ecuador. The technique of marinating raw fish or shellfish in citrus juice to 'cook' them is said to have been introduced to or from Polynesia (very similar to the Hawaiian *opihis*).

In Brazil, as the British and Spanish had done in the Caribbean and North America, the Portuguese shipped in thousands of black African slaves, primarily from Nigeria, to help build their colonies. This gave rise to a pronounced African influence on the cooking of the region. Palm or dende oil and black-eyed beans have become common ingredients in local dishes. Another ingredient common to both Africa and Brazil is manioc or cassava. All three ingredients are used in dishes such as *feijoada*, a speciality of Rio de Janeiro, and which has become the national dish of Brazil. It is a complicated amalgam of meats (beef, pork, pigs' ears and trotters, and sausages) with black beans, sprinkled with cassava meal, and served with rice, a pepper sauce and sliced oranges. I ate a wonderful *feijoada* on my first trip to Rio. A friend who was a chef at a local hotel took me to this very unassuming restaurant, where no tourist would ever dream of going, and the food was unforgettable.

To this day, the east coast of Brazil maintains strong cultural and especially culinary ties to North and West Africa, and this has given rise to a Brazilian saying that: 'The blacker the cook, the better the food.'

Three typical Brazilian ingredients – sweet potatoes, chillies and aubergines.

AFRICA

Africa is the second largest continent in the world. Its geography and climate reflect its size, and the extreme heat of the Sahara desert in the north is matched by the searingly hot sands of the Kalahari in the south. In between lie the lush tropical rainforests of the Congo basin and the extensive networks of freshwater lakes which mark what is known as the Great Rift Valley in the east. Africa is a land of great contrasts, but a land in which a multitude of peoples have made their homes for thousands of years – and indeed is probably where man himself originated.

The fertile north of Africa was always prey to exploration and invasion, and the first to make a mark were the sea-faring Phoenicians and Carthaginians who landed on the shores of the Meghrib (encompassing the modern states of Morocco, Algeria, Tunisia and Libya) during the first millennium BC. Here they encountered the nomadic Berbers with whom they traded ivory, gold and spices. The Carthaginians were to plant these northern areas with fruit, olive trees and grains. When Rome defeated Carthage, Roman Africa became an agricultural domain, providing supplies for the rest of the Empire.

Much later, in the seventh century after Christ, the Arabs were to claim the northern parts of Africa in their quest to spread the word of Islam. It was Arab merchants whose caravans crossed the Sahara to trade with West Africa, and whose dhows brought from the East cargoes of spices. However, in the sixteenth century, came influences that were to be the greatest on African cuisine. Arriving to the west and south, the Portuguese brought with them ingredients from the rest of the world – maize, pumpkins, peanuts, chillies and tomatoes (from the Americas) and citrus fruits. These enlivened a basic diet of millet, sorghum, melons and beans, including the black beans which were to travel later to the Caribbean and South America.

So began the European colonial scramble for Africa that brought French, British, German, Dutch, Belgian, Spanish and Italian nuances to what was basically a subsistence cuisine. Other influences were imported as well. Many African countries ruled by the British were settled by peoples of the British Raj, so Indian-style curries, rice and other dishes became common.

on hot chilli peppers, olive oil and garlic. Some Algerian and Moroccan stews are given a refreshing tang by the peel of preserved lemons or limes.

Harira, a soup of mutton and lentils, flavoured by onions, spices and fresh coriander, has become the commonest 'break fast' food of the Islamic Lent, Ramadan. *Chermoula* is another early flavouring, and it is particularly delicious with fish.

Because of religious prohibitions, the meat most commonly eaten in North Africa is lamb or mutton. It is stewed in tajines, or grilled as brochettes or kofta-type kebabs on skewers, and whole lambs are grilled over coals or baked in a pit.

Salads, often made with fruit or cooked vegetables, are a way of life in North Africa, and many of them will find their way on to the equivalent of a *mezze* table, a Middle-Eastern influence. Many of these salads are probably Andalusian in origin, as is what is considered to be one of the world's great dishes, *b'stilla, bastela*, or *pastela*. This is a layering of thin crispy pastry (*ouarka* or *warkha*, but filo can be used), with pigeon meat, eggs and spices, which is baked with a flavouring of ground almonds, sugar and cinnamon sprinkled on top.

The sweets of North Africa are famous throughout the world, and these – generally tissue-thin pastry wrapped around fillings of ground almonds, dates or figs with honey and sweet spices – are probably of Spanish or Middle Eastern origin.

NORTH AFRICA

The cooking of North Africa has absorbed many influences. One of the first was that of the nomadic Bedouin Arabs. Their diet included sheep and camel meat (some of it dried in strips as *khli* or *khadid*), milk, a cooked butter called *smen*, grains, dates and desert creatures such as locusts, scorpions and gazelles. Many of these are still eaten today. The indigenous Berbers also exerted a huge influence, using the wheat introduced by the Carthaginians and nurtured by the Romans for couscous, a grain 'made' from wheat semolina and flour. Other Berber dishes include *harira*, a pulse soup, and *tajines*, stews of meat, poultry or vegetables long-cooked in a pot with a conical lid, and bearing the same name. Arabs spreading the words of the Koran – some of them the Moors who were to rule in Spain for so many centuries – also introduced spices, and spices have since been assimilated into Meghribi cooking more insistently than elsewhere in the continent.

The Moors returning to North Africa after the Reconquest of Spain brought with

them an Andalusian style – the use of olive oil in cooking as opposed to *smen*, and the incorporation of nuts, fruits and herbs into dishes (dried fruits in a chicken *tajine*, for instance). After the discovery of the New World in the sixteenth century, new fruits and vegetables were also made use of in North African cooking, and paprika and cayenne, both products of the peppers of the Americas, play large roles in Moroccan cooking especially.

The most recent influences are those of France and Italy. France ruled Morocco, for instance, from 1913 until 1956, and Algeria from 1830 to 1962.

Couscous has become the national staple of much of the Meghrib, as well as the national dish. Couscous is eaten by itself with perhaps some dates or cheese added while it is steamed, or it can be used as a base for *tajines* of vegetables, meat or poultry (occasionally fish). The flavouring of these stews and other dishes differ from country to country in the Meghrib. However, many of these dishes are accompanied by harissa, a fiery condiment based

CENTRAL AND SOUTH AFRICA

Before the first explorers and colonists arrived, the basic foodstuffs of much of Africa were starches such as millet and sorghum which were pounded into meal for bread or for porridges or dumplings, as was maize much later. Maize porridges are still standard fare in Africa, similar to the *coo coo* of the West Indies, and the meal is made into loaves of bread called *mielie* in South Africa. (This is also the name of corn on the cob, a local delicacy.) Root vegetables such as cassava and yams were eaten, and sweet potatoes, peanuts and rice were quickly adopted as well.

It was the Dutch who settled in the southern part of Africa permanently in about 1650, 2,000 years after the north was populated, and where they planted vines, fruit trees, vegetables and herbs, which flourished in the fertile soil.

The indigenous people of the Cape, the Hottentots or 'Strandlopers' as they were

A bustling and colourful market in Central Africa.

christened by the colonists, did not cultivate crops or tend cattle, but lived simply off land and sea, on fish, shellfish and wild game that were abundant throughout the region. Although not hostile, the Hottentots did little to teach the settlers how to survive in their new environment (unlike the Indians in North America). The colonists' first attempts at planting grain crops were disastrous, as the well-documented storms of the area completely destroyed the first couple of harvests, and left the Dutch totally dependent on passing ships with their holds full of rice brought back from Malaysia, Indonesia and China. These ships also brought thousands of 'Malay' slaves who were to play a singular part in the cuisine of so-called Hottentot Holland.

Pies, stews, roasts and boiled vegetables were commonplace in seventeenth-century Holland, and recipes were lovingly recreated by the Cape housewives who adapted them to include local ingredients. Thus yams, plantains and sweet potatoes

began to be used as starches, and loquats, grenadillas, mangoes and Cape gooseberries (actually another import from South America) were used in desserts to replace traditional Dutch ingredients.

It was the Malay slaves, though, who were to be the prime influence on South African cooking. Their spices enlivened the bland Dutch food, and many dishes of Malay origin are still regarded as some of the most traditional of South African cuisine. Bobotie, which most regard as the national dish, is a kind of spiced cottage pie. *Sosaties* are cubes of lamb marinated in an apricot sauce, skewered and traditionally grilled over an open fire. Peoples from the Indian sub-continent have populated many parts of Africa, particularly in and around Durban, where curries predominate.

The Malay slaves were also skilful fishermen, and took advantage of the plentiful shoals of mackerel, Cape salmon, shad, *steenbrass*, *snoek* and stumpnose. Their

pickled fish, which often kept for up to three days, even in that heat, was vital to the diet of Dutch settlers who had travelled further inland and were too far away from the sea to obtain regular fresh supplies. Similarly meat was preserved, by drying, to make *biltong*, and fruits were pickled with spices in chutneys. In their wagon-train movements to the north and west, Dutch Voortrekkers initiated a great South African tradition of cooking outdoors over fire, thus the *braaivleis*, or barbecue, a cooking technique which is as important to the South Africans as it is to the Americans.

I have visited South Africa many times, principally to work – attending food fairs, cooking for special occasions. Once, for charity, we fed 10,000 children, which I found very touching. In April 1996, my London club launched Rainbow Cuisine, which is the South African 'nouvelle cuisine', a lighter version of all the various elements which characterise South African cooking – the Dutch, Malay and Indian. We served many lightly spiced hors d'oeuvres, then cooked springbok as we would venison, and the dessert was a milk tart, *Melktert*, an early Dutch introduction.

Subsequently, British, French and Portuguese colonists settled in central and western Africa, adding their own unique blend of cooking styles to those that were indigenous. The peanut, a staple ingredient in stews and sauces on the west coast, was actually brought from Brazil by Portuguese slavers who wanted to provide cheap and nourishing food for their captives while waiting for ships to carry them to the New World. The peanut is now used extensively as oil, when ground as a thickener, and whole in many snacks. Palm or dende oil is the major cooking medium, and it lends a pungent flavour and gold colour to every dish it is used in, and has since, along with the peanut, black beans and other ingredients, found its way via the slave routes to South America, southern North America, and the Caribbean.

I visited Mauritius for a holiday not so long ago, and ate the best curry I've ever had in my life. It was cooked by a local girl, Chef Mesh, who had obviously been profesionally trained but who, just as obviously, had absorbed the rich local tradition from her mother. I had squid curry for lunch one day, but so enjoyed its fresh flavour that I ordered it again for dinner. Food is my life both professionally and personally, but to have the same dish twice in one day shows how impressed I was.

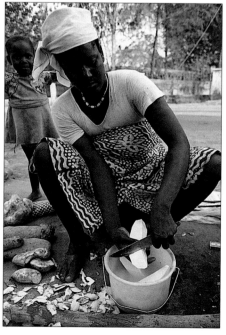

Preparing yam in Nigeria.

ASIA

Asia is the largest continent, occupying about one-third of the dry land in the world, and indeed, physically speaking, Europe is a peninsula of Asia.

Vegetables and grains are the focus of most Asian cuisines, with protein fish and meats forming a much smaller proportion of a meal than in the West. Wheat is a major ingredient, made into breads, buns, noodles and pancakes, but the prime grain of Asia is rice. Beans and pulses are important foodstuffs too, particularly the soya bean, which produces bean curd and the soy sauces and paste used in the easterly parts of Asia.

Flavourings feature enormously in Asian cooking, particularly spices, for most of the latter originated there. Ginger is a unifying flavour in the east of the continent, as is the chilli (although only introduced in the sixteenth century). The cuisines of India, China and South-East Asia have the most intense flavours, the countries to the far east and west being more muted.

THE MIDDLE EAST

It was in the fertile crescent at the eastern end of the Mediterranean that man the hunter is thought to have become man the farmer. Since then the area has been home to many civilisations. In modern times the area encompasses the states of Egypt, Israel, Lebanon, Syria, Jordan, Iraq, Iran, Saudi Arabia, Yemen, Oman, the United Arab Emirates and Kuwait, and in culinary terms stretches as far north as the Balkans, as far south as the Gulf of Aden.

All of these countries share a collective history, as the Middle East formed an integral part of the spice routes from the Far East and Central Africa to Europe. Many of the traders were in fact Arab, from the Middle East, and were responsible for the spread of spices and other ingredients around the Mediterranean.

The basis from which Middle Eastern food was to develop was a simple Bedouin one, but many Egyptian dishes such as *melokhia* soup and *fuls médames* are thought to date back to Pharaonic times. The region was much fought over, and many culinary traditions were absorbed into the cooking style. The Hellenic empire of Alexander the Great ruled over parts of Persia and India, thus the similarity of the Persian *polo*, the Indian *pullao*, the Turkish *pilav* and many other dishes. One of the great Persian empires was also very influential, building a lavish court cuisine upon the simple basics.

The spread of Islam after the death of the Prophet Muhammed in AD 632 heralded a new era of Middle Eastern cooking. The Muslim Arabs ate simply, of camel, sheep, milk, bread and dates, but they were to gradually adopt many of the culinary and social traditions of the Persians,

A typical selection of Middle Eastern *mezze* dishes.

and thus spread the 'haute cuisine' of Persia throughout the whole of their empire, which was to stretch over North Africa, and along the length of the Mediterranean into Iberia.

The Turkish Ottoman empire, which took over from the Persian in the fourteenth century, was to rule until the nineteenth century, when people from all over the world came to settle in, and colonise, the countries of the Middle East – the French, British and Italians – and these influences too have been absorbed.

Although details differ, particularly in spicing, there are more similarities than dissimilarities between the cuisines of the individual countries of the Middle East.

The singing green of Sri Lankan rice paddies.

Because of Islamic and Jewish law, lamb is the principal meat, and this is skewered to be cooked over charcoal, made into long-cooked stews with vegetables and/or fruit (rather like the North African *tajines*), or stuffed into vegetables. Lamb is also minced for meatballs and for *kibbeh*, the national dish of both Syria and Lebanon, which appears in Egypt and Iraq as well.

Other meats eaten in the Middle East are chicken, duck and turkey, and perhaps the most refined dishes are those of the Persians, relics of the haute cuisine of the court. *Faisinjan* is a stew of duck with a characteristic sweet-sour sauce made with walnuts and pomegranate.

But meat and poultry are the foods of the wealthy on the whole, and grains, pulses and vegetables are the major ingredients of most Middle Eastern dishes. Rice is important, particularly in the cities. Wheat is also very significant in the rural parts of the Middle East. It is made into semolina couscous in North Africa, but a couscous is also made and served in Israel. Cracked wheat is used in *kibbeh* and tabbouleh.

The brown beans of the Egyptian *fuls médames* are eaten as appetiser, tucked into the pouch of Arab flat bread, or as breakfast, by rich and poor alike. *Ta'amia* or falafel, rissoles made from ground white beans, are also an Egyptian speciality, but the idea has been adopted elsewhere – in Syria and the Lebanon, and particularly in Israel, where falafel made from chickpeas have virtually become the national dish. They are eaten along with salad, and a seasoning of tahina. Tahina itself, a sesame seed paste, is used in many Middle Eastern recipes, primarily in the appetiser hummus, and in sauces for vegetables.

Vegetables play a very important role in Middle Eastern cookery, and aubergines, grown all over the region, reign supreme. As well as being stuffed, they are puréed with flavourings for appetiser dips to be eaten with bread. Salads are common, made from fresh and cooked vegetables, and most are dressed with olive oil.

Other unifying factors in the Middle Eastern cuisines are the use of yoghurt – in cooked and uncooked sauces, and in

salads – and crisp sweet pastries in the manner of baklava and *kadaif*, most of them soaked in a sweet syrup. A sweet syrup is also the soaking medium for a salad of dried fruits, *khoshaf*.

Mezze are a way of life in the Middle East, and are common in virtually every country. A few years ago, I was invited to cook in Tel Aviv, and it was there that I had one of the most exciting *mezzes* I have ever tasted.

INDIA

Famous since antiquity as a source of spices, India was the goal of the early exploratory voyages which carried European sailors halfway around the world in search of spices. However, India's culinary history well predates this, and is related to its religious history.

The fair-skinned Aryans from Central Asia invaded northern India in about 2,000 BC, and settled, interbreeding with the remaining dark-skinned natives, the Dravidians. This intermingling of cultures led to the creation of Hinduism, still the religion of some 85 per cent of Indians. The

Ayurveda, the first Hindu text – concerning food, medicine and health – dates from 1,500 BC. In this the whole philosophy of present-day Indian eating is laid out: diseases should be treated first by food, and only then by medicine if needed. The six tastes – sour, sweet, salty, pungent, bitter and astringent – if in balance, can create and maintain a healthy body and mind.

Another basic tenet at the heart of Hindu doctrine is the theory of reincarnation, which encourages a respect for all animal life, thus most Hindus are vegetarian. Hindus also revere the cow, and do not eat beef. Buddhism, which was born in northern India in the sixth century BC, has since become one of the world's major religions, and strict Buddhists are vegetarian. Both Hindu and Buddhist beliefs have contributed largely to a huge proportion of the Indian population being vegetarian.

Other peoples were to come to India, among them the Moghuls or Mongols who invaded the north in the seventh century after Christ, under the leadership of Genghis Khan. They were Muslims from Persia and the Middle East, and they brought many culinary influences – meat-eating, rice, fruit and nuts, and garlic. They did not cook or eat pork. Fleeing Muslim rule in Persia, the Zoroastrians arrived in India in the eighth century, and settled around Bombay on the west coast. They became known as Parsees (Persians), and they too introduced unique Persian touches.

Europeans had introduced Christianity to India rather earlier, but it was the arrival of the Portuguese in the sixteenth century which strengthened its hold, particularly on the west coast. These early colonisers were also, of course, responsible for the introduction of the chilli pepper, perhaps the most significant in India's culinary history. This now provides the heat in food, a role previously taken by mustard seeds, ginger and black pepper.

The British contribution to the gastronomy of India has been minimal, despite the fact that it was an English colony for two centuries during the days of the Raj (from a Hindi word meaning to rule), but it did increase the awareness of spicy food in Europe, making curry a household name.

Curries (the word curry is a corruption of the south Indian word *kari*, meaning 'something in a spicy sauce') are the mainstays of Indian cuisine, and differ dramatically from region to region. There are thousands of different kinds, wet or dry, creamy or aromatic, but each is guaranteed its individuality by the inclusion of a *masala*, the sub-jective spice and herb combination that can create the fiery heat of the vindaloo in Goa or the fragrant tikkas of the north.

Inevitably vegetables play a prominent part in the diet of India. Potatoes, aubergines, onions, cucumbers, spinach, cauliflower and okra are all grown and eaten throughout India, as are pulses (lentils, beans, peas and chickpeas). These provide a rich source of protein and are collectively called gram or dhal (the latter also the name of the lentil curry served as a cooling side dish). Many pulses are ground to flour, and breads made from lentils and rice are common in the south.

Northern India and Pakistan

Northern India is a land of great geographical contrasts, from Kashmir and north Pakistan on the 'roof of the world' in the Himalayas, to the fertile plains of the western Punjab and the desert heat of Rajasthan. Until 1947, when Pakistan was created to satisfy the Muslim League's demand for a separate state for the Muslim minority, Pakistan was part of India, and shared its traditions, customs and cuisine, apart from obvious religious differences.

Each area has a culinary repertoire that depends heavily on local produce, yet all were greatly influenced by the Moghul style of cooking, which was lavish and meat based. Beef is proscribed by the Hindus, pork by the Muslims, so mutton or goat are the favoured meats, and are incorporated

Cooking chapatis in the tandoor oven in Lahore, Pakistan.

into a host of dishes. Many of these include ground nuts and sweet fruits, which is very Persian in essence. Meats can also be minced and rolled into spicy meatballs known as kofta or seekh kebab (made with beef in Muslim Pakistan), skewered as a kebab, or baked in the tandoor oven. The latter is a style which originated in the Punjab; the most famous dishes include tandoori chicken and chicken tikka.

Breads rather than rice accompany northern dishes, which are much drier than southern dishes. While the tandoor is still scorchingly hot, the leavened dough of naan bread is formed into circles or teardrop shapes, and slapped on to the side of the oven, where it sticks and bakes to a golden puffed brown. Once cooked, it is often smeared with ghee, a clarified butter prized for its purity and rich flavour; once made from buffalo milk, it is a principal cooking medium of the north. The plains of the Punjab grow the wheat for all Indian *roti* (bread); other northern breads are unleavened, and include chapati, puri and paratha.

Rice is eaten in the north, but it is considered a rare delicacy. The *pullaos*, which are so similar to the Persian *polos* – rice scented with saffron (the crocuses are grown in Kashmir) with meats and gentle spices – are dishes for feasts, as are *birianis*, the latter often topped with *warq*, sheets of gold or silver beaten to tissue thinness. *Birianis* are slowly steamed, very similar to the *chelo* and *polo* technique of Iran.

The Moghuls were also responsible for a number of the extraordinarily sweet dishes of north India. These are mostly based on milk, such as the famous ice cream, *kulfi*. This is made from full cream milk which is reduced by simmering and betrays its Moghul past by the inclusion of almonds and pistachios. Carrot *halwa* is another northern sweet, distantly related in flavour and name to the Middle Eastern *halva*.

Eastern India and Bangladesh

Eastern India encompasses the states of Bengal, Orissa, Bihar and Assam, the latter two sandwiching Bangladesh between them. A part of India until 1947, Bangladesh was known as East Pakistan until 1972 when it achieved independence. The flavours of the cooking are principally sweet, sour and bitter.

The entire area shares a love of fish, which are caught in vast quantities in the shallow, monsoon-whipped Bay of Bengal, and in the delta of the Ganges. Chefs can choose between the Indian shad or salmon, red snapper, seerfish and pomfret (black, white or silver), to name but a few. The fish is first rinsed in turmeric water (to sterilise it) and then fried in pure mustard oil – a cooking medium used mostly in Bengal – in an open pan to seal in the flavours before the sauce is added and the dish left to simmer.

Another popular eastern ingredient is *paneer*, the protein-rich soft curd cheese, not unlike cottage cheese. *Gulab jamun* is a popular Bengali sweet.

Southern India and Sri Lanka

In general, southern Indian food is much hotter and spicier than in any other region. This is necessary because very spicy food helps the body to perspire and thus lose heat. Other ways of cooling down involve the ubiquitous coconut, which has become synonymous with southern Indian food. Coconut milk is stirred into countless dishes, as well as making soothing drinks. The milk is obtained by grating the flesh of a fresh coconut and macerating it in about 300 ml hot water. This is then squeezed in a muslin cloth to remove the milky fluid, leaving behind the dry fibre pulp which in itself can be added to dishes.

Southern Indian food contains various flavours of the Ayurveda: sweet and bitter is contributed by asafoetida; salty and sour by tamarind; pungent by hot chillies; and astringent by fenugreek. Mustard seeds and curry leaves are common as well.

Vegetarianism is more common in the south than in the north, and this is due in part to the region's greater variety of vegetables, but also to the influence of the Hindu religion. Most of the chefs of the area are strict Brahmins: once an elite priestly order, they will not allow meat in any form into their kitchens, and contact with all meat eaters is banned.

Pulses provide valuable protein for non meat eaters, and dhals are common. Rice is eaten with every meal, and this helps to absorb the wetter dishes common in the south. Some sauces (curries) are so liquid that they are more like soup, including the pepper water which the British transformed into mulligatawny (from the Tamil words *molegoo*, pepper, and *tunes*, water).

The island of Sri Lanka has absorbed many influences from the peoples who have come and gone over the centuries, primarily the Dutch and Portuguese. The coconut, which is as prevalent in Sri Lankan cuisine as it is in Kerala, actually got its name from the Portuguese.

The Dutch introduced the idea of meat-balls, among others, and Sri Lankan *frikadells* (a name common to many meat-ball dishes in northern Europe) are deliciously spicy, now popularly served at a Sri Lankan feast called *lampries* (from the Dutch *lomprijst*). As with the Indonesian *Rijstaffel*, the central role is played by rice, and it is accompanied by several curries – some of the hottest in the sub-continent – and spice-hot *sambolas* (sambals).

Western India

This is arguably the most cosmopolitan region of the whole sub-continent. It incorporates Gujarat, Maharashtra, Karnataka, and Goa. India's principal seaport, Bombay, lies on the long coastline, and it was here that Portuguese explorers landed in the sixteenth century and founded Christian colonies. The area is predominantly Hindu but, because of its sea-faring history, it is also home to large minority groups of Jews and Christians, the latter residing mainly in Goa, famed for its searingly hot curries. Because Goa is Christian, pork is not proscribed, and this is about the only area in India in which pork is cooked as food. Goa remained a colony of Portugal until 1956, and Goanese food still is a blend of Portuguese and southern Indian influences, using cumin and fresh coriander, both very popular in Portugal.

The flavours and tastes of west-coast dishes are dictated by tamarind, coconut milk, chillies, cinnamon, lime juice and peanuts. Another seasoning often incorporated into curries is that of the bizarrely named Bombay duck, which is actually the dried fillet of a fish called the bummalow.

Very recently I was invited by the Taj group of hotels to visit India, and I stayed and worked in the Bombay Palace Hotel. I was amazed by the numbers of people who flocked to taste my food, and the whole trip was a huge success.

I also went to Goa, which I loved. I visited the hotel kitchens there as well, and each day I had at least four meals, so that I could try as many different things as possible! The Goa market was amazing, starting at about four in the morning, but the flavour highlight of the trip for me was a crab curry I ate in Bombay, so sweet, and so spicy.

CHINA

The ancient Chinese religion, Taoism, seeks harmony in every aspect of life, from the kitchen to the soul. This harmony is controlled by contrasting but complementary forces, known as *yin* (negative and passive) and *yang* (positive and dynamic), which should be properly and equally balanced. The human body, too, is regulated by such balance, and foods are defined as 'cooling' (*yin*) and 'heating' (*yang*), so that meals and dishes can enjoy an equal harmony. Another ancient 'rule' of Chinese gastronomy is similar to that of the Ayurveda: that five tastes should be intermingled to create a balance – salty, sweet, sour, bitter and pepper-hot.

China's vastness means that no one type of cookery predominates. No province shares the same geographical topography or even the same climatic conditions, which gives the cuisine a unique variety. This variety can be roughly categorised into four regional styles: Cantonese, Pekingese, Shanghainese and Sichwan. Although each differs marginally, sometimes dramatically, there are also many dishes which are prepared in almost identical ways throughout China. Rice, for instance, is a staple ingredient in all the regions, and is the focal point of most Chinese meals; indeed, in Chinese, an invitation to dine translates as 'come and have rice with me'. Rice is grown in the south primarily, and is also ground for flour and noodles, and used to make vinegars and wines.

Wheat is grown in more northerly parts of China, and wheat flour is used to make noodles, a symbol of longevity for the Chinese people. Noodles are also added to soups and salads, stir-fried, and the dough is wrapped around fish or meat to make dumplings or won-tons, or spring rolls.

The soya bean is native to China. It is as near to a complete protein as a vegetable food can be, so it is extremely valuable in the diet of the Chinese. The beans are very versatile. They are eaten fresh or dried as a vegetable, they are sprouted, and dried and ground into flour for noodles, and made into bean curd; the beans are also fermented to make soy sauce, and some of the many bean sauces and pastes (including black, yellow and sweet). Soy sauces of differing strengths are a staple in Chinese cooking, as are oils, particularly those made from peanuts and sesame seeds.

In a traditional Chinese meal there are many dishes to choose from, each carefully planned to achieve a harmony of taste, colour and texture. Texture is very important, and foods can be crisp or tender, gelatinous or slippery. These textural likes and dislikes, some very alien to western taste, are often supplied by equally alien ingredients such as snake, dog, birds' feet, fish lips, birds' nests and sharks' fins.

Cantonese

This style of cookery is based in the area around the south-eastern city of Canton (modern-day Guangzhou), but incorporates the whole province of Kwangtung as well as the bustling city of Hong Kong. Its climate is subtropical, so many fruits and vegetables grow in great profusion in the lush Pearl River delta. The coastline spreads for almost a thousand miles along the South China Sea, enabling fishermen to harvest such delicacies as abalone, crabs (used in crab fu-yung), ts'ang fish, shrimps, clams, scallops, crayfish and lobsters. Rice is grown here, with up to three harvests per year, as well as other staples such as wheat, sweet potatoes and chillies. Pigs and poultry, particularly ducks, are bred for the table, so Cantonese cooks have a huge choice of ingredients to draw on, more than in any other region of China.

This style of cooking is the best known in the West, because it was from Canton that emigrant Chinese travelled to better themselves in the nineteenth and twentieth centuries, to the South Seas and across the Pacific to America and San Francisco. Because of Hong Kong's relationship with Britain, most of the restaurants in Britain and Europe were opened by Cantonese cooks.

Cantonese dishes are mild and only lightly seasoned, for cooks want to bring out the individual taste of every ingredient to the full. The predominant herbs and spices, although they are used sparingly, are coriander, ginger, garlic, chillies, cloves, star anise and sesame seeds. Other seasonings include oyster sauce.

Stir-frying is probably the most popular method of cooking in Canton, and is the

A noodle maker at a Sunday market in Northern China.

most recent of Chinese techniques. Steaming is another favourite cooking method used for whole fish and for scallops. Yet another popular method of cooking is red or lacquer roasting: this is the basis for dishes such as *char siu*, a roast pork that is probably as important in Chinese gastronomy as Peking duck. Ducks are also roasted in this way. Other Cantonese dishes include sweet and sour pork, and spare ribs.

In Hong Kong, there are some 3,000 restaurants featuring the four principal culinary styles of China, as well as restaurants specialising in dim sum (see left). In Stanley, I remember I ate fresh grouper or garoupa (of the same family as sea bass) steamed with spring onions and ginger. I was too early for the snake season, but I gently declined a suggestion that I might sample a new Chinese delicacy – rat...

Pekingese

The cuisine centres around the Chinese capital Peking (or Beijing). In stark contrast to Canton, the area is rugged and its climate harsh. It is because of this that the food is more substantial and starchier than anywhere else in the country, and, as in northern India, wheat products – steamed breads, buns, dumplings and noodles – take preference over rice. Pork is a rarity on the menus of the north, as a large percentage of the population is Muslim, following the incursions of Genghis Khan and his

Mongols in the thirteenth century. Beef, too, is scarce, for the ox is more valued as a beast of burden than as food. Lamb is therefore the most popular meat, and is incorporated into countless recipes, most famously a Mongolian hot pot: paper-thin slices of mutton are dipped into boiling broth, and eaten instantly, with dipping sauces.

The techniques of cooking are essentially Middle Eastern or Mongol in style – barbecue grilling, spit-roasting, long low-heat simmering and deep-frying. Peking duck is a delicious adaptation of some of these techniques.

Sichwan (Sichuan, Szechwan)

Sichwan and its neighbouring province Hunan contain the most extensive fertile areas in the country, and Hunan is known as the rice bowl of China. Although landlocked, they are situated in the upper basin of the Yangtze River (the largest in the world), which provides the area with freshwater fish and shrimps in profusion, as well as ducks. Pig and poultry are common, and beef too is found.

Probably because the summers in Sichwan are very hot, as in India and elsewhere, the cuisine is characterised by its heat, achieved through the generous use of chillies, ginger and *fagara*, or Sichwan pepper. Salt is much used in the cooking, and also in vegetable pickles, a regional speciality, which are served with fresh foods to

---

DIM SUM

In Europe, *tapas*, *zakuski* and *mezze* are served with drinks; in China, small snacks are served with tea – the ceremony known as *yum cha*. It began over 1,000 years ago during the Sung Dynasty, and took place in special tea houses, where men gathered to relax and discuss business. The snacks became known as dim sum, or 'little heart' or 'heart warmer', and are served at lunchtime only, especially in Cantonese restaurants. Nowadays special dim sum chefs painstakingly prepare the small items, among them steamed buns stuffed with red-roasted pork, prawn toasts, spare ribs and a plethora of dumplings, of seafood or meat, wrapped in wheat or rice skins and steamed, grilled or deep-fried.

give them added piquancy, or as an hors d'oeuvre. Fermented soya bean sauces are also used, particularly yellow bean sauce and chilli bean paste.

Shanghainese

A distinctive cuisine has built up around the city of Shanghai in the north-east of China. All the ingredients in Shanghainese cookery are found locally, and are of the very highest quality. To let every taste shine through, the food is lightly seasoned and is accompanied by only the most delicate of sauces. Saltwater and freshwater fish come from the Yangtze River and delta, and many freshwater lakes.

The Shanghainese like sweetness, which accounts for the sugar added to pork, ham and seafood dishes; even the east-coast vinegar, *chingkiang*, is the sweetest and most fragrant in China.

Vegetables are used generously, along with the yellow rice wine which is a speciality of Shaohsing. This has been made and can be aged for from ten to 100 years. Shaohsing wine is also used in dishes which are defined as 'drunken'. An interesting Shanghai dish has chicken and vegetables, seasoned with soy, oyster sauce, garlic, ginger and shaohsing, wrapped in a paper parcel and baked or deep-fried.

SOUTH-EAST ASIA

The countries of South-East Asia include Thailand, Malaysia, Singapore, Indonesia, Vietnam, Cambodia, Laos, Burma (Myanmar) and the Philippines, all of which are clustered together between the Pacific and Indian Oceans. The area is huge, but consists principally of ocean, and only Laos has no coastline at all.

Situated in the southern shadow of China, and east of the land mass of India, the countries, islands, peninsulas and archipelagos of South-East Asia have been coveted and colonised for thousands of years by greater powers. Vietnam, for instance, was occupied by China for about ten centuries; nearer our own time France dominated much of Indochina – North and South Vietnam, Cambodia (or Kampuchea) and Laos – for nearly 100 years. Indonesia was ruled for decades, by first the Portuguese, then the Dutch, and was particularly valued because of the Spice Islands, or the Moluccas.

Although these diverse colonising influences have led to many individual nuances in the cooking techniques, ingredients and flavours of South-East Asian countries, the various cuisines share many characteristics. The principal shared ingredient is once again rice, the grain which feeds most of Asia.

The abundant seafood of South-East Asia also provides a basis for the pungent fermented fish sauces or pastes that are vital in most of the cuisines, adding depth of flavour as well as saltiness. Soy sauce and soy-based condiments are also comparatively important in a number of the cuisines, displaying the influence of China.

The distinctive spice and herb flavourings of South-East Asian cooking are generally those which were originally native to the region – onions, garlic, ginger, lemongrass, lime, mint, sesame and coconut. However, two of the region's most familiar and characteristic flavourings are not indigenous – chilli peppers from Central America and Mexico, and peanuts from Brazil and Peru. Tamarind, which adds a sweet sourness to so many South-East Asian dishes, is not indigenous either: African in origin, it was introduced early to India and thence to points east by Indian migrants. Coriander, too, is an import from

A typical 'stallholder' at the floating market near Bangkok, Thailand.

southern Europe, and it is the fresh herb rather than the spice that has become a principal flavouring of the area

Thailand

Thailand is geographically close to China, but in culinary terms it is just as influenced by the cuisines of India. The stir-frying in a wok was borrowed from China, but the searingly hot curries show the intense flavours of southern India.

The creamy and cooling sweetness of the ubiquitous coconut is vital because it is in Thailand that some of the hottest of the world's chillies are grown; there are about ten, including the tiny but lethal bird's eye chilli. Further heat is provided by three types of ginger – fresh root ginger, greater galangal, and the even stronger *krachai*, or lesser galangal. These are chopped and ground together with Thai garlic in a large mortar and pestle to make curry pastes, along with chillies (red or green, according to the colour of curry required), shallots, lemongrass, coriander, cumin, *nam pla* (fish sauce) and kaffir lime leaves or peel. Coconut milk or cream is used as the cooking medium and liquid. Much the same juxtaposition of ingredients goes to make up some of the Thai palette of dipping sauces; the most pungent is *nam prik*.

The four primary herbal flavours of Thailand are mint, coriander, lemongrass and basil. Lemongrass more than anything else typifies Thai cooking for me, and it is the clean and singing flavour predominant in many dishes, including the justly famed hot and sour soup containing shellfish or chicken. The green herbs star in most of the Thai salads known as *yom* or *yum*, for the cuisine has a wealth of cold or just-warm dishes, served with crisp and cooling raw vegetables.

There are two kinds of rice in Thailand, long-grain or fragrant rice, and short-grain glutinous rice which is grown in the north. All meals consist of rice, including breakfast. Rice is also made into noodles which feature in many of the country's most loved dishes; Pad Thai, rice noodles with eggs, is considered the national dish.

It is perhaps the fish that impressed me most: the massed colourful variety of seafood available in the markets of Bangkok is awe-inspiring and I loved the banks of fish tanks in almost every restaurant I visited, from which you could choose the particular fish you wanted to eat.

Fruits too are in abundance in the markets, and these are served after a meal, for there are few actual desserts in Thai cuisine. Apart from, of course, *sankhaya*, the famous custard introduced by the colonising Portuguese and Spanish, which the Thais make, inevitably, with coconut milk.

Vietnam and Cambodia

Vietnam and Cambodia (formerly Kampuchea) lie to the east of the South-East Asian mainland.

Both countries have been influenced by the Chinese, particularly North Vietnam. This has led to Chinese cooking techniques such as stir-frying and steaming, a liking for soy sauce and noodles, and the habit of eating from bowls with chopsticks. The flavours are milder in the north, where many Chinese still remain, and the cooking is lighter. Both countries became part of French Indochina in the nineteenth century, and have been influenced by French style. Breads are made as in France, and many French-style *daubes*, *soupes*, and *ragoûts* have the added accents of *nuoc mam* (fish sauce), chilli and lemongrass. Both cuisines are also very much in the Thai tradition, although they lack the fiery heat. Cambodia has actually absorbed a little Malay influence, particularly in the grilled pieces of meat, fish or shellfish which are similar to satay.

There are fertile rice-growing areas in both countries. Rice is cooked as a grain, but is also ground to make flour for noodles, to enhance broths made with chicken, beef, crab or pork, and flavoured with ginger, aniseed or star anise in Vietnam, lemongrass in Cambodia. *Pho* is one such dish, from Hanoi, using beef or chicken; it is eaten for breakfast, lunch or dinner all over Vietnam. Rice also makes transparent pancakes or wrappers which are moistened and wrapped round meats, salads and herbs for *banh trang* in Vietnam, or as a wrapping for Vietnamese spring rolls.

Fresh vegetables and herbs are greatly loved in both Cambodia and Vietnam (as well as in Laos and Thailand), and a raw platter of a variety of things is served with most meals, to accompany meat or to be wrapped in rice-paper wrappers.

Malaysia and Singapore

Malaysia is a long tropical peninsula pointing south towards Indonesia and separating the South China Sea from the Indian Ocean. Singapore is the island republic which sits on the southern tip of the peninsula; it is the smallest of all the Asian countries.

Many peoples have visited and stayed since the sixteenth century, among them Chinese, Indians and Arabs. It was the Arabs who were to have one of the most important and permanent influences, by introducing Islam, but all were to leave a mark on the cuisines of both Malaysia and Singapore. Malay cooking is based on rice and fish, and these are moistened with coconut and flavoured with many local seasonings such as *blachan* (shrimp paste), pepper, ginger, lemongrass or tamarind. The Portuguese were to bring chillies, and now the spicing of dishes is Indian; cumin, turmeric and chillies flavour Malay curries, but these same curries could also have additions of soy sauce, more than a hint of Chinese. Chutneys and Indian-style breads often accompany meals. The curries are still coconut based, but range in style from mild kormas to those with fiery Tamil and south Indian heat. Coconut milk or cream – *lemak* – also forms the basis of the famous *laksa* of both Malaysia and Singapore, a sour seafood soup flavoured with tamarind and/or lemongrass, containing noodles and bean curd, often with candlenuts as well.

The Chinese influence on the cooking of Malaysia reveals itself in many noodle dishes such as *mee goreng*, fried noodles served with shredded chicken, prawns and vegetables. Soy sauce and hoisin sauce are often used, as are pork and beef, for the Chinese have no religious restraints.

The Chinese influence is strongest, however, in Singapore. Chinese labourers came from Hokkien province and Canton to work on the construction of the city in the nineteenth century and stayed, marrying Malay women. This led to the creation of a unique cuisine, called Nonya or Straits Chinese, which combines Chinese ingredients with local Malay herbs and seasonings. Many dishes are still as mild as they might be in Canton, but as many are very hot. I have visited Singapore many times. Once when I was there I was entertained by Violet Oon, a top local food writer, and was first introduced to Nonya. I still remember the flavours of that first Nonya dinner, and the sense of honour I felt when she cooked yellow rice for me: in the old days it was used only to welcome royalty.

One of the dishes which most characterises Malaysia and Singapore is *satay* (although Indonesia claims it as well): thin strips of skewered meat – beef, pork or chicken – or prawns are marinated then chargrilled, and served with a peanut sauce. The technique is said to be traceable back to the Arab kebab.

Accompanying sambals are very common in both Malaysia and Singapore. These are cooked or uncooked, some mild, some hot. Coconut forms the base of many, as does chilli.

Indonesia

The three most well-known of over 13,000 islands belonging to Indonesia are Bali, Java and Sumatra. The Indonesian islands were the spice islands sought by so many in the fifteenth and sixteeenth centuries, and the spices once unique to them include cloves, nutmeg and mace, and pepper. As a result of spice incursions, as in Malaysia and Singapore, there are multifarious influences, primarily that of the Muslim Arabs, who brought Islam. The Portuguese were to introduce New World ingredients, among them the chilli pepper and peanut, now so characteristic of Indonesian cooking, and the Dutch were to graft many ideas on to the native cuisine during their three centuries of occupation.

As in Malaysia and Singapore, there is a meld of native Indonesian, Chinese and Indian influences. Rice is the staple, but there are some noodle dishes as well. *Nasi goreng* is fried rice with chillies, onions, spices, garlic and a fish sauce, *terasi*, the Indonesian equivalent of Malaysia's *blachan*. Curries are at the heart of the cuisine, which are coconut creamy, often with ground peanuts as a sauce thickener.

The East Javanese claim satay as their own, and satay is now considered the national dish of Indonesia. The peanut sauce accompaniment is flavoured with *kecap manis*, a thick sweet soy sauce.

Soy sauces are used in the making of sambals. They are usually very hot, made with chillies, coconut or peanuts and/or *terasi*, but some are mild, designed to calm the palate. Cooked vegetables are served in salads: for *gado gado*, a selection of vegetables is stir-fried or blanched, then coated with a hot nutty peanut sauce. Coconut milk provides the principal cooking medium and flavouring of other vegetable dishes.

The most famous Indonesian export is probably *Rijstaffel*, Dutch for 'rice table', and it is said to have been created when the original Dutch settlers wished to taste all the different dishes of Indonesia. One dish was brought at a time for approval and sampling, along with a central bowl of rice. This in essence is still what a *Rijstaffel* is: rice, along with many of the most characteristic dishes such as curries and *satay*, a myriad sambals, plus *krupuk*, prawn crackers. *Rijstaffel* can be sampled and

enjoyed in many cities in The Netherlands, as well as in Surinam in South America, another Dutch colony.

The Philippines

The Philippine Islands, more than 7,000 of them, lie between the Pacific Ocean and the South China Sea, directly south of Taiwan. As with most of South-East Asia, the islands have seen waves of settlers and conquerors, primarily the Chinese who intermarried, so that most of the country is of Chinese-Malay extraction. The Chinese also brought culinary influences – among them the spring roll (*lumpia* in the Philippines), soy sauce and noodles. Muslims from the Middle East and India arrived as well, bringing many spices plus the words of the Koran, but it was the Spanish, from the early sixteenth century, who were to have the greatest effect. They ruled for over 350 years, until 1898 (when the United States took over), and gave the country its major religion, Catholicism, and a more Mediterranean style of cooking.

The basis of the cuisine is still Chinese-Malay, with rice the staple. Coconut milk is used as cooking liquid, and fish pastes and sauces for flavouring (*bagoong* and *patis*, made from tiny shrimps). Local Pacific ingredients are used too, such as yams, *taro* and sweet potatoes. Most Filipino dishes are tart in flavour, due to the use of tamarind, and *kalamansi*, a local citrus fruit that is a cross between a lime and a lemon.

Vinegar also features in the cooking, particularly in fish dishes: *kilawin* is a method of 'cooking' fish by marinating it in coconut vinegar and *kalamansi* juice, which is very similar to the seviche of South America and to the Spanish 'curing' of fish in escabeche. Vinegar is also used in meat cookery, particularly in *adobo*: pork, chicken or seafood is marinated in vinegar with garlic and soy sauce, then stewed before frying and serving in the reduced sauce.

The prime influence of Spain, though, lies in the Filipino *merienda*. Undeniably based on the Spanish tapas, it is a selection of small tasty dishes served usually with drinks, and beginning at about four in the afternoon. It can also include sweet dishes, and rice dishes are particularly popular, one flavoured with chocolate, another Spanish introduction. A *merienda* can serve as a complete meal, as can tapas.

THE FAR EAST

Korea and Japan are the furthest east of all the Asian countries. The former is a mountainous peninsula, the latter is a chain of islands – part of the Pacific 'ring of fire' – running north to south. They share certain culinary characteristics, and both too have been influenced to a certain extent by their nearest neighbour, China. Both countries believe, like China, that every meal should include five tastes – bitter, salty, sweet, sour and hot (in Korea) or spicy (in Japan).

The basics of both cuisines are rice, fish and pickles, with a fondness for noodles (which may be a Chinese introduction), and a more recent passion for meat, especially beef. Vegetables are widely grown and revered, and pickled for use in the winter. Soya beans and the sauces, pastes and curd made from them, are vital in both cuisines. Garlic and chillies, fresh, dried or ground, are principal flavourings in Korea, but Japan must be the least spicy of all Asia's cuisines, using only chillies very occasionally, peppercorns and a type of horseradish for heat.

Korea

Korea, whose people are of Mongol ancestry, was occupied by Japan in the first half of the twentieth century, and then was divided after World War Two.

Korea's cuisine is hearty and robust, primarily because of climate. It is partly because of this that pickles play such a vital role in the cuisine, and they appear at every meal. *Kimchee* is the most ubiquitous of these; it is used as a condiment but it is also added as an ingredient of soups, braises, fritters, stuffings and fillings. Other fermented flavourings added to dishes are made from soya beans, grains and chillies, bean pastes, vary from mild like the Japanese *miso*, to searingly hot. Chilli heat is one of the main features of Korean cooking, as is plenty of garlic.

Geography plays an important part in Korean cooking, particularly the surrounding seas and their wealth of fish. These include abalone, octopus, squid, anchovies, herrings, oysters and crab, and they are commonly braised in table-top steamboats, or in combination with meats or bean curd.

Rice is grown in the plains of the north, vegetables in the mountains, and both are cooked as basics, as are noodles (made from wheat flour, buckwheat or mung beans) and beans. Sometimes rice is mixed with other grains such as millet or barley, as well as beans.

Poultry and pork are eaten, but it is beef which has recently become the universal favourite. *Bulgogi* is the most famous and popular beef dish. It consists of marinated thin strips of beef which are chargrilled at the table, and served with a garnish salad of spring onions, another common Korean flavouring.

Japan

The four main islands of Japan are Honshu, Hokkaido, Shikoku and Kyushu, all of them mountainous, with the highest peak, Mount Fujiyama on Honshu, rising to over 3,500 metres.

Japan's cuisine is unique in Asia, and indeed the world. It is based on the Zen Buddhist precepts absorbed from China, and those inherent in the native Japanese religion, Shinto. Simplicity and naturalness are the main principles, and presentation is as important to all cooks as is the ultimate taste of a dish. The simplicity is historic, in that once the majority of Japanese were very poor, with a limited choice of ingredients – no more, perhaps, than rice, pickled vegetables and fish. The naturalness comes from a Japanese love of nature and order; each ingredient is presented unadorned and unmasked, so that its origins can be seen and appreciated, with perhaps only a few simple seasonings to bring out and create a harmony of essential flavours. These few seasonings include dried chilli, *sansho* – Sichuan peppercorns – and *wasabi*, the mountain hollyhock, which has roots like horseradish and is even stronger in heated flavour. It is grated fresh or ground to a pale green paste and powder. Seasonality is part of the naturalness of Japanese food, and is very important in culinary terms.

From the sixteenth to the mid nineteenth century, Japan closed her ports to foreigners, so there have been few outside culinary influences. It was primarily a vegetarian cuisine, relieved only by fish (and perhaps some birds), but in the nineteenth century, the ideas of the West were to be introduced, among them the eating of red meat. It was only then that recipes for pork and beef were developed, including some of what are now the most famous of Japanese dishes – *sukiyaki*, *shabu shabu*, *tonkarsu* and *teriyaki*. Beef has now become so popular that special beef cattle are raised, the famous cattle of Kobe. I went to see some of these Kobe farms when I worked in Japan; there they massage the animals every day with a spirit such as sake, and give them drinks of beer.

Fish, however, remains the principal protein element of the diet of the Japanese, and they relish a large number of seafoods which are alien to the western palate and inclination, such as whale and krill. However, salmon, tuna, bass, horse mackerel or scad, eel, carp and bream are also eaten, plus a huge variety of other sea foods, such as abalone, prawns, lobsters, cuttlefish, squid and oysters. These are so fresh that the majority of them can be eaten raw in *sashimi*. *Fugu* or blowfish requires greater nerve, even for the Japanese, for if the flesh is not prepared correctly, it can kill within 5 minutes; *fugu* chefs have to be specially trained and licensed. Fish otherwise are simply grilled or steamed, or deep-fried in batter for tempura.

The fish markets in Japan – I visited those in Osaka and Tokyo – are quite astounding. At the Osaka fish market one morning, I had my first taste of what I call *udon pot*, a steaming bowl of flavoured fish stock with *udon* noodles and some of the freshest fish I have ever tasted.

Dashi, the fish stock which forms the basis of so many soups and other dishes in Japan, is made from flakes of dried *bonito* (a fish of the mackerel family, which is not valued or eaten fresh) combined with

Fresh tuna on offer in Tokyo.

kombu, a giant sea kelp, to give a flavour which is quite unique. *Kombu* and other marine plants are used a great deal in Japanese cookery – among them *nori* (known in the West as laver) and *wakame*; these are harvested fresh and then dried for culinary use. *Nori* is used as a wrapping for sushi; it can also be toasted and crumbled as a garnish.

The swaying green of rice paddies dots most of the available farming land around the coasts of Japan. Rice is so valued that the word for it is also the word for 'meal'. A bowl of rice with some pickled vegetables and green tea form the traditional end to every meal, whether eaten at home or more formally, in a restaurant. Rice is also made into sake, a mild rice wine, *mirin*, its sweetened form, and *harusame* noodles, which look like cellophane.

Noodles are very popular in Japan, particularly as a fast food. They are made primarily from wheat flour, as *udon* and *somen*, but *soba* include some buckwheat, and *sharataki* are quite unique, made from the paste of a root, a form of *taro*.

Soya beans are another basic of Japan, although they and their products originated with the Chinese. They are fermented to make soy sauces, *shoyu* and the darker *tamari*, as well as *miso*, a soya paste which is one of the most important ingredients of Japanese cooking. There are different varieties of *miso*, including red, yellow and white, which have different strengths and nuances of flavour. Soya beans also make bean curd or tofu; there are various types.

Vegetables and fruit are abundant in Japan. As in Korea, many vegetables are pickled as *tsukemono*, a relish which accompanies every meal. Vegetables are also cooked simply, perhaps in sesame oil, and garnished with sesame seeds, a classic Japanese flavouring.

Living and working in Japan had a great influence on my life and career. I was enormously excited to be working there, as executive chef of the Swiss Pavilion for Expo '70. My team of chefs, all of them Japanese, were talented and amenable, and I was very impressed by them. Very quickly they learned to cook Rösti (turning them in the pan with chopsticks!), and there was continual competition betweeen them – if two chefs were side by side chopping parsley, they would have a race to see who could finish first. Neither would want to lose face.

Everything about that trip was memorable. I have been a lover of Japan and Japanese food ever since.

AUSTRALASIA

Australasia – the name coming from the Latin for 'south' – is an imprecise term referring to various islands in the Pacific Ocean. We associate it mainly with the larger land masses of Australia, New Zealand, and Papua New Guinea, but it also includes Micronesia, Melanesia and Polynesia, which between them contain all the smaller South Pacific islands clustered to the east of Australia, islands like Tahiti, Samoa, Hawaii and Tonga. Early maps and journals categorise them as Oceania, an enormous area dominated by water.

The isolation of these islands meant that each community had centuries in which to evolve and develop completely independently of each other and of other cultures. By the time the Dutch and the English navigated the southern Pacific in the fifteenth and sixteenth centuries, the Aboriginal, Maori and South Pacific island cultures were well established.

THE SOUTH PACIFIC ISLANDS

The diet of these early communities is well documented. Early explorers brought back to Europe tales of strange and exotic animals and bloodthirsty cannibals. Wildly exaggerated though these stories often were, cannibalism was in fact common in the Pacific islands. Victims – or 'long pig' – included Christian missionaries sent to civilise the natives.

But even when missionary was off the menu, the Pacific islanders had a feast of natural ingredients from which to choose. The basic diet would have been based on fish, coconut, bananas and the three carbohydrates, sweet potatoes, breadfruit and taro. Another favourite ingredient was 'real' pig, which would be 'steamed' in an earth oven (ahimaa in Tahiti, imu in Hawaii). Yams, bananas, fish or chicken would also be cooked with the pig.

Coconut was and is probably the most important ingredient in South Pacific cooking, and the flesh and milk are added to hundreds of recipes. Much seafood in the islands is 'cooked' in lime juice, just as in seviche in South America.

Even today, hundreds of years later, the diet has changed only marginally, and this change is only due to the influx of foreign influences, which have created interesting regional differences among the islands. Tahiti and New Caledonia had the gastronomic good fortune to become French territories in the late nineteenth century, and there are French nuances in present-day Tahitian cuisine. Fiji's large Indian population has introduced the concept of curry; this is light on chillies, and uses a great deal of coconut cream to make it rich, mild and creamy. Hawaii has become somewhat of a melting pot, boasting influences from all over the world. The Americans introduced pineapples and sugar. The Chinese – who came to work in the sugar plantations – contributed soy sauce, noodles, rice, soya bean curd, ginger, water chestnuts, beansprouts and mangetouts or snow peas, and the Japanese brought the hibachi barbecue, sushi, tempura, sukiyaki and sake.

AUSTRALIA AND NEW ZEALAND

The Maoris of New Zealand share the Pacific island heritage; they had at one time been cannibals, and they still cook pork or fish in a deep-earth oven at their hargis or feasts. The Aborigines of Australia also open-fire-roast their foods like the Hawaiians.

However, with the arrival of Captain Cook in 1768, things began to change for the native Antipodeans. Australia soon became a penal colony for thousands of British convicts who, faced with problems of survival (their distrust of the local fauna – kangaroos, wallabies, koala bears and duck-billed platypus – was understandable), introduced rabbits and sheep. The rabbit population was later to be decimated by myxomatosis, but sheep-raising and breeding soon became a most profitable venture, and remains a major business in both New Zealand and Australia. Roasts of lamb are popular, as are steaks, for beef cattle are bred as well.

Neither Australia nor New Zealand have completely indigenous recipes. The earliest ones considered uniquely Antipodean date from the first half of the nineteenth century, and relate to cooking and eating in the bush. Damper, a soda bread (the idea perhaps introduced by Irish settlers?), is cooked in a pot or camp oven buried beside the fire with coals above and below.

More 'sophisticated' recipes include some desserts invented in Australia such as Peach Melba, created to honour the Australian soprano, Dame Nellie Melba (the surname itself adapted from Melbourne), Pavlova and Lamingtons.

These are all related in a sense to the British tradition, for both Australia and New Zealand were British colonies for over 200 years. However, one recipe very closely related to Australia – the carpetbag steak (fillet or rump stuffed with oysters) – is actually American in origin.

But things have changed again, especially for Australia. With immigration in the last few decades, the introduced food influences have been astounding. Italians have been the biggest group, followed by Greeks, Yugoslavs, Germans, Middle Easterners, South-East Asians, Chinese, Poles, Turks, French, Hungarians and Russians; some 36 major languages are said to be spoken in Australian cities, with many varying dialects, and the culinary fusion – of ingredients, ideas and cooking techniques – must be unique (similar to the melting pot that was America). Out of this has been born a new restaurant style which can surely be deemed the new Australian cuisine.

The principal distinguishing characteristic of this cooking is the marriage of European ideas with Asian flavours, and using some of the wonderful ingredients available in Australia, whether indigenous or introduced. Tasmanian or Sydney rock oysters might be served with a spicy salsa, or with buckwheat noodles and soy-based dressings. Kangaroo can be used in curries or enchiladas; ragoût of possum might be served with basil noodles, and a pot-au-feu of blue eye (or ling, snapper or dhu fish) could be accompanied by an anise-flavoured fish consommé.

In New Zealand, too, a revolution is now taking place, with a similar culinary style being developed – fresh, healthy, using wonderful ingredients, and singing with flavour. Lamb roasted on the rack has a pumpkin seed crust; Japanese kabocha pumpkins are also baked in Italian style, or used in a bread. Green shelled mussels – a New Zealand speciality – are steamed with lemongrass, coriander and coconut. Lambs' tongues are braised in Madeira, and served with a coconut sambal.

The cuisines of both countries are in their infancy in comparison to the rest of the world, but what they have achieved already is very exciting.

VEGETABLES AND SALADS

SOPA DE FAVAS
This broad bean soup comes from the wetter northern parts of Portugal; if young and fresh enough the pods are often used as well as the beans. It can be garnished with either fresh mint or fresh coriander, the latter a distinctive – and unusual – flavour of Portugal.

PORTUGAL   **SERVES 4**

1 kg broad beans in the pod

Shell the beans and place in a suitable saucepan.

1 x 15 ml spoon olive oil
2 medium potatoes, peeled and diced
1 medium onion, peeled and diced
1 garlic clove, peeled and crushed

Place in a sauté pan and heat together to soften, about 8 minutes. Do not colour. Add to the pan with the broad beans.

2 litres Chicken or Vegetable Stock
   (see pages 315 or 314)
1 sprig fresh marjoram

Add to the bean pan, and bring to the boil. Cover and simmer gently for about 15–20 minutes, until the potatoes and beans are tender. Process to a purée in a food processor or blender. Reheat gently.

2 x 15 ml spoons finely chopped fresh
   coriander or mint
salt and freshly ground pepper

Add the chosen herb to the soup just before serving, and season to taste with salt and pepper.

ASPARAGUS SOUP
Vegetable soups have been the mainstay of the working man in Britain and elsewhere in Europe for centuries, and in hard times, nettles and other herbs plucked from the wild would be the basic ingredient. This vegetable soup is rather more luxurious, good in early summer when English asparagus is at its best.

ENGLAND   **SERVES 4**

2 bunches asparagus

Wash the spears. Cut the tips off about 5 cm from the top and keep to one side. Trim the root ends, and then finely slice the stalks.

1 x 15 ml spoon olive oil
25 g butter
1 small onion, peeled and
   finely chopped
1 leek, trimmed and finely diced

Heat together in a large saucepan, and sweat until the onion and leek are soft, about 3–4 minutes. Add the finely sliced asparagus and stir.

1 x 15 ml spoon plain flour
1 litre Chicken or Vegetable Stock (see
   pages 315 or 314)

Stir in the flour, followed by the stock, then bring to the boil.

2 sprigs fresh parsley

Add to the pan, then simmer for about 10 minutes or until the asparagus is soft. Cool a little then blend the mixture in a liquidiser. Pass through a sieve for extra smoothness if required. Return the soup to the pan and bring back to the boil.

120 ml double cream
salt and freshly ground pepper

Add to the soup, seasoning to taste with salt and pepper, and simmer for a few minutes.
   Blanch the reserved asparagus tips in boiling salted water for a few minutes, then drain well. Pour the soup into soup bowls, and arrange the asparagus tips in as a garnish.

Opposite: Asparagus Soup with a garnish of fresh chervil leaves and pan-fried scallops.

BERNER MARKTSUPPE

A vegetable soup which comes from Berne, and which uses a pulse – yellow split peas – and many of the vegetables grown in the area and sold in the famous market. It is the Swiss equivalent of the famous French market soup, the onion soup associated with the old Les Halles.

SWITZERLAND

SERVES 4

50 g yellow split peas	Soak overnight in cold water to cover. Drain well.
1 small leek 1 celery stalk 1 medium carrot 1 small onion	Wash, trim and peel as appropriate, then cut in small dice.
25 g butter	Melt in a large pan, add the vegetable dice, and sweat for about 5 minutes to soften. Do not colour.
100 g smoked bacon, rinded and diced 150 g knuckle of pork, soaked 1.5 litres Vegetable Stock (see page 314) 1 bay leaf 1 sprig fresh thyme	Add to the pan, along with the split peas, and bring to the boil. Cover with the lid and leave to simmer gently for about 45 minutes.
125 g potatoes, peeled and diced	Add to the pan, and continue to simmer until cooked, about 10 minutes.
salt and freshly ground pepper	Taste the soup, add salt very sparingly, pepper more generously. Remove the knuckle of pork from the pot, and cut into largeish pieces. Return to the pan.
2 x 15 ml spoons finely cut fresh chives	As you serve (from a traditional tureen perhaps), sprinkle over the individual portions.

MELOKHIA

One of the national dishes of Egypt, this green soup is also known in Lebanon and Jordan. The leaves used are those of the *melokhia* plant, a member of the mallow family, and are available dried (occasionally fresh) in Middle Eastern shops. Spinach can be substituted.

EGYPT

SERVES 4

500 g meat or poultry (beef, lamb, veal, chicken, duck or rabbit), chopped 1.5 litres water 1 onion, peeled and chopped 1 garlic clove 1 leek, trimmed and chopped	Place in a large pot, bring to the boil, skim, then simmer for from 45 minutes to 1½ hours, or until the meat or poultry is tender. Strain, keeping the meat and the stock separate. Bone the meat, and discard the bones.
500 g fresh *melokhia* (or spinach) leaves, or 75 g dried *melokhia* leaves	Wash and dry the fresh leaves and remove the tough stalks. Cut them very finely. If using the dried leaves, crush them and reconstitute in a little hot water.
salt and freshly ground pepper	Season the stock to taste, and bring to the boil. Add the leaves and boil fresh for 5 or so minutes, dried for about 10 minutes.

2 garlic cloves, peeled 1½ x 15 ml spoons ground coriander	Crush together with a little salt.
40 g butter	Melt in a small pan then add the garlic paste. Sauté for a moment, then add to the soup. Stir in and cook for a minute or so longer.
100 g hot cooked rice (optional)	Serve in the soup if you like, along with the reheated meat or poultry pieces. Season again if necessary.

CREAM OF PUMPKIN SOUP
Many types of pumpkin are common in the Caribbean, as are soups made from them. The pumpkin must be very ripe for the best flavour. Jerk seasoning is available in many supermarkets; it combines a number of spices.

CARIBBEAN   **SERVES 4**

40 g butter 2 medium onions, peeled and finely chopped 1 garlic clove, peeled and crushed	Heat together in a large pan, and sweat until the onions have softened.
600 g pumpkin flesh 1 medium potato, peeled	Cut into small pieces and add to the onion. Cook for a minute or so.
150 ml dry white wine	Add to the pan and boil to reduce almost entirely.

750 ml Chicken or Vegetable Stock
    (see pages 315 or 314)
1 bouquet garni (thyme, celery,
    parsley, bay)
	Add to the pan and bring to the boil, then cover and simmer for about 35 minutes, or until the pumpkin is very soft. Remove the bouquet garni, and blend the soup until smooth. Reheat gently.

175 ml double cream 1 x 5 ml spoon jerk seasoning salt and freshly ground pepper freshly grated nutmeg Tabasco sauce	Add to the soup, stirring in well, and season to taste with salt, pepper, nutmeg and Tabasco (only a drop or so of the latter). Serve hot with croûtons or crusty bread.

Overleaf: Top, Minestrone (see page 47). Below left, Borscht (see page 48). Below right, Aubergine Salad with Dried Shrimps (see page 49).

MINESTRONE
Thick vegetable soups feature in almost every European cuisine, and the Italian versions are particularly good. The recipes vary all over the country. Tuscan minestrones are usually made in a large quantity so that there is enough for a different soup, *Ribollita* ('re-boiled'), the next day.

ITALY

SERVES 8

150 g fresh white (or red) kidney beans, or 100 g dried

> If using dried beans, soak them in cold water overnight. Rinse and drain well.

1 large onion, peeled and finely chopped
2 carrots, peeled and finely diced
3 celery stalks, finely diced
2 garlic cloves, peeled and crushed
60 ml olive oil

> Sweat together in a stockpot until softened and light brown.

2 litres hot Chicken or Vegetable Stock, (see pages 315 or 314)
200 g plum tomatoes, skinned, seeded and diced
1 bouquet garni (parsley, bay, rosemary)
100 g gammon or bacon in the piece

> Add to the stockpot, along with the beans. Simmer for 30 minutes. Remove and discard the bacon and bouquet garni.

½ small cabbage, shredded
200 g courgettes, trimmed and diced
100 g fresh podded peas

> Add to the stockpot, and simmer for a further 30 minutes until all the vegetables are quite soft.

salt and freshly ground pepper
grated Parmesan

> Season the soup to taste and sprinkle on some grated Parmesan. Offer a bowl of grated Parmesan as well.

GAZPACHO ANDALUZ
A chilled raw vegetable soup which has become famous all over the world. Almost every region in Spain has its own version; this one is from Andalucia, in the hot south, where all the gazpacho vegetables – tomatoes, peppers, cucumbers – grow in abundance.

SPAIN

SERVES 4

600 g ripe tomatoes, skinned
1 green and 1 red pepper, seeded
1 small onion, peeled
½ garlic clove, peeled
½ cucumber, peeled
1 slice fresh bread, crusts removed, made into breadcrumbs

> Chop the tomatoes, peppers, onion, garlic and cucumber roughly. Mix together with the crumbs in a large bowl or pan.

1½ x 15 ml spoons red wine vinegar
75 ml Brown Chicken Stock (see page 316)
60 ml olive oil
a few fresh oregano leaves
4 fresh basil leaves, finely cut
salt and freshly ground pepper

> Mix into the vegetables and breadcrumbs in the bowl, seasoning to taste with salt and pepper. Leave to marinate for 12 hours in the fridge.
> Liquidise in batches to a fine purée, then push through a sieve or a food mill into a serving bowl. Taste for seasoning, then chill.

croûtons and tomato, pepper and cucumber dice (optional)

> Use to garnish the soup if liked, or simply sprinkle with strips of fresh basil.

BORSCHT
Beetroot is one of the mainstay vegetables of the former USSR, available during the long winter when food is scarce. The number of soups made from beetroot is legion and they vary in style from pale pink broths to hearty thick vegetable mixtures. (Photograph page 46)

RUSSIA　　　　　　　　　**SERVES 4**　　　　**Oven: 150°C/300°F/Gas 2**

5 medium beetroot, raw	Wash well and dry, but do not peel. Place in a dish, cover with foil, and bake in the preheated oven for 2–3 hours, depending on size. When cool enough to handle, peel and cut the flesh into strips.
900 g lean beef brisket or chuck (plus beef bones if available), or 1 duck 1.5 litres water	Meanwhile, place together in a large soup pan, bring to the boil, then simmer, partly covered, for 1½ hours, skimming every now and then. Strain the broth, skimming off any fat. Keep the meat to one side.
20 g butter 3 small carrots, peeled and sliced 1 large onion, peeled and diced	Melt the butter in a large soup pan and gently sweat the vegetables until softened.
2 x 15 ml spoons red wine vinegar 2 x 15 ml spoons caster sugar, if necessary 200 g green kale or cabbage, roughly cut into strips salt and freshly ground pepper	Add, along with the beetroot strips and enough of the beef broth to cover the cabbage. Cover and simmer for about 15–20 minutes. Taste for seasoning, and add salt, pepper and more vinegar if necessary. 　　Slice or shred some of the meat used for the broth (reserve the rest for another use), and add to the soup to heat through.
120 ml soured cream 4 x 5 ml spoons caviar (optional) finely cut fresh chives	Place a spoonful of soured cream on top of each individual serving of soup, and top in turn with the caviar, if using, and chives.

STUFFED AVOCADO
Avocados are indigenous to Central and South America, and were enjoyed by the native peoples long before Europeans came to the continent. Avocados are stuffed – with chicken or seafood – in a number of South American countries, among them Guatemala and Bolivia.

SOUTH AMERICA　　　　　　　**SERVES 4**

4 small avocados	Peel, cut in half and remove the stones.
lemon juice salt and freshly ground pepper	Sprinkle to taste over the avocado halves.
2 small chicken breasts, cooked	Or you could use about 300 g cooked shelled shrimps or other seafood, or other cooked poultry. Skin and cut very finely.
1 small round lettuce, finely shredded 2 hard-boiled eggs, diced 4 x 15 ml spoons mayonnaise ½ fresh red chilli pepper, seeded and finely diced	Mix together with the chopped chicken. Season to taste. Spoon into the cavities in the avocado halves. Chill.
paprika	Dust over the top of the stuffed avocados, and serve two halves per person.

AUBERGINE SALAD WITH DRIED SHRIMPS

Dried shrimps are a common seasoning throughout South-East Asia, particularly in Indonesia, Malaysia and Thailand. Soak them in warm water before use; in many recipes, the liquid too is used. (Photograph page 46)

THAILAND **SERVES 4** **OVEN: 200°C/400°F/GAS 6**

2 medium aubergines

Grill or bake the aubergines (see below), but for about 40 minutes only. When cool enough to handle, skin and slice. Arrange on a platter.

1 x 15 ml spoon vegetable oil
2 x 15 ml spoons dried shrimps, soaked and drained
2 garlic cloves, peeled and sliced

Meanwhile, heat together in a small frying pan and fry until golden. Remove from the pan using a slotted spoon. Sprinkle over the aubergine slices.

1 hard-boiled egg, sieved
2 shallots, peeled and finely sliced

Sprinkle over the aubergine slices.

2 x 15 ml spoons lime juice
1 x 15 ml spoon *nam pla* (fish sauce)
1 x 15 ml spoon (dark brown) sugar
salt and freshly ground pepper

Mix together in a small bowl, and drizzle over the aubergine slices. Season to taste.

1 x 15 ml spoon fresh coriander leaves
2 fresh red chilli peppers, seeded and sliced (optional)

Use as a garnish.

AUBERGINE PUREE

The aubergine is native to Asia, was introduced to Europe by the Moors, and is a major ingredient in Greece and the Middle East. Several cuisines have similar purées, with varying additions. Bake the aubergines, purée the flesh, and then choose your individual flavouring.

MIDDLE EAST **SERVES 4** **OVEN: 200°C/400°F/GAS 6**

2 aubergines, about 225 g each
salt and freshly ground pepper

Prick the skins all over with a fork. Bake in the preheated oven until the insides are soft and the skins are blackened, about 50–60 minutes. You could also grill the aubergines over charcoal (or under a conventional grill): this gives a smokier flavour to the aubergine flesh, which is traditional. Skin while still hot, and mash the pulp. Leave to cool, then season.

LEBANESE AUBERGINE PUREE
1 garlic clove, peeled and crushed
salt to taste
60 ml lemon juice
45 ml olive oil, or tahina (sesame seed paste)
pomegranate seeds (optional)

This purée is called Baba Ghanoush ('spoiled old man'), because it was said to have been made by a son to please his ancient (and presumably toothless) father.
    Mix the garlic, salt, lemon juice and oil or tahina into the chopped aubergine, then garnish with pomegranate seeds if using.

GREEK MELITZANOSALATA
1 small onion, peeled and grated
2 garlic cloves, peeled and crushed
1 large tomato, skinned, seeded and diced
150 ml olive oil
1 x 15 ml spoon white wine vinegar

Mix into the chopped aubergine. Garnish, if liked, with olives and rings of sweet pepper.

SLICED AUBERGINE AND GOAT'S CHEESE 'SANDWICH' The flavours here are essentially Mediterranean, but they are gaining currency almost everywhere, including Australia, from where some of the most exciting ideas are coming now.

AUSTRALIA   **SERVES 4**   **OVEN: 200°C/400°F/GAS 6**

1 large aubergine, cut into 8 slices widthways
salt

Sprinkle the slices with salt and leave for 1 hour or so to 'sweat' out any sour juices. Pat dry with kitchen paper.

olive oil

Brush over the aubergine slices and grill on both sides until golden.

2 x 15 ml spoons Pesto (see page 306)

Spread evenly over four of the aubergine slices.

2 small round goat's cheeses, each cut in half horizontally
2 plum tomatoes, skinned, seeded and finely diced
freshly ground black pepper

Place a slice of cheese on top of the pesto, and then sprinkle with the tomato dice. Season with pepper and top with the remaining aubergine slices. Place in the preheated oven for a few minutes, just until the cheese starts to sizzle.

2 x 15 ml spoons finely cut fresh basil

Sprinkle over the 'sandwiches' and serve.

STUFFED SWEET PEPPERS Stuffed peppers are popular throughout the Middle East, the Balkans, and in the Mediterranean area. A vegetarian version, found in Greece and Turkey, uses rice as the bulk of the filling, which is spiked with herbs and tomatoes, and given texture and taste by the pine kernels, nuts or currants. (Photograph opposite)

MIDDLE EAST   **SERVES 4**   **OVEN: 180°C/350°F/GAS 4**

8 medium peppers, assorted red, orange, yellow and green

Cut a lid off the top of each, and remove the cores and seeds. Rinse well and drain.

2 medium onions, peeled and finely chopped
2 x 15 ml spoons olive oil

Sweat together in a shallow pan for a few minutes until soft. Allow to cool.

600 g mixed lean pork and beef, minced
150 g long-grain rice, cooked
2 eggs, beaten
1 garlic clove, peeled and crushed
2 x 15 ml spoons mixed dried herbs
salt and freshly ground pepper

Mix into the onions, and season to taste with salt and pepper. Fill the peppers with the mixture, replace the lids, and arrange in an ovenproof dish, standing up side by side.

500 g tomatoes, finely diced
200 ml Vegetable or Chicken Stock (see pages 314 or 315)

Combine, place around the peppers, and season to taste. Cover with a lid of foil and bake in the preheated oven for about 45 minutes or until the peppers are just becoming tender.
   Remove the peppers carefully from the dish. Liquidise the sauce, then push through a fine sieve. The sauce should be just spooning consistency; if too thin, boil to reduce a little.

4 large sprigs fresh basil, finely cut

Mix into the tomato sauce just before serving. Pour over the stuffed peppers.

ROASTED PEPPERS

These fragrant, softened peppers usually form part of an Italian *antipasti*. They can also be served as a vegetable accompaniment, good with grilled meats or fish. If no fresh oregano is available, crush 2 x 15 ml spoons fennel seeds and add to the dressing.

ITALY   SERVES 4   OVEN: 200°C/400°F/GAS 6

600 g peppers, preferably red, green and yellow

Cut in half and remove seeds and white cores. Place pepper halves side by side on a baking tray, skin downwards. Bake in the preheated oven for about 15 minutes, then turn over and bake for a further 15 minutes.

2 garlic cloves, peeled
1–3 very thin slices fresh chilli pepper, seeded (optional)
½ x 15 ml spoon finely chopped fresh oregano
25 ml white wine vinegar
85 ml olive oil
salt and freshly ground pepper

Meanwhile, make a spicy dressing. Crush one of the garlic cloves and mix with all the remaining ingredients, except the other garlic clove. Season to taste.
   Remove the peppers from the oven and spray with cold water, after which they can be easily peeled. Cut each piece in half and place in a dish. Pour the dressing over the warm peppers, add the remaining peeled and sliced garlic, and leave to marinate overnight in the fridge.

2 x 15 ml spoons finely chopped fresh parsley

Mix in just before serving.

MARINATED GRILLED VEGETABLES

A dish of the 'new' Italian cooking, and one which is delicious either as a salad or a first course. Use different vegetables if you like – try courgettes, plum tomatoes, broccoli florets, slices of red onion.

ITALY   SERVES 4

85 ml extra virgin olive oil
3 sprigs fresh thyme
1 garlic clove, peeled and crushed

Heat together gently in a small pan to perfume the oil. Leave to cool and infuse, then strain.

1 medium aubergine
salt and freshly ground pepper

Cut the aubergine lengthwise into four thick slices. Sprinkle with salt and leave to drain in a colander for about 15 minutes. Halve the slices.

8 baby sweetcorn
2 yellow and 2 red peppers
4 large spring onions
8 cherry tomatoes
8 oyster mushrooms

Trim the vegetables as appropriate, cutting the peppers in quarters and seeding them. Wipe the mushrooms.
   Brush the vegetables all over with a little of the perfumed oil, using the thyme sprigs as brushes.
   Grill on both sides on a barbecue or a ridged cast-iron grill pan, or under a conventional grill. The corn, pepper and aubergine will need about 6–7 minutes, the tomatoes, mushrooms and onions about 1 minute.
   Drizzle with the remaining olive oil (plus more if required), and season to taste with salt and pepper.

2 x 15 ml spoons finely cut fresh chives
juice of 1 lemon or 2 x 15ml spoons of balsamic vinegar

Sprinkle over the vegetables and serve warm or cold.

CREAMED CABBAGE
Cabbage as an accompanying vegetable has had a bad reputation in the UK, due entirely to the fact that it has almost always been overcooked. But, simply braised, stir-fried or steamed, it can be delicious, and goes magnificently with roast meats or with game, especially grouse (see page 205).

GREAT BRITAIN

SERVES 4

1 small Savoy cabbage, about 500 g	Discard torn outer leaves, and cut the cabbage in half. Remove the core and shred the leaves. Wash briefly then dry.
2 rashers bacon, rinded and finely sliced 1 small onion, peeled and finely chopped 1 x 15 ml spoon vegetable oil	Place in a large shallow pan and sweat together for a few moments.
1 medium carrot, trimmed	Score channels down the sides using a cannelle knife and then cut into thin slices. Add with the cabbage to the bacon pan.
salt and freshly ground pepper 4 x 15 ml spoons double cream	Add to the pan, cover and cook for 5–6 minutes, stirring once or twice. Serve immediately.

SAUERKRAUT
Virtually every country of northern continental Europe has its pickled cabbage dish, and it is not uncommon in Asia. The cabbage can be prepared at home, but good uncooked German or French versions – the latter known as *choucroûte* – are available in jars and vacuum packs in good delicatessens.

GERMANY

SERVES 4

500 g uncooked *sauerkraut*	Drain off any brine, and rinse thoroughly in cold water. Drain well again.
2 x 15 ml spoons olive oil 1 onion, peeled and sliced 1 garlic clove, peeled and crushed	Heat together gently in a suitable saucepan until soft, about 5 minutes. Add the sauerkraut and mix together. Cook for about 5 minutes.
500 ml Vegetable Stock (see page 314) 150 ml white wine of the region	Add half the stock and all the wine, cover, and braise slowly for about 45–60 minutes, adding more stock as needed.
1 large potato, peeled and grated 1 x 15 ml spoon caraway seeds (or juniper berries) 1 sour apple, peeled, cored and grated (optional) salt and freshly ground pepper	Add for the final 10 minutes of cooking, mixing in well, and seasoning to taste with salt and pepper. Serve hot.

BOK CHOY AND MUSHROOMS WITH OYSTER SAUCE

One of the most delicious – and simple – of Cantonese dishes is lightly steamed bok choy served with oyster sauce. This recipe is slightly more elaborate, adding some spiced mushrooms, but the freshness and flavours are similar. You could use Swiss chard, spinach or Chinese cabbage instead of the bok choy.

CHINA　　　　　　　　　　　　　　　　　**SERVES 4**

450 g fresh bok choy

Separate the leaves and trim off only the toughest parts of the stalks. Slice the thick stalks. Cut the leaves in half. Wash and dry very well.

100 ml Brown Chicken Stock (see page 316)
2 x 15 ml spoons oyster sauce
2 x 5 ml each of light soy sauce, sake (Japanese rice wine), and sesame oil
2 x 5 ml spoons cornflour

For the sauce, stir together until the cornflour has dissolved. Leave to one side.

peanut oil
2 large garlic cloves, peeled and crushed
1 x 15 ml spoon sake

Heat 1 x 15 ml spoon oil in a wok and stir-fry the bok choy and half the garlic with the sake until wilted, no more than 2–3 minutes. Transfer, using a slotted spoon, to a platter. Arrange in a circle, leaving a space in the middle. Keep warm.

5 cm piece of fresh root ginger, peeled and grated
6 spring onions, trimmed and finely sliced

Add to the wok, along with the remaining garlic and another 15 ml spoon of oil, and stir-fry for about 1 minute.

250 g button or halved shiitake mushrooms, trimmed
salt and freshly ground pepper

Add to the wok, and stir-fry for 2–3 minutes before adding the sauce and cooking for a few minutes more, until the sauce has thickened and the mushrooms are nearly cooked. Arrange the mushrooms and sauce in the centre of the bok choy and serve immediately. Season to taste.

SPINACH JAPANESE STYLE

The essence of simplicity, and a method employed elsewhere in the East. In Korea, ground sesame seeds and sesame oil are added to the *shoyu*. In Thailand and China, fish sauce or oyster sauce would be used respectively instead of the *shoyu*. Eight bunches of watercress could be substituted for the spinach.

JAPAN　　　　　　　　　　　　　　　　　**SERVES 4**

500 g spinach

Wash very well and trim off any tough stalks.

salt and freshly ground pepper

Bring a large pan of salted water to the boil, and boil the spinach until wilted. Plunge into cold water to set the colour, then drain well, and squeeze dry.

1 garlic clove, peeled and finely sliced
2 x 15 ml spoons vegetable oil

Heat together gently, then add the spinach and fry for a few minutes. Drain the spinach very well.

2 x 15 ml spoons *shoyu* (Japanese soy sauce)

Sprinkle over the spinach, mix well, then serve as an appetiser or accompanying green vegetable. Season to taste.

Opposite: Top, Coconut Spiced Vegetables (see page 56). Below, Bok Choy and Mushrooms with Oyster Sauce.

COCONUT SPICED VEGETABLES
A vegetable 'stew' cooked with the flavourings so characteristic of Indonesia – *blachan*, a shrimp paste, mild spices such as turmeric and cumin and, first and foremost, coconut milk. You could use other vegetables to taste – baby sweetcorn, for instance. (Photograph page 55)

INDONESIA

SERVES 4

1 garlic clove, peeled and crushed
1 x 5 ml spoon *blachan* (shrimp paste)
1 x 15 ml spoon vegetable oil

Cook together in a sauté pan for a minute or two.

1 x 5 ml spoon each of salt,
  ground turmeric and cumin
175 ml Chicken Stock (see page 315)
3 curry leaves
8 small new potatoes, scrubbed and
  halved

Add to the pan and bring to the boil. Simmer for 4–5 minutes.

1 red pepper, seeded
1 carrot, peeled
50 g mangetout peas, topped and
  tailed
6 large spring onions
25 g water chestnuts, halved

Cut into julienne strips, add to the liquid, and cook for about 6 minutes.

175 ml thick coconut milk
salt and freshly ground pepper
lime or lemon juice

Add to the pan, seasoning to taste with salt, pepper and citrus juice. Heat through gently, then serve.

GREEN BEANS IN A CREAM SAUCE
Serve this creamy bean dish with ham or roast or boiled meats. Summer savory, an annual herb popular on the Continent, is known as the 'bean herb', as it complements all pulses, and helps in their digestion.

GERMANY

SERVES 4

400 g green beans (string or runners)
salt and freshly ground pepper

Trim as appropriate and cut into 5 cm lengths. If using runners, cut into strips. Place in a pan of boiling salted water.

2 sprigs fresh summer savory

Add to the pan and cook the beans, uncovered, until nearly tender, about 4–6 minutes, depending on thickness. Refresh in cold water to retain the green colour.

4 rashers bacon, rinded and cut into
  small lardons

Sauté in a dry frying pan until crisp, and the fat has been rendered.

200 ml double cream
freshly grated nutmeg

Add to the bacon pan and heat, stirring, to thicken a little. Season to taste with salt, pepper and nutmeg.

a little chopped fresh summer savory

Add, along with the cooked beans, and reheat gently before serving.

TURKISH CARROTS
A wide use of yoghurt is characteristic of eastern Turkey, linking the cuisine to those of its Middle Eastern and Asian neighbours. This carrot and yoghurt recipe, with its seasoning of caraway seeds, would make a delicious addition to a Middle Eastern *mezze*.

TURKEY   **SERVES 4**

450 g carrots, trimmed and peeled	Cut into thin julienne strips.
1½ x 15 ml spoons plain flour 1 x 15 ml spoon ground coriander salt and freshly ground pepper	Mix together, with a little salt and pepper to taste, then toss with the carrot strips.
1 x 15 ml spoon olive oil	Heat in a pan and sauté the carrots until they are light brown. Drain very well on kitchen paper, then place in a dish. Cool.
250 g natural (Greek or set) yoghurt	Spoon over the cool carrot strips. Season to taste.
1 x 5 ml spoon caraway seeds	Sprinkle over the yoghurt, then serve.

STIR-FRIED BROCCOLI WITH SESAME SEEDS
A typically quick Chinese vegetable dish – full of flavour and crispness. Cooking the broccoli this way retains its colour and crunchiness, and enhances its flavour. Bok choy could be substituted for the broccoli.

CHINA   **SERVES 4**

450 g broccoli	Trim and peel the stalks if necessary, and break the broccoli into small florets. Cut the stalks into similarly sized pieces.
2 x 15 ml spoons sherry 1 x 15 ml spoon dark soy sauce 1 x 15 ml spoon cornflour	Mix together carefully and leave to one side.
2 x 15 ml spoons sesame seeds	Heat in a dry pan or wok, tossing, until golden. Put to one side.
1 x 15 ml spoon each of groundnut and sesame oils	Heat together in a wok.
6 spring onions, trimmed and sliced 1 fresh red chilli pepper, seeded and finely sliced 2 garlic cloves, peeled and crushed 2.5 cm piece of root ginger, peeled and grated	Add to the wok, and stir-fry in the hot oil for about 1 minute.
75 g fresh shrimps, shelled (optional) salt and freshly ground pepper	If using, add along with the broccoli pieces, both stalk and florets, and stir-fry for 1–2 minutes. Pour in the sauce, mix well, then cover and simmer for a couple of minutes. Season to taste. Transfer to a serving dish, sprinkle with the toasted sesame seeds, and serve immediately.

STANGEN SPARGEL
A simple and very elegant, way of presenting boiled (or steamed) asparagus. White asparagus is a great gourmet treat in Austria, appearing before the green. You could garnish the spears with a fried egg and/or shavings of Parmesan.

AUSTRIA   **SERVES 4**

1 kg asparagus, stems and ends peeled
salt and freshly ground pepper

Cook, uncovered, in boiling salted water for about 5–10 minutes (depending on thickness), or until tender. (It's best to do this in an asparagus pan, so that the tender tips steam rather then boil.) Drain and place on a warm platter.

75 g best-quality unsalted butter

Melt in a small pan, then pour two-thirds of it into a separate pan.

4 x 15 ml spoons fresh breadcrumbs

Sauté in the larger portion of butter until golden and crisp. Sprinkle over the asparagus, and then pour over the remaining melted butter and season.

FRIED TOMATOES
Green (or indeed red) tomatoes, if cut thickly enough, fry very successfully when encased in a protective coating such as flour or breadcrumbs. The great French chef, Escoffier, fried tomato slices in a light batter and, in Italy, firm red tomatoes are treated in much the same way as below.

USA   **SERVES 4**

4 medium green tomatoes

Cut horizontally into slices about 1 cm thick. Remove the seeds carefully.

2 x 15 ml spoons cornmeal
    (or plain flour)
a pinch each of mild chilli powder
    and ground cumin
salt and freshly ground pepper

Mix together then place in a flat plate, seasoning to taste with salt and pepper. Dip the tomato slices in this.

1 large egg, beaten with
    1 x 5 ml spoon water

Place on a flat plate and moisten the floured tomato slices.

100 g fine dry breadcrumbs

Place in a flat dish and coat the tomato slices well.

bacon fat (or olive oil)

Heat a generous amount in a frying pan and fry the tomato slices on both sides until crisp, about 5 minutes. Drain the slices very well on kitchen paper.

150 ml whipping cream (optional)

If liked, use to deglaze the frying pan, then serve as a sauce for the tomatoes.

Opposite: Stangen Spargel.

LEBANESE CAULIFLOWER

The combination of tahina, garlic, parsley and avocado makes an exciting sauce for a simply cooked vegetable; other cooked vegetables could be substituted for the cauliflower. The sauce can also be used as a dip.

MIDDLE EAST   **SERVES 4**

1 medium cauliflower, about 500g
salt and freshly ground pepper

Discard leaves, and cut into small florets. Place in a pan and cover with boiling salted water. Bring back to the boil, then simmer for 2–3 minutes until al dente. Drain well.

225 g light tahina (sesame seed paste)
1 garlic clove, peeled and crushed with
　½ x 5 ml spoon salt
120 ml lemon juice
2 x 15 ml spoons finely chopped fresh
　parsley

Meanwhile, for the sauce, mix together to a paste, adding water as necessary to get a consistency like that of double cream. Season to taste.

1 large avocado

Peel and remove the stone. Mash with a fork, then mix together with the tahina sauce. Blend, if necessary, for a completely smooth sauce. Pour over the warm cauliflower and serve.

POTATO CAKES WITH PEANUT SAUCE

Potatoes are native to Peru, but they are popular elsewhere in South America, particularly in combination with cheese (which the conquering Iberians taught the natives how to make). This recipe make a good accompaniment to the Beef Bogota on page 148.

ECUADOR   **SERVES 4**

600 g floury potatoes
salt and freshly ground pepper

Cook in their skins in boiling salted water until tender, then drain, and cool before skinning, slicing and mashing.

1 large onion, peeled and finely diced
75 g butter

Heat together in a sauté pan and sauté until the onion is golden. Mix into the mashed potato.

200 g Cheddar or other similar
　cooking cheese

Grate and add to the warm potato and onion mix. Season to taste with salt and pepper. Divide the mix into eight balls, and flatten into cakes. Chill.

vegetable oil
1 x 5 ml spoon annatto seeds
　(optional)

Meanwhile, for the peanut sauce, heat 1 x 15 ml spoon oil and the seeds together in a pan until the seeds colour the oil a rich red-orange. Strain the oil and discard the seeds.

1 medium onion, peeled and finely
　chopped
1 garlic clove, peeled and crushed
4 medium tomatoes, skinned, seeded
　and diced

Sauté in the red oil until soft, about 10 minutes.

120 g shelled peanuts, finely ground

Add to the sauce and cook for a few minutes longer. Season to taste with salt and pepper.
　Pour a little more vegetable oil into a frying pan and shallow-fry the potato cakes on each side until golden brown. Drain well, and serve hot and crisp with the peanut sauce.

CREAMED MUSHROOMS
The Finns are very enthusiastic seekers of wild mushrooms, which abound in Finnish woodland and forests in the autumn. You can use cultivated mushrooms instead, as they do in Hungary (although the Hungarians would add lots of paprika).

FINLAND

SERVES 4

600 g wild mushrooms

Trim, wash or wipe as appropriate, then slice.

50 g butter
1 medium onion, peeled and finely chopped

Sweat together in a large pan to soften the onion.

salt and freshly ground pepper
freshly grated nutmeg

Add the mushrooms to the onion and season to taste with salt, pepper and nutmeg. Cook gently, stirring, for about 15 minutes, or until most of the mushroom juices have evaporated. Remove the pan from the heat.

300 ml soured cream

Stir into the mushrooms and reheat gently. Do not allow to boil.

1 x 15 ml spoon finely cut fresh chervil or dill

Sprinkle over the mushrooms and serve immediately.

POTATO AND CEP GRATIN
Gratin dauphinois from the Dauphiné may be more famous, but the principle behind the dish – a layering of potato with flavourings to be baked – is popular in other mountainous districts of south-east France: *gratin savoyard* from near the Swiss border and this gratin, from the Auvergne, which uses the wild mushrooms that grow there in such profusion. You can use cultivated or other wild mushrooms instead of the ceps.

FRANCE

SERVES 4   **OVEN: 110°C/225°F/GAS ¼**

butter

Generously grease a gratin dish.

1 garlic clove, peeled and halved

Rub the cut edges around the dish.

400 g potatoes, peeled and finely sliced
250 g ceps, cleaned and sliced
1 small onion, peeled and very finely chopped
100 g Gruyère cheese, grated
2 x 15 ml spoons finely chopped fresh parsley
salt and freshly ground pepper

Layer the potatoes and ceps in the greased dish, sprinkling each layer with onion, 75 g of the cheese, the parsley and salt and pepper to taste.

300 ml whipping cream
50 ml milk

Mix together in a small pan and bring to just below the boil. Pour into the gratin dish. Dot the top of the gratin with the remaining cheese and about 25 g butter cut into small pieces. Bake for about 1 hour in the preheated oven until the top of the gratin is golden and the potatoes are cooked through. Serve hot.

NEW POTATOES COOKED WITH YOGHURT

Yoghurt plays an enormous part in the cooking of western, central and southern Asia. In Indian households, it is made fresh every day and is used in cooking, in many cooling garnishes such as Raita (see page 124), and as a drink, Lassi.

INDIA

SERVES 4

25 g ghee or butter 1 small onion, peeled and finely chopped 2.5 cm piece of fresh root ginger, peeled and grated	Heat together in a frying pan, and sweat until the onion is golden, about 5 minutes.
1 x 15 ml spoon ground coriander 1 x 5 ml spoon turmeric	Add to the pan and sauté for a further 30 seconds.
2 fresh green chilli peppers, seeded and finely sliced 2–3 plum tomatoes, skinned and diced 250 g thick natural yoghurt	Add to the pan, and stir well. Simmer very gently until the sauce is thick.
a pinch of ground mace, salt and pepper 25 g raisins, soaked in a little water 450 g small new potatoes, cooked	Add, stir and simmer for about 5–6 minutes or until the potatoes are heated through. Turn into a serving dish. Season to taste.
1 x 15 ml spoon chopped fresh coriander leaves	Sprinkle over the potatoes as a garnish.

POTATOES COOKED WITH GREENS

In northern India, potatoes are very often cooked with greens. Fenugreek greens – leaves of the pea-like plant that produces the spice seeds – are usually preferred, but young leaves of spinach can happily substitute.

INDIA

SERVES 4

50 g ghee or butter 1 large onion, peeled and finely sliced 2.5 cm piece of fresh root ginger, peeled and grated 2 fresh green chilli peppers, seeded and finely sliced	Heat together in a large frying pan, and sweat, stirring, until the onion is golden, about 5 minutes.
1 x 5 ml spoon turmeric 400 g potatoes, peeled and cut into 1 cm slices	Add to the pan and stir to coat the potatoes with ghee and turmeric. Reduce the heat to low, cover the pan, and cook until the potatoes are just tender, about 10–15 minutes.
400 g spinach, washed and tough stalks removed	Add to the potatoes in batches, turning the heat to high. Cook until the spinach wilts and all excess moisture has evaporated.
salt and freshly ground pepper 2 spring onions, finely sliced 1 fresh red chilli pepper, seeded and finely sliced	Season to taste with salt and pepper, then serve garnished with the spring onion and chilli.

Opposite: New Potatoes Cooked with Yoghurt and Potatoes Cooked with Greens.

POTATO AND APPLE PUREE
Potatoes are eaten a great deal in Germany and they are cooked and mashed with apple in a dish that traditionally accompanies Frankfurters or fried slices of *Blutwurst* (black pudding). It is called *Himmel und Erde* (heaven and earth).

GERMANY

SERVES 4

400 g potatoes, peeled and coarsely
   chopped
500 g cooking apples, peeled, cored
   and coarsely chopped
2 x 5 ml spoons white wine vinegar
1 x 5 ml spoon caster sugar
salt and freshly ground pepper

Place in a large saucepan, cover with salted water, and bring to the boil. Cover and simmer for about 15 minutes, or until the potatoes are tender when pierced. Drain well and mash until smooth.

25 g butter

Add to the mashed potato and melt in, along with more salt and pepper to taste. Serve hot.

ROSTI
A traditional Swiss dish utilising the potato which is very much a basic food in Switzerland. Each canton has a slightly different recipe for Rösti: some use only potatoes, some add onion and bacon, or grated apple or cheese, or cream. This variation is from Zurich, and its natural partner is the Zurich speciality, *Emincé de Veau* (see page 166).

SWITZERLAND

SERVES 4

600 g medium waxy potatoes, peeled
salt and freshly ground black pepper

Boil the potatoes for 10 minutes. Drain, cool a little, then grate into a bowl. Season lightly.

50 g butter
75 g onions, peeled and finely chopped
50 g good bacon, rinded and cut
   into small strips

Sweat together in a medium to large non-stick frying pan for a few minutes.

1 x 15 ml spoon finely chopped
   fresh parsley
freshly grated nutmeg

Add to the pan, along with the grated potato, and salt and pepper to taste. Mix well, then spread over the bottom of the frying pan like a pancake, pressing down. Cook for a few minutes until the bottom of the potato is brown. Turn over carefully, using a plate, and brown the other side.

1 x 15 ml spoon finely cut fresh chives

Sprinkle over the Rösti, and cut into wedges. Serve hot.

CANDIED SWEET POTATOES
You can use yams instead of sweet potatoes if you like. Candied vegetables, particularly sweet potatoes, are traditionally served in the southern states as an accompaniment to ham, and they are also very good with roast chicken and roast turkey.

USA

SERVES 4

600 g sweet potatoes
salt and freshly ground pepper

Parboil in salted water. Cool a little, then peel, quarter and sprinkle with a little salt and pepper.

80 g soft brown sugar
40 g butter
85 ml water

Heat together in a large sauté pan, add the sweet potato quarters, and cook, turning often, until coated with the sugary liquid, about 15 minutes. Serve hot.

JANSSON'S TEMPTATION
Raw potatoes, sliced or cut into strips, then layered in a dish with flavourings and baked, appear in a number of cuisines – the French *gratin dauphinois*, the American scalloped potatoes, and a Welsh onion cake, *teisen nionod*.

SWEDEN **SERVES 4** **OVEN: 220°C/425°F/GAS 7**

675 g potatoes, peeled	Cut into strips or thin slices, and leave in some cold water until ready to cook.
50 g butter	Use a little to grease a suitable casserole.
2 large onions, peeled and sliced into rings	Sauté gently in about half of the butter until slightly softened, but not coloured. Drain well. Drain the potato slices or strips and dry them well. Arrange half of them in the buttered casserole, and place half of the softened onion on top.
6 Swedish anchovies, filleted and sliced, or 12 anchovy fillets in oil **freshly ground black pepper**	Arrange on top of the onions, then cover with the remaining onion and potatoes. Season the layers with pepper. You could add some of the oil from the anchovies too, if liked. Put pieces of the remaining butter on the top layer of potatoes.
200 ml double cream **100 ml milk**	Heat together, and then pour half of this into the casserole. Bake in the preheated oven for 20 minutes, then reduce the oven to 190°C/375°F/Gas 5. Pour in the remaining cream and milk, and bake until the potatoes are tender, about another 20–30 minutes.

PAPET VAUDOIS
This famous dish, using the 'king' of Swiss vegetables, the leek, comes from the Vaud, the region lying on the north side of Lake Geneva. It is traditionally served with local smoked pork sausages or cabbage and liver sausages; these are pre-cooked, then placed on top of the leeks to cook for about 15 minutes.

SWITZERLAND **SERVES 4**

1 kg leeks, washed, trimmed and cut into 2 cm pieces **1 medium onion, peeled and sliced** **40 g lard** **salt and freshly ground pepper** **freshly grated nutmeg**	Place in a large pan, seasoning to taste with salt, pepper and nutmeg, and sweat to soften. Do not colour.
100 ml Beef Stock (see page 316) **250 ml dry white wine**	Add to the pan, bring to the boil, then cover and simmer for 15 minutes, until very soft.
450 g potatoes, peeled and thinly sliced	Add to the pan (along with a partly cooked pork sausage if liked), cover again, and simmer for about 30 minutes.
75 ml double cream	Stir in gently, and allow to heat through.
a dash of white wine vinegar	Stir in just before serving hot. Season to taste.

COLCANNON
This Irish dish of puréed potatoes and cabbage or kale, above, is traditionally served at Hallowe'en, and often contains some sort of token, a thimble or ring, the finding of which foretells the recipient's future. There are many similar potato and cabbage dishes all over the UK, and in Holland as well.

IRELAND

SERVES 4

350 g potatoes (Golden Wonders or
  Kerr's Pinks), scrubbed
salt and freshly ground black pepper

Cook in boiling salted water until soft, then cool slightly and skin. Push through a sieve or food mill.

225 g cabbage or kale, shredded

Cook in boiling salted water until cooked but still crisp, then drain well.

3 spring onions, trimmed and finely
  sliced
25 ml milk, scalded
25 g butter (optional)

Add to the sieved potato along with the cooked cabbage or kale. Mix well until smooth. Season to taste. Serve as an accompaniment to meat dishes – good with fried slices of black pudding.

SALADE LIEGEOISE
This potato salad is one of a number of warm salads in the Belgian repertoire which are similar to salads enjoyed in northern France to the west. Garnish it at the last minute with some chervil, a herb which is particularly popular in Belgium.

BELGIUM   **SERVES 4**

500 g small new potatoes | Scrub and boil in salted water until tender. Cool a little then slice. Place in a dish and keep warm.
salt and freshly ground pepper

250 g green beans | Trim as appropriate and cut into 5 cm lengths (and into strips if using runner beans). Cook in boiling salted water until cooked but still crisp, then drain and add to the potatoes. Keep warm.

120 g streaky bacon in the piece | Cut into lardons and fry in a dry frying pan until crisp and the fat has been rendered. Remove the lardons from the fat, using a slotted spoon, and add them to the potatoes and beans.

1 medium onion, peeled and finely diced | Add to the bacon fat in the pan and cook for a few minutes just to soften a little. Pour into the potatoes.
½ x 15 ml spoon olive oil

1 x 15 ml spoon finely chopped fresh parsley | Add to the potatoes and taste for seasoning.
4–6 fresh tarragon leaves, finely cut

50 ml white wine vinegar | Add to the sauté pan, stir over gentle heat, then pour over the potato and bean salad. Mix all the ingredients together gently, check the seasoning, and serve warm.

CABBAGE SALAD
A Russian salad is quite different in concept to a British or French one, and generally consists of a mixture of cooked vegetables. Cabbage is one of the two principal vegetables available in the former USSR, and a salad such as this would be served as an appetiser, or *zakuska*.

RUSSIA   **SERVES 4**

675 g white cabbage | Cut roughly, then blanch in boiling salted water for 2–3 minutes. Drain well, cool a little, then squeeze out excess water. Cut very finely indeed.
salt and freshly ground pepper

2 medium dessert apples (tart rather than sweet) | Peel, core then grate and add to the cabbage. Mix well.

4 spring onions, trimmed | Finely chop, and add to the cabbage and apple.
4 sprigs each of fresh parsley and dill

2 hard-boiled eggs, shelled (optional) | If using, cut into eighths, and add to the cabbage.

3 x 15 ml spoons sunflower oil | Mix together, with some salt and pepper, to make a dressing. Pour over the salad and toss lightly.
1 x 15 ml spoon lemon juice
a pinch of caster sugar

JERSEY ROYAL POTATO SALAD

Every year I look forward to the arrival in May of Jersey Royal new potatoes. These are almost the first new potatoes to arrive in Britain every year and, tasting of the volcanic soil in which they were grown, are a truly seasonal treat.

GREAT BRITAIN   **SERVES 4**

300 g Jersey Royal new potatoes, scrubbed
salt and freshly ground pepper

Boil in salted water for about 15 minutes, or until barely tender. Halve and season with salt and pepper.

½ cucumber, seeded and diced

Sprinkle with salt and leave in a colander to drain.

200 g tomatoes, seeded

Cut the halves into four wedges.

1 bunch radishes, trimmed and quartered
1 bunch spring onions, trimmed and finely sliced

Place in a bowl, and add the potatoes, cucumber and tomatoes.

1 x 15 ml spoon grain mustard
150 g Greek yoghurt
1 x 15 ml spoon sherry vinegar

Mix together, and pour into the bowl with the vegetables.

1 x 15 ml spoon each of finely chopped fresh parsley and cut chives

Sprinkle on top of the salad and mix well. Correct seasoning then serve.

FATTOUSH

This is a 'peasant' bread salad from the Lebanon. It traditionally includes purslane and chickweed, both of which are considered very nourishing. Sumak berries, the seeds of decorative bushes which are found in the Lebanese mountains, often add their sour, lemony flavour.

MIDDLE EAST   **SERVES 4**

1 round Lebanese (or pitta) bread

Toast until very crisp on both sides, then break into small pieces. Sprinkle with a little water then place in a bowl.

2 small cucumbers, sliced
½ soft round lettuce, washed and shredded
1 bunch watercress, washed, or a handful of rocket leaves
2 medium tomatoes, diced
4 spring onions, trimmed and sliced
1 small green pepper, seeded and diced
1 x 15 ml spoon each of finely chopped fresh parsley and mint

Add to the bread in the bowl and toss.

120 ml olive oil
juice of 1 lemon
1 garlic clove, peeled and crushed
salt and freshly ground pepper

Mix together for the dressing, adding salt and pepper to taste. Pour over the salad and toss again. Serve immediately.

WARM FUNGHI PORCINI SALAD

Gently warming fresh sliced ceps, and then coating them with a cep and garlic sauce, is a delicious idea, but only if you can get hold of fresh ceps. It's also very important to clean them well: cut in half first to check for firmness and freshness.

ITALY
SERVES 4   OVEN: 150°C/300°F/GAS 2

500 g small fresh funghi porcini (ceps or penny buns)	Brush off earth and trim the stems. Wipe if necessary, but do not wash if you can help it. Slice very thinly and arrange 400 g of them attractively on individual small ovenproof plates. Arrange on a baking sheet.
1 x 15 ml spoon olive oil **1 garlic clove, peeled and halved**	Heat together gently in a pan to flavour the oil, then remove and discard the garlic. Chop the remaining porcini very finely and add to the oil.
salt and freshly ground pepper	Add a pinch of salt, and cook, covered, very gently for a minute or so. Process to a purée.
50 g unsalted butter, diced	Beat into the oil and porcini paste, little by little, until amalgamated, thick and hot.
2 x 15 ml spoons finely cut fresh parsley, thyme or basil	Stir into the sauce and check again for seasoning. Place the baking sheet with the plates on it in the low oven for 2 minutes to warm the porcini, then remove. Pour the warm sauce over the warm porcini and serve immediately.

CARROT AND ORANGE SALAD

A fresh salad to accompany meat and poultry dishes which is typically Moroccan – colourful, full of texture and exciting flavours. An alternative is to use radishes – the small long ones preferably – instead of carrots.

MOROCCO
SERVES 4

500 g carrots	Wash, trim and peel, then coarsely grate into a bowl.
2 oranges	Peel and segment one orange, adding the halved segments to the carrots, then squeeze in the juice of the second.
½ x 5 ml spoon each of salt, ground cinnamon and icing sugar **½ x 15 ml spoon orange-flower water** **1 small bunch fresh chives, finely cut** **1 x 15 ml spoon finely chopped fresh coriander**	Add to the salad, and toss thoroughly.
a little lemon juice	Add if necessary. Chill.

CRISPY SEAWEED

The vegetable used here is not seaweed at all, but any sturdy green leaf such as spring greens, cabbage (preferably Savoy) or kale. The leaves are very finely shredded and then thoroughly dried before deep-frying. You can add and deep-fry some split almonds as well.

CHINA **SERVES 4**

450 g green leaves (see above)

Separate the leaves, then roll into a cigar shape and shred very, very finely with a very sharp knife. Wash then drain well. Leave spread out in a tray on kitchen paper to become as dry as possible.

vegetable oil for deep-frying

Deep-fry the shreds in batches in hot oil, for about 45 seconds, until crisp. Remove from the oil, using a slotted spoon. Drain well on kitchen paper. Place on a hot platter.

salt
soft brown sugar

Mix a little together to taste, and sprinkle over the top of the seaweed. Serve immediately as an appetiser.

PLANTAIN CHIPS

A close relative of the banana, the plantain never sweetens as do bananas, and it has to be cooked before it is edible. This simple 'crisp' recipe can be found on many of the islands, as well as in countries in Africa, such as Tanzania. The chips are eaten with pre-dinner drinks. Unripe bananas can be used instead of the plantains, as can cassava and sweet potatoes.

CARIBBEAN **SERVES 4**

2 plantains

Peel and cut, crosswise, into very thin slices.

vegetable oil for deep-frying

Deep-fry the plantain slices, a few at a time, in hot oil until crisp, which takes a few minutes. Drain very well on kitchen paper.

salt and freshly ground pepper

Season to taste and serve hot.

OKRA STEW

Stews of okra are common throughout Africa, as well as the southern states of North America and parts of South America where African slaves were introduced during the years of the slave trade. In Ghana, this stew also contains dried prawns and pieces of meat or fish.

WEST AFRICA **SERVES 4**

400 g okra

Wash, trim the ends carefully, and cut into slices about 1 cm thick.

150 ml vegetable oil
1 x 5 ml spoon turmeric
3 medium onions, peeled and
  finely chopped
1 garlic clove, peeled and crushed

Place in a large saucepan, and fry until the onion is slightly coloured.

Top: Okra Stew and Coocoo (see page 89).

4 small aubergines, trimmed and finely chopped
2.5 cm piece of fresh root ginger, peeled and chopped
2 fresh red chilli peppers, seeded and finely sliced

Add to the pan and cook gently for about 2–3 minutes. Add the okra and cook for another 2–3 minutes.

6 very ripe medium tomatoes, skinned and coarsely chopped

Add to the pan, mash into the mixture, and cook for a further 20 minutes or so, stirring frequently. Add a little water if it starts to stick on the bottom.

salt and freshly ground pepper

Season to taste, and serve hot with rice or boiled potatoes. In Africa, the accompaniments might be yam, cassava, boiled plantains or cornmeal dumplings.

VEGETABLE CURRY

Any vegetable can be used in this basic sauce, which consists of onion, garlic and some basic spices. Just add the vegetables to the sauce in the rough order of cooking time – hard vegetables like potatoes and carrots first, with softer vegetables like aubergines or courgettes last.

INDIA

SERVES 4

1 large onion, peeled and finely sliced
2 x 15 ml spoons vegetable oil
2 garlic cloves, peeled and crushed

Sauté together gently in a large pan until the onion is golden, stirring for about 10 minutes.

1 x 5 ml spoon each of white mustard, cumin and coriander seeds
5 black peppercorns
2.5 cm piece of cinnamon stick
1 dried red chilli pepper, crumbled

Toast in a dry pan, then blend to a coarse powder in a spice mill.

1 x 5 ml spoon turmeric

Mix with the toasted ground spices and then stir in enough cold water to make a paste. Add the paste to the onion and garlic and simmer together gently for about 10 minutes.

600 g mixed vegetables

Choose from carrots, potatoes, aubergines, green beans, cauliflower, broccoli, courgettes etc. Trim or peel as appropriate, then cut into bite-sized pieces.

Vegetable Stock (see page 314) if necessary

Add to the sauce, along with the vegetables in order of cooking time – enough to barely cover the vegetables. Cook, without a lid, over a low heat until the vegetables are just tender.

salt and freshly ground pepper
lime or lemon juice

Add to taste, mixing in well. Serve hot.

RATATOUILLE

Some form of vegetable stew-salad is common to many southern European countries, and ratatouille, from Provence, is probably the most familiar. It has definite affinities with the Italian *peperonata*, the Sicilian *caponata*, the Spanish *pisto* and the Basque *pipérade*.

FRANCE

SERVES 4   **OVEN:200ºC/400ºF/GAS 6**

3 x 15 ml spoons olive oil
2 garlic cloves, unpeeled and slightly crushed
1 bay leaf
1 small sprig fresh thyme or rosemary

Heat gently together in a large sauté pan.

2 small onions, peeled and roughly chopped

Add to the pan and gently soften for a minute or so. Remove from the pan, using a slotted spoon, and drain in a colander over a bowl, to catch the juices.

2 peppers, 1 green, 1 red, seeded and cut into 1.5 cm dice	Lightly sauté, separately and in turn, the peppers, courgettes, tomatoes and aubergines, adding more oil if necessary.
250 g small courgettes, trimmed and sliced	Place all the vegetables and their juices in a casserole.
500 g good tomatoes, skinned, seeded and cut	
250 g small aubergines, trimmed and cut into large dice	
85 ml Vegetable Stock (see page 314)	Use to deglaze the sauté pan, then add to the vegetables.
salt and freshly ground pepper	Season the vegetables well, then cover the casserole and place in the preheated oven for 20 minutes, on the lowest shelf.
	Strain out the liquid and reduce quickly in a separate pan. Return to the vegetables. Remove the garlic, and serve warm or cold.

SPRING ROLLS

As with any 'wrapped' food (such as won-tons, or ravioli in Italy, *pelmeni* in Russia and *börek* in Turkey) the filling can vary. You could use vegetables only, replacing the meat with more of one of the vegetables, or with something else.

CHINA

MAKES 12

125 lean pork or chicken fillet	Cut into fine shreds.
75 g bamboo shoots	
1 red pepper, seeded	
1 medium carrot, peeled	
4 spring onions, trimmed	
vegetable oil	Heat 1 x 15 ml spoon vegetable oil and the sesame oil until very hot in a wok.
1 x 15 ml spoon sesame oil	
1 garlic clove, peeled and crushed	Add to the oil in the wok and stir-fry for 30 seconds before adding the shredded ingredients above. Stir-fry for another 2 minutes.
1.5 cm piece of fresh root ginger, peeled and shredded	
a pinch of five-spice powder	
150 g beansprouts	Toss into the pan and briefly stir-fry.
1 x 5 ml spoon cornflour	Mix together quickly, then pour into the wok, stirring continuously. Cook until the liquid has evaporated. Spread out on a plate and leave to cool.
2 x 5 ml spoons light soy sauce	
½ x 5 ml spoon each of salt and caster sugar	
2 x 15 ml spoons Brown Chicken Stock (see page 316)	
1 x 15 ml spoon finely cut fresh coriander	Stir into the spring roll filling. Season to taste.
salt and freshly ground pepper	
12 spring roll wrappers	Spread a portion of the cooled filling diagonally across the centre of each wrapper. Fold the sides in then roll up. Seal the end using a little beaten egg. You might need to secure with a wooden cocktail stick.
1 egg, beaten	
	Deep-fry the spring rolls in hot vegetable oil for 3–4 minutes, turning once. Drain very well then serve hot.

GADO GADO
This cooked salad with peanut sauce is a favourite lunch dish or mixed vegetable accompaniment in Indonesia. However, the vegetables can also be served raw, when the salad is known as *karedok*; choose those most suitable and cut them into smaller pieces. Use the Peanut Satay Sauce on page 313, but replace the fish paste with *kecap manis* (sweet soy sauce).

INDONESIA   **SERVES 4**

600 g assorted vegetables
salt

Choose from sweet potato, potato, green beans, cauliflower, white cabbage, aubergines, carrots and spring onions. Prepare as appropriate, then cut into small pieces. You want them all to be approximately the same size. Steam, separately, over boiling salted water until just tender. Arrange on a platter or divide between individual plates. Cool.

½ cucumber, sliced
100 g beansprouts, washed
salt and freshly ground pepper

Arrange with the other vegetables. Season to taste.

Peanut Satay Sauce (see above and
page 313)

Pour over the vegetables.

2 limes, halved
2 x 15 ml spoons mixed cut fresh
herbs (basil, mint, coriander)

Use to garnish the vegetables, then serve.

DOLMAS
A good dish for a *mezze*, these vine-leaf parcels, opposite, are popular throughout the whole of the Middle East, particularly Greece, Turkey, the Lebanon, and Iran. *Dolmas* to be served hot are usually made with meat: those to be served cold, with rice and flavourings only. Garnish the dish with diced tomato. (See photograph opposite)

TURKEY   **SERVES 4**

175 g preserved vine leaves

To get rid of the salt, blanch in boiling water for about 5 minutes, then drain. Cool and separate the leaves. (If using fresh leaves, soften them in much the same way.)

50 g long-grain rice
salt and freshly ground pepper

Place in a pan of water with a little salt, and bring to the boil. Simmer for about 5 minutes until softened a little, then drain and cool.

1 medium onion, peeled and finely
diced
1 x 15 ml spoon olive oil

Sweat together until the onion is softened. Drain.

175 g lean lamb, minced
1 garlic clove, peeled and crushed
2 x 15 ml spoons chopped fresh
parsley
1 x 15 ml spoon Tomates Concassées
(see page 312)
1 x 5 ml spoon ground cinnamon

Mix into the rice, along with the onion and some salt and pepper to taste.
Lay the leaves out on the work surface, vein side up. Place a heaped 5 ml spoon of the filling in the centre of the leaf and fold over the sides, then roll up loosely (the rice will swell). Squeeze a little, then place in a pan, loose edge down. Do the same with the remainder of the leaves and filling. Pack them in tightly so that they do not move about during the cooking.

2 lemons
tomato juice or water

Squeeze the lemon juice over the *dolmas* and add enough tomato juice or water to come about half way up the *dolmas*. Cover with a lid and cook very gently on top of the stove for at least 1 hour, or until the leaves are tender. Add a little more juice or water from time to time as it is absorbed. Serve hot, or leave to get cold. Season to taste.

PULSES
AND GRAINS

SUCCOTASH

This mixture of lima (butter) beans and sweetcorn kernels could not be more American, using vegetables which are indigenous to the continent. Hominy grits – processed dried and ground, corn kernels – is the grain that would traditionally be used here, and it is available in packets; it is most commonly served for breakfast with bacon and eggs. Couscous – processed wheat semolina – makes an interesting alternative.

USA   SERVES 4   OVEN: 240°C/475°F/GAS 9

4 corn on the cob, with husks and silks

Open up the husks of the corn and try and remove as much of the silks as you can. Put the husks back in place, wrap the cobs individually in foil, and bake in the preheated oven for 15–20 minutes. When cooled a little, remove the foil, husks and any remaining silks. Cut the kernels off the cobs.

50 g butter
100 g spring onions, trimmed and sliced
150 g sweet peppers, seeded and sliced

Heat together in a pan, and sweat for a few minutes, stirring.

120 g fresh butter beans, or dried butter beans, soaked and cooked
120 g fresh podded peas
150–300 ml Vegetable Stock (see page 314)

Add to the pan, along with the corn kernels, and bring to the boil. Cook until the vegetables are tender, about 3–4 minutes.

120 g couscous grain, cooked (see page 90)
salt and freshly ground pepper

Stir into the pan at the end, season to taste with salt and pepper, and allow to heat through.

BOSTON BAKED BEANS

This is possibly the recipe which characterises traditional American cooking more than any other. It uses the indigenous bean and some salt pork. In Boston and other parts of Massachusetts, molasses is the sweetening element: in Vermont it would be maple syrup.

USA   SERVES 4   OVEN: 140°C/275°F/GAS 1

300 g dried white beans

Soak in cold water overnight, then drain.

Vegetable Stock (see page 314)
1 bouquet garni (bay, thyme, parsley)

Add enough stock to the pan to cover the beans, plus the bouquet, bring to the boil, then turn down the heat and simmer for about 1 hour until the beans are barely tender.

350 g salt belly pork in the piece

Soak in cold water for about 1 hour, then blanch in boiling water for 10 minutes. Skin, reserving the rind, then cut off 2 slices, and arrange these in the bottom of a casserole with a tight-fitting lid. Chop the rest of the pork.

50 g each of carrot and leek, finely diced
2 x 5 ml spoons dry mustard powder
50 g soft brown sugar
50 g black treacle or molasses
1 large onion, peeled and quartered
salt and freshly ground pepper

Add to the beans, along with the chopped pork, seasoning to taste with salt and pepper. Pour into the casserole on top of the pork slices, and top with the rind of the pork. Pour in boiling stock or water if necessary, to come almost to the top of the ingredients. Cover securely with the lid, and cook in the slow oven for about 6 hours, adding more stock (or water) as and when necessary. Remove the lid and the rind for the last 30 minutes, and turn the oven up to 180°C/350°F/Gas 4 to brown the top. Check the seasoning and serve hot.

Succotash

FUL MEDAMES
Ful médames are brown broad beans which have given their name to one of the national dishes of Egypt. The beans can be bought in Greek shops, and are available canned. *Hamine* eggs (long-boiled eggs) are traditionally served with the beans rather than ordinary hard-boiled eggs.

EGYPT

SERVES 4

300 g brown broad beans	Soak overnight in cold water to cover.
2 garlic cloves, peeled and crushed 1 sprig fresh thyme	Place in a suitable pot, along with the soaked drained beans, and cover with water. Bring to the boil, cover and simmer until tender, about 2 hours. Drain and discard the garlic and thyme.
85 ml olive oil 2 garlic cloves, peeled and crushed juice of 2 lemons salt and freshly ground pepper	Mix together to make a dressing, seasoning to taste. Pour over the beans, and then divide between the plates.
4 hard-boiled eggs	Shell, quarter and place on top of the beans.
30 g fresh parsley, finely chopped 1 lemon, quartered	Sprinkle the parsley over the beans and eggs, and garnish each plate with a lemon quarter.

BLACK BEAN SOUP
These black beans, which belong to the kidney bean family, are shiny, very black, and have a full, meaty flavour. They are used a great deal in the Caribbean and the southern United States. (They are not the same beans as those fermented for use in Chinese and Japanese cooking.) Variants of this soup are popular in Cuba, Puerto Rico, Trinidad and other islands.

CARIBBEAN

SERVES 4

200 g dried black beans, soaked
    overnight

Drain, rinse and drain again. The beans should be fairly dry.

2 x 15 ml spoons olive oil
1 large onion, peeled and finely chopped
2 garlic cloves, peeled and crushed
100 g salt pork, soaked, drained and
    finely diced

Sweat together in a large saucepan for a few minutes. Add the black beans and stir.

1.5 litres Chicken or Vegetable Stock
    (see pages 315 or 314)

Add to the saucepan, and bring to the boil. Reduce the heat to a simmer.

1 celery stalk, trimmed and sliced
1 large carrot, peeled and sliced
2 sprigs fresh thyme
2 bay leaves
a pinch each of ground cloves, mace
    and cumin

Add, and cook for approximately 1¼–1½ hours until the beans are soft. Add more stock or water if necessary.
    Cool the mixture slightly. Remove the herbs, place the mixture in a food processor and blend until smooth. Return the mixture to the saucepan to reheat.

salt and freshly ground pepper
4 x 15 ml spoons soured cream
2 fresh red chilli peppers, seeded and
    cut into fine dice
1 x 15 ml spoon finely chopped fresh
    coriander

Correct seasoning with salt and pepper, then serve in warm bowls with soured cream and a sprinkling each of chopped chilli and coriander.

FRIJOLES
Dried beans are a Mexican and Central American staple, and are usually eaten as an accompaniment, with grated cheese on top, or in tortillas. Most households will make more than is necessary for one meal in order to have some left over for *frijoles refritos* (beans mashed over heat with some lard until a coarse dry purée with crisp bits on the bottom).

MEXICO

SERVES 4

350 g dried beans (black, red kidney
    or pinto)

Soak in water to cover overnight, or for at least 3 hours. Rinse thoroughly and discard any that float or that are shrivelled. Drain and place in a large pot or casserole.

1 medium onion, peeled and chopped
25 g lard or bacon fat
2 fresh green chilli peppers, seeded
2 garlic cloves, peeled and crushed
1 bay leaf

Add to the beans, along with enough water to barely cover, and bring to the boil. Turn the heat down to a gentle simmer, cover and cook for about 1½–2 hours or until the beans are tender. Add some boiling water occasionally if necessary. The cooked beans should be thick and soupy, but not too wet.

salt and freshly ground pepper
4 spring onions, finely sliced

Add and mix in well. For a thicker sauce, remove 1–2 x 15 ml spoons of the beans, mash them and return them to the bulk of the beans. Serve hot.

PEA SOUP

This yellow pea soup is often called 'habitant' soup because it was made by, and made famous by, the *habitants*, or farmers, of French Canada. Interestingly, it echoes many similar soups in Europe, from where the majority of the French (and other) Canadians came.

CANADA

SERVES 4

300 g yellow (or green) split peas

Soak in cold water overnight, or for at least a couple of hours, rinse well, then drain and put in a large soup pot.

1 onion, peeled and finely sliced
300 g salt pork, smoked bacon in the piece, or a ham shank, soaked
2 celery stalks, finely sliced
1 sprig each of fresh thyme and parsley

Add to the pot, cover with water, at least 1.5 litres, and bring to a boil over high heat. Cover, reduce the heat, and simmer slowly, stirring occasionally, for 2 hours, or until the peas are tender.
    Purée or sieve the soup after removing the herbs and pork. Chop the latter into small pieces and use to garnish the smooth yellow soup.

salt and freshly ground pepper
finely chopped fresh parsley

Taste for seasoning, then sprinkle the parsley over each bowl.

FALAFEL

Falafel, or *ta'amia,* originated in Egypt, where they are made with dried white broad beans. The Israelis have adopted the idea, but use chickpeas instead, and these little patties have become almost the national dish of Israel. They are eaten as an hors d'oeuvre with fresh and tahina-based salads, or bought from street vendors, popped into the pouch of an Arab pitta bread, along with chopped salad ingredients and a seasoning of tahina (sesame seed paste), and eaten as a snack.

ISRAEL

SERVES 4

250 g chickpeas, soaked for 24 hours

The peas must be soft enough to bite into after soaking. Drain them very well, then pound to a smooth paste or purée them in a food processor.

1 small onion, peeled and grated
1 garlic clove, peeled and crushed
1½ x 5 ml spoons each of ground cumin and coriander
½ x 5 ml spoon cayenne pepper
1½ x 15 ml spoons each of finely chopped fresh parsley and coriander
salt and freshly ground pepper

Mix into the chickpea paste well, and season generously to taste with salt and pepper. (In the Lebanon, they would add a finely sliced chilli pepper.) To make the mixture absolutely smooth, pound again or purée it again in the blender. Rest for about 10 minutes. Shape into small patties or rounds, 2–4 cm in diameter.

vegetable oil

Shallow- or deep-fry the falafel slowly in hot oil until deep golden brown, turning once. Drain very well on kitchen paper, and serve hot and crisp.

ONION BHAJIA
Vegetable fritters occur in many cuisines across the world, and it is usually the batter that is the distinguishing characteristic. The gram or *besan* flour (ground chickpeas or peas) and spice batter here is unmistakeably Indian, quite different from the Italian or French batters, or the Japanese tempura batter.

INDIA

SERVES 4

1 egg, beaten
4 x 15 ml spoons water
1 x 15 ml spoon lemon juice

For the batter, combine well in a large bowl.

100 g gram or *besan* (chickpea) flour
½ x 5 ml spoon each salt, chilli powder, garam masala and cumin seeds
1 x 5 ml spoon ground cumin
a good pinch of turmeric

Mix together, then stir well into the liquid in the bowl.

1 each fresh green and red chilli pepper seeded and finely sliced
2 x 15 ml spoons finely chopped fresh coriander

Mix into the batter and then leave to rest for about 10 minutes.

200 g onions, peeled and finely sliced
1 carrot, peeled and shredded

Mix thoroughly into the batter.

vegetable oil for deep-frying

Heat until hot, but not smoking. Take spoonfuls of the mixture and drop into the hot oil a few at a time. Deep-fry for 5–6 minutes or until golden in colour. Remove, drain well on kitchen paper and serve hot.

HUMMUS
Hummus, a chickpea spread or dip, is common to several cuisines in the Balkans and the Middle East. Tahina is a paste of sesame seeds, another common Middle Eastern ingredient, and is easily available in jars in delicatessens and good supermarkets. You can buy it roasted or unroasted; the darker roasted tahina gives a slightly more bitter flavour to the hummus.

GREECE

MAKES 650–700 g

200 g dried chickpeas

Soak overnight in cold water to cover, then drain well and cover generously with fresh cold water. Bring to the boil, cover and cook gently until the beans are completely soft, about 1–1½ hours. Drain, keeping the liquid.

4 x 15 ml spoons tahina (see above)
2 garlic cloves, peeled and roughly chopped
75 ml lemon juice
45 ml extra virgin olive oil
salt and cayenne pepper

Place in a food processor along with the chickpeas, and about 150 ml of the cooking water. Season to taste with salt and cayenne and process until smooth. If too thick, add a little more cooking water; add more oil, lemon juice or seasoning to taste. The texture should be light and creamy, similar to a light mayonnaise.

1 x 15 ml spoon finely chopped fresh parsley (optional)

Stir into the hummus if liked, or use as a garnish. Serve with hot pitta bread or with crudités as a dip.

Opposite: Onion Bhajia. Above: Spiced Fruity Lentils (see page 84).

SPICED FRUITY LENTILS

The lentil is thought to be one of the world's oldest vegetables, and it has been cultivated in the West since about 6,000 BC. It was not introduced to the New World until the sixteenth century, but lentils are now used in Mexico, like the indigenous beans and pulses, in a variety of interesting ways. (Photograph page 83)

MEXICO   **SERVES 4**

250 g brown or green lentils	Place in a large pan, and cover with water, about 1.25 litres. Bring to the boil, then cover and simmer for about 45 minutes. Drain the lentils, reserving the cooking water.
150 g lean bacon, rinded and chopped 150 g each of spicy sausage (chorizo) and black pudding, skinned and roughly cut at an angle	Sauté the bacon for a few minutes in a dry pan to render the fat, then add the sausage and black pudding pieces. Cover and cook for a few minutes longer.
150 g onions, peeled and finely chopped 2 garlic cloves, peeled and crushed 1 x 15 ml spoon corn oil	Add the onion and garlic to the meats in the pan, along with the oil if necessary, and fry for about 5 minutes to soften.
2 circles fresh pineapple, diced 1 plantain, peeled and sliced salt and freshly ground pepper	Add to the meats and vegetables in the pan along with the lentils, and cook, covered, on a low heat for about 10 minutes.
6 spring onions, trimmed and sliced	Add to the pan along with about 450 ml of the lentil liquid, and cook, covered, for a further 30 minutes. The texture should be quite thick, not runny.
a handful of fresh flat-leaf parsley leaves	Scatter over the lentils and serve warm.

TARKA DHAL

Dhals occupy a central place in Indian cuisine, and they can be served wet to acompany a dry curry or dry to accompany a wet curry. You can use different types of dhal (such as lentils or split peas), but you must alter the cooking times. (Photograph page 171)

INDIA   **SERVES 4**

225 g red split lentils (*masoor dhal*)	Pick over, wash well, then place in a pan.
2 bay or curry leaves 1 x 5 ml spoon each of chilli powder, turmeric and salt 1 small onion, peeled and finely chopped 2.5 cm piece of fresh root ginger	Add to the pan, along with 675 ml water, and bring rapidly to the boil. Turn the heat down, cover and simmer very slowly until the dhal is completely soft and mushy, and the water has evaporated. Add more water if it gets too dry. Remove bay or curry leaves and ginger.
2 x 15 ml spoons finely chopped fresh coriander	Stir into the soft dhal and pour into a serving dish. Keep warm.
2 x 15 ml spoons vegetable oil 1 x 5 ml spoon each of white cumin seeds and mustard seeds 1 garlic clove, peeled and crushed	Heat the oil in a frying pan and add the other ingredients. Sauté until the seeds pop, then immediately pour over the dhal. Stand back, as the oil splatters. Cover, then after 5 minutes stir and serve hot.

SPICY CHICKPEAS

Chickpeas and other pulses such as lentils are a useful source of protein for the largely vegetarian population of India. They are curried as here, split and made into dhals, or eaten as a snack sold by street vendors in the bazaars of large cities.

INDIA

SERVES 4

200 g dried chickpeas, washed

Soak overnight in cold water to cover. Drain, place in a large pot, and cover with water. Simmer until tender, about 1–1½ hours. Drain, keeping the liquid.

1 fresh green chilli pepper, seeded and sliced
2.5 cm piece of fresh root ginger, peeled and chopped
2 garlic cloves, peeled and chopped

Grind together to a paste in a mortar.

2 x 15 ml spoons vegetable oil or ghee
1 onion, peeled and finely sliced

Heat together and gently sauté until the onion is soft.

½ x 5 ml spoon cumin seeds, crushed
1 x 5 ml spoon coriander seeds, crushed
1 x 5 ml spoon chilli powder, or to taste
½ x 5 ml spoon turmeric

Add, along with the chilli paste, and sauté for another minute.

4 tomatoes, skinned and chopped
juice of ½ lemon

Add, and cook until the tomatoes blend well with the onion and spices. Add the drained chickpeas and cook gently for 10 minutes, adding some of their cooking liquid if needed.

salt and freshly ground black pepper
finely chopped fresh coriander and mint leaves

Season to taste with salt and pepper, and serve hot, sprinkled with herb leaves. The chickpeas are good cold as well.

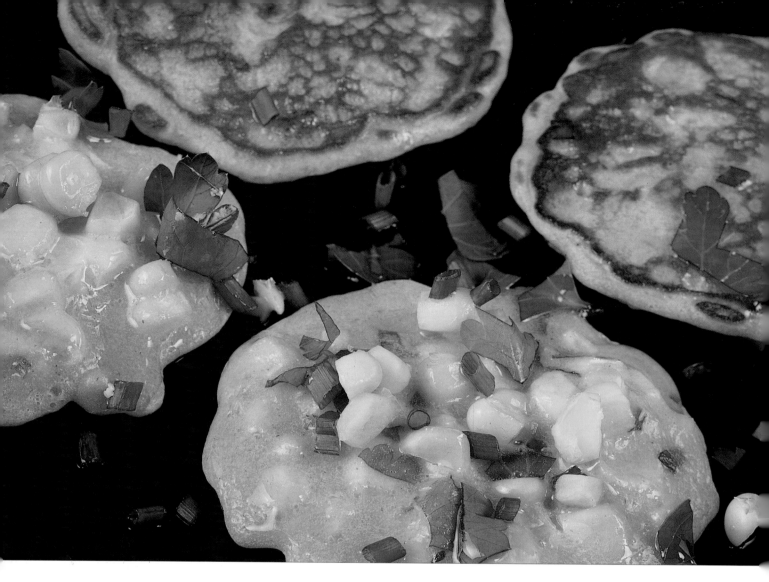

SWEETCORN PANCAKES
The recipe below is American in concept, but with some judicious additions and spicing, it can become more akin to the corn fritters of South-East Asia. Garlic, onion, celery and coriander are added to an Indonesian version, and the milk used is coconut milk; chopped prawns flavour an *empanada de mais* from the Philippines.

USA

SERVES 4

300 g fresh sweetcorn kernels, removed from the cob
150 ml milk

Place in a saucepan and bring to the boil together. Remove from the heat, and drain the kernels, but retain the milk. Chop the kernels roughly.

120 ml double cream (or fromage frais)
1 egg plus 1 egg yolk
60 g plain flour

Mix together in a bowl with the reserved milk and the chopped corn kernels.

1 x 15 ml spoon finely cut fresh chives
salt and freshly ground pepper
freshly grated nutmeg

Add, and season the mixture to taste.

unsalted butter or corn oil

Heat a little in a pan and fry spoonfuls of the corn mixture on both sides until golden brown.

SOYA BEAN PASTE SOUP

The *dashi* below is an essential ingredient in Japanese cooking, and is very much better in flavour then instant *dashi* mixes. This basic soup, *miso shiru*, is very common in Japan, often served for breakfast with rice, pickles and tea. It can be enriched with pieces of meat, fish, shellfish and vegetables. Cook these in the *dashi* before adding the *miso*.

JAPAN
SERVES 4

25 g piece *kombu* (kelp), wiped with a damp cloth
1 litre water

To make the *dashi* (soup stock), put into a medium pan and leave overnight or for at least 2–3 hours. Heat slowly to just below a simmer, and remove and discard the *kombu*.

25 g *hana-katsuo* (dried *bonito* flakes)

Add to the stock, bring to the boil, and simmer for a couple of minutes. Remove from the heat and allow to stand for about 5 minutes. Strain and reserve the *dashi*.

3 x 15 ml spoons *aka miso* (red soya bean paste)
salt and freshly ground pepper

Place in a small sieve and hold it in the hot *dashi*; it should not be submerged. Press as much of the *miso* through the sieve as possible and allow to melt in the *dashi*. Season if necessary.

100 g tofu, cut into small cubes
2 spring onions, very thinly sliced

Add to the *miso* soup and heat through at a simmer very briefly.

fresh root ginger, peeled (optional)

Grate a little over the top of the soup just as you are about to serve, if you like.

TOFU AND OYSTER SOUP

A soup typical of Korea, with robust flavours and good natural ingredients. Korea has a wealth of seafood from the surrounding seas, and other shellfish could be used here instead of the oysters.

KOREA
SERVES 4

400 ml Fish Stock (see page 315)

Place in a flameproof serving pot, and bring to the boil.

100 ml sake (Japanese rice wine)

Add to the stock, reduce the heat, and mix well.

75 g *aka miso* (red soya bean paste)

Add to the simmering liquid, reduce the heat, and mix well.

8 spring onions, trimmed and cut into 2cm lengths

Add to the simmering liquid, and cook for 2–3 minutes.

300 g firm tofu, cut into 2 cm lengths

Add to the simmering liquid and cook for a further 2 minutes.

24 oysters, shelled (but keep their liquor)

Add to the soup, along with the oyster liquor, and remove almost immediately from the heat.

salt and freshly ground pepper

Season to taste – probably with pepper only – and serve immediately.

POLENTA

Polenta is a staple in northern Italy, and is remarkably similar to the *mamaliga* of Romania, and indeed the *coocoo* of the Caribbean and the maize porridges of Africa. Served hot and wet, polenta is an excellent accompaniment to meat and vegetable dishes with sauces; dry and grilled or fried, it goes well with tart salads, cheeses, prosciutto and oil-based sauces. (Photograph page 262)

ITALY
SERVES 4

250 g polenta

Place in a jug with a pouring lip.

1.25 litres water
salt and freshly ground pepper

Bring to the boil in a large pan and add salt to taste. Turn the heat down to a simmer and pour in the polenta flour in a thin stream, stirring vigorously with a whisk. Blend completely then continue stirring occasionally, over a very gentle heat, for about 20 minutes. The polenta is ready when it comes away from the sides of the pan.
  If you wish to serve the polenta grilled or fried, pour on to a flat dish or baking sheet, smooth out a little, and leave to cool and set.

100 g butter
80 g Parmesan, grated

Add to the wet polenta and stir in if you want to serve it as a hot accompaniment. Season to taste with salt and pepper.

olive oil

To grill or sauté cold polenta, cut into thin slices. Brush with a little olive oil and grill until crisp and brown on the outside, tender within; or shallow-fry in olive oil, then drain well.

PARSLEY TABBOULEH

Wheat is revered by the peoples of the Arab world, and is the staple cereal. Bulgar or cracked wheat (also known as bulghur or burghul) is an essential ingredient in many soups and stews, is made into a breakfast porridge, and is a component of *kibbeh*, the national dish of Syria and Lebanon (see page 177). This much loved bulgar salad, originating from the same cuisines, is to me the essence of freshness and flavour.

MIDDLE EAST
SERVES 4

100 g fresh parsley
50 g fresh mint

Remove the herb leaves from the stalks (discard the latter), and cut in the food processor, pulsing the blade carefully to stop the leaves from becoming a purée.

200 g finely ground bulgar

Bring some water to the boil, and soak the bulgar in this for 10 minutes. Drain and press out excess water. Put in a bowl. (Or follow the instructions on the packet; some types vary.)

juice of 1½ large lemons
4 x 15 ml spoons fragrant olive oil
salt and freshly ground pepper

Mix the lemon juice and oil together. Season the bulgar with salt and pepper to taste, and add some of the dressing. Leave to absorb the dressing for 30–40 minutes. Add more oil if necessary. Just before serving, mix the bulgar with the chopped parsley and mint, a little at a time, for a speckled effect.

100 g spring onions, finely sliced
4 ripe sweet tomatoes, skinned,
  seeded and diced

Add to the bulgar, along with the remaining dressing, and mix well. The salad should be distinctly and refreshingly sharp. Check seasoning. Place in a mound on a plate.

2 heads chicory or cos lettuces, leaves
  separated

Arrange around the mound of tabbouleh. Serve as soon as possible as the lemon juice can discolour the green herbs. The salad is scooped up in the chicory or cos leaves; vine leaves are used in some country areas.

COOCOO
Barbados is said to be the island of origin of this cornmeal and okra recipe (minus the corn kernels, which are a Trinidadian addition). Cornmeal porridges, usually with okra, are common throughout the Caribbean, and interestingly are very similar to the African maize meal porridges, perhaps brought to the Caribbean during the years of the slave trade. *Coocoo* is very like polenta *mamaliga*. (Photograph page 71)

CARIBBEAN   **SERVES 4**

12 small young okras	Wash, trim the ends and cut into slices about 5 mm thick.
1 litre Chicken Stock (see page 315) salt and freshly ground pepper	Bring to the boil in a large pan, season to taste with salt and pepper, then add the okra. Cook for about 1 minute.
175 g cornmeal (or polenta)	Add to the stock in a thin stream, stirring constantly in order to avoid lumps. Cook over a gentle heat, stirring, until the cornmeal has absorbed the liquid, about 12–15 minutes.
100 g cooked sweetcorn kernels (optional)	Add about halfway through the cornmeal's cooking.
25 g butter 1 x 15ml spoon finely cut fresh chives	Stir into the cornmeal. Check seasoning. Serve hot as an accompaniment to fish or meat.

ISRAELI COUSCOUS SALAD
A fresh flavoured salad which draws together flavours of the Middle East and North Africa. This type of couscous has much larger grains than that used in North Africa. Use more herbs if you like, but the mint and coriander are particularly important. (Photograph page 91)

ISRAEL   **SERVES 4**

olive oil 2 shallots, peeled and diced 2 garlic cloves, peeled and crushed	Heat 1 x 15 ml spoon of the oil, the shallot and garlic together in a saucepan, and sweat until the shallot is soft, about 5 minutes.
250 g Israeli couscous	Add to the pan and stir to coat with the oil.
600 ml Chicken Stock (see page 315)	Pour into the pan and bring to the boil. Reduce the heat to low, cover with the lid and simmer for about 20 minutes or until cooked. Stir every so often, and add more liquid if necessary. Pour on to a dish to cool, draining off any liquid if necessary.
a pinch of turmeric ½ x 5 ml spoon ground cumin 60 ml lemon juice salt and freshly ground pepper	For the dressing, mix together in a bowl along with 75 ml olive oil, seasoning to taste with salt and pepper.
250 g red and yellow cherry tomatoes, quartered 150 g feta cheese, crumbled 1 small red onion, peeled and diced 2 x 15 ml spoons mixed fresh herbs (parsley, mint, chives, coriander)	Place in a bowl, and add the cooled couscous. Pour in the dressing and toss. Check seasoning. Serve at room temperature.

COUSCOUS

Couscous is made from wheat semolina, and the name is applied to both the 'grain' and the dish made from it. Couscous is the most familiar and famous carbohydrate of the Maghreb – Morocco, Tunisia, Algeria and Libya – and the accompanying stew can be of meat, chicken or vegetables alone. The following are only suggestions.

MOROCCO

SERVES 4

50 g butter
1 garlic clove, peeled and crushed
2 onions, peeled and finely chopped
1 small fresh red chilli pepper,
    seeded and sliced
2 bay leaves
1 x 5 ml spoon ground cumin
½ x 5 ml spoon each of freshly ground
    pepper and ground ginger
1 cinnamon stick

Place in a large stewing pan, and gently heat together, stirring well.

450 g lean lamb, cut into 5 cm pieces
    (optional)
100 g chickpeas, soaked and cooked

Add to the pan, stir well, and pour in water to cover. Bring to the boil, then turn the heat down and simmer, covered, for 45 minutes.

2 each of carrots, small turnips and
    courgettes, trimmed and quartered
4 tomatoes, quartered and seeded
1 small aubergine, coarsely diced
2 x 15 ml spoons finely chopped fresh
    coriander
3 x 15 ml spoons finely chopped fresh
    parsley

Add to the stew in the pan, along with more water to cover if necessary. Mix carefully, and continue to cook for a further 20–30 minutes until the vegetables and meat (if using) are tender.

450 ml stock
250 g couscous

Meanwhile, bring the stock to a boil in a pan, and stir in the couscous. Remove from the heat and cover with the lid. Leave to stand for 20 minutes, and the couscous will be ready.

50 g butter

Stir into the couscous, allowing it to melt in. Fluff the couscous up with a fork. Keep warm.

200 g piece of pumpkin, skinned,
    seeded and diced

Meanwhile, in a separate pan, braise in a little of the stew liquid until just tender. It must be cooked separately from the stew as it can disintegrate very quickly. Watch it carefully.

salt and freshly ground pepper

Season the stew and couscous to taste. Add the pumpkin and its liquid to the stew. To serve, pile the hot couscous around the edges of a large heated platter and pile the vegetables and meat and some of the sauce in the middle. Offer the remaining sauce separately. Serve with Harissa (see page 308): mix a little Harissa with a spoonful of the stew broth and then pour over the plate of food.

Opposite: Top, Couscous with a vegetable stew. Below: Israeli Couscous Salad (see page 89).

CHELO

You can add to this basic steamed rice dish – mixing in handfuls of fresh herbs (of which the Iranians are very fond), or toasted pine kernels. When the rice is cooked with other ingredients it is called *polo* (see page 193), a linguistic relative of the Turkish *pilav* and the Indian *pullao*.

IRAN

SERVES 4

260 g basmati rice	Wash well in boiling water then cover with boiling water.
salt and freshly ground pepper 1 x 15 ml spoon white wine vinegar	Add to the water, then leave for several hours. Drain well and rinse.
boiling Chicken or Vegetable Stock (see page 315 or 314) 1 bay leaf	Place the rice in a pan and cover with boiling stock. Add the bay leaf and some salt. Bring to the boil and boil for about 7–8 minutes, uncovered – the rice must be slightly undercooked. Strain the rice. Reserve the stock.
60 g butter, melted, or 60 ml olive oil	Place on the bottom of the cleaned-out rice pan with 1–2 x 15 ml spoons of the reserved stock. Pour in the rice and sprinkle with another 2 x 15 ml spoons of the stock. Cover the pan with a cloth and then the lid. Place over a very, very low heat and steam for another 12–15 minutes. The grains will be separate and fluffy, and there will be a golden crust of rice on the base of the pan. This is scraped off and offered as a special treat along with the rice. Season to taste.

SHRIMP JAMBALAYA

The Creole dish, jambalaya, evolved in Louisiana, where a large proportion of American rice is grown. It is Spanish in concept, though, being very similar to paella. You could use meat, poultry or other shellfish as the protein element, or spicy sausages, but not a mixture as in paella.

USA

SERVES 4

50 g butter 1 medium onion, peeled and finely chopped 1 garlic clove, peeled and crushed	Heat together in a large heavy saucepan, and cook until the onion and garlic are pale gold.
200 g long-grain rice 1 green pepper, seeded and diced 2 celery stalks, trimmed and diced	Add to the pan, and sauté, stirring, until the rice too is golden.

4 medium tomatoes, skinned,
    seeded and diced
2 x 15 ml spoons Tomates Concassées
    (see page 312)
500 ml Chicken Stock (see page 315)
2 bay leaves
a large dash of Tabasco sauce
a pinch each of chilli powder and
    ground cumin
salt and freshly ground pepper
	Add to the pan, stir, bring to the boil, then cover and leave to simmer for 15–20 minutes until the rice is tender and has absorbed most, but not all, of the stock. Remove the bay leaves.

500 g cooked shrimps, peeled	Add to the jambalaya about 5 minutes before it is ready, stir in, cover and continue cooking until hot. Adjust the seasoning. Serve immediately.

BOILED RICE
The rice in Japan and Korea is plump and short-grained, which becomes slightly sticky when cooked, thus the grains adhere to one another. No other rice can adequately replace it – whether as a grain or the basis of *sushi* – nor can any other rice be so easily picked up in chopsticks! Use a 300 ml cup to measure rice and water.

JAPAN/KOREA   **SERVES 4**

1 cup Japanese short-grain rice

Put into a large bowl and wash under cold running water until the water becomes clear instead of milky. Drain the rice in a sieve for 30 minutes; it will also absorb a little of the water clinging to it.

1¼ cups water
salt and freshly ground pepper

Put in a heavy-based pan with the rice. Bring to the boil over high heat, then cover tightly and simmer very, very slowly for 20 minutes. Turn the heat to high for 30 seconds or so, then turn it off. Let the rice sit, still covered, for another 10–15 minutes. It will continue to 'cook' in its own steam.

JALOFFA
A rice and protein dish, also known as *jollof* rice, which hails from several countries in the west of Africa. It can be served as a main course or an accompaniment, and is a good dish for a hot buffet. You could also garnish the finished dish with parsley, sliced hard-boiled eggs and shredded lettuce.

WEST AFRICA   **SERVES 4**

400 g lean meat or boneless poultry
salt and freshly ground pepper

Cut into 5 cm cubes and season to taste with salt and pepper.

2 x 15 ml spoons peanut oil

Heat in a sauté pan, and sauté the meat until sealed and brown all over. Remove the meat from the pan using a slotted spoon and place in a large saucepan.

500 ml Beef or Chicken Stock
   (see pages 316 or 315)

Add to the saucepan, and simmer the meat gently for about 10 minutes.

2 large onions, peeled and finely
   chopped
2 garlic cloves, peeled and crushed

Add to the oil in the sauté pan and sauté until golden.

a pinch each of cayenne pepper and
   ground allspice
½ fresh red chilli pepper, seeded and
   sliced
4 large tomatoes, skinned, seeded
   and diced
2 x 15 ml spoons Tomates Concassées
   (see page 312)

Add to the onions and stir well to amalgamate. Add to the meat and stock in the saucepan.

200 g long-grain rice

Stir into the pan, season with salt and pepper, cover and simmer on a low heat for 20–25 minutes or until the rice has absorbed all the liquid. You may need to add a little more stock. Turn on to a hot platter when ready.

2 x 15 ml spoons finely chopped fresh
   coriander

Use as a garnish. Serve hot.

PAELLA

A true paella is primarily a rice dish, rather as is the Italian risotto, spiked and flavoured with small pieces of available meat or fish and green vegetables. A Valencian paella usually consists of chicken or rabbit and snails with dried and green beans. A Barcelona paella might use squid, chorizo sausage, prawns or clams and red pepper, as in the photograph opposite. Paella is named after the flat-bottomed metal pan in which it is cooked.

SPAIN

SERVES 4

---

1 x 1.4 kg chicken (or rabbit), cut into 8 pieces
salt and freshly ground pepper
olive oil
200 g lean pork, cut into small pieces (optional)

Dry the chicken pieces well, then season. Heat 100 ml of the oil in the chosen pan, and fry the chicken pieces for 2 minutes or until golden. Add the pork a few minutes before the chicken if using.

---

1 medium onion, peeled and finely chopped
2 garlic cloves, peeled and crushed
125 g tomatoes, skinned, seeded and diced
½ medium red pepper and ½ medium green pepper, diced
100 g green beans, cut into pieces
100 g podded peas

Add to the pan and sauté gently for a minute or two.

1.25 litres Chicken Stock (see page 315)
2 x 5 ml spoons paprika
a large pinch of powdered saffron
12 snails, mussels, pieces of eel, or raw shelled prawns (optional)

Add to the pan and bring to the boil.

---

250 g short-grain rice (use Valencia or risotto)

Stir into the stock, cover and bring to a simmer. Reduce the heat to very low and cook very gently for 20 minutes until the rice is tender and the stock has evaporated. Stir every now and again.

Remove from the heat and leave to stand for a few minutes before serving. Adjust seasoning.

FRIED RICE
A flavourful way of using up leftover boiled or steamed rice, and small pieces of protein (meat, poultry or fish). The Indonesian Nasi Goreng (see below) is very similar. Cook the rice freshly if you like, but this is best done some 3–4 hours before frying it.

CHINA

SERVES 4

1 x 15 ml spoon peanut oil
1 large onion, peeled and chopped
1 garlic clove, peeled and crushed
½ each of red and green pepper,
   seeded and diced

Heat together in a wok or heavy frying pan and cook for about 5 minutes.

400 g long-grain, sticky or basmati
   rice, cooked
2 x 15 ml spoons light soy sauce
175 g cooked meat or poultry,
   cut into pieces
some cooked and shelled shrimps or
   prawns (optional)
salt and freshly ground pepper

Stir in and continue to fry gently until the rice and other ingredients are thoroughly heated through and nicely browned. Adjust seasoning.

1 fresh red chilli pepper, seeded and
   cut into fine rings
2 spring onions, cut into fine rings
1 egg, made into a thin omelette (see
   below), cut into strips
1 x 15 ml spoon finely chopped fresh
   coriander or parsley

Use to garnish the rice, and serve hot as an accompaniment.

NASI GORENG
This fried rice dish is one of the most famous of Indonesian dishes, and is an essential part of a *Rijstaffel*. It can be cooked with coconut milk, and sliced onions fried until brown and crisp are another possible garnish. Shrimp or prawn crackers, or *krupuk*, are a good accompaniment. (Photograph page 99)

INDONESIA

SERVES 4

vegetable oil

Heat about ½ x 15 ml spoon in a small frying pan.

2 eggs, beaten

Add half to the pan and let it set into a thin omelette. Cook until golden, then slide on to a plate. Repeat with another ½ x 15 ml spoon oil and the remaining beaten egg. Roll each omelette up tightly and cut into thin strips. Set aside.

2 onions, peeled
2 garlic cloves, peeled
2 fresh red chilli peppers, seeded
1 x 15 ml spoon *blachan*
   (shrimp paste)

Place in the food processor and blend to a purée.
   Heat 3 x 15 ml spoons vegetable oil in a wok or large frying pan and stir-fry the onion purée until golden.

1 chicken breast, skinned and diced
225 g medium king prawns,
   shelled and deveined

Add to the onion purée, and continue to stir-fry over a gentle heat until both are cooked, about 5–6 minutes.

450 g cooked long-grain rice
2 x 15 ml spoons light soy sauce
1 x 5 ml spoon brown sugar
juice of ½ lemon
salt and freshly ground pepper

Add to the pan, seasoning to taste with salt and pepper, and continue to stir-fry until the rice is thoroughly heated through. Spoon into a warmed serving dish.

100 g cooked ham, shredded
2 x 15 ml spoons fresh coriander
    leaves

Use to garnish the rice, along with the omelette strips.

WILD MUSHROOM RISOTTO

The right sort of rice is vital for risotto, as is a good stock; after that the additions can be virtually anything, from bone marrow and saffron (risotto Milanese, a perfect accompaniment for an Osso Buco, see page 164), to asparagus, young spring vegetables or clams. I like to make risotto in two stages, but if you're confident that your guests are on time, you can cook yours in one stage. (Photograph page 103)

ITALY

SERVES 4

10 g butter
1 medium shallot, peeled and
    finely chopped

Heat together in a suitable saucepan, and cook gently without colouring for about 4 minutes, or until the shallot is transparent.

150 g risotto rice (arborio, carnaroli
    or vialone)

Add, and stir well with a spatula to allow each grain of rice to be coated with oil, about 3 minutes. Do not allow anything to brown.

250 ml hot strong Brown Chicken
    Stock (see page 316)

Add 150 ml to the rice and stir in well over gentle heat. Continue stirring for about 10 minutes. By this time, the stock will have been absorbed. Remove the pan from the heat, and then leave the rice to cool on a tray. It will be part cooked, still with a crunch to it. This can be done in the morning, and it will take only minimal time to finish the cooking.
    When ready to serve, return the rice to the saucepan.

Wild Mushroom Sauce (see page 313)

Add to the part-cooked rice in the pan, along with the remaining stock, a little at a time. Stir and begin to heat through. The rice should need about 4 minutes in all, including the additions below, to become al dente.

40 g trumpet mushrooms,
    cleaned

Add to the rice and stir in.

40 g Parmesan, freshly grated
25 ml double cream, lightly whipped

Add the cheese to the rice and stir in, followed by the cream.

2 x 15 ml spoons Champagne
2 x 15 ml spoons freshly cut chives
salt and freshly ground pepper

Add at the very last moment, seasoning to taste with salt and pepper. Serve the risotto immediately with more grated Parmesan served separately.

Pumpkin Risotto with Prosciutto

PUMPKIN RISOTTO WITH PROSCIUTTO
Pumpkin is used seasonally in many parts of Italy – notably in gnocchi. Here it is cooked with rice in a risotto. As with the Wild Mushroom Risotto overleaf, the risotto can be started ahead of time, and then finished at the last minute.

ITALY

SERVES 4

2 x 15 ml spoons olive oil
1 small onion, peeled and finely
  chopped

Heat together in a suitable pan, and cook gently without colouring for about 4 minutes, or until the onion is transparent.

150 g risotto rice (arborio, carnaroli
  or vialone)
120 g pumpkin flesh, diced

Add, and stir well with a spatula to coat the rice with the oil, about 3 minutes. Do not brown.

250ml Chicken or Vegetable Stock
  (see pages 315 or 314)

Add, and stir in well over a gentle heat. Continue stirring for about 10 minutes. By this time the stock will have been absorbed. Remove the pan from the heat, and then leave the rice to cool on a tray. It will be part cooked, still with a crunch to it. This can be done in the morning, and it will take only minimal time to finish the cooking.

Nasi Goreng (see page 96).

175 g cooked mashed pumpkin	Place in a suitable saucepan along with the cooled part-cooked rice. Stir over gentle heat to warm through, about 8 minutes, or until the rice is nicely al dente.
50 ml Champagne or dry white wine	Just seconds from when the risotto is ready, add to stop the cooking. Remove from the heat.
2 x 15 ml spoons grated Parmesan **25 g butter** **salt and freshly ground pepper**	Add to the risotto, seasoning to taste with salt and pepper. Spoon into shallow serving bowls.
4 slices prosciutto **deep-fried sage leaves (optional)**	Use as a garnish.

SUSHI

These morsels of vinegared rice and raw fish or vegetables, one of the most popular foods in Japan, are increasingly served in western countries. They make a very interesting canapé. Sushi falls into several basic categories which are outlined below.

JAPAN

MAKES ABOUT 30 PIECES

75 ml Japanese rice vinegar
30 g caster sugar
½ x 5 ml spoon salt

For the sushi rice dressing, mix together and leave to steep overnight.

300 g Japanese short-grain rice

Wash well under cold running water for 5 minutes until the water runs clear rather than milky, then leave in a sieve to drain for at least 30 minutes.

Cook as described on page 93, using 850 ml water for this amount of rice.

Pour the sushi dressing to taste over the hot rice. Use a rice paddle to mix the dressing and rice in a cutting motion. Fan the rice to cool it rapidly to body temperature. Mound it in a bowl and cover with a damp cloth.

100 g each of three types of fresh
    seafood, prepared (fish filleted,
    squid skinned, molluscs shelled etc.)

Seafood for sushi should be the finest and freshest: it can be pre-cooked or uncooked, more usually the latter. Cut the fish portions into pieces, some thin slices, some small squares.

1½ x 15 ml spoons *wasabi*
    (green horseradish paste)

The simplest sushi (*oshi-zushi*) are made from rice formed in a suitable mould, topped with *wasabi* and fish, and then cut into little blocks. Hand-made sushi – rice formed in the palm of the left hand into an oval – are known as *nigiri-zushi*; the rice oval is topped with *wasabi* and fish.

several sheets of *nori* (dried laver
    seaweed), toasted
cucumber, peeled and seeded
green and red pepper strips

To make rolled sushi – *maki-zushi* – have ready a traditional bamboo mat. Place the sheets of seaweed on the mat and cover with sushi rice. Put a line of fish or vegetable or a filling of choice in the centre, and then roll the bamboo mat to enclose rice and filling in the *nori*. Press into a roll, then remove the bamboo mat and cut the roll into pieces about 3 cm long.

sesame seeds
finely cut chives
red lumpfish roe
fresh parsley leaves

Use to garnish the sushi if liked.

250 ml dark soy sauce
25 ml *mirin* (Japanese sherry)

Simmer together in a small pan for 2–3 minutes, then cool. Serve as a dipping sauce for the sushi.

RICE AND BARLEY WITH MIXED BEANS
As it is all over Asia, rice is the basic grain of Korea, but barley and beans of various types are popular as well. When roasted, barley is the basis of Korea's national drink, *poricha*, a tea. (Photograph page 103)

KOREA   **SERVES 4**

225 g Korean rice 25 g pearl barley	Wash in several changes of water, then place in a large saucepan.
400 ml water	Pour into the pan and bring to the boil.
75 g each of black beans and red kidney beans, cooked	Add to the rice and barley, stir, cover, then turn the heat to low. Cook for 15–20 minutes until the rice and barley are tender and the water has evaporated. Remove from the heat and leave to stand for 10–15 minutes without removing the lid. Fluff up with the back of a wooden spoon or a pair of chopsticks.
1 x 5 ml spoon finely chopped fresh parsley (optional)	Use as a garnish and serve hot.

MOROS Y CHRISTIANOS
The name of this recipe translates as 'Moors and Christians', and refers to the conquest of Spain by the Moors as well as to the colour combination of the white rice and dark beans. Although Spanish in name, the dish is African in concept; in Ghana it is served with fried plaintains, just as it is in Cuba.

CUBA/SOUTH AMERICA   **SERVES 4**

250 g black beans	Soak overnight in cold water. Drain, rinse, then cover with fresh cold water.
1 bouquet garni (bay, thyme, parsley) 1 ham bone (optional)	Add to the pan, then bring to the boil and simmer for 20–30 minutes until the beans are part-cooked. Drain the beans, reserving the water.
2 garlic cloves, peeled and finely chopped 1 onion, peeled and finely chopped 1 green pepper, seeded and finely chopped 2 x 15 ml spoons corn oil	Cook together in a pan until the onion begins to soften, about 4 minutes.
200 g long-grain rice	Add to the onion in the pan, and sauté for about a minute. Add 500 ml of the reserved bean water, stir well, and simmer for 10 minutes.
salt and freshly ground pepper	Add to taste, along with the part-cooked beans and a little more bean water if necessary. Cook slowly on a very low heat until the beans are cooked, another 15–20 minutes. Check the seasoning. Serve with fried plantains if you like.

KEDGEREE
Kedgeree is an Anglo-Indian adaptation of the original Hindi *khicharhi* or *chichri*, which consisted of rice, onion, lentils, spices, fresh limes, ghee and fish or meat. The idea was adopted in culinary terms during the many years of the British Raj. This is a simpler breakfast version, and is served with a mild, but interesting, curry sauce.

GREAT BRITAIN　　　　　　　　　　**SERVES 4**　　　**OVEN: 190°C/375°F/GAS 5**

700 ml Fish Stock (see page 315)
　　or water
1 sprig fresh parsley or thyme,
　　or a few chives

Bring to the boil together in a shallow pan.

300 g smoked Finnan haddock
　　with skin

Add and poach in barely simmering liquid for about 3–4 minutes. Remove the fish and leave to cool. Skin, bone and flake. Set aside. Strain the stock and set aside.

100 g onions, peeled and finely
　　chopped
1 garlic clove, peeled and crushed
2 x 15 ml spoons olive oil

To make the curry sauce, sweat together until the onion and garlic are soft, about 5 minutes.

50 g carrot, finely chopped
50 g celery, finely chopped
100 g apple, finely chopped
2 x 5 ml spoons curry powder
½ x 5 ml spoon turmeric

Add to the pan, mix well, and sauté gently for 5 minutes.

1 bouquet garni (bay, thyme, parsley
　　stalks)
1 medium tomato, roughly chopped

Add, along with 200 ml of the reserved stock, and bring to the boil. Cover and allow to cook until reduced by half, about 15 minutes.

100 g whipping cream
salt and freshly ground pepper

Stir in, and allow to cook together for 5–7 minutes, then season to taste with salt and pepper. Push everything through a sieve, or liquidise and sieve. Keep warm.

1 x 15 ml spoon olive oil
50 g onions, peeled and finely
　　chopped

Meanwhile, for the rice, sweat together in a suitable pan for a few minutes to soften the onion.

200 g basmati rice

Stir in, and mix well with the onion. When the rice starts to look transparent, add the remaining reserved fish stock, about 500 ml, and bring to a simmer. Cover and cook in the preheated oven for about 15–16 minutes, until the rice is tender and fluffy and has absorbed the stock. Use a fork to separate and loosen the rice.

1 x 15 ml spoon finely chopped fresh
　　parsley

Add, along with the flaked haddock and seasoning to taste.

8 quail's eggs, medium boiled
　　and shelled

Serve the kedgeree in a warm dish or on individual plates, garnished with the halved eggs, on top of the warm curry sauce.

Opposite: Above, Rice and Barley with Mixed Beans (see page 101). Below left, Wild Mushroom Risotto (see page 97). Below right, Kedgeree.

PASTA AND NOODLES

FRESH PASTA

There has been considerable debate for centuries about the origins of pasta – whether it began with the Chinese or the Italians, and whether Marco Polo really discovered it in the East and brought it to the West. However, the basic flour and water, often with egg, combination is a feature of many more cuisines than just the Italian and Chinese. This basic dough can be used for other national 'pastas', but it is in essence Italian. Flavour and colour it in a variety of ways. Make it with plain white flour, or with wholemeal flour.

ITALY

SERVES 4

200 g strong plain white flour or fine
    wholemeal flour
25 g semolina

Sieve into a bowl and make a well in the centre.

1 egg, beaten
1 x 15 ml spoon olive oil
a good pinch of salt
3–4 x 15 ml spoons hot water

Mix together, then place in the well in the flour, and gradually work the flour in towards the middle. Knead to a very firm, smooth dough. Cover with a damp cloth and rest in a cool place for at least 2–3 hours.

    Divide into convenient pieces and roll as thinly as possible. Use a rolling pin or a pasta machine. Cut the dough into the shape required, and use straightaway or leave to dry for a while. Cook fresh pasta for 2–3 minutes in salted boiling water, slightly dried pasta for about double that time. Drain well in a colander.

TOMATO PASTA
1 x 15 ml spoon tomato purée

Add to the dough instead of the hot water.

SPINACH PASTA
50 g cooked, puréed spinach,
    squeezed dry

Add to the dough instead of the hot water – but you may need a little extra water.

SAFFRON PASTA
a large pinch of powdered saffron

Dissolve in the hot water before making the dough.

HERB PASTA
25 g fresh finely chopped herbs
    (mixed if desired)

Sorrel pasta and basil pasta are particularly successful. Mix the herb with the eggs before making the dough.

BLACK INK PASTA
40 ml squid ink

Add to the dough instead of the hot water.

BUCKWHEAT PASTA

Replace half of the plain white or wholewheat flour with buckwheat flour.

Opposite: Above, Tagliatelle with Peas and Prawns. Below, Penne with Radicchio and Bacon (For both see page 108).

TAGLIATELLE WITH PEAS AND PRAWNS
In the north of Italy, tagliatelle is the name for flat long strips of pasta. In Rome and the south, virtually the same pasta shape is known as fettuccine. In this pea sauce, some of the more tender pods could be used as well, if you first remove the film or skin from the inside of the pods, as this can be tough. (Photograph page 107)

ITALY   **SERVES 4**

olive oil 1 small onion, peeled and finely chopped 1 garlic clove, peeled and crushed	Heat 2 x 15 ml spoons of the oil, the onion and garlic together in a medium saucepan, and sweat until the onion is soft, about 5 minutes.
225 g podded peas	Add to the pan, stir and cook for about 2 minutes.
150 ml Chicken Stock (see page 315)	Add to the pan, then bring to the boil and simmer for about 25 minutes, or until the peas are tender. Transfer to a mixing bowl and mash coarsely. Heat another 2 x 15 ml spoons oil in a large sauté pan.
20 tiger prawns, peeled and deveined salt and freshly ground pepper	Season the prawns with salt and pepper, then add to the oil in the pan. Sauté until the prawns turn pink. Remove the prawns and set aside. Add the pea mixture to the pan and heat gently.
450 g fresh tagliatelle	Cook in boiling salted water until al dente, about 4–5 minutes. Drain and add to the pea mixture, along with the prawns.
1 x 15 ml spoon each of chopped fresh mint and flat-leaf parsley	Add to the pasta, toss well, and season to taste with salt and pepper. Add more olive oil if necessary, and serve hot.

PENNE WITH RADICCHIO AND BACON
Radicchio, a member of the chicory family, originates from Italy, and is either a small round globe or a cos lettuce shape. The latter is a radicchio from Treviso in the Veneto, sometimes known as trevise. (Photograph page 107)

ITALY   **SERVES 4**

2 x 15 spoons olive oil 175 g lean bacon or pancetta, cut into bite-sized pieces	Heat together in a sauté pan, then sauté until the bacon is golden.
450 g radicchio, finely shredded	Add most of the shreds to the pan and stir over a medium heat until starting to wilt, about 3–4 minutes.
150 ml double cream	Stir into the pan, and bring to a gentle boil.
175 g Gorgonzola cheese, crumbled into small pieces salt and freshly ground pepper	Add all but 2 tablespoons to the pan, and stir until melted, seasoning to taste with salt and pepper. Remove from the heat.
250 g penne	Cook in boiling salted water until ready, about 4–5 minutes for fresh, 9–11 minutes for dried. Drain well, and toss in the sauce. Adjust the seasoning, and add more cream or water if the sauce seems too dry.
2 x 15 ml spoons grated Parmesan	Use as a garnish along with the reserved radicchio shreds and Gorgonzola pieces.

WON-TONS IN SOUP
The Chinese are thrifty people, and can make a little food go a long way. This explains to a certain extent the plethora of dishes which involve a 'pasta' dough as a wrapping for other ingredients – won-tons as here, dumplings, spring rolls, the pancakes for Peking duck. Won-ton skins are widely available in oriental food stores, and they freeze well.

CHINA **SERVES 4**

250 g plain flour
1 egg, beaten
salt and freshly ground pepper

To make the dough for the won-ton 'skins', mix the flour and 1 x 5 ml spoon salt with the egg and enough water to make a stiff dough. Cover with a damp cloth and set aside to rest.

250 g prawn or shrimp flesh, finely diced, or minced pork
150 g bamboo shoots, finely diced
½ garlic clove, peeled and crushed
a pinch of grated fresh root ginger
1 x 15 ml spoon finely chopped fresh coriander
½ x 15 ml spoon light soy sauce
1 x 15 ml spoon shaohsing (yellow rice wine) or sherry
½ x 15 ml spoon sesame oil

For the filling, mix all the ingredients together.
Roll the won-ton dough out to a thin sheet on a lightly floured surface, and cut into 7.5 cm squares. If not using straightaway, cover again with a damp cloth. Put a teaspoon of the filling on each square and squeeze the sides together to form a pouch shape. Use a little water to help the dough stick to itself.

1 litre good Brown Chicken Stock (see page 316)
1 x 15 ml spoon light soy sauce
1 small piece fresh root ginger

Bring to the boil together in a large pan, then drop in the won-tons. Boil for 2–3 minutes only. Pour hot into individual bowls, discarding the ginger.

4 spring onions, finely sliced

Sprinkle on to each bowl as a garnish.

PELMENI
These meat dumplings are the Russian equivalent of Italy's ravioli and China's won-tons – little pieces of dough, wrapped round a savoury filling, which are poached in water or stock to cook. *Pierogi* and *vareniki* are similar stuffed pastas from Eastern Europe.

RUSSIA **SERVES 4**

dough as for won-ton 'skins' (see above), replacing the water with soured cream, if liked

Make the dough as described above, using soured cream instead of water if liked, but mix to a soft but firm dough. Cover with a damp cloth and set aside to rest.

175 g each of minced beef and pork
1 onion, peeled and minced
2 x 15 ml spoons finely cut fresh dill
salt and freshly ground pepper

Mix together, adding salt and pepper and taste.
Roll the dough out very thinly, and cut into small 5 cm rounds or squares. Put a 1 x 5 ml spoon of filling on to each piece of dough and fold over to a triangle or crescent shape. Crimp the edges securely, using a little water to make them stick. Put in the fridge to chill for 30 minutes.
Bring a large pan of salted water to the boil and cook the *pelmeni* for 5–6 minutes, or until they float to the surface of the water.

melted butter

Serve with the hot *pelmeni*, which should be sprinkled with lots of freshly ground pepper as well.

RAVIOLI OF SMOKED SALMON WITH BASIL DRESSING
Ravioli is perhaps the most familiar of Italian stuffed pastas, although tortellini and cappelletti are also made. It is interesting to compare these ravioli with the stuffed pastas of other countries – the *pierogi*, *pelmeni* and *vareniki* of Eastern Europe, and the won-tons and dumplings of China.

ITALY

SERVES 4

**1 quantity Fresh Pasta dough
(see page 106)**

Make as described on page 106, then cover with a damp cloth and chill for 30 minutes.

**100 g smoked salmon, finely sliced
75 g each of ricotta and mascarpone
  cheeses
salt and freshly ground pepper
16 fresh basil leaves, finely cut**

For the filling, stir all the ingredients together. Cover and chill until the mixture has set.
    Roll the dough out, using a pasta machine or rolling pin, to make four thin sheets of pasta. Place two of these on top of each other, cover with a damp cloth, and set aside briefly.

1 egg, beaten with a little water

Brush some over one sheet of the uncovered pasta dough, and mark lightly with a round 8 cm cutter (or mark into squares). Put about 1 x 5 ml spoonful of the filling on to each lightly etched circle or square. Lay the second piece of pasta dough on top and press down between the mounds to form the shapes of the ravioli. Cut with a suitable circular or square cutter. Press the edges well together to seal. Do the same with the remaining two sheets of pasta, and the remaining filling.

1 red pepper, seeded and skinned	Cut into very thin strips and blanch in boiling water to soften. Drain well and allow to cool.
150 ml olive oil 4 x 15 ml spoons white wine vinegar 4 x 15 m spoons dry white wine 1 x 15 ml spoon grain mustard 2 x 15 ml spoons finely cut fresh basil	Mix together to form the basis of the dressing. To cook the ravioli, drop them, two or three at a time, into boiling salted water. Cook for seconds only after they float to the top of the pan, then remove using a slotted spoon and drain well.
	Mix into the dressing. To serve, place three ravioli per person on heated plates, pour over a little of the dressing, and sprinkle with the red pepper strips.

FETA AND SPINACH RAVIOLI FILLING

2 x 15 ml spoons olive oil 1 garlic clove, peeled and finely chopped 1 shallot, peeled and finely chopped 2 spring onions, finely sliced	Sweat together for 2–3 minutes without colouring. Remove from the heat.
150 g young leaf spinach, blanched and squeezed dry 200 g feta cheese, crumbled	Place with the shallot mixture into a food processor and process finely.
50 g Parmesan cheese, finely grated salt and freshly ground pepper	Add, and correct seasoning with salt and pepper.

Opposite: Ravioli of Smoked Salmon with Basil Dressing. Below, Zucchini and Ricotta Cannelloni (see page 112).

ZUCCHINI AND RICOTTA CANNELLONI

Cannelloni, tubes of pasta, can be bought dried, but taste much better if made from sheets of home-made pasta (see page 106). Any ravioli filling could be used instead of the courgette filling here. (Photograph page 111)

ITALY   SERVES 4   OVEN: 190°C/375°F/GAS 5

25 g butter
75 g onion, peeled and finely chopped
2 garlic cloves, peeled and crushed

Heat together in a pan, and sweat until the onion is soft, about 5 minutes.

450 g courgettes, trimmed and sliced
2 sprigs fresh thyme
salt and freshly ground pepper

Add to the pan, seasoning to taste with salt and pepper, and stir well. Add a little water, cover and cook until the courgette is tender, about 7–8 minutes. Drain off any excess moisture, discard the thyme stalks, and coarsely chop the mixture in a food processor. Scrape out into a bowl.

1 egg
225 g ricotta cheese
50 g Parmesan, freshly grated
1 x 15 ml spoon chopped fresh parsley

Add the egg, ricotta, 15 g of the Parmesan and the parsley to the bowl and mix well, seasoning to taste with salt and pepper. Spoon into a piping bag.

12 dried cannelloni tubes, or sheets
   of fresh pasta

Pipe the filling into the dried tubes, or on to the pasta sheets, roll up and moisten to stick.

Tomato Sauce (see page 311)

Pour into a suitable gratin dish and neatly arrange the cannelloni on top.

25 g butter
25 g plain flour
300 ml milk

Make a roux with the butter and flour, then stir in the milk, and cook to a smooth béchamel sauce, seasoning to taste with salt and pepper. Pour over the top of the cannelloni and sprinkle with the remaining Parmesan. Bake in the preheated oven until the tops of the cannelloni are golden, about 30–35 minutes. Serve hot.

PHO

Pho is actually the name of the fresh rice noodles used in this soup. Traditionally a vehicle for raw or very rare beef, *Pho* can also be made with chicken as below, and it is always accompanied by *nuoc cham*, a fermented fish sauce condiment. The rice noodles can be found in Eastern grocers; fresh they only need blanching in hot water; dried they need to be soaked first before brief cooking. (Photograph page 114)

VIETNAM

SERVES 4

1 fresh green chilli, seeded and sliced
1 garlic clove, peeled and diced
1 x 5 ml spoon caster sugar

For the *nuoc cham* or fish sauce condiment, grind together in a mortar until smooth.

2 x 15 ml spoons *nuoc mam* (fish sauce) or *nam pla*
2 x 15 ml spoons water
2 x 5 ml spoons lime juice

Add to the chilli mixture and stir until smooth. Place in a bowl on the table.

5 cm piece of fresh root ginger, peeled
3 shallots, peeled

Over an open flame or in a dry non-stick pan, using a metal skewer, blacken the ginger and shallots. Place in a large saucepan.

1 litre Chicken Stock (see page 316)
½ star anise
1 cinnamon stick

Add to the pan, bring to the boil, then reduce the heat to low.

2 chicken breasts with bones
salt and freshly ground pepper

Add to the hot stock and simmer for about 10 minutes or until the chicken is cooked. Remove from the stock, cool slightly, then skin and shred into pieces. Keep to one side.

120 g beansprouts

Blanch in boiling water for 30 seconds. Refresh in cold water and drain well.

350 g rice noodles

Soak for 30 minutes if dried. Drop fresh or soaked dried into a pan of boiling water and boil for a minute or two until cooked. Drain and divide between four large deep soup bowls. Sprinkle the chicken shreds over the noodles.

2 spring onions, finely sliced
2 x 15 ml spoons each of finely chopped fresh coriander and mint
1 x 15 ml spoon fried garlic slices
1 x 15 ml spoon fried shallot rings
2 fresh red chilli peppers, seeded and finely sliced

Sprinkle evenly over the chicken and the noodles. Strain the stock and bring to the boil. Check seasoning.

8 baby bok choys

Add to the boiling stock and cook for a few seconds only. Divide the bok choy and beansprouts between the bowls, then fill the bowls with hot stock.

2 limes, halved

Squeeze into each bowl of soup as serving, and offer the *nuoc cham* separately.

Pho (see page 113).

PAD THAI
This is the Thai version of the beef and broccoli recipe on page 120. It shows the Chinese influence, in the use of noodles, eggs and tofu, but also the accents which are so typically Thai – the peanuts, chillies and *nam pla* (fish sauce).

THAILAND

SERVES 4

---

300 g rice noodles, dried

Soak in hot water for 20 minutes to soften.

---

vegetable oil
2 eggs, beaten
salt and freshly ground pepper

Heat 3 x 15 ml spoons oil in a frying pan and add the seasoned beaten egg. Sauté very quickly, stirring, so that you have a cross between an omelette and scrambled eggs. Remove from the heat and the eggs from the pan. Drain the egg well, and clean the pan. Add another 3 x 15 ml spoons oil to the pan and heat gently.

---

50 g firm tofu, cut into strips

Stir-fry in the oil for a minute or so to brown lightly.

Pad Thai

16 shrimps, peeled and deveined
2 garlic cloves, peeled and finely diced
6 spring onions, trimmed and cut into short lengths

Add to the pan along with the noodles, and stir-fry for 1–2 minutes.

3 x 15 ml spoons shelled peanuts, coarsely ground
3 x 15 ml spoons *nam pla* (fish sauce)
2 fresh red chilli peppers, seeded and sliced
1 x 15 ml spoon lemon juice
sugar and freshly ground pepper

Add to the noodles, seasoning with sugar and pepper to taste, and stir-fry for a minute or two before adding the pieces of egg. Warm through thoroughly, and serve.

120 g beansprouts, washed and drained
2 x 15 ml spoons fresh coriander leaves

Sprinkle over the dish as you serve.

AUBERGINE AND BEANSPROUT NOODLE SALAD
In influence, this noodle salad could also be classified as Javanese or Indonesian – they use much the same ingredients, and techniques. Chicken, meat or prawns could be cooked instead of the aubergine, and the salad served hot or cold. Sometimes meat or poultry noodle dishes are served topped with shredded omelette.

CHINA　　　　　　　　　　　　　　　　**SERVES 4**

2 x 15 ml spoons rice vinegar
4 x 5 ml spoons balsamic vinegar
1 x 5 ml spoon caster sugar
100 ml light soy sauce
40 ml sesame oil
60 ml light olive oil
2 fresh red chilli peppers, seeded and
　finely cut
salt and freshly ground pepper

Mix together for the dressing, and season with a little salt and pepper.

100 g mangetouts or snow peas
50 g carrots

Top and tail the mangetouts, and peel the carrots. Cut both into long fine strips and blanch for a few seconds only in boiling salted water. Drain and cool. Season with a little of the dressing, and keep to one side.

1 garlic clove, peeled
2 slices fresh root ginger, peeled

Chop together very finely.

2 x 15 ml spoons peanut oil
200 g long thin aubergines, cut into
　slices then fine strips

Heat half the oil in a pan and add half the garlic and ginger mixture and the aubergines. Cook until soft, drain very well using a slotted spoon, then transfer to a large bowl.

200 g beansprouts, washed and dried

Cook briefly in the remaining oil with the remaining garlic and ginger. Drain very well, as above, then add to the aubergines.

300 g fresh fine Chinese egg or
　cellophane noodles (or vermicelli)

Cook in a large pan of boiling water. Stir to separate. This only takes a few minutes, so be careful not to overcook. Put into a colander and rinse in cold water. Shake off any excess liquid and place in the bowl with the aubergine and beansprouts. (If using dried noodles or vermicelli, follow the cooking instructions on the packet.) Pour in the remainder of the dressing.

25 g fresh coriander leaves, roughly
　chopped
½ bunch spring onions, finely sliced

Add, and toss the noodle mixture well together. Adjust seasoning. Transfer to a large serving bowl or individual plates. Scatter the mangetout and carrot strips on top of the bowl(s) of noodles.

1 x 15 ml spoon each of white and
　black sesame seeds, toasted

Sprinkle over the salad, and serve.

UDON POT

Udon means a basic wheat and water noodle in Japanese, and the noodles are available in round or flat lengths. They are generally used in soup-noodle dishes such as this one. You could use other noodles to vary the recipe – Chinese egg noodles or cellophane vermicelli, for instance – but they would need only the merest of cooking at the beginning. You could also use vegetables alone instead of the seafood.

JAPAN

SERVES 4

250 g *udon* noodles

Drop into a large pan of boiling water, bring back to the boil, then add 250 ml cold water. Bring back to the boil and add another 250 ml cold water. Do this twice more, testing after the third time: the noodles should be just soft, not al dente. Drain then pour boiling water over them and drain again.

150 each of fresh squid, fresh monkfish fillet, and fresh salmon fillet
8 cooked mussels in their shells

Clean and slice the squid into small rings or squares. Thinly slice the fish fillets.
Arrange the squid, fish and mussels in one large or two small flameproof pots on top of the noodles.

100 g thin leeks
100 g carrots, peeled
100 g shiitake mushrooms

Clean and trim as appropriate. Cut the leeks diagonally into thin slices; score channels along the carrots with a cannelle knife, then slice very thinly. Divide all the vegetables between the two pots.

600 ml *dashi* or Brown Chicken or Fish Stock (see pages 87, 316 or 315)
1 x 15 ml spoon sake (Japanese rice wine)
2 x 15 ml spoons *shoyu* (Japanese soy sauce)
salt and freshly ground pepper

Bring to the boil together, taste for seasoning (it probably won't need salt), then divide between the pots. Heat the pots on top of the stove until the stock is simmering again.

1 x 15 ml spoon finely cut spring onion or seeded fresh red chilli pepper
2 x 15 ml spoons fresh parsley or coriander leaves

Add to the pots, then divide their contents evenly between four heated soup bowls. Serve straightaway, piping hot.

CHOW MEIN

Meaning 'fried noodles', this is possibly the most famous noodle dish from China, fried noodles with a variety of meats – here chicken and prawns – vegetables and flavourings. Instead of the chicken you could use beef, pork or ham, and you could add other vegetables. The important thing is contrast in texture and colour.

CHINA

SERVES 4

12 tiger prawns	Peel and devein.
1 chicken breast	Remove the skin, then cut the meat into thin slices.
vegetable oil	Heat 2 x 15 ml spoons in a wok or large frying pan, then add the prawns and chicken. Stir-fry for about 4–5 minutes, until cooked. Remove from the wok and set aside. Keep warm. Heat 2 more 15 ml spoons oil in the wok.
225 g beansprouts	Add to the wok and stir-fry for about 3 minutes.
350 g egg noodles, par-boiled 2 x 15 ml spoons light soy sauce salt and freshly ground pepper	Add to the beansprouts, seasoning to taste with salt and pepper. Toss and turn, cooking until the noodles are thoroughly heated.
50 g watercress leaves	Add to the noodles, along with the prawn and chicken mixture, and reheat briefly. Adjust seasoning.
2 x 5 ml spoons sesame oil 2 spring onions, sliced 2 fresh red chilli peppers, seeded and sliced	Drizzle the oil over the noodles, and serve garnished with the spring onion and chilli.

COLD BUCKWHEAT NOODLES
The Japanese like cold noodle dishes like this *zaru soba*, especially in summer. The classic way of serving *soba* or *somen* noodles is cooked and cold on ice with a soy dipping sauce, a cucumber relish (see page 307), and scattered with crumbled seaweed (or sliced spring onion).

JAPAN

SERVES 4

300 g dried *soba* (buckwheat) noodles	Cook as for *udon* noodles (see page 117). Drain, rinse in cold water and drain again very well. Arrange on four plates (in Japan they are served in slatted bamboo boxes). Season to taste.
2 sheets *nori* or laver seaweed	Toast over a flame until dry and crisp. Crumble over the top of the noodles. (Or use 4 spring onions, finely sliced.)
250 ml *dashi* (see page 87) 125 ml *mirin* (Japanese sherry) 125 ml dark soy sauce salt and freshly ground pepper	For the dipping sauce, mix together in a small pan, and bring to the boil. Allow to cool, then divide between four small bowls.
5 cm piece of fresh root ginger, peeled and grated 2 spring onions, very finely sliced	Place in separate small bowls. The noodles are dipped into the individual bowls of sauce, which can be spiked to taste with ginger and/or spring onions.

RICE NOODLES WITH BEEF AND BROCCOLI
Rice ribbon noodles are eaten in many countries in South-East Asia as well as in China. This is perhaps their most popular Chinese usage – with tender beef and tiny florets of broccoli. Pad Thai (see page 114) is the Thai equivalent.

CHINA

SERVES 4

3 x 15 ml spoons vegetable oil	Heat half in a large wok or frying pan.
2 eggs, beaten salt and freshly ground pepper	Add to the frying pan, and as soon as it starts to set, stir to scramble into small pieces. Season.
450 g soft fresh rice noodles	Add to the eggs, mix well, and cook for about 2–3 minutes. Transfer to a serving platter and keep warm. Heat the remaining oil in the same wok.
2 garlic cloves, peeled and crushed	Add to the oil and stir-fry until golden.
225 g rump steak, finely sliced	Add to the garlic and stir-fry until it changes colour, about 1 minute.
225 g broccoli, cut into tiny florets	Add to the beef and stir-fry for another minute.
2 x 15 ml spoons yellow bean sauce 1 x 15 ml spoon soy sauce 1 x 5 ml spoon caster sugar	Add to the beef, and stir well.
1 x 15 ml spoon cornflour 120 ml stock or water	Mix the cornflour with the stock or water, and add to the beef. Cook gently, stirring, until it thickens. Pour the beef mixture over the warm noodle and egg mixture, season to taste, and serve immediately.

SPINACH AND POTATO GNOCCHI WITH GORGONZOLA

Gnocchi are a type of dumpling, here consisting primarily of potato (as are other national dumplings further north and east). They can be flavoured in a variety of ways, both with additions to the basic mix and in the accompanying sauces, but they can also be made from pumpkin, wheat flour and maize flour (polenta).

ITALY

SERVES 4

600 g potatoes, washed	Cook in their skins, peel whilst hot, then push through a fine sieve into a bowl.
150 g plain flour 2 eggs, beaten	Blend in carefully, and stir well until smooth.
1 x 15 ml spoon finely cut fresh basil 100 g cooked spinach, dried well and puréed salt and freshly ground pepper freshly grated nutmeg	Mix in the herb, then add enough of the spinach purée to achieve a good colour. Season to taste with salt, pepper and nutmeg. Pipe or roll the mixture into a long log approximately 2.5 cm in diameter and cut into 3.5 cm pieces. Dust well with extra flour and roll each piece in your hands. Press with the tines of a fork to make a corrugated pattern. Poach in boiling salted water for about 5 minutes and then drain carefully.
100 ml each of fromage frais and double cream 150 g Gorgonzola cheese, crumbled	For the sauce, heat the fromage frais and cream gently together in a pan, allow to reduce a little, then add the crumbled cheese, stirring over a low heat until melted. Reheat the gnocchi gently in the sauce for about 2 minutes.
3 x 15 ml spoons mixed finely cut fresh herbs (chives, basil, parsley)	Add to the sauce, season to taste again, and serve hot.
25 g shelled walnuts, chopped	Sprinkle over the gnocchi when serving, to add texture and flavour.

HERB SPÄTZLE

A cross between dumplings and pasta, these can be simmered in soups, mixed with vegetables, added to stews or served as an accompaniment. They can also be served as a pasta, with a sauce and shavings of Parmesan. They are found in Germany and Switzerland as well.

EASTERN EUROPE

SERVES 4

50 g young spinach leaves	Wash and place in a food processor with the water attached to the leaves and about 1 x 15 ml spoon extra. Process to mash well but not purée.
50 g mixed fresh green herbs (parsley, basil, sage)	Wash, dry, add to the processor and whizz briefly.
4 eggs, lightly beaten 250 g plain flour salt and freshly grated nutmeg	Place in a bowl and season to taste with salt and lots of nutmeg. Beat together with a wooden spoon before mixing in the green purée.
up to 25 ml milk	Add just enough to make a soft dough. Beat well, then chill for 20 minutes.
1 x 15 ml spoon sunflower oil	Add to a large pan of boiling salted water (not needed if cooking *Spätzle* in a soup or stew). Spread the herb dough over the surface of a small chopping board then, using a spatula, cut off small lines of the dough and drop into the water. Or grate the dough on a grater with wide holes (or push through a colander). When the *Spätzle* float back to the surface of the liquid, they are ready.

MILK, CHEESE AND EGGS

HOME-MADE YOGHURT

Making yoghurt at home is an everyday task in central and southern Asia, the Middle East and parts of Europe. It is an essential for making relishes and salads in India, Iran, Turkey and Greece, soups in the Balkans, and cheeses, breads, cold drinks and any number of other dishes all over the area. It is a highly versatile and nutritious food, a good source of protein for many people.

INDIA/MIDDLE EAST

MAKES 850 ML

850 ml milk (cow', sheep' or goat')

Place in a heavy pan, bring to just below the boil, then cool down to blood heat or anything between 37–43°C/98.6–110°F. It should still feel slightly warm to the touch.

2 x 15 ml spoons live natural yoghurt

Whisk in a large non-metallic bowl until perfectly smooth. Pour in the cooled milk gradually, whisking to amalgamate. Cover the bowl (clingfilm will do), and wrap in a large heavy towel or cloth (for warmth). Leave completely undisturbed for at least 6–8 hours; moving the bowl will cause the whey to separate. When well thickened, remove clingfilm and chill for a few hours before serving.

YOGHURT CHEESE

Home-made yoghurt is a good basis for a soft curd cheese. This is lighter and less fatty than full cream milk cheeses. In Iran and other parts of the Middle East, fresh herbs are mixed into it or olive oil poured over it; little balls of cheese are also rolled in herbs or paprika. *Labna*, the Arab yoghurt cheese, is popularly eaten at breakfast. Whole milk yoghurt makes the most creamy cheese. (Photograph page 126)

INDIA/MIDDLE EAST

MAKES ABOUT 500 ML

750 ml fresh home-made yoghurt

Place in a muslin-lined sieve or colander and suspend over a bowl. Cover lightly and leave to drip in a cool place for about 6 hours until all the whey has drained out.

salt
other flavouring(s) of choice
(see above)

Add to taste, mixing in well, then refrigerate. Use as soon as possible.

CUCUMBER AND YOGHURT RAITA

Yoghurt raitas are what serve as salads in India, and they are usually presented with the main course. They are fresh and cooling, but may also be spiced to taste. Other vegetables you can use instead of the cucumber are small aubergines, tomato dice, baby courgettes, carrots and spinach, or a mixture. Similar yoghurt dishes are served all over Asia, the Middle East, and in parts of Europe, particularly the Balkans – think of the *tzatziki* of Greece, and the *çaçik* of Turkey. Prepare shortly before eating, or the cucumber will give off moisture and make the yoghurt too watery.

INDIA

SERVES 4

½ large cucumber

Slice thinly, dice or grate into a bowl.

225 g natural yoghurt

Lightly whisk until smooth, then stir into the cucumber.

salt and freshly ground pepper
6 spring onions, trimmed and finely
sliced (optional)

Add and stir in. Place in a serving bowl.

½ x 5 ml spoon paprika, chilli powder
or white cumin seeds (optional)

Sprinkle on the top, and serve immediately.

YORKSHIRE PUDDING

The traditional accompaniment to Roast Beef (see page 140). Once it was cooked in a dish under the spit-roast meat, benefiting from all the juices and fats that dripped from the meat. Cook the pudding with the meat for its last 30 minutes in the oven, before it is brought out to rest.

ENGLAND **SERVES 8** **OVEN: 200°C/400°F/GAS 6**

beef dripping

When poured from the beef roasting tray, sieve and place in a small roasting tin, about 25 cm square. Put into the oven to heat.

350 g plain flour
salt and freshly ground pepper

Sift into a bowl, seasoning to taste with salt and pepper, and make a well in the centre.

5 medium eggs, lightly beaten
600 ml milk
300 ml water

Beat together, then pour about a third into the well in the flour, and mix from the middle, gradually incorporating the flour. Beat well to get rid of any lumps. Stir in the remainder of the liquid.

2 x 15 ml spoons finely chopped mixed
    fresh herbs (sage, thyme, parsley etc.)

Add to the smooth batter.
    Pour into the smoking hot tin, and place in the oven. Cook alongside the meat for its last 30 minutes. When you remove the beef, after that 30 minutes, turn the oven down to 180°C/350°F/Gas 4. Cook the pudding for a further 20 minutes. Serve, cut in squares, with the beef.

ANTON'S CAESAR SALAD

Caesar Salad is believed to have originated in Tijuana, Mexico, on the border just south of San Diego. It has since become an all-American classic. This is my version.

USA **SERVES 4**

2 heads cos lettuce

Remove and discard the outer green leaves and separate the remaining leaves from the heart of the lettuce. Wash and dry thoroughly, and keep cool.

1 small garlic clove, peeled
2 egg yolks
2 anchovies
100 ml sherry vinegar
40 g Parmesan cheese, finely grated

For the Caesar dressing, place in a blender, and blend until smooth and creamy.

200 ml olive oil
100 ml Vegetable Stock (see page 314)
salt and freshly ground pepper
a drop of Worcestershire sauce

Trickle the oil into the dressing and thin down with the stock. Season to taste with salt, pepper and Worcestershire sauce. Keep cool until needed.

1 large garlic clove, peeled and bruised
4 x 15 ml spoons clarified butter

For the croûtons, cook the garlic in the butter over a low heat until just beginning to colour. Remove the garlic from the pan.

2 slices bread, cut into 5 mm cubes

Add to the garlic-flavoured butter and cook until golden brown in colour. Drain well on kitchen paper. Place back in a clean pan.

60 g Parmesan cheese, finely grated

Toss 20 g of the cheese into the croûton pan while the croûtons are still hot. Heat, if necessary, to melt the cheese.
    Arrange 3–4 lettuce leaves on individual plates. Drizzle some of the dressing over the lettuce, along with a sprinkle of the remaining Parmesan. Repeat this lettuce, dressing and cheese procedure twice more, making three layers on the plates. Serve.

ROLLED OMELETTE
This omelette, lightly seasoned with *dashi* and soy, is made into a log shape of several layers. *Datemaki* is sliced and sold as an appetiser in speciality shops in Japan. It is often served with finely grated radish – *daikon oroshi* – or used as a sushi topping.

JAPAN

SERVES 4

8 eggs, beaten
50 ml *dashi* or Vegetable Stock
  (see pages 87 or 314)
1 x 15 ml spoon *shoyu* (Japanese
  soy sauce)
salt

vegetable oil

Mix in a bowl, seasoning to taste with salt.
  Heat a rectangular Japanese frying pan over a medium heat. (Or use a non-stick round frying or omelette pan, and then cut the omelette to shape after cooking).

Moisten the pan with oil very lightly, and pour in about one-third of the egg, to thinly cover the whole base of the pan. When set, tilt the pan towards you and roll the omelette up into a log shape. Oil the pan again, and place the egg log at the far end of the pan. Pour in a further third of the egg and let it run all over the base and under the egg log. When set, repeat as above, tilting and rolling, so that the first log is rolled up within the second omelette. Repeat again with the remainder of the egg. Remove from the pan, and wrap in a traditional bamboo mat (if available) to mark it with little ridges. To serve, cut 1 cm slices for appetisers, 5 cm slices for a first course. Offer a dipping sauce or soy sauce.

SPANISH POTATO OMELETTE

A properly cooked Spanish *tortilla de patata* is a delight, at least 4 cm thick, golden and crisp on the outside, and soft and succulent on the inside. Serve it in wedges with a salad for lunch, or cut into small squares as a *tapa*. It is non-traditional, but you could use red peppers and mushrooms, or sliced courgettes, as a 'filling' for the omelette instead of potato (see below).

SPAIN

SERVES 4, 8 AS A TAPA

olive oil
400 g potatoes, peeled and diced or thinly sliced
250 g onions, peeled and finely chopped
salt and freshly ground pepper

Heat about 100 ml oil in a heavy, medium non-stick frying pan, then add the potato and onions, seasoning to taste with salt and pepper. Cover the pan and cook very slowly until the potatoes are soft. They must not brown or become crisp. Shake the pan occasionally to prevent sticking. You may want to add more oil.

6 large eggs

Beat lightly in a large bowl. Remove the potato and onion from the pan using a slotted spoon so that as much oil as possible is left behind in the pan. Mix the potato and onion into the beaten egg.

2 x 15 ml spoons finely chopped fresh parsley (optional)

Add to the egg mixture, and season again. Remove all but a thin layer of oil from the pan, heat this, then pour the egg and potato mixture into the frying pan. Cook for 1–2 minutes until one side is golden. Put a plate over the top of the pan, and invert it so that the omelette slips on to the plate, cooked side up, adding a little more oil if necessary, and continue cooking until the base is golden. Serve in wedges or small squares for tapas.

Opposite: Yoghurt Cheese. Below: Spanish Potato Omelette.

CRAB FU-YUNG
In Chinese restaurants, *fu-yung* usually means eggs cooked in some way, but in reality it means 'lotus-white', indicating that egg white alone has been used. Here crab is cooked in a scramble with both yolks and whites. The recipe is based on a famous Peking version.

CHINA

SERVES 4

250 g crab meat, white and brown

Pick over, discarding any pieces of shell, and break into small pieces.

6 eggs, beaten
1 x 15 ml spoon dry sherry or
    shaohsing (yellow rice wine)
salt and freshly ground pepper

Mix with the crab meat, and season to taste with salt and pepper.

4 spring onions
25 g bamboo shoots, shredded
5 cm piece of fresh root ginger, peeled
    and finely grated
1 x 15 ml spoon each of peanut and
    sesame oils

Sauté together in a wok or sauté pan for a few minutes. Add the egg and crab mixture, and stir, scrambling until a creamy consistency. Adjust seasoning.

1 x 15 ml spoon finely chopped fresh
    parsley

Sprinkle over the egg and serve hot, in small bowls on top of banana leaves.

SPICY SCRAMBLED EGGS
Ekoori is a traditional dish of the Parsees, the people who fled Muslim rule in Persia and who settled on the west coast of India, but scrambled eggs in some form or other are popular all over the sub-continent. (Photograph page 131)

INDIA

SERVES 4

80 g butter
1 medium onion, peeled and grated
2 garlic cloves, peeled and crushed
2 cm piece of fresh root ginger, peeled
    and very finely chopped
1 fresh green chilli pepper, seeded and
    finely sliced

Place in a saucepan and heat gently together, cooking until the onion and chilli are soft, about 8 minutes.

8 large eggs
1 x 5 ml spoon each of ground cumin
    and turmeric
salt and freshly ground pepper

Whisk together, seasoning to taste with salt and pepper. Pour into the onion pan, and begin to stir. Scramble a little; the mixture should still be soft.

2 medium tomatoes, skinned,
    seeded and diced
2 x 15 ml spoons finely chopped fresh
    coriander

Add to the eggs just before they are ready. Stir in, and almost immediately remove from the heat. Serve hot with toast or an Indian bread (see Naan, page 259).

GLAMORGAN SAUSAGES
These cheesy sausages can be made smaller as a canapé, and can be grilled *en brochette* with vegetables. You could also roll the mixture into ball or cake shapes. You can dip them in egg white and fresh breadcrumbs before grilling or sautéing.

WALES

SERVES 4

2 leeks, washed and finely chopped
vegetable oil

Sweat gently in 1 x 15 ml spoon vegetable oil, for a couple of minutes until the leek is soft.

150 g Caerphilly cheese, grated
2 x 15 ml spoons finely chopped fresh
   parsley
½ x 5 ml spoon thyme
½ x 5 ml spoon dry mustard powder
75 g fresh white breadcrumbs
2 eggs, beaten
salt and freshly ground pepper

Mix together with the leek mixture, adding the egg to bind everything together, and then season well with salt and pepper. Leave to chill for 30 minutes.
   Shape into 4 sausage or cake shapes, and grill or sauté in a little oil on both sides until cooked, 5 minutes or so altogether.

CHEESE RAMEKINS
These small cheese and bread soufflés are made in many of the cantons of Switzerland, to be served as snacks or starters. Some local versions include other ingredients, such as ham. Vacherin cheese, from Fribourg, could also be used.

SWITZERLAND

SERVES 4   OVEN: 180°C/350°F/GAS 4

20 g butter

Use to grease 4 medium-sized ramekins or individual baking dishes.

6 small slices bread, toasted
90 g each of Gruyère and Emmenthal
   cheeses

Cut both toast and cheese into small triangles and arrange overlapping around the bases of the greased dishes.

50 ml dry white wine

Sprinkle over the cheese and toast.

4 eggs, separated
150 ml double cream
200 ml milk
salt and freshly ground pepper
freshly grated nutmeg

Beat the yolks with the cream and milk to make a custard, then season to taste with salt, pepper and nutmeg.
   Whip the egg whites until stiff, then fold into the custard. Pour over the cheese and toast in the dishes, then bake in the preheated oven until golden in colour and slightly puffed up, about 20 minutes.

FONDUE
A special earthenware pot is used for fondue in Switzerland, called *caclon* or *caquelon*. Instead of the bread, you could use raw or cooked vegetables, or cooked new potatoes. There are many varieties of fondue, using tomatoes, mushrooms – even chocolate!

SWITZERLAND   **SERVES 4**

1 garlic clove, peeled and halved	Rub over the inside of the pot, then place the pot on the stove.
200 ml dry white wine	Pour into the pot and bring almost to the boil.
200 g each of Gruyère and Emmenthal cheeses	Grate, then add gradually to the pot. Stir continuously with a wooden spoon until the cheese has melted and amalgamated with the wine. Heat to boiling point.
1 x 15 ml spoon cornflour dissolved in 1 x 15 ml spoon Kirsch salt and freshly ground pepper freshly grated nutmeg a pinch of cayenne pepper	Add, stirring in well, and season to taste with salt, pepper, nutmeg and cayenne. Transfer the pot to a burner with a low flame on the table.
about 800 g bread with crust	Cut into 2.5 cm squares and place in a bowl. Skewer these with fondue forks and dip into the fondue.

HOT FETA CHEESE
Feta, a salty cheese which should properly be made from ewes' milk, is rarely grilled as it is so crumbly. It is usually the savoury element in the omnipresent Greek salad, but tastes quite different when grilled as below. Serve as an hors d'oeuvre, or part of a *mezze*.

GREECE   **SERVES 4**

1 x 250 g block feta cheese, drained	Cut in half lengthways and then through the depth of the two pieces to make four thinner pieces.
olive oil	Place the cheese pieces in one layer in a lightly oiled heatproof dish and sprinkle with a little oil.
½ fresh red chilli pepper, seeded and finely sliced 1 x 5 ml spoon fresh oregano freshly ground pepper	Sprinkle evenly over the cheese.
2 medium tomatoes, sliced	Arrange over the top of the cheese and sprinkle again with a little olive oil. Sit under a hot grill until the tomato has softened, and the cheese is beginning to sizzle at the edges. Serve immediately, using a fish slice.

Opposite: Above, Spicy Scrambled Eggs (see page 128). Below, Hot Feta Cheese.

WELSH RAREBIT

The uniquely British savoury is in essence a sharp little dish designed to clear the mouth after dessert, in preparation for the serving of the port. It was primarily a male tradition, but Queen Victoria is said to have been very partial to bone marrow on toast. (Photograph page 134)

UK   SERVES 4

15 g butter	Melt in a pan over low heat.
100 g each of Caerphilly and Cheddar cheeses, grated 1 x 15 ml spoon beer 1 x 15 ml spoon made English mustard a dash of Worcestershire sauce salt and freshly ground pepper	Add, seasoning to taste with salt and pepper. Stir until the cheeses have melted and the mixture is smooth. Draw off the heat and allow to cool slightly.
4 slices hot buttered granary bread, toasted on one side	Spread the untoasted side with the cheese mixture. Place under a hot grill to brown lightly, then serve sizzling hot.

BOREK

Pastry pies, large and small, are made all over the Balkans, the Middle East and North Africa. The pastry can be flaky or rough puff, warkha or filo as here, and a bread dough is sometimes used. The *sanbusak* of Syria, Lebanon and Egypt are generally half-moon shaped, the *pasteles* of Turkey are like little meat pies, and the *brik* of Tunisia are cigar-shaped. *Burekakia*, the filo pastries of Greece, are usually triangular as here. (Photograph page 134)

TURKEY/MIDDLE EAST   MAKES ABOUT 24–30   OVEN: 180°C/350°F/GAS 4

6–8 large sheets filo pastry	Lay on top of each other. Cut them all simultaneously into 4 cm wide strips. Cover with a barely damp cloth while you make the filling.
250 g crumbly white feta cheese 100 g cooked spinach, finely chopped 1 x 5 ml spoon fresh oregano 1 x 15 ml spoon finely chopped parsley freshly grated nutmeg salt and freshly ground pepper	Mix together in a bowl to make the filling; it should be paste-like. Season to taste with nutmeg and pepper, but be careful with salt, as feta is very salty already.
50 g butter, melted	Brush over one of the filo strips, keeping the others still under the cloth while you work. Place a spoonful of the cheese mix on the top corner. Fold over into a triangle and fold over again and again until you have reached the end of the pastry strip, resulting in a tight triangular package. Place on a baking sheet. Continue in the same fashion with the remaining filo strips, butter and filling.
1 egg yolk, mixed with 2 x 5 ml spoons water	Brush over the tops of the little pastries and bake in the preheated oven for 10–12 minutes until puffed up and golden in colour. Serve hot.

SPINACH AND GOAT'S CHEESE QUESADILLAS

Another use for the omnipresent Mexican corn pancakes or tortillas. *Quesadillas* are often tube- or crescent-shaped, and can be deep-fried instead of shallow-fried. A Mexican Salsa Verde (see page 312) could be served with the *quesadillas*. (Photograph page 135)

MEXICO

MAKES 4

olive oil
2 shallots, peeled and finely sliced
1 garlic clove, peeled and crushed

Sweat 1 x 15 ml spoon oil, the shallot and garlic together in a frying pan until the shallot is softened, about 3 minutes. Transfer to a bowl and leave to cool.

600 g spinach, washed and tough stalks removed

Sweat half in another 2 x 15 ml spoons oil; it will cook down very quickly. Push to one side of the pan, add the remaining spinach and cook briefly.

salt and freshly ground pepper
freshly grated nutmeg

Season the spinach to taste with salt, pepper and nutmeg. Transfer the spinach to a colander to drain off any excess liquid. Leave to cool, then combine with the shallot and garlic.

8 Flour Tortillas (see page 256), 15 cm in diameter

Arrange four on a work surface.

175 g soft goat cheese

Spread over the tortillas, then cover with the spinach, leaving a clean edge.

1–2 jalapeño chilli peppers, seeded and finely sliced
175 g Monterey Jack cheese (or Cheddar), grated

Sprinkle the chilli over the spinach, followed by the grated cheese. Cover with the four remaining tortillas, wet the edges, and press together to seal.
  Pan-fry the *quesadillas* one at a time in a little olive oil until golden on both sides and heated right through. Keep warm in a low oven while you finish the cooking. Cut into wedges to serve, with soured cream or a fresh tomato salsa if you like.

Photographs overleaf: Above left, Welsh Rarebit, with a little chutney on top, and some herbs. Below left, Börek, sprinkled with black poppy seeds. Right, Spinach and Goat's Cheese Quesadillas.

MEAT

STEAK, KIDNEY AND OYSTER PUDDING
The inclusion of kidney in an English steak pudding is a comparatively recent innovation, dating from about the middle of the nineteenth century. Use mushrooms or oysters, not both (see method).

UK

SERVES 4 **OVEN: 150°C/300°F/GAS 2**

675 g chuck steak or ox cheek	Trim off all gristle and fat, and cut into small pieces, about 2.5 cm square.
200 g veal or ox kidney	Remove skin and white core, then cut kidney into medium dice.
1 x 15 ml spoon plain flour **salt and freshly ground pepper**	Sprinkle over the meats, seasoning to taste.
2 x 15 ml spoons vegetable oil	Heat in a frying pan and quickly and separately brown the meat and kidney on all sides. Drain and place in a suitable casserole.
1 large onion, peeled and finely chopped **3 sprigs each of fresh rosemary and thyme**	Sweat in the fat remaining in the frying pan, then add to the casserole.
1 bouquet garni (bay, parsley) **250 ml Beef Stock (see page 316)** **200 ml red wine**	Add to the casserole, bring to the boil on top of the stove, then braise in the preheated oven for about 1–1½ hours. Leave the meats to go cold. Remove the herbs. Check the seasoning. When cold, remove any fat from the surface, and if there is too much liquid, separate meat and liquid and boil the latter to reduce it a little. Return most of it to the meat, keeping the rest separate to accompany the pudding later. (This part of the dish can be done two days in advance, and the stew chilled until ready to use.) Adjust seasoning.
200 g self-raising flour **25 g fresh fine white breadcrumbs** **100 g beef or veal suet, very finely diced**	For the suet-crust pastry, place in a bowl, and mix together well, using your hands. Add a little cold water, just enough to bind the dry ingredients together. On a floured surface roll out to a large circle, then cut out a quarter of the circle (the lid).
butter	Use a little to grease a 1.75 litre pudding basin. Use the larger piece of suet-crust pastry to line the bowl, pressing the cut edges together well, and allowing a small overhang at the top. Roll out the remaining pastry to a circle to fit the top of the pudding.
225 g mushrooms, sliced (optional)	If you choose to use the mushrooms instead of the oysters, fry them quickly in about 25 g butter, then add to the meat stew. Fill the lined bowl with the steak, kidney and mushroom mixture. Fold over the pastry overhang, top with the circle rolled for the lid, and press together, using a little water to make it stick. Cover the bowl with a large piece of foil, the side nearest the pastry buttered, and tie on loosely with string. Place the bowl on a trivet in a large saucepan, and pour in boiling water to come half-way up the sides of the bowl. Or put the bowl in a steamer above boiling water. Cover then boil or steam for about 3 hours, checking the water level occasionally, and topping up with boiling water. Remove the pudding from the steamer.
18 oysters, shelled, plus their juices (optional)	If using the oysters instead of the mushrooms, lift the lid off the pudding very carefully when cooked, and insert the oysters and their juices. By the time you serve, the oysters will have heated through. Serve the pudding from the bowl at table, offering a jugful of any gravy left over.

MEAT

CARPETBAG STEAK
Although thought of as indisputably Australian, carpetbag steaks originated in America, where such ranch 'n' reef or surf 'n' turf combinations are popular. A good accompaniment, demonstrating the new 'fusion' in Australian cooking, would be stir-fried bok choy.

AUSTRALIA

SERVES 4

4 thick fillet steaks,150 g each, about
  4 cm thick
salt and freshly ground pepper

Using a very sharp knife, make a horizontal cut into the side of each steak to make a pocket. Season inside the pocket.

8 fresh oysters, shelled
lemon juice

Insert two oysters into the slit in each steak, with a squeeze of lemon juice.

4 thin rashers good bacon (optional)

Sew the slits shut, secure with wooden cocktail sticks, or hold closed with a tightly wrapped piece of bacon (and a wooden cocktail stick if necessary).

50 g butter, melted

Brush the top of the steaks with butter and place under a preheated hot grill. Grill for 4–5 minutes then turn. Brush with butter again, and grill for a further 4–5 minutes. Remove threads or sticks.

8 fresh oysters, shelled
2 x 15 ml spoons plain flour or
  cornmeal
vegetable oil for deep-frying

Toss the garnish oysters in flour to coat, then deep-fry in hot oil for about 1 minute only. Drain well.

To serve, arrange the steaks on hot serving plates, and garnish with the warm fried oysters.

ROAST RIBS OF BEEF AND GRAVY

The roast beef for which England is most famous. Try to buy Aberdeen Angus. Serve it with Yorkshire Pudding (see page 125), roast potatoes, roast parsnips if you like, and a green vegetable. The pudding was once baked under the spit-roasted meat, in the fatty juices from the meat.

UK **SERVES 8** **OVEN: 240°C/475°F/GAS 9**

1 beef forerib, about 4–5 ribs, trimmed
    and tied
20 tiny herb sprigs (rosemary or thyme)
salt and freshly ground pepper

Push the herbs in all over the meat between flesh and fat. Season well with salt and pepper.

beef dripping

Heat a little in a roasting tin on top of the stove.

1.75 kg extra beef bones (if available),
    cut in pieces

Add to the dripping in the tin then place the prepared joint on top. Baste with the dripping then roast in the preheated oven for 20 minutes. Turn the heat down to 200°C/400°F/Gas 6, and roast for a further 20 minutes.
    Remove the bones and dripping from the pan and return the meat to the oven. Roast for a further 1¼ hours. Then remove from the oven and the tin and rest for 20–25 minutes, covered with foil, in a warm place.

1 medium onion, peeled
1 medium carrot, trimmed
1 celery stalk, trimmed
½ leek, washed

Meanwhile, for the gravy, cut roughly and place in a stockpot along with the roasted bones and a little dripping. Sweat for a few minutes to colour.

up to 2.5 litres Beef Stock
    (see page 316)
1 bouquet garni (rosemary, bay, thyme)

Add about 300 ml stock to the pot along with the herbs, and boil to reduce to a syrup. Add another 300 ml and do the same. Barely cover the vegetables and bones with further stock, simmer until the beef is ready and rested. Strain the sauce, and reduce further if necessary. Check the seasoning, then serve with the beef.

BOEUF A LA BOURGUIGNONNE

Burgundy is a region of France long famed for the quality of its food, and this dish is a classic example, preferably made with the local Charolais beef. The bacon lardons, button mushrooms and small onions are essential; you could also fry some croûtes in butter to garnish the finished dish. Serve with boiled potatoes (or rice or noodles).

FRANCE **SERVES 4** **OVEN: 150°C/300°F/GAS 2**

1 kg lean stewing beef (chuck, leg or
    shin)

Cut into 5 cm cubes, trimming away any fat or gristle. Place the cubes in a large bowl.

750 ml red wine, preferably Burgundy
1 large onion, peeled and sliced
1 large carrot, sliced
2 garlic cloves, peeled and crushed
1 bouquet garni (thyme, bay, parsley)
olive oil

Add to the meat in the bowl, along with 2 x 15 ml spoons olive oil, mix, cover and leave to marinate in a cool place for from 6–24 hours, turning occasionally.
    Drain the meat from the marinade, using a slotted spoon, and dry it very well. Keep the wine and other ingredients to one side.

200 g green bacon in the piece, rinded
    and cut into lardons (keep the rind)

Blanch the lardons and rind in boiling water for a few seconds, then dry well and fry in about 1 x 15 ml spoon olive oil in a frying pan until brown. Place in a suitable casserole. Add the onion and carrot slices from the marinade to the frying pan and sauté until golden. Add to the casserole, along with the bouquet garni.
    Add a little more oil to the pan and sauté the meat in the hot oil until browned on all sides.

1 x 15 ml spoon plain flour salt and freshly ground pepper	Add to the meat and toss to coat, continuing to sauté until the flour is golden. Place the meat in the casserole. Discard any excess fat from the frying pan, then pour in the marinade wine and garlic. Stir to dissolve any pan juices, then add to the casserole.
300 ml Beef Stock (see page 316)	Add 250 ml to the casserole, and bring to the boil on top of the stove. Cover tightly, then place in the low oven. Leave to simmer, stirring occasionally, for about 3 hours, or until the meat is tender but still keeping its shape.
16 pickling onions, peeled 50 g butter	Meanwhile, cook the onions for the garnish. Place them in a pan in one layer with 25 g of the butter and the remaining stock. Heat gently, tossing, until softened, about 10 minutes.
150 g small button mushrooms, wiped	Sauté in the remaining butter until tender and lightly browned.
sugar	When the meat is tender, taste for seasoning, adding salt, pepper and sugar if necessary. Pick the beef from the sauce and set aside. Strain the sauce and discard the vegetables, bacon rind and bouquet garni. Reduce if neccasary. Stir the meat, garnish onions and mushrooms into the sauce, and simmer together for a few minutes. Taste again for seasoning.
4 x 15 ml spoons finely chopped fresh parsley	Use to garnish the beef. Serve hot.

CARBONNADE A LA FLAMANDE
This is perhaps the most famous of all Belgian dishes, using local beef and more significantly, the local beer. For the finest possible flavour, it is best to use a beer still manufactured in traditional ways, particularly *gueuze*, a strong beer made from a mixture of wheat and barley.

BELGIUM

SERVES 4

1 kg lean stewing beef (a neck cut is traditional)	Trim well and cut into large 100 g steaks.
vegetable oil	Heat 3 x 15 ml spoons in a large sauté pan and brown the meat pieces on all sides. Remove with a slotted spoon and place in a suitable casserole.
500 g onions, peeled and sliced	Add to the oil in the sauté pan, and cook until lightly brown.
2 x 15 ml spoons white wine vinegar 2 x 15 ml spoons plain flour	Add to the onions, stir around to dissolve any meat deposits, and pour into the casserole.
1 bay leaf 2 garlic cloves, peeled and crushed 1 sprig fresh thyme 500 ml dark beer salt and freshly ground pepper	Add to the casserole, stir, and bring to the boil, seasoning to taste with salt and pepper.
Beef Stock (see page 316) if necessary	Add as needed if the meat and onions are not generously covered with the beer. Turn the heat down, cover tightly with the lid, and cook very gently on top of the stove for 2–2½ hours, or until the meat is tender. Serve with boiled potatoes.

CHILLI CON CARNE
Despite the Spanish name, *chilli con carne*, chilli with meat, is more American now than Mexican. It is said to have been first made by missionaries in what was then part of Mexico, now Arizona or New Mexico – a good way of using up the local stringy beef.

USA

SERVES 4

2 x 15 ml spoons corn oil
2 large onions, about 450 g, peeled and finely chopped

Heat the oil in a large casserole and sauté the onion until soft and transparent.

350 g lean beef, minced
300 g pork, minced

Add to the onion and break up with a wooden spoon. Stir to brown.

2 garlic cloves, peeled and crushed
1 x 5 ml spoon chilli powder or a few drops Tabasco sauce
2 x 15 ml spoons dried oregano
1 x 15 ml spoon cumin seeds, crushed lightly
400 g plum tomatoes, skinned, seeded and chopped

Add to the casserole, stir in well, and bring to the boil.

salt and freshly ground pepper
1 x 15 ml spoon red wine vinegar
1 x 5 ml spoon caster sugar

Add to the casserole, and partially cover with the lid. Simmer gently for about 1 hour. Remove any fat carefully from the surface.

300 g cooked red kidney beans

Stir into the casserole and cook for a further 15 minutes. Adjust seasoning.

4 x 15 ml spoons soured cream
4 x 15 ml spoons Guacamole (see page 306)
a handful of fresh chives, snipped
paprika

Serve the chilli, with rice if liked, with a spoonful each of soured cream and guacamole on top. Sprinkle with the snipped chives and paprika.

SAUERBRATEN
A marinated spiced pot roast of beef appears in almost every region of Germany, but details differ. Sometimes the meat is pot-roasted in beer or buttermilk instead of wine and vinegar; sometimes lemon and single cream are the sauce additions. In the north of the country the sauce is thickened by the addition of *Lebkuchen* or spiced gingerbread crumbs.

GERMANY

SERVES 4

1 kg topside or silverside of beef in the piece, boned and rolled
salt and freshly ground pepper

Place in a suitable deep casserole, and season with salt and pepper.

400 ml each of red wine and red wine vinegar
600 ml water
1 medium onion, peeled and sliced
1 carrot, sliced
1 celery stalk
1 bay leaf
1 x 5 ml spoon each of black peppercorns or juniper berries (or pickling spice), slightly crushed
2 cloves

Place in a saucepan and bring to the boil. Simmer for about 15 minutes, then leave to cool.
   Strain the marinade over the meat in the casserole, and leave in a cool place, turning the meat occasionally, for up to 2 days. Remove the meat from the liquid and dry it well. Strain the marinade and reserve. Discard the vegetables.

vegetable oil

Heat about 2 x 15 ml spoons in a large sauté pan and brown the meat all over. Return to the casserole, and pour over the strained marinade. It should come half way up the meat.

1 large onion, peeled and sliced
1 carrot, sliced
2 celery stalk, sliced

Sauté in the oil remaining in the pan until golden, then add to the meat and marinade. Bring to the boil, then cover and simmer gently on top of the stove for 2–3 hours or until the meat is very tender. Baste regularly. When ready, remove the meat to a dish and keep warm with the vegetables.

1 x 15 ml spoon plain flour

Mix with the liquid, and pour into a saucepan. Reduce gently to a sauce consistency.

50 g raisins, soaked in water and strained
150 ml soured cream

Add to the sauce and heat through gently. Adjust the seasoning.
   Slice the meat and serve with the sauce, accompanied by boiled potatoes, potato dumplings, noodles, red cabbage, apple purée or cranberry sauce.

BEEF GOULASH
A true goulash is almost a soup, and is very similar to many other national one-pot beef stews, differing only in its use of paprika, the sweet pepper spice that is so characteristic of Hungary and its cuisine. Caraway seeds are used a great deal in this area as well.

HUNGARY

SERVES 4

1 kg stewing beef (e.g. shin)

Trim well and cut into 2.5 cm cubes.

2 x 15 ml spoons vegetable oil
1 large onion, peeled and chopped

Place in a suitable casserole and heat gently to soften the onion. After a few minutes, add the meat pieces and continue to sauté together until the meat is brown. Remove from the heat.

1 x 15 ml spoon paprika
2 garlic cloves, peeled and crushed
¼ x 5 ml spoon caraway seeds, lightly crushed
salt and freshly ground pepper

Add to the pan, and stir in well, seasoning with salt and pepper to taste.

Beef Stock (see page 316) or water

Add enough to cover the meat, then cover with the lid and simmer on top of the stove for about an hour.

1 green pepper, seeded and cut into strips
3 tomatoes, skinned and cut
350 g small potatoes, peeled

Add to the casserole and simmer for another 30 minutes, or until the meat and potatoes are tender. You may need to add more stock or water – the goulash should be of a soupy consistency. Taste for seasoning and add more paprika or caraway seeds if desired.

Herb Spätzle (see page 121)

Cook separately, then add to the goulash when serving.

BEEF STROGANOV
Named after a high-ranking merchant nobleman in St Petersburg, this recipe is the result of the Imperial Russian passion for all things French during the nineteenth century.

RUSSIA

SERVES 4

500 g fillet of beef (the tail end, which is traditional and less expensive)

Cut into 5 cm slices, flatten with a meat bat, then cut into strips.

50 g butter
2 medium onions, peeled and finely sliced

Melt the butter in a frying pan, and fry the onion until soft and golden, about 5 minutes.

salt and freshly ground pepper

Add the beef strips to the pan, season, and shake and toss them until they are brown all over, about 5 minutes.

1 x 15 ml spoon plain flour

Sprinkle over the meat, stir in, then sauté, stirring, for a further minute.

200 ml soured cream (or crème fraîche)

Pour into the pan, and stir over gentle heat until warm, about 2–3 minutes. Divide between four warmed plates.

4 gherkins, sliced
soured cream

Sprinkle the gherkins over the beef, and put a dollop of soured cream on top. Serve with fried potatoes or on a bed of rice.

BULGOGI

Marinated beef is popular throughout the whole country, beef being an especial favourite. (It can be prepared using pork or lamb instead.) It is usually cooked on a portable table-top barbecue, but a cast-iron frying pan or a conventional grill will do.

KOREA

SERVES 4

500 g lean tender beef steak in the piece

Place in the freezer for a while, which makes it easier to slice. Cut against the grain into very thin slices about 5–8 cm in length. Place in a bowl.

2 x 15 ml spoons sake (Japanese rice wine)
2 x 15 ml spoons caster sugar
60 ml dark soy sauce
2 garlic cloves, peeled and crushed
4 x 15 ml spoons sesame seeds, toasted and ground
50 g spring onions, trimmed and finely sliced
1 x 5 ml spoon freshly ground pepper
2 x 5 ml spoons sesame oil

Add to the bowl, and mix to coat the meat slices. Leave for 8 hours.

When ready to cook, remove the meat from the marinade. Grill or pan-fry to taste in a non-stick pan; the meat can be cooked rare.

200 g spring onions, trimmed

For the spring onion salad, cut into 5 cm lengths, and halve lengthwise. Wash and drain well.

a good pinch of cayenne pepper
½ x 5 ml spoon caster sugar
1 x 5 ml spoon sesame seeds, toasted and coarsely ground
4 x 15 ml spoons sesame oil
2 x 5 ml spoons light soy sauce

Mix together in a bowl, then pour over the spring onion pieces.

soft lettuce leaves (optional)
soy sauce (optional)

The slices of beef are occasionally wrapped in the lettuce leaves, along with some of the onions (or other accompanying vegetable or rice) and dipped into soy sauce before eating. Serve warm.

THAI BEEF SALAD

Salads, known as *yam* or *yum*, are important in Thai cooking, accompanying almost every meal, and this lightly cooked beef salad contains the majority of the characteristic Thai flavours such as lemongrass, *nam pla* (fish sauce), lime juice, chillies, mint and coriander.

THAILAND

SERVES 4

1 x 15 ml spoon vegetable oil
2 x 225 g sirloin steaks

Heat the oil in a frying pan, add the steak and fry until medium rare, about 2 minutes on each side. Remove from the pan and set aside to cool. Thinly slice across the grain and place in a large bowl.

1 red onion, peeled and finely diced
½ cucumber, shredded
1 lemongrass stalk, finely sliced
2 x 15 ml spoons *nam pla* (fish sauce)
60 ml lime juice
2–4 fresh red chilli peppers, seeded and sliced
10–15 mint leaves
2 spring onions, finely sliced
salt and freshly ground pepper

Add to the beef in the bowl and toss to mix well. Serve chilled or near room temperature. Season to taste.

2 x 15 ml spoons fresh coriander, basil or mint leaves, or Japanese cress

Use to garnish the salad.

PARRILLADA MIXTA

A simple barbecue or mixed grill of various meats can be transformed by the addition of some of the unique flavours of Mexico – here a hot salsa, the subtle smoothness of guacamole, a simple pepper and onion stir-fry, tortillas and beans.

MEXICO

SERVES 4

1 x 225 g spicy sausage (chorizo, peperoni etc), cut into four
2 small pork cutlets
4 chicken legs or wings
4 small thin sirloin steaks
salt and freshly ground pepper

Season the meats with salt and pepper then grill – on a ridged cast-iron grill pan or over barbecue coals – until cooked (the steaks until medium only). Keep warm.

1 red and 1 green pepper, seeded and cut into strips
1 large onion, peeled and thinly sliced
1 x 15 ml spoon vegetable oil

Stir-fry together for a few minutes; the pepper and onion should still be fairly crisp. Keep warm.

Guacamole (see page 306)
Frijoles (see page 80)
Salsa Verde (see page 312)
Flour Tortillas (optional, see page 256)

Have ready in bowls on the table.
    To serve, arrange the meats on individual plates, with the pepper and onion stir-fry. Eat, accompanied by the avocado, beans, sauce, and tortillas if using.

Opposite: Thai Beef Salad.

BEEF BOGOTA

After its introduction by Europeans, beef became the staple meat of South America. This Colombian winter dish uses beef skirt or flank, which are coarse but very flavourful cuts. They may have to be ordered especially from the butcher.

COLOMBIA **SERVES 4** **OVEN: 160°C/325°F/GAS 3**

1 kg beef skirt or topside in the piece

Trim well but leave a little fat on. Place in a casserole.

1 medium onion, peeled and coarsely
    chopped
2 garlic cloves, peeled
1 bouquet garni (bay, thyme, parsley)
1 carrot, trimmed and sliced
1 celery stalk, trimmed and sliced
Beef Stock (see page 316)
salt and freshly ground pepper

Add to the casserole, alone with enough stock to cover, and season to taste with salt and pepper. Bring to the boil, then cover, reduce the heat, and cook gently in the preheated oven for about 2 hours, or until the meat is tender.
    Remove the meat from the casserole and pat dry. Arrange in a pan that will go under the grill. Preheat the grill.
    Strain the stock, discarding the vegetables and herbs and then begin to reduce the stock to a sauce consistency.

50 g butter, softened
2 x 15 ml spoons chopped fresh
    parsley

Mix together, then spread over the top of the meat.

fresh fine breadcrumbs

Season to taste with salt and pepper, then sprinkle generously over the parsley butter. Press to adhere, and then grill until the breadcrumbs are golden. Serve, in slices, with the sauce and the potato cakes on page 60.

BOLLITO MISTO

Bollito misto is a favourite dish in the north of Italy, where beef cattle are bred. The 'boiled mixed meats' are served sliced, moistened with a little of their broth, along with a sharp sauce and, occasionally, boiled potatoes. Use the leftover broth in soups or risotti.

ITALY **SERVES 8**

1 large fresh cotechino sausage

Soak in cold water for at least a couple of hours, then cover with fresh water and simmer very slowly for 2½ hours. (A part-cured cotechino will only need cooking for 30 minutes).

2 large carrots, peeled
2 large celery stalks, trimmed
2 large onions, peeled and halved
1 small beef tongue, about
    1 kg in weight
500 g boiling beef in the piece
    (brisket, rump or chuck)
1 calf's foot or pig's trotter
salt and freshly ground pepper

Place in a separate pot, one that is large enough to hold all the ingredients apart from the cotechino, and season to taste with salt and pepper. Cover with boiling water, bring quickly back to the boil, then reduce the heat to a simmer. Skim very well. Simmer very gently for about 1 hour.

500 g boned veal shoulder in the piece

Add to the pot, cover again, and continue to simmer for another hour.
    Remove the tongue from the pot, and peel off the skin and trim away any fat and gristle from the root end. Return the skinned tongue to the pot.

1 x 1 kg chicken

Add to the pot, cover again, and continue to simmer for another 45 minutes. Halfway through this time, add the cooked cotechino to the large pot of meats. When the chicken is tender, the *bollito* is ready.
    Slice or carve the meats as appropriate and arrange on a large heated platter. Baste with a little of the hot broth, and serve with Salsa Verde 1 (see page 312) and *mostarda di frutta* (fruits preserved in a mustard syrup).

RAWON SOUP
A soup commonly made in the island of Java and containing many flavourings – *blachan* (shrimp paste), lemongrass, *kecap manis* and tamarind – which are characteristic of Indonesia. Instead of the beans, the seeds of the tropical kaluak tree are usually used to give the soup its distinctive black colour.

INDONESIA

SERVES 4

500 g lean beef

Remove any fat and sinews, and cut into 3 cm cubes. Place in a large saucepan.

1 litre water
salt and freshly ground pepper

Add to the pan, seasoning to taste with salt and pepper, and bring to the boil. Skim then simmer until the meat is cooked, about 45 minutes. Remove the meat to a plate. Keep the stock.

25 g black beans, soaked overnight

Place in a mortar, and grind to a paste. Keep to one side.

2 x 15 ml spoons vegetable oil
2 shallots, peeled and finely sliced
3 garlic cloves, peeled and crushed
5 cm piece of fresh root ginger, peeled and diced
1 x 5 ml spoon turmeric
2 x 5 ml spoons ground coriander
1 x 15 ml spoon brown sugar
1 x 15 ml spoon *blachan* (shrimp paste)

Heat together in a large saucepan along with the black bean paste for about 5 minutes.

2 lemongrass stalks
2 lime leaves (or bay leaves plus zest and juice of 1 lime)
2 x 15 ml spoons *kecap manis* (sweet soy sauce)
2 x 15 ml spoons tamarind water

Add to the pan, along with the beef and beef stock. Bring to the boil, then reduce the heat and simmer for 15 minutes. Add some salt if necessary. Serve hot.

SEEKH KEBABS
Very finely minced meat is used in a number of kebab dishes throughout the Middle East, North Africa and the Indian sub-continent. Some mixtures are made into meatballs and fried; some are shaped around skewers and grilled. See also Kofta Kebab on page 176.

PAKISTAN

SERVES 4

700 g lean rump beef, minced twice
200 g onions, peeled and chopped
2 fresh red chilli peppers, seeded
5 x 15 ml spoons chopped fresh coriander
5 cm piece of fresh root ginger, peeled and finely chopped
1 x 5 ml spoon garam masala
salt and freshly ground pepper
½ x 5 ml spoon each of ground cloves, cinnamon, cumin and nutmeg

Place in a bowl, and mix well together, seasoning to taste with salt and pepper. Put in batches into the mincer (or food processor) to make a very fine paste.

vegetable oil

Oil your hands, and divide the meat into four or eight portions. Wrap each portion tightly around the top end of a flat metal skewer to a sausage shape about 20 cm long. Support the kebabs with your hand as you lift to the grill. Grill under a conventional grill or over barbecue coals, turning, until cooked, about 10 minutes. Serve with chutney and bread.

BERNER PLATTE
The Swiss version of *cocido* or *bollito*, above, said to have been served for the first time to victorious Swiss troops, having beaten the French in battle in 1798. Everyone brought what they could to cook, thus there is a huge variety of meats and sausages included. Dried French beans are a traditional accompaniment, soaked then added along with the bacon and pork.

SWITZERLAND

SERVES 8

1 knuckle of salt pork
200 g ox tongue, salted or smoked
200 g lean bacon, salted or smoked
400 g smoked pork chops

Soak the salted meats in cold water to cover for at least 12 hours. Drain very well.

400 g boiling beef in the piece (brisket or topside)
2 bouquets garnis (thyme, bay, marjoram, savory, parsley stalks)

Place the beef and 1 bouquet garni in a large saucepan with the tongue and knuckle of pork, and cover with water. Simmer for about 1½–2 hours.

25 ml vegetable oil
100 g onions, peeled and chopped

Heat together in a separate large saucepan and sweat until the onion has softened.

200 g Bernese sausage (known as tongue sausage), or any good garlic sausages
800 ml Beef Stock (see page 316)

Add to the onions, along with the bacon, pork chops, and the remaining bouquet garni. Cover with the lid, and simmer for about 1 hour.

200 g Emmenthaler sausages (similar to *Knackwurst*)
8 small pieces beef marrow bone

Add to the bacon and pork chop pan about 10 minutes before the meats are ready. Drain the meats well, slice as appropriate, and arrange on a large platter. Serve with boiled potatoes and Sauerkraut or freshly cooked dried French beans.

PORK VINDALOO

Pork is only eaten in Christian India, particularly in the eastern area of Goa, which was once administered by the Portuguese. The name 'vindaloo' actually comes from the Portuguese words for vinegar and garlic. Chilli heat is normally associated with vindaloo, but you can control that to taste by seeding the chillies or using fewer and milder chillies. Other meats can be cooked in a vindaloo.

INDIA

SERVES 4

1 x 5 ml spoon each of cumin, fenugreek and cardamom seeds
2–6 fresh red chilli peppers, seeded if wished
10 black peppercorns
3 cloves
3 cm piece of cinnamon
100 ml white wine or cider vinegar

Place in a blender or spice mill and grind to a paste. Pour into a large bowl.

700 g boneless lean pork

Cut into 3 cm cubes, trimming off any excess fat, and then mix with the spice paste. Leave to marinate for at least an hour. Remove the meat from the marinade and drain well, keeping the marinade.

2 medium onions, peeled and very finely chopped
75 ml vegetable oil

Heat together in a large frying pan, and cook until the onion is soft and golden.

2 garlic cloves, peeled and crushed
5 cm piece of fresh root ginger, peeled and finely grated

Add to the onion along with the spice-paste marinade, and cook for a few minutes before adding the meat. Sauté for 5 or so minutes.

1 x 5 ml spoon each of turmeric and ground cumin
salt and freshly ground pepper

Add to the meat, along with about 300 ml water, and bring to a simmer. Cover and simmer until the meat is tender, about 30 minutes, stirring occasionally and adding more water if necessary. Serve hot with rice.

fresh coriander

Use as a garnish.

FRIKADELLER

These meatballs are the national meat dish of Denmark, where there are as many different recipes as there are cooks. The Dutch also make similar meat balls, and were responsible for introducing the idea to Sri Lanka, where *frikadells* are highly spiced.

DENMARK

SERVES 4

3 x 15 ml spoons soft white
    breadcrumbs
1 x 15 ml spoon plain flour
1 small onion, peeled and grated
60 ml double cream
2 x 15 ml spoons milk or water
salt and freshly ground pepper
freshly grated nutmeg and/or ground
    allspice

Mix together, seasoning to taste with salt, pepper, nutmeg and/or allspice. Leave to stand for a while.

225 g lean pork, minced
50 g lean beef, minced
2 x 15 ml spoons finely chopped fresh
    parsley

Add to the breadcrumb mixture, and mix well until smooth. Add a little more milk or water if the mixture seems too firm.

75 g butter

Melt a little in a sauté pan, and sauté a 5 ml spoon of the meatball mixture to check on texture and taste. Shape the mixture into small balls, and sauté in batches in the butter until golden, shaking the pan to cook all sides and keep the round shape. Serve hot with potatoes or cold, sliced, for *smørrebrød*.

ADOBO

This famous Filipino dish is more Spanish in influence than South-East Asian, for Spain ruled the Philippines for over 350 years (the name being that of a Spanish king). 'Adobo' comes from an Arabic word for marinade, recalling the former Moorish rule over Spain.

THE PHILIPPINES

SERVES 4

300 g boneless lean pork

Cut into 4–5 cm cubes. Place in a large bowl.

400 g chicken pieces (thighs or
    breasts)

Cut into 4–5 cm pieces, then add to the pork in the bowl.

120 ml white wine vinegar
2 garlic cloves, peeled and crushed
1 bay leaf, crumbled
2 x 15 ml spoons dark soy sauce
salt and freshly ground pepper

Add to the bowl, seasoning to taste with salt and pepper. Leave to marinate for 1 hour, turning occasionally. Place meats and marinade in a large saucepan.

Brown Chicken Stock (see page 316)

Add to the pan to just cover the meats, and bring to the boil. Cover and simmer for 15 minutes. Remove the chicken, which should be tender, and keep warm. Continue simmering the pork for a further 20 minutes. Add more stock if necessary. Remove the tender pork, keep warm with the chicken, and boil the stock to reduce it to about 200 ml.

corn oil

Heat in a large sauté pan and sauté the pork and chicken until golden. Strain off the fat. Strain the reduced stock over the meats, and simmer together for a few minutes. Serve hot with rice.

SWEET AND SOUR PORK

This is probably the most famous Chinese dish of all. It is Cantonese in origin, and it was mainly the Cantonese who were to emigrate in the nineteenth century to the South Seas, to San Francisco, London and elsewhere. The sauce can be used with other meats such as stir-fried lamb or poultry, spare ribs and with fish.

CHINA

SERVES 4

450 g belly of pork, in the piece, skinned
2 x 15 ml spoons dry sherry

Cut the pork into 2 cm cubes, and then marinate in the sherry for 30 minutes.

1 x 15 ml spoon sesame oil
1 small onion, peeled and finely chopped
75 g each of diced red and green pepper
1 medium garlic clove, peeled and finely chopped
1 cm piece of fresh root ginger, peeled and finely chopped

To make the sauce, heat the oil in a pan and sauté the vegetables and seasonings until softened, a few minutes only.

1 x 15 ml spoon dark soy sauce
1 x 15 ml spoon white wine vinegar
2 x 5 ml spoons rice vinegar
50 g tomato ketchup
40 ml pineapple juice
20 g clear honey

Add to the pan, mix well, then bring to the boil.

150 g peeled pineapple flesh, diced

Add to the pan, reduce the heat, and simmer for 10 minutes.

1 x 15 ml spoon cornflour, diluted in a little water
1 x 15 ml spoon chilli sauce
salt and freshly ground pepper

Add to the sauce, seasoning to taste, stir in well, then simmer for another 5 minutes.

1 x 15 ml spoon cornflour
1 egg

Mix together to make a light batter. Coat the pork pieces.

vegetable oil

Shallow-fry the pork cubes over high heat for 3–5 minutes. Drain very well. Add the pork to the warm sweet and sour sauce and stir to heat together. The pork should remain crisp. Serve with rice.

PORK WITH CLAMS
An unlikely combination, perhaps, but one of Portugal's most famous tastes, a speciality of the Alentejo. Prepare the clams by leaving in water for half an hour with some cornmeal; this gets rid of sand. Serve the stew with a green salad, some *broa* (corn bread), and red wine.

PORTUGAL

SERVES 4

800 g boned pork loin

Cut into 2.5 cm cubes. Place in a large bowl.

1½ x 15 ml spoons paprika
2 garlic cloves, peeled and crushed
olive oil
salt and freshly ground pepper

Mix together, using just enough oil to make a paste, and seasoning to taste with salt and pepper. Coat the meat cubes with this.

2 bay leaves
300 ml dry white wine

Add to the bowl, mix well, then leave to marinate overnight in the fridge, turning from time to time. Remove the pork from the marinade, and reserve both. Dry the meat cubes.

2 medium onions, peeled and sliced

Fry in a casserole in a little olive oil until soft, but not brown. Remove from the casserole. Add the pork and more oil if necessary and sauté until brown on all sides. Return the onion to the casserole, pour in the marinade, then cover and cook over a very low heat until the pork is tender, about 20–30 minutes. Add a little more wine if necessary.

500 g small clams in the shell

Clean and scrub thoroughly, then add to the casserole, cover and cook until they open, for about 5–10 minutes, depending on size. (Discard any that do not open.)

2 x 15 ml spoons finely chopped fresh parsley

Sprinkle over the meat and clams, and serve hot.

POT-ROAST PORK WITH PRUNES
Pork is by far the most favoured meat in Denmark, and pork products such as bacon and salami are a major industry. This dish is not dissimilar to the French pork stuffed with prunes. These help counteract the richness of the meat.

DENMARK

SERVES 4

2 pork tenderloins (fillets)

Trim well, and then cut into them lengthwise to open out to one larger piece. Flatten slightly, using a meat bat.

1 x 5 ml spoon ground mace
salt and freshly ground pepper

Season both inner sides with mace and salt and pepper to taste.

2 small Cox type apples, peeled, cored and roughly sliced
12 plump prunes, soaked (if necessary), pitted and halved

Arrange over the pieces of meat. Roll up carefully, and tie firmly with string.

50 g butter

Melt in a casserole that will hold both pork rolls in one layer. Add the rolls and sauté to brown on all sides.

50 ml each of Brown Chicken Stock (see page 316) and dry white wine
150 ml double cream

Add to the casserole, and stir carefully around the rolls to mix with the butter and juices. Cover with a lid and pot-roast for 30–45 minutes until the pork is tender, turning occasionally. Remove the pork rolls to a platter and keep warm. Reduce the juices in the casserole to a coating consistency then check the seasoning. Slice the pork rolls and pour the sauce over.

CAJUN ANDOUILLE
The *andouilles* of Cajun country in the southern states of America are believed to have originated from those of France, brought over by settlers from Normandy and Brittany – who formed a major proportion of the original inhabitants of Acadia.

USA

MAKES 4 LARGE SAUSAGES

600 g pork leg, skinned
150 g green bacon, rinded
150 g pork fat

Cut into pieces and finely mince or work in the food processor until smooth.

1 garlic clove, peeled and finely chopped
½ x 5 ml spoon black peppercorns, ground
¼ x 5 ml spoon each of cayenne pepper, chopped fresh parsley and thyme
a pinch of dry mustard powder
1 x 15 ml spoon coarse salt

Place in a large bowl, along with the minced meats, and mix very thoroughly.

about 75 cm sausage skin or 200 g caul fat

Wash well, then fill with the stuffing. Tie both ends and make three other ties along the length of the sausage to make four sausages. Divide and secure.
　　For authenticity, place in a smoker and smoke at approximately 150°C/300°F for 2 hours.
　　To cook, slice into 1 cm slices and cook in gumbos, jambalayas, in pasta or vegetable dishes, or sauté or grill whole as a breakfast sausage.

STIR-FRY TERIYAKI PORK WITH MUSHROOMS
The classic *teriyaki* sauce consists of a mixture of *shoyu*, sake and *mirin*, and here it is used first as a marinade for the pork. You can use any mushrooms, cultivated or wild. (Photograph page 158)

JAPAN

SERVES 4

400 g lean pork, cut into thin strips
1 x 15 ml spoon *shoyu* (Japanese soy sauce)
1 x 15 ml spoon sake (Japanese rice wine)
1 x 15 ml spoon *mirin* (Japanese sherry)

Mix together in a bowl, and leave to marinate for 30–60 minutes. Drain well, retaining the marinade.

2 x 15 ml spoons vegetable oil
5 cm piece of fresh root ginger, peeled and grated
2 garlic cloves, peeled and crushed

Heat together in a wok or large frying pan, and stir-fry for 30 seconds, stirring. Add the drained pork and stir-fry over high heat for about 5 minutes or until the pork is cooked and golden brown in colour.

225 g shiitake mushrooms
120 g *shimiji* mushrooms
50 g *enokitake* mushrooms

Add to the wok, toss and stir, and cook for about 3–4 minutes until the mushrooms are tender.

2 x 15 ml spoons oyster sauce
salt and freshly ground pepper

Stir in, with the marinade, and heat through, seasoning if necessary.

2 spring onions, finely sliced

Sprinkle over as a garnish.

CHAR SIU
This Cantonese pork dish, also known as barbecued pork, is traditionally spit-roasted, hung from a hook inside an oven. Serve it thinly sliced, hot or cold, or use in other dishes such as fried rice. Beef fillet could also be cooked in this way.

CHINA

SERVES 4   **OVEN: 200°C/400°F/GAS 6**

800 g fillet of pork, in the piece

Place in a dish and halve lengthways.

5 cm piece of fresh root ginger, peeled and finely grated
1 medium onion, peeled and finely grated
2 garlic cloves, peeled and crushed
75 ml light soy sauce
60 ml rice wine or sherry

Mix together and add to the pork, turning to coat. Leave to marinate in a cool place, covered, for at least 8 hours.

2 x 15 ml spoons clear honey
1 x 15 ml spoon each of soy sauce, shaohsing (yellow rice wine) or dry sherry, and vegetable oil
salt and freshly ground pepper

Mix together to use as a basting sauce. Drain the pork, reserving the marinade. Place on a rack in a roasting tray (with a little water in the base), and brush with some of the basting sauce. Roast in the preheated oven for 10–15 minutes then turn and baste again. Reduce the oven to 180°C/350°F/Gas 4, and continue roasting for a further 20 minutes, basting occasionally. Remove from the oven and baste again to give it a shine.
Leave to dry. Slice very thinly just before serving, and arrange overlapping on a platter. Heat the roasting pan juices and water with the marinade, strain, then serve as a dipping sauce. Season if necessary.

Stir-fry Teriyaki Pork with Mushrooms (see page 157).

BARBECUED SPARE RIBS
The meat of the pig features in seven out of ten meat recipes in China, and it is so popular that the Chinese character for pork is simply 'meat', whereas that for lamb is 'sheep meat', for instance. The Chinese character for home consists of 'roof' over 'pig'.

CHINA

SERVES 4

12–16 meaty Chinese-style pork ribs

Trim, and if the ribs are still in the rack, slice into separate ribs, always close against the right-hand bone.

2 garlic cloves, peeled
25 g (1 oz) fresh root ginger, peeled

Finely chop then, using your hands, rub into the ribs. Place the ribs in a dish in one layer.

Barbecued Spare Ribs

2 x 15 ml spoons each of hoisin sauce
  and yellow bean sauce
2 x 15 ml spoons each of light and
  dark soy sauce
juice of 1 small orange
3 tomatoes, skinned, seeded and very
  finely diced
2 x 15 ml spoons shaohsing (yellow
  rice wine) or dry sherry
1 star anise, crushed
a pinch of caster sugar
freshly ground black pepper

1 x 15 ml spoon clear honey, warmed

For the marinade, place all the ingredients in a saucepan and bring to the boil. Leave to cool, then pour over the ribs. Leave to marinate overnight.

Remove the ribs from the marinade, which you retain. Grill the ribs on a barbecue for 15–25 minutes, according to size, basting with the marinade and turning occasionally. (Or cook in the marinade in the oven, at 180°C/350°F/Gas 4 for about 45 minutes, turning halfway through.)

Brush over the ribs about 10 minutes before they are ready. Continue cooking until the ribs are a rich brown colour.

COCHINILLO ASADO
Suckling pig is a holiday or festival food, served as a banquet centrepiece, in many countries of the world, from the Caribbean islands such as Cuba (a Spanish influence perhaps), to Brazil, Bavaria, the Philippines, Poland and China.

SPAIN/PORTUGAL

SERVES 8

1 x 3–3.5 kg suckling pig

Wipe inside and out, and cover the ears and tail with little cones of doubled foil.

1 garlic clove, peeled and minced
1 medium onion, peeled and grated
3 x 15 ml spoons finely chopped fresh
　parsley
olive oil
salt and freshly ground pepper

Mix together, adding enough olive oil to make a thick paste, and seasoning to taste with salt and pepper. Smear over the inside of the pig. Smear the skin of the pig with some olive oil, and sprinkle with salt.

120 ml white wine

Pour into a suitable roasting tray, and add the same amount of water. Place a rack in the tin and place the pig on top, on its back. Roast in the preheated oven for about 1 hour, then turn, pour off excess juices, and baste with some of the juices. Roast for a further 2¼–2¾ hours, basting occasionally (roughly 30–35 minutes per 500 g). Do not baste during the last half hour of cooking.
　　Make a thin sauce from the skimmed juices in the pan and some more wine if necessary. Season to taste with salt and pepper. Remove the pig's head, and carve the meat, giving each guest some of the crisp crackling.

VITELLO TONNATO
One of the most famous of Italian combinations – tender veal fillet, gently poached then partnered with a tuna sauce – to be served cold. (You could use veal loin; poach for 25 minutes). A good accompaniment is the tuna and bean salad on page 218, with some extra capers and black olives. (Photograph page 162)

ITALY

SERVES 4

1 whole veal fillet, about 500–600 g
salt and freshly ground pepper

Trim the veal of excess fat and sinew, and tie with string. Season to taste with salt and pepper.

1 x 15 ml spoon olive oil

Heat in a frying pan and brown the veal fillet on all sides.

1 litre strong Veal Stock (see
　page 316)
1 bouquet garni (parsley, bay,
　marjoram/oregano)

Bring to the boil together in a suitable pan, then add the veal and poach it for about 10–15 minutes. Remove from the heat and leave the veal to cool in the stock.

150 g tuna in oil, drained
1 garlic clove, peeled
2 anchovy fillets
1 x 15 ml spoon Dijon mustard
1 x 15 ml spoon drained capers, rinsed
1 egg

For the tuna sauce, place together in a food processor and blend for about 30 seconds or until smooth.

125 ml sunflower oil 125 ml olive oil	With the machine running slowly, gradually add the sunflower oil followed by the olive oil, thinning down with a little of the poaching stock if it gets too thick.
lemon juice	Add to taste, along with more salt and pepper if necessary. Cut the veal into thin slices and arrange on a bed of the sauce. Garnish with some rocket leaves and some tuna and bean salad, if liked.

FILO MEAT PIE
Finely ground or minced meat is common in the Balkans, and is usually made into kebabs or rissoles. Here meat is encased in filo pastry and baked, the use of filo revealing an affinity with the cuisines of Greece and Turkey. The idea is similar to the *b'stilla* of Morocco. (Photograph page 163)

YUGOSLAVIA   **SERVES 4**   **OVEN: 180°C/350°F/GAS 4**

2 x 15 ml spoons vegetable oil 1 onion, peeled and finely diced 2 garlic cloves, peeled and crushed	Heat together in a large saucepan and sweat until the onion is soft, about 5 minutes.
350 g each of minced pork and veal salt and freshly ground pepper	Add to the pan, seasoning to taste with salt and pepper. Stir to break up any lumps, and fry until golden brown. Remove from the heat.
1 x 15 ml spoon each of chopped fresh marjoram, dill and parsley 2 eggs, beaten	Stir in, and transfer to a bowl. Allow to cool slightly. Adjust seasoning.
75 g butter, melted	Brush a little over the base of a loose-bottomed 20 cm cake tin.
10 large sheets filo pastry	Place one sheet over the base of the cake tin and brush with melted butter. Top with another sheet of pastry but at a slightly different angle, and brush again with melted butter. Continue stacking the sheets of pastry in the same way, at a slightly different angle each time, until you have used five sheets. Spoon half the meat filling into the centre of the pastry in a neat round. Cover with two more pastry sheets, still brushing with butter, then spoon in the remaining filling. Top with the remaining three pastry sheets, still brushing with butter. Draw up the overhanging pastry edges and scrunch them on top. Brush with butter. Bake in the preheated oven for about 30 minutes until golden.
soured cream	Serve as a sauce for the pie.

Overleaf: Left, Vitello Tonnato. Above right, Osso Buco with Gremolata (see page 164). Below right, Filo Meat Pie.

OSSO BUCO WITH GREMOLATA

Osso buco, slow-cooked shin of veal, is a speciality of Lombardy, a major cattle-breeding region of Italy. The traditional accompaniment is *risotto alla milanese*, a risotto made with marrow and saffron, but wet polenta (see page 88) is also good. (Photograph page 163)

ITALY   **SERVES 4**   **OVEN: 180°C/350°F/GAS 4**

4 x 350–400 g osso buco pieces (shin of veal) salt and freshly ground pepper plain flour	Season the *osso buco* pieces and lightly dust with flour.
2 x 15 ml spoons olive oil	Heat in a casserole large enough to take the veal pieces in one layer, and brown the meat on all sides. Take care not to lose the marrow from the bones. Remove the meat from the casserole and keep warm.
75 g onions, peeled and finely diced 1 garlic clove, peeled and crushed 150 g in total of trimmed carrot, celeriac, celery and leek, very finely chopped 1 x 5 ml spoon each of finely chopped fresh thyme and basil	Sauté in the oil remaining in the casserole for a few minutes, until the vegetables soften a little.
20 g Tomatoes Concassées (see page 312) 100 g tomatoes, skinned, seeded and diced 150 ml dry white wine	Add and cook gently until reduced by a third.
Brown Veal Stock (see page 316)	Add about 1.5 litres, along with the meat, to the casserole, bring to the boil on top of the stove, cover then cook in the preheated oven for about 2 hours, or until the veal is tender. If necessary, add some more veal stock. Adjust seasoning.
1 x 5 ml spoon grated lemon rind ½ garlic clove, peeled and crushed 1 x 15 ml spoon chopped parsley	Mix together and sprinkle this *gremolata* over the *osso buco*. Serve from the casserole, remembering to eat the marrow from the bones.

WIENER SCHNITZEL
One of the most famous dishes of Vienna. These veal escalopes are delicious with a beurre noisette – 60 g of butter melted and heated until golden with the juice of ½ lemon and 1 x 15 ml spoon finely chopped parsley. The best accompaniment is a green salad.

AUSTRIA

SERVES 4

4 large thin escalopes of veal, approx. 100 g each, cut against the grain

Place between pieces of greaseproof paper or clingfilm, and beat well to make them thin and flat.

salt and freshly ground pepper

Season the escalopes well.

2 x 15 ml spoons plain flour
1 egg, beaten with 1 x 15 ml spoon each of water and olive oil
4 x 15 ml spoons dry, very fine breadcrumbs

Place on separate plates. Press the escalopes separately into first the flour, shake and pat off any excess, then brush with the egg. Roll them in the crumbs, pressing in well.

100 ml clarified butter

Divide between two frying pans and heat. Fry the escalopes until crisp and golden, about 3–4 minutes per side, constantly moving the pan. Drain well.

4 slices lemon

Serve immediately with the lemon.

ROAST KNUCKLE OF VEAL
Veal is a common meat in Germany, the most popular after pork, especially in Bavaria, of which this *gebratene Kalbshaxe* is the national dish. The veal knuckle is first poached, then roasted to a golden crispness. The traditional accompaniment is bread dumplings.

GERMANY

SERVES 4   **OVEN: 200°C/400°F/GAS 6**

1 large knuckle of veal, about 1.75 kg, with the meat on it

Trim well, and place in a large pan. Cover with water, at least 1 litre.

2 onions, peeled
2 carrots
3 celery stalks
1 leek
1 bouquet garni (bay leaf, parsley, thyme)
finely grated rind of ½ lemon
1 clove
5 black peppercorns, crushed

Add to the pan and bring the water to the boil. Skim well, then cover and simmer for about 45 minutes. Remove the knuckle from the stock (strain this and use as a veal stock), and dry well. Place in a roasting tray.

50 ml vegetable oil
salt and freshly ground pepper

Pour the oil over the meat, and season with salt and pepper. Place in the preheated oven and roast for about 30–40 minutes, basting occasionally, until the skin is golden and crisp, and the meat is coming away from the bone. Pour a little of the hot poaching stock over the meat as it is being taken out of the oven.

EMINCE DE VEAU ZURICHOISE

This recipe is one of the most famous national dishes of my homeland, Switzerland. It originates from Zurich, in the German-speaking parts of the country, where it is known as *züri Gschnätzlets* or *geschnätzeltes Kalbfleisch*. The veal strips are usually served with Rösti (see page 64).

SWITZERLAND

SERVES 4

600 g fillet or rib of veal	Cut the meat into thin slices, 1.5 x 3 cm.
salt and freshly ground pepper butter	Season the meat slices, then sauté carefully in 20 g hot butter. Do not brown. Place the meat slices in a sieve over a saucepan to catch the juices.
200 ml dry white wine	Add to the meat juices in the pan, and boil to reduce a little.
100 ml Brown Veal Stock (see page 316) 300 ml double cream	Add the stock to the pan and bring to the boil, then add the cream. Simmer to reduce to a thin coating consistency.
150 g mushrooms	Choose a mixture of mushrooms, preferably 50 g each of small chanterelles, yellow boletus or ceps, and cultivated mushrooms. Wash thoroughly, dry and slice.
1 small shallot, peeled and very finely chopped	Sweat, with the sliced mushrooms, in a further 25 g butter until softened.
2 x 15 ml spoons finely cut chives	Add most to the pan holding the sauce, along with the meat and mushrooms, and heat together gently for a minute or so. To finish the sauce, melt in about 25 g hard butter, cut into small dice. Taste for seasoning, and serve, sprinkled with the remaining chives.

Emincé de Veau Zurichoise with Rösti (see page 64).

ROAST BABY LAMB
Over the centuries, lamb has become associated with religious festivals. Milk-fed, four-month-old lamb is an Easter speciality in Italy. The Pascal lamb is also associated with Christian and Jewish tradition – lamb is eaten at Passover. There are many ways in which it can be cooked.

ITALY **SERVES 4** **OVEN: 180°C/350°F/GAS 4**

1 leg of lamb	The day before, trim the lamb. Place in a roasting tray. Cut some small slits all over and around the meat.
juniper berries	Press a berry into each slit in the leg.
3 garlic cloves, peeled salt and freshly ground pepper	Crush the garlic with some salt and pepper.
1 x 15 ml spoon fresh rosemary leaves	Chop very finely, then mix with the garlic paste.
olive oil	Add some to the garlic and herb mixture to make a fairly fluid paste. Smear this over the meat, pressing into the slits. Leave to stand in a cool place overnight.
2 medium onions, peeled and sliced 1 celery stalk, sliced 1 carrot, sliced 300 ml white wine	Add to the roasting tin, along with some more oil. Roast in the preheated oven for about 30 minutes, turning the meat when it is brown on top, and basting occasionally with the wine. Make a sauce with the vegetables and juices, adding more water if necessary.

SCOTCH BROTH
A substantial soup, using whatever vegetable was available (dried pulses in winter), which was made to last over a least a couple of days – the meat and a little broth first one day, the remaining 'matured' broth the next. The broth can be made with beef as well.

SCOTLAND **SERVES 4**

1 lamb or mutton shank 100 g lean lamb or mutton in the piece 50 g pearl barley 2 sprigs fresh thyme	Place in a large pot, cover with water (at least 1 litre), and bring to the boil. Skim well, then simmer gently for about an hour. Remove the bone and meat from the broth, and cut the meat into dice. Reserve.
25 g butter 1 small onion, peeled and finely diced 1 small carrot, peeled and diced 1 small leek, trimmed and diced 2 celery stalks, peeled and diced	Sweat together for a few minutes to soften.
60 g finely shredded cabbage	Add to the other vegetables and stir briefly before pouring into the broth. Bring to the boil, then turn down the heat.
salt and freshly ground pepper	Add to taste, along with the lamb dice. Simmer for a few minutes.
2 x 15 ml spoons finely chopped fresh parsley	Add as you serve the broth, piping hot.

MOUSSAKA

This must be the best-known of all Greek dishes. You could use cold cooked lamb, cut in dice, instead of lamb mince, and sliced cooked potatoes are often included as well. A little finely grated cheese could be mixed into the soufflé sauce topping.

GREECE   SERVES 4   OVEN: 200°C/400°F/GAS 6

2 medium aubergines salt and freshly ground pepper	Wash and slice into circles, then place in a colander, sprinkle with salt, and leave for 30 minutes. Drain and pat dry.
olive oil	Heat about 1 x 15 ml spoon in a frying pan and fry as many slices of aubergine as will fit in the pan until golden on both sides. Remove and drain very well on kitchen paper. Use more oil as needed.
500 g lean lamb, minced 1 large onion, peeled and chopped 2 garlic cloves, peeled and crushed	Heat 2 x 15 ml spoons olive oil in a separate large frying pan, add the meat, onion and garlic, and cook until the meat has started to colour.
120 g Tomato Sauce (see page 311) 1 x 5 ml spoon fresh oregano ½ x 5 ml spoon freshly grated nutmeg 150 ml red wine or Lamb Stock (see page 316)	Add to the meat, along with salt and pepper to taste, and heat through until simmering. Cover and simmer for about 25 minutes. Place a layer in the bottom of a suitable casserole and top with a layer of aubergine slices.
6 tomatoes, skinned, quartered and seeded	Arrange half on top of the aubergine slices, rounded side up, then repeat the meat, aubergine and tomato layers again to use them up.
25 g butter 20 g plain flour 250 ml milk	Cook together to make a béchamel or white sauce. Season to taste with salt and pepper.
1 x 5 ml spoon ground cinnamon 1 egg, separated	Off the heat, stir the cinnamon and egg yolk into the sauce. Whip the egg white until stiff, then fold into the sauce. Spoon this over the ingredients in the casserole, and bake in the preheated oven for about 15 minutes or until the interior is hot and the soufflé top is risen and golden.

Overleaf: Above left, Bobotie (see page 172). Below left, Lamb Cassoulet (see page 173). Right, Lamb Korma (see page 172) with Tarka Dhal (see page 84).

MEAT

BOBOTIE

Workers from South-East Asia were brought to South Africa by the occupying Dutch to help farm the land. They included Muslims from Madagascar and the islands of Indonesia, and people from southern India. The result, in a culinary sense, was a spicy blend of eastern and western ingredients and techniques, as in this curry dish with a baked custard topping. (Photograph page 170)

SOUTH AFRICA   SERVES 4   OVEN: 190°C/375°F/GAS 5

500 g lean lamb or mutton (or beef), minced
1 x 15 ml spoon sunflower oil

Heat together in a large frying pan, then stir over high heat until the meat is brown and crumbly. Remove the meat using a slotted spoon. Keep to one side.

1 large onion, peeled and chopped
1 garlic clove, peeled and crushed
1 bay leaf
½ x 5 ml spoon each of mustard seeds, turmeric and garam masala
1 x 15 ml spoon curry powder

Add to the oil remaining in the pan and sweat gently until the onion has softened. Return the meat to the pan.

60 ml white wine vinegar
1 x 15 ml spoon brown sugar

Add to the pan and allow to simmer for 10 minutes.

15 g soft white breadcrumbs
25 g flaked almonds
25 g seedless raisins
2 x 15 ml spoons Cape Apricot (or mango) Chutney (see page 308)
salt and freshly ground pepper

Add to the pan, and season to taste with salt and pepper. Mix well. Divide between four greased individual ovenproof bowls or large ramekins. Level the tops.

1 large egg, beaten
250 ml milk

For the topping, combine, and pour over the meat.

4 small fresh lemon or bay leaves

Tuck a leaf into each dish, then place the dishes on a baking sheet. Bake in the preheated oven for about 20 minutes or until the topping is lightly browned. Serve with rice and chutney.

LAMB KORMA

'*Korma*', which comes from the north of India, means a dish that is fragrant and aromatic, with a creamy sauce and little heat. It is a Moghul dish, thus the inclusion of almonds which reveals the Persian influence. (Photograph page 171)

INDIA   SERVES 4   OVEN: 190°C/375°F/GAS 5

1 medium onion, peeled
2 garlic cloves, peeled
seeds of 6 cardamom pods
25 g ground almonds
5 cm piece of fresh root ginger, peeled
a pinch of cayenne pepper

Place together in a blender or food processor and blend to a purée. Place in a large bowl.

700 g lean neck end of lamb

Cut into 3 cm cubes, and mix with the marinade in the bowl. Leave to marinate for at least 1 hour.

150 g clarified butter
1 medium onion, peeled and sliced

Heat together in a casserole and cook until the onion is soft. Add the meat and marinade and cook for a few minutes.

MEAT

172

5 cm cinnamon stick 2 bay leaves 1 x 5 ml spoon cumin seeds	Add to the casserole, along with 100 ml water, then cover and bake in the preheated oven for 30 minutes.
250 g natural yoghurt 150 ml double cream salt and freshly ground pepper	Mix together, then stir into the lamb in the casserole. Return to the oven and continue to cook very gently for a further 20 minutes or until the lamb is tender. If the meat sticks, add more water. Season to taste.
4 x 15 ml spoons finely chopped fresh coriander 1 x 15 ml spoon flaked almonds, toasted	Sprinkle over the meat in the casserole, and serve hot with rice.

LAMB CASSOULET

Cassoulet, the bean and meat stew of the Languedoc, is often made with pork, but recipes vary from one town to another. The Castelnaudary version consists of pork; that of Carcassonne adds mutton and game birds in season; *confit* of duck is added to the cassoulet from Toulouse. (Photograph page 170)

FRANCE **SERVES 4** **OVEN: 180°C/350°F/GAS 4**

350 g haricot beans	Soak overnight in cold water, then drain and put in a large casserole.
225 g piece green streaky bacon, roughly diced 1 onion, peeled and stuck with 4 cloves 1 carrot, trimmed and sliced 2 garlic cloves, peeled 1 bouquet garni (parsley, thyme, bay)	Add to the casserole, cover with water, and bring to the boil. Reduce the heat, cover, and simmer for 1 hour until the beans are tender but still whole. Check the water occasionally and replenish with boiling water if necessary.
4 lamb loin chops 2 neck fillets of lamb, cut in half 225 g garlic or meaty sausages (preferably 4) salt and freshly ground pepper	Season the meat and sausages to taste.
1 x 15 ml spoon olive oil	Heat in a large frying pan and brown the meat and sausages on all sides.
350 g tomatoes, skinned and chopped 1 x 15 ml spoon Tomates Concassées (see page 312)	Stir into the beans, then place the meat and sausages on top.
50 g fine fresh breadcrumbs 50 g butter, melted	Spread the breadcrumbs over the top of the meat and beans, then sprinkle with the melted butter. Put the casserole in the oven, uncovered, and cook for a further 1–1½ hours. The breadcrumbs will become crisp and golden, and in many regions are stirred in, and more breadcrumbs added during the cooking.

LAMB AND LENTIL SOUP

There are many versions of *harira*, the classic soup of Morocco, which is of Berber origin. This one, perhaps the most famous, is traditionally served during Ramadan, the Arab Lent. After a day of fasting, without food or water, when the *muezzin* announces that the sun has set, everyone can sit down to some hot *harira*, their first meal of the day.

MOROCCO

SERVES 4

150 g red lentils
50 chickpeas

Soak overnight in cold water to cover, then drain well.

300 g lean lamb or mutton, cut into 1 cm dice
lamb bones, if possible
1 large onion, peeled and finely chopped

Place in a large saucepan along with the lentils and chickpeas (if using). Cover with water, at least 1 litre, and bring to the boil. Skim well, then cover and simmer gently for 1½–2 hours, or until the meat and pulses are cooked. Add more water, if necessary, to keep the ingredients covered.

1 x 5 ml spoon plain flour
½ x 5 ml spoon each of ground cinnamon, powdered saffron and paprika
150 ml water

Mix together until smooth.

450 g tomatoes, skinned, seeded and diced
3 x 15 ml spoons finely chopped fresh parsley
2 x 15 ml spoons finely chopped fresh coriander
salt and freshly ground pepper

Place in a saucepan, seasoning to taste with salt and pepper. Add the flour liquid and a little soup stock, bring to the boil, then simmer, stirring, for about 10 minutes. Pour this slightly thickened liquid back into the soup. Taste and adjust the seasoning.

2 lemons, halved

Squeeze a little juice into each bowl of hot *harira*.

LANCASHIRE HOTPOT

The traditional pot for this lamb stew (once made with mutton) was brown earthenware, and tall, almost flowerpot shaped, so that the lamb chops could stand upright. Oysters were once traditionally added, much as was and is the case with Steak and Kidney Pudding.

ENGLAND

SERVES 4 **OVEN: 160–180°C/325–350°F/GAS 3–4**

4 lamb loin chops
4 middle neck lamb chops
4 lamb's kidneys

Trim the chops of fat; halve, clean and core the kidneys.

salt and freshly ground pepper

Season the meat to taste with salt and pepper, and place the loin chops, 'tails' up, on the base of a suitably large tall pot.

2 bay leaves
2 sprigs fresh thyme
olive oil

Tuck half of the herbs in to the bottom of the pan.

300 g onions, peeled and finely sliced

Sweat and lightly colour the onion in a little oil. Add about half to the chops, and season with salt and pepper.

Lamb and Lentil Soup

300 g carrots, trimmed and sliced
200 g button mushrooms, trimmed (or 8 oysters, shelled)

Add about half of the carrots, along with the kidneys, and all the mushrooms, to the pot and season again. (If using the oysters, don't add until the very end, just under the potato crust.) Add the middle neck chops, laying them flat and pressing down. Cover with the remaining onion and carrot, and season.

600 g medium potatoes, peeled and thickly sliced

Arrange neatly, slightly overlapping like tiles on a roof, over the top of the ingredients. Season and brush with a little oil.

350 ml Lamb Stock (see page 316)

Pour in until it reaches the level of the potato topping. Tuck the remaining herbs down the side of the potatoes. Cover tightly with the lid and bake slowly in the preheated oven for 1½–2 hours. Half an hour before serving, turn the temperature up to 190°C/375°F/Gas 5. Remove the lid, and allow the potato topping to brown for the remaining 30 minutes' cooking time.

Add the oysters (if using) when the hotpot is ready, slipping them and their juices carefully under the potato topping. They will quickly be heated through. Add some fresh herbs too, if you like.

SHISH KEBAB

Meat grilled on skewers is common throughout the Balkans, Middle East and Eastern Europe, and is often known as *shashlik*, or, in Greece, *souvlaki*. The meat used is usually lamb, occasionally beef or pork, and the various international differences depend on the spicing; in India, ginger, cumin and/or garam masala would be used; in the Balkans paprika and yoghurt.

TURKEY   **SERVES 4**

700 g neck fillet of lamb, trimmed
    and cut into 5cm cubes
4 lamb's kidneys, skinned and halved
2 onions, peeled and cut into pieces
1 red and 1 green pepper, seeded and
    cut into pieces
1 garlic clove, peeled and crushed
2 x 15 ml spoons dried thyme or mint
4 dried bay leaves, crumbled
juice of 2 large lemons

Place in a bowl, and leave to marinate for at least 2 hours, or overnight, turning occasionally.
　　When ready to cook, drain the meats from the marinade, and thread on to metal skewers, alternating meat, onion and pepper slices for a colourful effect.

olive oil
salt and freshly ground pepper

Oil the grill and brush a little over the meat and vegetables. Season to taste with salt and pepper, then grill under a conventional grill or over charcoal until cooked to taste, turning once, and basting with the juices.

lemon wedges
fresh parsley and mint

Serve as a garnish to the kebabs, along with a salad and warm pitta bread.

KOFTA KEBAB

The North African version of Seekh Kebabs (see page 149), using ground meat, spices and herbs characteristic of Morocco. The Pakistani version uses hotter spices; the Balkan version would be much plainer, seasoned with parsley and onion only, perhaps.

MOROCCO   **SERVES 4**

700 g boneless shoulder of lamb

Cut in small pieces, trimming off excess fat, but keeping some in place, as this helps keep the kofta soft, and will melt away during the cooking. Place in a bowl.

200 g onions, peeled and roughly
    chopped
6 x 5 ml spoons finely chopped fresh
    parsley
3 x 15 ml spoons finely chopped fresh
    coriander
1 x 15 ml spoon finely cut fresh mint
1 x 5 ml spoon each of ground
    cinnamon, cumin and paprika
¼ x 5 ml spoon chilli powder or
    cayenne pepper
salt and freshly ground pepper

Add to the bowl, and mix well together, seasoning to taste with salt and pepper. Put in batches into the food processor to blend to a very fine paste. Prepare and cook thereafter exactly as for Seekh Kebabs (see page 149).

STIR-FRIED LAMB WITH MINT
Many different types of mint are used in Vietnamese cooking. One is called caraway mint, and is actually the leaves of sprouted caraway seeds.

VIETNAM

SERVES 4

3 x 15 ml spoons vegetable oil
2 garlic cloves, peeled and crushed

Heat half the oil and the garlic together in a wok or large frying pan, and sweat until the garlic is golden.

450 g lean lamb, thinly sliced
salt and freshly ground pepper

Add to the wok, and stir-fry until brown, about 2 minutes. Remove from the wok, and set aside. Heat the remaining oil in the wok.

1 medium aubergine, cut into bite-sized pieces

Add to the oil in the wok and stir-fry for about 5 minutes or until tender. Return the lamb and garlic to the wok.

2 x 15 ml spoons *nuoc mam* (fish sauce)
1 x 15 ml spoon brown sugar
60 ml water

Add to the wok, and heat gently to dissolve the sugar. Stir-fry for another 1–2 minutes. Place in a warmed serving dish. Adjust seasoning.

2 fresh red chilli peppers, seeded and sliced
20 mint leaves

Sprinkle over to garnish. Serve with rice.

NINEVEH KIBBEH
Kibbeh is greatly loved all over the Middle East, particularly in Syria and the Lebanon. It consists of pounded lamb and cracked wheat, and is presented in many ways. These stuffed *kibbehs* are unusual in that the casing is of cracked wheat only, and the 'balls' are poached rather than deep-fried. (Photograph page 179)

MIDDLE EAST

SERVES 4

225 g cracked wheat
250 ml boiling water
salt and freshly ground pepper

For the outer casing, place in a bowl, adding a pinch of salt, and allow to stand for 30 minutes.

2 x 15 ml spoons olive oil
1 onion, peeled and finely chopped
2 garlic cloves, peeled and finely chopped

Meanwhile, for the stuffing, heat together in a frying pan, and sweat until the onion is soft, about 5 minutes.

225 g lean lamb, cut into small dice

Add to the pan and cook, stirring constantly, until almost browned.

1 x 5 ml spoon ground allspice
50 g sultanas
50 g pine kernels, toasted
1 x 15 ml spoon finely chopped fresh parsley

Add to the pan, seasoning to taste with salt and pepper, and stir to mix thoroughly. Remove from the heat and leave to cool for 10 minutes.
   Drain the cracked wheat if necessary, then process in a food processor to a smooth purée. Form into eight balls. Take one in your hand, and make a hole with your forefinger. Starting from the centre work outwards enlarging the hole as much as possible to open out a cup-like shape. Stuff the hollowed-out balls with the meat mixture, then pinch the ends to seal and close securely; the stuffing must not leak out.
   Poach the balls in a large pot of boiling water for about 5 minutes or until they float. Serve warm with Tomato Sauce (see page 311) or crème fraîche with chopped mint.

FEGATO ALLA VENEZIANA
This is the ultimate recipe for calves' liver and onions, a speciality of the beautiful northern city of Venice. The success of this Venetian recipe lies principally in slicing the liver as thinly as possible, to no thicker than 5 mm. The best livers should be pale and rosy, not dark, in colour.

ITALY

SERVES 4

700 g calves' liver, very thinly sliced

Discard any skin and large tubes from the liver slices, and leave the slices as they are, or cut into bite-sized pieces. Set aside.

90 ml olive oil
30 g butter

Heat half the oil and half the butter together in a large frying pan.

4 medium onions, peeled and thinly sliced

Add to the pan and fry gently until transparent and brown, about 10 minutes. (You could do this ahead of time.) Remove the oil.

250 ml Brown Veal Stock (see page 316)
salt and freshly ground pepper

Add to the onion pan, seasoning to taste with salt and pepper, then continue to simmer until thickened.
   Heat the remaining oil and butter in a separate pan. The pan must be hot.

1 x 15 ml spoon plain flour

Sprinkle over the liver pieces, then fry quickly on both sides – it's a very speedy process. Add the onions and stock to the liver pan, and turn the heat down.

2 x 15 ml spoons finely chopped fresh parsley and sage

Add to the pan, along with some more salt and pepper to taste. Stir, and serve immediately. The Venetians like it with grilled polenta.

Opposite: Above, Nineveh Kibbeh (see page 177). Below, Fegato alla Veneziana with grilled Polenta (see page 88).

RINONES AL JEREZ
This kidney and sherry dish, which is found in Puerto Rico and many other Spanish-influenced islands, is directly in the Spanish tradition. In Spain, veal kidneys would probably be used instead of lamb's kidneys.

CARIBBEAN

SERVES 4

700 g lamb's kidneys

Trim and core and remove skin and any gristle. Cut into quarters.

juice of 1 lemon

Place in a bowl, add the kidney pieces and enough water to cover. Soak together for about 15 minutes. Drain the kidney pieces, and pat thoroughly dry with a kitchen cloth.

2 x 15 ml spoons cornflour
salt and freshly ground pepper

Mix together, then sprinkle over the kidney pieces.

75 g butter
1 medium onion, peeled and chopped
leaves of 1 sprig each of fresh thyme
**   and rosemary**

Heat together in a large frying pan and cook until the onion is lightly browned. Add the kidney and cook, stirring, for about 5 minutes or until the kidney pieces are tender.

150 ml dry sherry

Add to the pan and bring to the boil. Simmer for about 2 minutes. Check the seasoning, and serve hot, either on a bed of rice or on hot buttered toast.

DEVILLED KIDNEYS
These formed part of the substantial breakfasts served in Victorian and Edwardian households. Make a good supper dish, by adding a small onion fried in butter with 2 x 5 ml spoons curry powder; add 2 x 15 ml spoons mango chutney, and a little crème fraîche at the end.

UK

SERVES 4

1 x 15 ml spoon plain or wholemeal
**   flour**
1 x 15 ml spoon dry mustard powder
salt and cayenne pepper

Sift together on to a plate, adding salt and cayenne pepper to taste.

8 lamb's kidneys

Clean well, trimming off gristle, fat and skin. Cut into small cubes and roll in the spicy flour.

50 g butter

Melt in a small frying pan and sauté the kidney cubes over a low heat for about 1 minute, turning them occasionally. Remove the fat from the pan, patting the kidneys dry.

100 ml Lamb Stock (see page 316)

Add to the pan, and simmer uncovered for about another minute, until the sauce thickens a little. Taste for seasoning. Add the kidneys to the pan.

4 slices hot buttered toast

Place on individual plates, then top with the hot kidneys. Cut each slice diagonally in half.

BRAISED OXTAIL
A classic winter braise, which releases all the full flavour of the oxtail. Cattle store surplus fat in their tails, and these are particularly meaty in winter. Cook it the day before so that you can remove as much fat as possible from the top of the juices.

UK

SERVES 4

16 pieces oxtail, well trimmed
salt and freshly ground pepper

Season the oxtail to taste with salt and pepper.

50 ml vegetable oil

Heat in a large frying pan and brown the oxtail pieces well, in batches. Remove from the pan, and set aside.

20 g plain flour

Sprinkle over the browned oxtail pieces. Clean the pan with kitchen paper.

25 g butter
1 large onion, peeled and finely chopped
2 large carrots, trimmed and finely diced
4 celery stalks, very finely diced

Add to the cleaned pan and sauté lightly together.

300 ml red wine

Pour into the pan and stir to deglaze. Transfer wine and vegetables to a large casserole.

up to 2.5 litres Beef Stock (see page 316)
50 g tomatoes, diced

Add about 500 ml stock to the casserole along with the tomato and pieces of oxtail. Boil to reduce to a syrup. Repeat once more, with another 500 ml stock, then add enough stock just to cover the oxtail.

1 bouquet garni (bay, 2 sprigs thyme, 1 sprig rosemary, parsley stalks)

Add to the casserole, cover with the lid, and simmer on top of the stove for 2½–3 hours, until the oxtail is tender and the meat is coming away from the bones. Add more stock as necessary to prevent the meat sticking to the bottom or getting dry on the top.
 Remove the oxtail from the sauce and keep warm. Discard the herbs. Strain the stock, bring to the boil and skim until all grease is removed. Adjust seasoning. Return the oxtail to the sauce, heat through and serve with seasonal vegetables on top for a colourful effect.

POULTRY
AND GAME

ROCK CORNISH HEN STUFFED WITH WILD RICE

I first came across this popular North American combination when I worked in Montreal, during the Expo of 1967. A Rock Cornish hen is virtually the same as a poussin – therefore a six week-old chicken, weighing about 450 g.

CANADA   **SERVES 4**   **OVEN: 190°C/375°F/GAS 5**

4 poussins
salt and freshly ground pepper

Cut down the back with a sharp knife and remove the bones. Remove the breast bones and pull out the upper thigh bone. Season with salt and pepper. Chill until ready to use.

75 g wild rice

Place in a bowl and pour boiling water over to cover. Leave to soak for an hour or overnight. Drain well. Cover with three times the volume of fresh water (or chicken stock). Add a little salt, cover, bring to the boil then simmer for 1 hour. Drain (if necessary) and cool.

1 x 15 ml spoon finely diced shallot
15 g butter
4 chicken livers, diced
25 g peeled and diced apple
40 ml double cream
1 egg yolk
a little fresh thyme

For the filling, sweat the shallot in the butter, then season the liver dice and sauté them. When cool, mix with the cooked wild rice and the apple dice. Add the cream and bind with the egg yolk. Season with thyme, salt and pepper. Stuff into the poussins, return all the birds to their original shape, and tie with small pieces of string. Season with salt and pepper.

40 ml olive oil

Heat in a roasting pan, put in the stuffed poussins and sauté on both sides.

25 g each finely diced carrot and
    celery
1 x 15 ml spoon finely diced shallot
8 juniper berries, slightly crushed

Add to the poussin pan, then transfer to the preheated oven and roast until golden brown, about 30 minutes, basting constantly. Remove the birds from the pan and keep warm. Remove the fat from the pan, leaving the juices.

50 ml Madeira
200 ml Brown Chicken Stock (see page
    316)

Add to the juices in the pan, then boil to reduce to half the original volume. Strain, then season with salt and pepper. Skim well of fat. Arrange the poussins on a suitable dish, and cover with the finished sauce. Serve immediately.

COCK-A-LEEKIE

One of Scotland's most famous and oldest dishes, this chicken soup-stew is flavoured by local leeks and sweetened by prunes. It was a traditional way of using an old and tough rooster or layer, and would once have been cooked slowly on a peat fire overnight.

SCOTLAND   **SERVES 8**

1 boiling fowl

Clean well, wiping inside and out, then place in a large stockpot. Pour over boiling water to cover, then drain very well.

Brown Chicken or Beef Stock (see page
    316)
    or water

Pour in enough liquid to cover the fowl comfortably, then bring to the boil. Turn the heat down to a simmer, and skim very thoroughly.

1 bouquet garni (thyme, bay, parsley)
1 marrow bone
2 medium onions, peeled and roughly
    chopped
salt and freshly ground pepper

Add to the pan, seasoning to taste with salt and pepper.

10 leeks, washed and trimmed	Cut 7 of the leeks into 5 cm pieces and add to the pot. Keep the remainder to one side. Cover the pot and simmer on a very low heat for about 2 hours, or until the chicken is tender. Remove the chicken from the pot, and skin and bone it. Cut the meat into julienne strips. Strain the stock and discard the vegetables, herbs and bones. Return the stock and chicken to the pan.
16 prunes, soaked overnight and pitted	Add to the liquid in the pan and cook for 30 minutes more. Slice the remaining leeks into julienne pieces and add to the pan a few minutes before serving. Check the seasoning.
4 x 15 ml spoons finely chopped fresh parsley	Sprinkle over each portion of soup, chicken, prunes and crisp leeks.

SOUTHERN FRIED CHICKEN
Perhaps one of the most famous of southern dishes, Southern Fried Chicken is also very easy to prepare and cook. It is traditionally served with 'mush', a cornmeal 'polenta', fried as little cakes, but the Sweetcorn Pancakes on page 86 would go well too.

USA   Serves 4   Oven: 110°C/225°F/Gas ¼

1 x 1.5 kg chicken	Cut into 8 serving pieces, and skin them. Wash or wipe, then dry well with paper towels. Place in a plastic or paper bag.
120 g plain flour 1 x 5 ml spoon each of ground cinnamon and curry powder salt and freshly ground pepper	Add to the bag, seasoning to taste with salt and pepper and shake the bag to coat the chicken pieces thoroughly. Shake them free of excess flour.
100 g fat (traditionally lard, but bacon fat or vegetable oil could be substituted)	Heat in a large frying pan and briskly fry the chicken pieces until brown on one side. Turn over with tongs and fry the second side until brown. Reduce the heat, cover the pan, and cook gently until the chicken is tender, 25–30 minutes (the breast pieces will be ready first). Remove from the pan, drain well, and keep warm in the low oven. Pour off all but 2 x 15 ml spoons of the fat from the pan.
6 medium tomatoes, skinned, seeded and diced 1 fresh chilli pepper, seeded and diced	Mix together to make a fresh chilli sauce. Season with salt and pepper. Serve the chicken on a heated platter, with the sauce separately.

HAWAIIAN BARBECUED CHICKEN

The Chinese came to Hawaii to work in the sugar cane plantations, and they stayed. Because of this pervasive influence, many Hawaiian dishes now include soy sauce. (Photograph, opposite above)

HAWAII

SERVES 4

100 ml light soy sauce
1 x 15 ml spoon dry mustard powder

For the marinade, mix together in a china or glass container.

1 x 15 ml spoon clear honey
5 cm piece of fresh root ginger, peeled and grated
1 medium onion, peeled and grated
2 garlic cloves, peeled and crushed
1 star anise, crushed

Add to the soy sauce and leave to stand for at least 8 hours or overnight.

1 chicken, cut into 8 joints

Coat with the marinade and leave for at least an hour, turning occasionally, and basting.

salt and freshly ground pepper

When ready to cook, sprinkle over the chicken and grill under a preheated grill or on a barbecue for 5–6 minutes, then turn and cook for another 5–6 minutes. Baste with the marinade occasionally. Serve with coconut rice, on banana leaves if you like.

CHICKEN AND JELLYFISH SALAD

The northern Chinese like to eat the salted and sun-dried mantle skin of the marine jellyfish. It is available in the piece or in packets in shreds. It has to be rinsed and soaked before use. It lends a slight sea flavour to salads, and a rubbery consistency. (Photograph, opposite below)

CHINA

SERVES 4

350 g dried jellyfish

Rinse well to get rid of excess salt, then soak in generous cold water for at least 6 hours or overnight. Change the water several times. Drain and cut into strips about 5 mm wide. Pour boiling water over, and the shreds will curl up instantly. Rinse and drain again as quickly as you can (to avoid toughness), then leave to cool.

2 chicken breasts, poached

Skin, then cut into strips. Place in a serving dish and leave to cool.

½ cucumber

Cut into similar strips and add to the chicken.

1 shallot, peeled and finely diced
1 garlic clove, peeled and crushed
5 cm piece of fresh root ginger, peeled and grated
1 x 5 ml spoon hot mustard
2 x 15 ml spoons light soy sauce
3 x 15 ml spoons rice vinegar
1 x 5 ml spoon caster sugar
3 x 15 ml spoons sesame oil
salt and freshly ground pepper

For the dressing, mix together in a separate bowl, seasoning to taste with salt and pepper.
   Add the jellyfish to the chicken and cucumber in the dish, then pour over the dressing. Mix well.

1 x 15 ml spoon black sesame seeds, toasted
2 spring onions, finely sliced

Sprinkle over the salad as a garnish.

CHICKEN WATERZOOI
The Flemish people – of Flanders in the north of Belgium – make famous soup-stews called *waterzooi* or *water sootje*, from fish or shellfish, rabbit or chicken. Serve with boiled potatoes or bread and butter.

BELGIUM

SERVES 4

1 x 1.5 kg chicken

Cut into 8 pieces, and discard skin. Place in a suitable saucepan. Blanch in boiling water, then drain well.

about 1 litre Brown Chicken Stock (see page 316)
1 bouquet garni (bay, thyme, parsley stalks)

Pour in enough stock to cover the chicken, add the bouquet garni, then bring to the boil. Cover and poach gently for 20 minutes. Remove the chicken from the poaching stock, then bone and slice. Discard the bouquet garni.

50 g butter
2 celery stalks, trimmed and sliced
2 leeks, trimmed and sliced
2 onions, peeled and chopped

Melt the butter in a large soup pan and add the vegetables. Sauté gently for 5–6 minutes, without colouring.
   Pour in the chicken poaching liquid, plus the pieces of chicken, and simmer for about 5 minutes.

2 egg yolks, beaten with 1 x 15 ml spoon water

Add a little of the hot liquid to the egg yolks, and stir well together. Pour back into the bulk of the stock, and stir over gentle heat until the stock thickens. Do not let it boil.

salt and freshly ground pepper
1 x 15 ml spoon each of finely chopped parsley and chervil

Season to taste and garnish with herbs.

POULET A L'ESTRAGON
The tarragon chicken recipe which has become so famous is a poached chicken served cold with a cold tarragon and cream sauce made with some of the poaching stock and wine. This version, which comes from the Franche-Comté, braises the bird instead of poaches it, and is served hot.

FRANCE

SERVES 4

1 x 1.75 kg chicken
½ lemon
salt and freshly ground pepper

Wipe the outside and inside of the chicken with the lemon, and season to taste with salt and pepper.

25 g fresh tarragon leaves

Cut finely, and place all but 1 x 15 ml spoon of it inside the bird.

75 g butter

Place 25 g inside the bird, and melt the remainder in a deep casserole. Brown the chicken all over in the casserole.

200 ml Chicken Stock (see page 315)
200 ml white wine

Add to the casserole, then cover tightly and simmer slowly for about 45 minutes, or until the chicken is thoroughly cooked. If necessary, add more chicken stock to the sauce. Remove from the casserole, and discard the tarragon from the cavity. Leave to rest for a few minutes before cutting into serving pieces. Keep warm.
   Blot any fat off the juices in the casserole, using kitchen paper.

200 ml double cream

Stir into the pale, degreased chicken juices, and simmer to reduce by half. Taste for seasoning, then stir in the remaining tarragon and pour over the chicken. Serve hot.

CHICKEN WITH ALMONDS
To the Chinese, chicken is the 'pig of the poultry world', and it is cooked in innumerable ways, not least for soup stocks. This is a Cantonese dish, which is popular in Hong Kong.

CHINA

SERVES 4

400 g white chicken meat	Cut into strips about 1 cm wide and 3–5 cm long.
1 x 15 ml spoon peanut oil	Heat in a wok, and stir-fry the chicken strips for a few minutes.
2 celery stalks, finely sliced 50 g bamboo shoots, diced 50 g water chestnuts, sliced 1 medium onion, peeled and finely chopped salt	Add to the wok, along with salt to taste, and stir-fry for a few minutes longer.
200 ml Brown Chicken Stock (see page 316)	Add to the wok, bring to the boil, then cover and simmer for a few minutes.
1 x 15 ml spoon oyster sauce 2 x 15 ml spoons light soy sauce 1 x 15 ml cornflour mixed with 50 ml water	Mix together, then add to the wok. Cook for a few minutes longer to thicken the sauce.
80 g split almonds, toasted 1 x 5 ml spoon sesame oil	Add to the wok, and stir in, then serve hot with fried or steamed rice.

STEAMED CHICKEN WITH SESAME SAUCE
This sesame sauce, often augmented by garlic, ginger and spring onions, is also used with green beans or cold cooked noodles. Sesame paste is different from tahina, in that it is made from untoasted seeds.

JAPAN

SERVES 4

8 chicken thighs, boned	Score the skin side of the meat fairly deeply. Arrange skin side up in the top of a steamer pan.
6 x 15 ml spoons sake (Japanese rice wine) salt	Sprinkle over the chicken and season to taste with salt. Place the steamer over the pan of hot water, cover and steam for 15–20 minutes, over a high heat. Allow the chicken to cool to room temperature then refrigerate.
2 x 15 ml spoons white sesame paste, or white sesame seeds, ground 2 x 15 ml spoons dashi or Brown Chicken Stock (see pages 87 or 316) 1 x 15 ml spoon dark soy sauce ½ x 15 ml spoon lemon juice ¼ x 5 ml spoon caster sugar	For the sauce, mix together until smooth, seasoning with ¼ x 5 ml spoon salt. Cut the chicken into 7–8 cm slices, discarding the bones and skin. Arrange on individual plates and top with the sesame sauce. Serve.

Chicken and Dried Fruit Tajine

CHICKEN AND DRIED FRUIT TAJINE
Tajine is the name of both the earthenware dish with pointed lid and the stew which is served in it. The combination of meat with sweet ingredients – here the dried fruit and honey – is common in many Moroccan recipes, as well as further north and east, in Iran and other countries of the Middle East. Serve with bread, rice or couscous (see page 90).

MOROCCO

1 x 1.6 kg chicken, cut into pieces
1 lemon, halved
salt and freshly ground pepper

2 medium onions, peeled and very
 finely chopped
1 garlic clove, peeled and finely
 chopped
½ x 5 ml each of powdered saffron
 and ground cumin
olive oil

SERVES 4

Wipe the chicken pieces with the cut lemon halves, and then season with salt and pepper. Place in a dish in one layer.

Mix together, adding 2 x 15 ml spoons olive oil and the juice from the lemon halves. Pour over the chicken, mix to coat thoroughly, and leave to marinate for about an hour in a cool place.
 Heat the marinade oil (or more if needed) in a frying pan and fry the chicken pieces, onion and garlic until golden. Place in a large saucepan.

Green Chicken Curry (see page 192).

1 cinnamon stick
1 strip lemon peel
Brown Chicken Stock (see page 316)

Add to the pan, using just enough chicken stock to cover the chicken, then bring to the boil. Lower the heat, cover the pan, and simmer for 45 minutes, or until the chicken is tender. Remove from the pan and keep warm.

200 g prunes, dried apricots or dried dates, halved and stoned
3 x 15 ml spoons clear honey

Add to the saucepan, and simmer for a further 15 minutes, uncovered. Strain out the dried fruit and add to the chicken. Reduce the liquid to a coating consistency. Return the chicken and dried fruit to the sauce and reheat together.

2 x 15 ml spoons finely chopped fresh coriander
1 x 15 ml spoon flaked almonds, sautéed in a little butter

Use to garnish the chicken and fruit.

GREEN CHICKEN CURRY
One of the classics of Thai cooking, using a green curry paste the colour (and heat) of which results from the use of fresh green chillies and coriander. For authenticity, use the washed stems and roots of the coriander as well as the leaves. (Photograph page 191)

THAILAND

SERVES 4

400 g chicken thighs, skinned
vegetable oil

Fry the chicken thighs in 1 x 15 ml spoon of the oil over a fairly high heat until golden brown. Remove chicken from the pan.

6 fresh green chillies, seeded and
    sliced
3 x 15 ml spoons chopped fresh
    coriander
2 stalks fresh lemongrass, dry outer
    husk discarded, sliced
6 spring onions, trimmed and sliced
4 garlic cloves, peeled
2.5 cm piece of fresh root ginger
2 x 5 ml spoons ground cumin
1 x 5 ml spoon each of coriander
    seeds and black peppercorns, toasted and
    ground
1 lime (or lemon)

For the green curry paste, mix all the ingredients together in a blender, adding about half the pared rind of the lime (or lemon), and as much juice as will help the mixture to become paste-like.

    Heat 1 x 15 ml spoon oil in a casserole and add the green curry paste. Simmer for 2–3 minutes, then add the chicken, and simmer for 4–5 minutes.

450 ml coconut milk, mixed with a
    little cornflour
6 kaffir lime leaves (or a few extra
    stalks of lemongrass)
salt

Add to the casserole, seasoning to taste with salt. Cover with a lid and simmer on top of the stove until the chicken is tender, about 45 minutes. Serve on Thai sticky or fragrant rice, scattered with roughly torn coriander leaves.

CHICKEN TIKKA
Nothing at home can quite substitute for the high and dry heat of the tandoor oven, but grilling chicken tikka is nearly as effective. Eat the chicken pieces as a starter, or on Naan bread (see page 259), with diced fresh vegetables and herbs, as a main course or snack.

INDIA

SERVES 4

4 large chicken breasts

Skin, cut out any bone, and cut into 2.5 cm pieces. Place in a dish.

juice of 2 lemons
salt

Sprinkle over the chicken pieces, seasoning to taste with salt.

100 g natural yoghurt
25 g chilli paste
1 x 5 ml spoon each of ground
    coriander and garam masala
1 x 5 ml spoon each of crushed garlic
    and freshly chopped root ginger
½ x 5 ml spoon turmeric

Mix together, along with a pinch of salt, and then pour over the chicken in the dish. Mix well, and leave to marinate for 2 hours.
    To cook, brush off most of the marinade and place the meat on skewers.

50 ml vegetable oil

Brush over the meat, and place on a piece of foil on a grill rack. Grill under a hot grill until tender, about 10 minutes, turning once.

2 lemons, halved

Use as a garnish.

DRUNKEN CHICKEN
'Drunken' in Chinese culinary terms usually means that the food has been cooked in or sauced by wine. Here, in a Pekingese dish, the local shaohsing wine is used in a marinade. It is an unusual dish in that it is served cold.

CHINA

SERVES 4

1 chicken, about 1.5 kg in weight

Clean well, then blanch in boiling water. Rinse in cold water and place in a clean pan. Cover with fresh cold water.

4 spring onions, cut
5 cm piece of fresh root ginger, sliced
1 x 5 ml spoon Sichuan peppercorns
2 star anise
salt

Add to the water, bring to the boil, then reduce the heat, cover and simmer for about 35 minutes. Leave the chicken to cool in the stock (retain for another use). Cut the chicken into small pieces and arrange in a dish, skin side down.

2 x 15 ml spoons dark soy sauce
1 x 15 ml spoon soft brown sugar
100 ml shaohsing (yellow rice wine) or
    sherry

Heat together to melt the sugar, then pour over the chicken. Leave to marinate in a cool place for several hours. Drain well.

4 spring onions, finely cut

Sprinkle over the chicken and serve cold.

CHICKEN POLO
A lamb *polo* can be made in much the same way. Interestingly, a Moghul *biriani* from the north of India, not too far distant from Iran, is very similar in concept, using Indian spices instead of the dried fruit. The *polos* of Iran are related to the *pilavs* of Turkey and *pullaos* of India.

IRAN

SERVES 4

1 x 1.5 kg chicken

Clean and cut into 8 serving pieces.

olive oil
1 onion, peeled and finely chopped

Heat 2 x 15 ml spoons oil in a pan and lightly brown the onion and chicken pieces. Place in a saucepan.

Brown Chicken Stock (see page 316)

Pour in enough to cover the chicken, and bring to the boil.

½ x 5 ml spoon each of ground
    cumin, cardamom and cinnamon
salt and freshly ground pepper

Add to the pan, seasoning to taste with salt and pepper, then cover and simmer for about 20–30 minutes, or until the chicken is tender. Remove the chicken pieces from the stock, and bone them. Keep warm.

200 g basmati rice

Prepare and cook in the boiling stock as for Chelo, using reduced quantities in proportion (see page 92), but do not steam. Strain, reserving the stock.

60 g butter, melted

Place in the bottom of a large pan or casserole (or use 60 ml olive oil), along with 2 x 15 ml spoons of the reserved stock. Add a layer of part-cooked rice.

120 g dried apricots, soaked in 2 x 15
    ml spoons white wine, quartered
2 x 15 ml spoons raisins
2 x 15 ml spoons pine kernels, lightly
    toasted

Add on top of the rice. Top with the chicken pieces, and cover with the remainder of the rice. Sprinkle over 90 ml of the reserved stock, cover with a cloth and the lid, and steam over a very, very low heat for about 30 minutes. Adjust seasoning. Serve hot.

SINGAPORE SATAY

Skewers of marinated, aromatically seasoned poultry, meat or seafood are common to many cuisines in South-East Asia. Satays are generally grilled over charcoal and served with a peanut sauce (see page 313). To prevent the bamboo or wooden skewers from burning, soak them in water for about an hour before threading on the meat and cooking it. (Photograph page 195)

SINGAPORE   **SERVES 4**

500 g boneless chicken (beef, pork or prawns)
Cut into thin slices, approximately 2 cm wide by 4 cm long.

1 x 5 ml spoon each of coriander and cumin seeds
2 garlic cloves, peeled and crushed
4 slices fresh root ginger, peeled
1 fresh red chilli pepper, seeded and sliced
1 x 15 ml spoon curry powder
1 x 5 ml spoon turmeric
salt to taste
1 x 5 ml spoon clear honey
1 x 15 ml spoon light soy sauce
3 x 15 ml spoons corn oil
Pound together to a paste, or process in a spice mill. Pour over the chicken pieces and leave to marinate for 2 hours in a cool place.
Thread the chicken pieces on to soaked wooden skewers and grill over charcoal, or under a preheated grill, turning occasionally and brushing with the remaining marinade, until cooked, about 5 minutes.

Peanut Satay Sauce (see page 313)
Serve warm with the satay, which are dipped into the sauce.

PAPER-WRAPPED CHICKEN

This dish from the Shanghai area sometimes includes ham, and the vegetables can be varied too, of course. The paper envelopes are usually deep-fried, but can be oven-baked just as successfully. Break open the envelopes with chopsticks. (Photograph page 194)

CHINA   **SERVES 4**   **OVEN: 200°C/400°F/GAS 6**

2 chicken breasts
Skin, and cut the flesh into thin strips. Place in a bowl.

1 x 15 ml spoon each of diced fresh root ginger and garlic
2 x 15 ml spoons oyster sauce
1 x 15 ml spoon each of light soy sauce and shaohsing (yellow rice wine) or sherry
1 x 5 ml spoon cornflour
Add to the bowl. Mix and then leave the chicken to marinate for 1 hour.

1 red onion, peeled
1 yellow and 1 red pepper, seeded
Cut in strips roughly the same size as the chicken strips.

225 g baby bok choy
120 g baby sweetcorn
1 bunch spring onions
Split both bok choy and sweetcorns in half lengthways. Cut the spring onions into 5 cm lengths.
Cut four greaseproof or waxed paper sheets, about 30 cm square. Place on a flat surface, and put a quarter of the chicken, marinade and vegetables on one side of the square.

Previous pages: Above left, Yakitori (see page 197). Below left, Paper-wrapped Chicken. Right, Singapore Satay.

sesame oil
oyster sauce
salt and freshly ground pepper

Season with oil, sauce, salt and pepper to taste. Fold the paper up to cover the filling, as if making an envelope, tucking the last flap in. Tie with string if you like into a loose parcel. Place the four parcels on a greased baking sheet and brush with some oil. Bake in the preheated oven for 10–12 minutes until the chicken and vegetables are cooked. Serve hot in the parcels.

YAKITORI
Yakitori and *teriyaki* are grilling and barbecuing techniques: the meat is basted with the sauce during grilling so that it acquires a rich, dark glaze. Many *yakitori* recipes add chicken livers, squares of green pepper and pieces of onion as well. (Photograph page 194)

JAPAN

SERVES 4

800 g boned chicken meat (breast or thigh)

Skin, then cut the meat into 2 cm cubes. Thread on to long bamboo skewers that have been soaked in water.

120 ml sake (Japanese rice wine)
120 ml *mirin* (Japanese sherry)
120 ml *shoyu* (Japanese soy sauce)
1 x 15 ml spoon caster sugar

Mix together in a small saucepan, and bring to the boil. Simmer until the sugar has dissolved. Cool a little.
　　Brush the sauce thoroughly over the chicken skewers. Grill the chicken over charcoal or under a grill, turning once or twice and basting constantly, until cooked and richly dark and glossy from the sauce, about 8–10 minutes.

POLLO ALLA ROMANA
'*Alla romana*' means 'in the style of Rome' literally, but also 'with peppers' in Italian culinary language. Sometimes a little ham is added as well. This is one of the recipes I encountered when I worked in Rome, my first job away from Switzerland.

ITALY

SERVES 4　　　　**OVEN: 180°C/350°F/GAS 4**

1 chicken, about 1.5 kg

Clean thoroughly and cut into 8 portions.

40 ml olive oil

Melt in a suitable casserole, and sauté the chicken pieces until turning golden on all sides.

50 g onions, peeled and sliced
1 garlic clove, peeled and crushed
100 g button mushrooms, cleaned

Add to the casserole, and sauté for a few minutes.

100 g each of red, green and yellow pepper, seeded and quartered
200 g tomatoes, seeded and diced
200 ml dry white wine
600 ml Brown Chicken Stock (see page 316)
salt and freshly ground pepper

Add to the casserole, seasoning to taste with salt and pepper. Bring to the boil.

2 sprigs fresh rosemary
1 sprig fresh thyme or marjoram
4 fresh basil leaves

Add to the casserole, cover with the lid, and cook in the preheated oven for 10 minutes. Remove the chicken and vegetables from the liquid and keep warm. Reduce the liquid by about one-third to a good sauce consistency. Return the chicken to the sauce, then adjust the seasoning.

2 x 15 ml spoons finely chopped fresh parsley

Sprinkle over the chicken, and serve immediately. Serve with freshly cooked noodles.

SICHWAN DUCK WITH GREEN BEANS
The province of Sichwan (Szechwan) lies in Central China, in the upper basin of the Yangtze River, and its cuisine's principal characteristic is chilli heat. The bean paste here, which is much used in the area, can also be found as chilli bean paste.

CHINA

SERVES 4

4 duck breasts

Thinly slice, then place in a dish.

2 x 15 ml spoons light soy sauce
1 x 15 ml spoon shaohsing (yellow rice wine) or sherry
1 x 5 ml spoon cornflour
a pinch of sugar

Mix together, then pour into the dish with the duck. Marinate for about 30–40 minutes.

2 x 15 ml spoons vegetable oil
2 shallots, peeled and finely chopped
2 garlic cloves, peeled and crushed
5 cm piece of fresh root ginger, peeled and finely chopped
2–4 fresh red chilli peppers, seeded and sliced

Heat the oil, the shallots, garlic, ginger and chilli in a wok or large frying pan, and stir-fry for 30 seconds before adding the duck slices. Stir-fry for 3–5 minutes, then remove the duck to a bowl and set aside.

| 2 x 15 ml spoons spicy brown bean paste | Add to the vegetables in the wok and stir-fry for 30 seconds. |
| 350 g mixed green beans
salt and freshly ground pepper | Prepare and chop as appropriate, then add to the wok. Stir to coat the beans with sauce, then add a little water. Cover and cook for about 5 minutes.
Return the duck to the wok and continue cooking until most of the moisture has been absorbed and the duck and beans are cooked. Serve hot with rice. Adjust seasoning. |

TURKEY IN CHILLI AND CHOCOLATE SAUCE *Mole poblano* of turkey is virtually

Mexico's national dish, and is said to have been created by the nuns of Puebla, the gastronomic centre of Mexico. Traditionally the pre-cooked turkey is simmered for a while in the sauce; here it is simply coated with the sauce. Use a variety of chillies if you can: *mulatos, anchos, pasillas* and *chipotles*.

MEXICO   **SERVES 4**   **OVEN: 180°C/350°F/GAS 4**

750 g boneless turkey breast salt and freshly ground pepper vegetable oil	Sprinkle the turkey with seasonings and a little oil, and roast in the preheated oven for about 40 minutes, or until cooked and golden. Keep warm.
6 small dried chilli peppers (see above) 3 cloves 1 small piece cinnamon stick 1 x 5 ml spoon each of coriander and anise seeds	Meanwhile, start the sauce. Toast in a dry pan to release the spice aromas, then cover with 350 ml boiling water. Leave to soak for 1 hour. Strain thoroughly, reserving the soaking water. Discard all the spices except for the chillies. Remove and discard as many of their seeds as you can.
50 g sesame seeds 50 g blanched almonds	Toast in a dry pan for a few seconds only. Place in a food processor.
50 g raisins	Cook in about 1 x 15 ml spoon of oil for a few minutes. Remove, using a slotted spoon, and place in the processor.
1 onion, peeled and roughly cut 1 garlic clove, peeled and crushed 2½ x 15 ml spoons Tomates Concassées (see page 312)	Place in the processor with the seeded soaked chillies, and blend until smooth. If too thick to blend well, add some of the chilli and spice soaking water. Heat 2 x 15 ml spoons oil in a frying pan and add the chilli mixture. Simmer until it is hot.
50 g Mexican or dark bitter chocolate	Chop into small pieces, then melt into the sauce.
250 ml Brown Chicken Stock (see page 316)	Stir into the sauce, a little at a time, until the consistency is correct. Season to taste with salt and pepper. Slice the turkey breast, and divide between the serving plates, or arrange on one large platter. Coat with the sauce.
1 x 15 ml spoon finely cut fresh coriander	Use as a garnish. Serve with rice.

PEKING DUCK

Perhaps the most famous Chinese dish of all, which comes from the Peking or Beijing in the north-east. Choose duck as near to the special Peking one as possible – with a very meaty breast. The pancakes may be made in advance, interleaved with paper or clingfilm and frozen, then steamed to reheat.

CHINA **SERVES 4** **OVEN: 200°C/400°F/GAS 6**

1 x 2 kg duck, cleaned

Immerse in boiling water, or pour boiling water over. Drain and dry very well. Hang up in an airy place to drip and dry overnight.

1 x 15 ml spoon soft brown sugar
   or honey
1 x 5 ml spoon each of salt and
   five-spice powder
270 ml warm water

Mix together and brush over the duck. Hang again to dry – or use a hairdrier if time is short!
   Roast the duck in the preheated oven for 1½ hours on a rack over a roasting tin of water. Brush with the marinade every 15 minutes or so.

450 g plain flour
1 x 5 ml spoon salt
350–375 ml boiling water

For the pancakes, sift the flour and salt into a bowl, and very carefully mix in the boiling water.

sesame oil
plain flour for dusting

Add 2 x 5 ml spoons oil to the flour and water mix, and stir together well. When dough is cool enough to handle, knead on a lightly floured surface until firm, then divide into three equal portions. Roll each into a sausage, then cut into eight equal slices. Pat each of these out to a flat disc. Brush a little sesame oil over one side of each disc, then press two oiled sides together to make a 'sandwich' (12 in all). Roll these out to very thin pancakes of about 15 cm in diameter. Cook on both sides of 'sandwich' in a very hot, ungreased pan or griddle, until brown spots show on the cooked surface. Remove from the heat, carefully separate the two layers of each pancake (24 in all) and store under a damp cloth until needed.

2 x 15 ml spoons caster sugar
4 x 15 ml spoons sweet bean paste
125 ml water

For the sauce, mix together in a small pan, along with 2 x 15 ml spoons sesame oil, and heat gently to melt the sugar. Place in a small dish. (You could use bought plum or hoisin sauce instead of this home-made version.)

12 spring onions, trimmed
½ cucumber

Cut into very thin strips of about 5 cm in length. Place in a small dish.
   When the duck is cooked, rest, then carve and cut and shred into small pieces. Place on a platter. Heat the pancakes through in a steamer. The sauce is spread on a pancake, then topped with a little greenery, then some duck and skin. The pancake is rolled up and eaten in the hands.

CONFIT DE CANARD

Confit, 'preserve' of duck or goose, refers to a meat that has been cooked in its own fat, then stored in that fat to keep out the air. It is a speciality of South-West France, and evolved as a way of using the birds which had been fattened for *foie gras*.

FRANCE **SERVES 4**

8 duck legs
50 g coarse salt
3 x 5 ml spoons freshly ground black
   pepper
4 dried bay leaves, crumbled
6 sprigs dried thyme
4 cloves
freshly grated nutmeg

Place in a bowl, and mix together, separating the thyme leaves from the stalks, and seasoning to taste with nutmeg. Cover and leave in a cool place for 8–10 hours. Turn the pieces occasionally.
   The next day, wipe the duck legs free of spices and herbs and place in a deep casserole large enough to hold the legs in one layer.

at least 1 kg duck or goose fat
1 fresh bay leaf
4 sprigs fresh thyme
4 sprigs fresh rosemary

Heat together in a pan to melt the fat, then pour over the duck legs which should be covered by the fat. Bring to the boil, then cover and simmer very, very slowly for 1–1½ hours until the duck is very tender.

Have ready two smallish jars (each should hold 4 duck legs). Wash and dry thoroughly, then strain in a layer of fat. Chill until set, then add 4 duck legs to each (bone first if you like). Strain in enough fat to cover the legs completely, then tap to get rid of any air holes. Chill to set, then cover the top with clingfilm or foil. Store for at least a week before use, in a cool place.

To use, stand the jar in hot water until the fat liquifies and the legs can be extracted. Wipe and use them in a cassoulet (see page 173), or dry-fry until crisp and use in a salad.

FAISINJAN

This special-occasion stew, or *khoresh*, is typical of Iran, with a sauce thickened by ground nuts and soured by pomegranate juice, to be eaten with Chelo (see page 92). It could be made with chicken or lamb as well. Dried barberries could replace the pomegranate: soak in hot water until plump. (Photograph page 202)

IRAN

SERVES 4

1 duck

Cut into 8 serving pieces.

150–200 g shelled walnuts

Skin and then grind roughly, reserving a few whole for garnish.

60 g butter
1 onion, peeled and chopped

Heat half the butter in a casserole, add the onion, and sweat until it is golden, about 5 minutes.

600 ml Brown Chicken or Beef Stock (see page 316)
150 ml pomegranate juice (squeezed from fresh fruit)
juice of ½ lemon
½ x 5 ml spoon turmeric
salt and freshly ground pepper

Add to the onion in the casserole, along with the ground walnuts, and stir together to make a thick sauce, seasoning to taste with salt and pepper. Simmer uncovered for 15 minutes.

Meanwhile, sauté the duck pieces on both sides in the remaining butter until golden and nearly cooked, about 5 minutes. Add the duck, boned if you wish, to the sauce, and simmer for 10–15 minutes.

caster sugar (optional)

Add to taste, depending on how sour the pomegranates were.

Arrange the duck pieces on a platter on top of rice, with a little of the sauce poured over. Serve the remaining sauce separately.

seeds of 1 pomegranate

Sprinkle over the duck and rice, along with the reserved walnuts, roughly chopped.

Overleaf: Above left, Faisinjan. Below left, Partridges with Lardons and Grapes (see page 204). Right, Breast of Grouse with Grouse Sausage (see page 205).

PARTRIDGES WITH LARDONS AND GRAPES

Grapes from the vineyards of the Loire are often used in recipes for duck as well as in recipes for game birds such as pigeon or partridge. A white muscatel or large seedless grape would be good. (Photograph page 202)

FRANCE   **SERVES 4**   **OVEN: 230°C/450°F/GAS 8**

4 partridges, cleaned
salt and freshly ground pepper
1 x 15 ml spoon vegetable oil

Season the birds well and rub with the oil.

12 rashers streaky bacon (optional)

If the birds are not already dressed with a covering of barding fat, tie on the bacon. Place the birds on one side in a roasting tin.

8 button onions, peeled and blanched
    for 5 minutes

Dry well, then add to the roasting tin. Place the tin in the preheated oven and roast for 3 minutes before turning the birds on to their other sides, for another 6 minutes. Remove from the oven and remove the bacon. Baste birds and onions and continue to roast for a further 3–4 minutes or until golden brown or done to your liking. Remove the birds and onions to a serving dish and keep warm. Spoon out any excess fat from the roasting tin.

120 ml red wine
250 ml Game or Brown Chicken Stock
    (see page 316)

Pour into the roasting tin and stir well, scraping up any residue from the tin. Simmer to reduce by half. Season to taste with salt and pepper.

cornflour (optional)

Use a little to thicken the sauce if necessary.

25 g butter
120 g lean bacon, cut into lardons and
    blanched

Heat together in a frying pan, and sauté until the lardons are golden.

50 g seedless grapes, peeled
1 x 15 ml spoon chopped fresh parsley

Add to the lardon pan, heat through briefly, then sprinkle over the partridges. Serve with the sauce.

BREAST OF GROUSE WITH GROUSE SAUSAGE

A roast fresh grouse is perfection to me, and it is a seasonal treat I look forward to each year, but this dish is one I evolved for the weeks following the Glorious Twelfth. (Photograph page 203)

GREAT BRITAIN

SERVES 4   OVEN: 220°C/425°F/GAS 7

4 grouse	Clean the birds, and carefully cut off the breast and legs. Set aside in a cool place. Use the carcasses to make a Game Stock (see page 316). When the stock is ready, boil in a clean pan to reduce to about 200 ml. Reserve.
50 g duck leg meat 30 g pork back fat	Finely mince along with the leg meat of the grouse (of which you need about 250 g). Place in a bowl.
30 g fresh white breadcrumbs 12 juniper berries, finely diced 1 x 15 ml spoon finely chopped fresh herbs (parsley, rosemary, thyme) 4 eggs salt and freshly ground pepper	Add to the bowl and mix, binding together with the egg. Season well with salt and pepper to taste. Divide into 4 even balls and roll each ball into a sausage shape.
4 sage leaves	Place a leaf on top of each sausage.
50 g pork caul fat, washed well and cut into 4 pieces	Wrap each sausage and its leaf in a piece of the caul.
50 ml peanut oil 50 g butter	Melt in a sauté pan and colour the sausages evenly all over. Transfer to a roasting tin, and place in the preheated oven. Season the grouse breasts well, and sear on both sides in the remaining butter and oil. Add to the sausages in the oven and roast for 2–3 minutes, basting constantly. (The sausages should have 8–10 minutes in the oven altogether.) Remove both from the oven and the tin, and keep warm. Discard any fat from both sauté pan and roasting tin.
175 ml red wine	Use to deglaze the sauté pan and then the roasting tin, incorporating any meat juices. Boil to reduce, then add the reserved reduced stock. Simmer together to reduce a little more, then strain and season with salt and pepper to taste.
Creamed Cabbage (see page 53)	Divide between four warmed plates, and arrange the breasts and sausages on top or alongside. Serve with the sauce and some game chips if you like.

ROAST SCOTTISH GROUSE

A particular and unique seasonal joy of the late British summer occurs on and after the 12th of August, the 'Glorious Twelfth', when the grouse shooting season begins. There are several varieties of grouse throughout Europe, but the red grouse (*Lagopus lagopus scoticus*) is only found in Scotland, Ireland, and some northern parts of England and Wales.

SCOTLAND · SERVES 4 · OVEN: 230°C/450°F/GAS 8

4 young Scottish grouse, about 450 g each, hung for 2–3 days and cleaned	Wipe the grouse inside and out, and then season inside and out.
50 g butter 1 x 15 ml spoon sour berries (cranberries, bilberries)	This is optional. Crush together and divide between the insides of the birds.
80 g barding fat, cut into thin slices	Tie over the breasts of the birds.
100 ml peanut oil	Heat until very hot in a suitable roasting tin, and place the grouse in on one side. Sauté for a few minutes, then turn on to the other side to sauté for a few minutes more.
100 g fine *mirepoix* (finely diced carrot, onion and turnip)	Add to the roasting tin, and mix to coat with the fat. Turn the birds on their backs, breasts up, and sit on top of the *mirepoix*. Place in the preheated oven and roast for about 8 minutes. Remove from the oven, take the birds out of the tin, and keep warm. Pour the excess fat out of the tin.
175 ml red wine	Add to the cooking juices and *mirepoix* in the tin, and boil to reduce.
400 ml Game or Brown Chicken Stock (see page 316)	Add to the tin and boil to reduce to the required consistency. Season with salt and pepper, strain, then keep warm. Discard the *mirepoix*. Remove the barding fat from the grouse and return them to the hot oven to brown the breasts a little, another 5–8 minutes.
4 bread croûtes (spread with the mashed cooked livers if you like) browned breadcrumbs bread sauce or a berry jelly or sauce	Use to garnish the grouse. Serve the sauce separately.

RABBIT COOKED WITH MUSTARD

This is a fairly simple way of cooking rabbit with mustard, bacon and onion, and garnished with croûtes. Elsewhere in France rabbit is braised with prunes, apples, raisins, green almonds or apricots, and in Normandy the liquid used can be cider instead of wine.

FRANCE · SERVES 4 · OVEN: 160°C/325°F/GAS 3

1 rabbit, cleaned, about 2 kg	Cut into neat pieces, and wipe clean.
French mustard	Coat the dried pieces well with mustard and leave in a bowl overnight in a cool place.
plain flour salt and freshly ground pepper	Season the flour with some salt and pepper and dip the mustardy rabbit pieces into this.

2 x 15 ml spoons olive oil	Heat in a large casserole and fry the coated rabbit pieces until brown all over. Remove and keep to one side.
75 g lean smoked bacon in the piece	Cut the rind off, and cut the flesh into lardons. Fry in the fat remaining in the casserole until golden.
1 medium onion, peeled and finely chopped 1 garlic clove, peeled and crushed	Add to the lardons and sweat for a few minutes to soften.
100 ml each of Chicken Stock (see page 315) and dry white wine	Add to the casserole, along with the rabbit pieces, cover and cook in the preheated oven for 30 minutes.
200 ml crème fraîche	Stir into the juices in the casserole, re-cover and return to the oven for another 45 minutes. Remove from the oven and test for doneness and seasoning.
8 small bread croûtes 2 x 15 ml spoons finely chopped fresh parsley	Use as a garnish, and serve hot with noodles or potatoes.

RAGOUT OF YARRA VALLEY VENISON
Venison is farmed in Australia, in the Yarra Valley, near Melbourne – from where many fine wines come as well. A classic garnish would be local glazed shallots.

AUSTRALIA **SERVES 6** **OVEN: 180°C/350°/GAS 4**

olive oil 50 g lean bacon, diced 100 g button mushrooms, cleaned	Heat about 1 x 15 ml spoon olive oil in a large frying pan and sauté the bacon and mushrooms for 5 minutes. Remove from the pan using a slotted spoon, and reserve to one side. Add a further 100 ml olive oil to the pan and heat.
750 g stewing venison, cut into 5 cm pieces salt and freshly ground pepper	Add to the oil in the pan in batches, and seal until browned, drain well and place in a casserole. Season. Discard excess fat from the frying pan.
300 ml red wine	Add to the frying pan and scrape up all the meat juices. Pour into the casserole.
600 ml Venison Stock (see page 316) 2 medium carrots, peeled and cut into circles 1 onion, peeled and thinly sliced 2 garlic cloves, peeled and crushed 1 bouquet garni (lemon thyme, rosemary, bay)	Add to the casserole, stir, cover with a tight-fitting lid, and stew in the preheated oven for 45 minutes. About 5 minutes before the end of cooking, add and stir in the bacon and mushrooms. Remove the bouquet garni.
juice of ½ lemon 2 x 15 ml spoons soured cream (optional)	Stir into the casserole, seasoning to taste with salt and pepper. Good accompaniments are saffron noodles (see page 106) and glazed shallots.

FISH AND SHELLFISH

CLAM CHOWDER
New England or Boston chowders are divided into three groups according to the liquid used in their cooking: milk or milk and cream chowders, stock chowders, or stock and cream chowders. Manhattan chowders include some tomatoes and some broken cream crackers stirred in at the last moment.

USA

SERVES 4

24 cherrystone clams	Scrub well, and rinse.
750 ml Fish Stock (see page 315)	Place in a large pan and add the clams. Cover the pan and cook over a high heat until all the clams open, about 5–10 minutes. Remove the clams from the stock and leave to cool. Strain the stock through muslin or a fine sieve and reserve. Remove the clams from their shells. Discard any hard tendon, and chop the flesh.
120 g salt pork (or green bacon), soaked, drained and diced	Sauté in a large soup pan to render the fat.
25 g each of diced onion, leek, carrot and celery 1 garlic clove, peeled and crushed	Add to the pan and sauté in the bacon fat until softened, without browning, about 5 minutes.
1 small bay leaf 25 g diced green pepper 100 g potato, peeled and diced	Add, along with the reserved stock, and simmer for about 10 minutes.
1 x 5 ml spoon each of chopped fresh thyme and parsley 4 x 15 ml spoons whipping cream (optional) salt and freshly ground pepper	Add, along with the chopped clams. Remove the bay leaf, and season to taste with salt and pepper. Serve hot.

SWEETCORN AND FINNAN HADDOCK CHOWDER
Finnan haddock is a cold-smoked haddock, the name of which derives from Findon, a fishing village south of Aberdeen. Simple soup-stews are a feature of the cooking all along the east coast; I have added a few little extras.

SCOTLAND

SERVES 4

1 litre Fish Stock (see page 315) 225 g Finnan haddock on the bone	Place the stock in a large saucepan, bring to the boil, then add the haddock. Remove immediately from the heat and leave for 10–15 minutes. Lift the haddock out and when cool enough to handle, remove bones and skin, and flake the flesh.
25 g butter 1 small onion, peeled and finely diced	Heat together in a large saucepan and sweat until the onion is soft, about 5 minutes.
175 g new potatoes, scrubbed and sliced 1 large leek, washed and sliced	Add to the saucepan, stir to coat with the butter, and cook for 3–5 minutes.
2 corn on the cob	Remove the kernels from the cobs and add to the pan.

Sweetcorn and Finnan Haddock Chowder

1 sprig fresh thyme
4 x 15 ml spoons dry white wine

1 x 15 ml spoon finely chopped flat-
   leaf parsley
1 x 15 ml spoon finely cut chives
2 x 15 ml spoons whipping cream
   (optional)
salt and freshly ground pepper

Add to the vegetables in the pan, along with the strained fish stock, and bring to the boil. Simmer gently until the potato is cooked, about 15 minutes.

Just before serving, stir into the hot soup, along with the flaked haddock, seasoning to taste with salt and pepper. Serve hot.

BOUILLABAISSE
This is an adaptation of what must be the most famous of all the French fish soups – a cross between a soup and a stew, emanating from Marseilles where the principal flavourings are saffron, tomatoes and fennel. It is served with Rouille (see page 311), with its pungent flavours of garlic and chilli.

FRANCE   **SERVES 4**

1.25 kg mixed fish (white fish and oily fish)

Clean the fish, scaling, cutting off heads, tails and fins (use to make the stock), and removing innards. Cut the flesh into 5 cm squares, and place in a suitable dish.

juice of 1 lemon
salt and freshly ground black pepper

Add to the fish, to taste, and leave to marinate for a while.

50 g white of leeks
100 g fennel bulb
50 g carrots

Trim or peel, as appropriate, then cut into fine strips.

50 ml olive oil

Heat in a large wide casserole, then sweat the leek, fennel and carrot for 4–5 minutes, stirring constantly.

1 garlic clove, peeled and crushed
a few saffron threads
4 tomatoes, skinned, seeded and diced

Add to the vegetables, and sauté for 3–5 minutes.

120 ml dry white wine
450 ml Fish Stock (see page 315)

Add to the casserole, and bring to the boil. Reduce to a simmer and poach the fish pieces for a few minutes only.

2 x 5 ml spoons Pernod
1 x 15 ml spoon finely cut herbs

Add to the soup, and remove from the heat. Taste and season if necessary.

Rouille (see page 311)

Serve with the hot soup.

BERMUDAN FISH CHOWDER
This fish soup uses many of the fish native to Bermudan water, such as hog fish, rock fish, wahoo, snapper or shark, as well as Bermudan dark rum. If you like it spicier, add more rum and chilli peppers to taste.

BERMUDA   **SERVES 4**

1 kg fresh fish fillets, skinned

Use a mixture of white and oily (the above, or whiting and mackerel, say).

1 green pepper and 1 red pepper, seeded
1 medium leek, trimmed
1 small onion, peeled
100 g carrots, peeled
2 celery stalks, trimmed
2 garlic cloves, peeled
a handful of parsley

Finely dice all the vegetables, including the garlic, and finely chop the parsley.

2 x 15 ml spoons olive oil

Heat in a large pot, add the vegetables and garlic, and sweat until softened, about 5 minutes. Do not colour.

1.5 litres Fish Stock (see page 315)
75 ml Bermuda dark rum
3 small hot fresh chilli peppers,
  seeded and kept whole
1 x 15 ml spoon each of curry powder
  and Worcestershire sauce
100 g Tomates Concassées (see page
  312)
50 g tomatoes, skinned, seeded and
  diced
a pinch of powdered saffron
salt and freshly ground pepper

Add to the pot, seasoning to taste with salt and pepper, then boil to reduce by half.

Add the fish and simmer for 5 minutes. Remove the peppers before serving hot. Sprinkle with the chopped parsley.

HOT AND SOUR PRAWN SOUP
A soup typical of Thailand, chilli-hot (use less if you wish) and fragrant with lemongrass, kaffir lime leaves (available in oriental groceries) and coriander. It would probably be served with rice, the blandness of the grain helping to offset the fieriness of the soup.

THAILAND

SERVES 4

16 green prawns

Shell and devein, leaving the tails in place. Transfer to a large bowl.

3 lemongrass stalks, cut into 5 cm
  lengths
4 kaffir lime leaves

Crush slightly, then add to the prawns.

140 g button mushrooms, sliced
50 ml *nam pla* (fish sauce)
6 spring onions, trimmed and cut into
  5 cm lengths
4–8 small fresh red chilli peppers,
  optionally seeded
juice of 6 limes
2 x 5 ml spoons chilli paste

Add to the prawns, and mix well. Leave to marinate together for about an hour. Remove the prawns.

2 litres Fish or Chicken Stock (see
  page 315)

Bring to the boil in a large saucepan, then add the vegetables and flavourings. Simmer for about 5 minutes, then add the prawns. Simmer until they turn pink.

25 g finely chopped fresh coriander
  leaves
salt and freshly ground pepper

Add to the soup, seasoning to taste, and serve hot.

CHARCOAL-GRILLED SEA BASS WITH FENNEL

The essence of Italian cooking is simplicity, and nothing could be easier than this grilled fish dish. Fennel is said to be *the* fish herb, and all parts of the plant – leaves, stems and seeds – are aromatic, and can be used in cooking.

ITALY

SERVES 4

1 sea bass, approx. 1 kg

Trim the sharp spines and fins. Clean through the gills, then rinse thoroughly until the water runs clear. Dry well.

2 small fennel bulbs

To prepare the stuffing, remove and keep the feathery tops of the bulbs. Cut bulbs in half lengthways, remove and discard hard cores, and finely slice.

2 onions, peeled and finely sliced
50 ml olive oil
salt and freshly ground pepper

Sweat together with the bulb fennel slices in 1 x 15 ml spoon of the olive oil until just tender, then season with salt and pepper. Add the chopped fennel fronds and leave to cool. Spoon and pack the stuffing into the fish through the mouth, or pipe in, using a piping bag.

dried fennel stalks, pounded
½ lemon, zested in strips, and juiced

Place the fish on a suitable tray with the dried pounded fennel stalks, and add 2 large pieces of lemon peel and the lemon juice, along with the remaining oil. Leave to marinate for 2–3 hours. Turn in the marinade every so often.

Brush a wire barbecue rack with oil to prevent sticking, and heat over the barbecue coals. Place the fish on the rack above the grid of the barbecue – the fish must cook slowly, so should not be in direct contact with the heat.

Place the rack on the barbecue and cook for 8 minutes. Turn, then repeat 8 minutes later. After about 20 minutes, check to see if the fish is cooked. If not, cook directly on the barbecue grid for a few more minutes. Just before serving, take the fennel stalks used in the marinade and place them over the barbecue to toast slightly, which brings out their flavour. Place on a platter with the fish on top and take to the table.

100 ml olive oil
4 x 5 ml spoons fennel seeds, slightly crushed

Heat together gently to imbue the oil with the fennel flavour. Just before serving, drizzle a few drops over the fish.

STEAMED SEA BASS

This is probably the most popular way of cooking fish in China, and a whole steamed fish (it could also be a perch, sea bream or garoupa) is treated rather like a roast in the West, something to be carved and shared with family or friends on a special occasion. You will need a large bamboo steamer or a trivet inside a wok or saucepan, or you can steam in a fish poacher.

CHINA

SERVES 4

1 sea bass, about 1 kg, cleaned, but leave head and tail on	With a sharp knife, make four or five diagonal slashes on each side of the fish.
salt	Rub sparingly all over the fish and into the slashes and cavity.
lemon juice soy sauce	Mix together a 15 ml spoon of each, and rub into the slashes in the fish.
4 spring onions 3 garlic cloves 4 slices fresh root ginger, about 5 mm thick	Trim or peel as appropriate, and cut into fine julienne strips. Put a few slivers of each into the slashes in the fish. Reserve the remainder. Place the fish on an oval plate that will fit into the steamer. Place in the steamer over rapidly boiling water and steam for about 10–12 minutes, until the flesh along the backbone is opaque.
2 x 15 ml spoons sesame oil	Heat in a pan and sauté the reserved spring onion, garlic and ginger for about 10 seconds. Remove the fish from the steamer, and spoon the vegetable mixture over it. Serve immediately.

BAKED SARDINES

The sardine is almost as popular in Portugal as salt cod: it is sold plainly grilled by street vendors. Sardines are said to be at their best in the summer months, when they are fat and sweet.

PORTUGAL

SERVES 4   **OVEN: 200°C/400°F/GAS 6**

12 fresh medium sardines salt and freshly ground pepper	Scale, clean and trim. Wash, pat dry, then season to taste with salt and pepper.
50 ml olive oil	Brush a little over a shallow ovenproof dish, and arrange the sardines in it. Place in the preheated oven and bake (no longer than 15 minutes) while you prepare the tomato sauce.
1 small onion, peeled and finely chopped 1 garlic clove, peeled and crushed ½ x 5 ml spoon fennel seeds, crushed	Add to a small pan along with the remaining oil and sweat together until the mixture is soft, about 5 minutes.
200 g tomatoes, skinned, seeded and diced 60 ml white wine	Add to the pan and bring to the boil. Pour over the sardines in the dish and continue cooking in the oven until the sardines are ready, about another 5 minutes.
2 x 15 ml spoons finely chopped fresh parsley 1 x 15 ml spoon finely chopped fresh coriander	Sprinkle over the fish and serve, preferably with boiled potatoes or good country bread.

DACE, ZUG STYLE
The canton of Zug lies in the middle of Switzerland, and it contains many lakes and rivers. Freshwater fish such as dace, *féra* (a member of the salmon family) and *rötel* are great culinary specialities there. You can use perch instead of the dace.

SWITZERLAND　　　　　　　**SERVES 4**　　　**OVEN: 180°C/350°F/GAS 4**

4 small whole dace	Clean and scale, then wash well and dry.
8 sage leaves **10 g plain flour** **salt and freshly ground pepper**	Divide the leaves between the cavities of the fish, then sprinkle with flour and salt and pepper to taste.
butter	Use a little to grease a baking dish large enough to hold the fish in one layer.
4 shallots, peeled and finely chopped **1 clove** **2 bay leaves** **2 x 15 ml spoons finely chopped parsley**	Place in the bottom of the dish and arrange the fish on top. Dot the fish with a few knobs of butter.
150 ml dry white wine **150 ml Fish Stock (see page 315)** **1 x 15 ml spoon lemon juice**	Pour into the dish, then bake in the preheated oven for about 8 minutes. Baste the fish occasionally. Adjust seasoning. Remove skin and serve with the sauce, accompanied by boiled potatoes.

RED SNAPPER WITH FRESH SALSA
The fresh flavours of salsas enhance fish in many Californian recipes, revealing one of the many influences, that of Mexico. Turbot could be served instead of the snapper, although it is not a fish caught in American waters.

USA　　　　　　　　　　**SERVES 4**

2 large ripe tomatoes, skinned and seeded **1 medium onion, peeled** **1 green pepper, seeded** **1–2 fresh green chilli peppers, seeded** **2 garlic cloves, peeled**	To start the salsa, very finely dice all the vegetables. Place together in a large glass bowl.
1 x 15 ml spoon red wine vinegar **2 x 15 ml spoons finely chopped fresh coriander** **Tabasco sauce** **salt and freshly ground pepper**	Add to the vegetables in the bowl, seasoning to taste with Tabasco (only a dash or two), salt and pepper. Cover and chill. Stir occasionally.
4 x 150 g red snapper fillets	Spread a little of the salsa on the base of a heatproof dish, and place the fish fillets on top in one layer.
25 ml olive oil **paprika**	Brush over the fillets, seasoning to taste with paprika, salt and pepper. Grill until cooked, about 6 minutes. There is no need to turn the fish over. Serve the hot fish on a platter with the remaining cold salsa.

CHERMOULA FISH

This classic Moroccan marinade – consisting of garlic, onion, parsley, coriander and an assortment of spices – is delicious with fish, but can also be used for poultry, meat or game; the *chermoulas* for these are usually a little spicier.

MOROCCO

SERVES 4

2 x 15 ml spoons each of finely chopped
fresh parsley and coriander
2 shallots, peeled and finely chopped
1½ x 5 ml spoons each of paprika and
ground cumin
½ x 5 ml spoon chilli powder
3 x 15 ml spoons olive oil
2 x 15 ml spoons lemon juice
salt and freshly ground pepper

Mix together in a dish, seasoning to taste with salt and pepper.

1 x 1 kg fish

Choose from sea bream, sea bass, sea trout or any firm fleshed fish (or smaller fish like mullet). Scale and trim, then cut off the head and tail. Divide into four good steaks (or leave whole, for smaller fish). Place in the dish with the *chermoula* marinade and coat thoroughly. Leave to marinate in a cool place for at least 2 hours.

plain flour

Season with a little salt and pepper to taste. Lift the fish steaks (or fish) from the marinade and dust with the flour on all sides.

vegetable oil

Heat a little in a large frying pan and shallow-fry the fish or steaks until cooked and golden brown, from 5–8 minutes, depending on thickness.

BLACKENED GRILLED SWORDFISH

In the Cajun heartland in the South, there is an abundance of seafood. In true Cajun style, this blackened fish could be served with black beans and rice. Tuna or catfish could be used instead of the swordfish.

USA

SERVES 4

½ x 5 ml spoon each of garlic salt,
onion powder, cayenne pepper,
ground white pepper and black
pepper
¼ x 5 ml spoon each of dried basil,
thyme and sage, well crushed

Mix together and sprinkle evenly over a large flat platter.

4 x 225 g thick swordfish steaks
50 g butter, melted

Brush the steaks on both sides with the melted butter, then dip into the spice and herb mixture. Coat well on both sides.

Grill on a very hot barbecue, close to the coals, for about 5 minutes on each side. Or grill on a very hot ridged cast-iron pan for about 5 minutes on each side.

1 lemon, quartered

Serve with the seared swordfish steaks.

Seared Tuna Niçoise

INSALATA DI TONNO E FAGIOLI This most famous salad links two typical Italian ingredients,
cannellini beans and tuna, but here the tuna is fresh rather than tinned. It goes well with Vitello Tonnato (see page
160). Salads like this are usually served as an antipasto in Italy. (Photograph page 162)

ITALY

1 x 225 g tuna steak
salt and freshly ground pepper

175 g cooked cannellini beans
120 g green beans, trimmed and
    blanched
1 small red onion, peeled and finely
    chopped

4 x 15 ml spoons extra virgin olive oil
3 x 15 ml spoons red wine vinegar
1 x 15 ml spoon finely cut fresh
    chives

SERVES 4

Season the tuna well on both sides with salt and pepper to taste. Heat a
ridged cast-iron grill pan or a heavy frying pan to very hot, and sear the tuna
for 1–2 minutes on each side, depending on thickness. Set aside to cool.

Place together in a bowl and season with salt and pepper to taste. Toss.
Flake the tuna into the mixture.

Add to the bowl and toss together. Taste for seasoning. Chill before serving.

SEARED TUNA NICOISE
Salade Niçoise, a salad made with flaked tuna, green beans, tomatoes, hard-boiled eggs and olives, is a classic Provençal recipe. Here it is given a modern twist with fresh seared tuna steaks.

FRANCE   **SERVES 4**

120 g small new potatoes
salt and freshly ground pepper

Scrub and cook in salted water until tender. Cool, then slice into a bowl.

120 g green beans

Trim as appropriate, and cook in salted water until tender. Refresh in cold water, then cool and place in the bowl with the potatoes.

1 red onion, peeled and finely chopped
2–3 plum tomatoes, quartered
12–15 black olives, pitted
6 anchovy fillets, diced
1 x 15 ml spoon finely cut fresh chives

Add to the potatoes and beans in the bowl.

4 x 15 ml spoons balsamic vinegar
175 ml olive oil

Mix together with salt and pepper to taste, then pour enough into the vegetables to just moisten them. Divide the vegetables between individual plates.

olive oil
4 x 150 g tuna steaks

Heat a very little oil on a ridged cast-iron grill pan, then add the tuna steaks. Cook to medium, about 1 minute per side, but according to thickness.
   Put a seared tuna steak on top of each mound of salad.

2 hard-boiled eggs, quartered

Arrange on top of the fish and salad, and drizzle with a little more dressing.

THAI FISHCAKES
A popular appetiser which contains many characteristic Thai flavours. You can buy commercial red curry paste, or use some of the green chilli paste on page 192, substituting red chillies for the green. Serve the cakes with a tart Cucumber Relish (see page 307).

THAILAND   **MAKES ABOUT 12**

300 g firm white fish fillet, cut into
   pieces
1 x 15 ml spoon red curry paste (see
   above)
1 egg

Place in the food processor and blend well together. Transfer to a bowl.

2 x 15 ml spoons *nam pla* (fish sauce)
1 x 15 ml spoon caster sugar
2 x 15 ml spoons cornflour
3 kaffir lime leaves, shredded
1 x 15 ml spoon finely chopped fresh
   coriander
50 g green beans, topped, tailed and
   finely diced
salt and freshly ground pepper

Add to the bowl and mix together well. Season to taste. Using your hands, mould and shape the mixture into patties about 5 cm in diameter and 2 cm thick.

vegetable oil for deep-frying

Heat in a wok or deep-fryer and sauté the fish cakes, a few at a time, for about 4–5 minutes, turning once, or until golden brown. Remove from the oil and drain well on kitchen paper. Serve hot with cucumber relish.

MOHINGHA
This is the national dish of Burma, and it is very similar to others in South-East Asia, the *khao phoune* of Vietnam, and the *laksa* of Malaysia and the Philippines. Banana tree hearts would traditionally be used, added at the last minute.

BURMA

SERVES 4

400 g oily fish (e.g. mackerel) fillets — Place in a medium pan, and cover with water.

1 lemongrass stalk, sliced
3 x 15 ml spoons *nam pla* (fish sauce)
1 fresh red chilli pepper, seeded and sliced — Add to the water, bring to the boil, and simmer for 10 minutes. Remove the fish and flake. Reserve the stock, and keep both warm.

1 onion, peeled and chopped
1 garlic clove, peeled and crushed
5 cm piece of fresh root ginger, peeled and grated
1 x 15 ml spoon vegetable oil — Heat together in a pan, then sauté until the onion is coloured.

250 ml thick coconut milk
salt and freshly ground pepper — Add to the fragrant stock along with the onion mixture and the flaked fish. Simmer to warm through. Season to taste.

250 g rice vermicelli, soaked in boiling water to soften
25 g beansprouts, soaked in cold water — Drain and add to the soup.

2 limes, halved
2 x 15 ml spoons finely chopped fresh coriander — Serve as garnishes for the hot soup.

GRILLED FISH BALLS
The distinguishing feature of many Laotian dishes is the consistency – fish or poultry is pounded to pastes to use as below or to be scooped into salad leaves.

LAOS

SERVES 4

600 g firm white fish, cut into pieces
5 cm piece of fresh root ginger, peeled
50 g spring onions, sliced
½ fresh green chilli pepper, seeded
½ lemongrass stalk, sliced — Place in the food processor and blend to a smooth paste. Scrape out into a bowl.

120 ml water
salt and freshly ground pepper — Add to the bowl, seasoning to taste with salt and pepper. Form the mixture into small balls. Drop these into lightly salted boiling water and poach until they float. Drain well and thread on to greased wooden skewers.

sesame or vegetable oil — Brush over the balls, and then grill under a conventional grill – or over barbecue coals – until golden.

lemon juice — Sprinkle over the fish balls, and serve them hot with a chilli dipping sauce.

COULIBIAC OF SALMON

Also known as *koulebiaka* and *kulibyaka*, this salmon pie belongs to the same family of pies and pastries which are called *pirogi* when small, *pirozhki* when large. Coulibiac is a 'court' dish, and it is ideal for serving at a large party or buffet.

RUSSIA **SERVES 8** **OVEN: 190°C/375°F/GAS 5**

olive oil
1 small onion, peeled and finely
   chopped

Heat 1 x 15 ml spoon olive oil and the onion together in a casserole, and cook gently for 2 minutes. Do not colour.

165 g long-grain rice
300 ml Fish Stock (see page 315)
1 sprig fresh thyme
1 bay leaf
salt and freshly ground pepper

Stir in, and season to taste with a little salt and pepper. Bring to the boil, then cover with a greased piece of paper. Cook in the preheated oven for about 15 minutes. When ready, transfer the drained rice to a tray, then spread out to cool. Remove the herbs.

150 g button mushrooms, wiped and
   sliced

Meanwhile, fry gently in a further 1 x 15 ml spoon olive oil until almost dry.

50 ml dry white wine
250 ml double cream

Add to the pan and continue to simmer until reduced and thick. Place the rice in a bowl and bind with the mushroom cream mixture.

2 x 15 ml spoons finely cut dill

Stir in, and adjust the seasoning.

1 recipe Brioche dough (see page 262)

Roll out one-third to the size of a baking tray, about 23–25 x 33–35 cm, and about 3 mm thick. Place on the greased *reverse* of the baking tray, the unlipped side.

1 egg, beaten

Brush some over the rolled-out brioche dough.

4 x 20–23 cm round herb Crêpes (see
   page 260)

Arrange two of the pancakes, slightly overlapping, in the centre of the rolled-out brioche. Spread on one-third of the rice mixture, making a neat layer, and leaving a 3 cm border all round.

6 medium-hard boiled eggs, sliced
   thinly
2 x 750 g pieces smoked haddock or
   fresh salmon fillet, skinned and
   boned
fresh dill sprigs

Build up more layers using half of the sliced egg, a piece of fish, and another third of the rice, followed by the second piece of fish, remaining egg and rice. Tuck in the dill sprigs. Cover with the remaining pancakes and fold them neatly under the filling, shaping to make a tidy and firm topping.

Roll out the remaining larger piece of brioche dough to roughly 1½ times the size of the original piece. Brush the edges of the brioche with beaten egg, and lift the top piece with the aid of a rolling pin. Ease it into position, and lightly press all round to seal. Trim the excess pastry at the edges. You can flute the edges with your thumb and forefinger, or simply press with the tines of a fork. Brush all over with egg wash and decorate the top with leftover dough. Bake in the preheated oven for 35–40 minutes until golden brown. Serve immediately.

SMOKED SALMON TORTINO
This pizza-type tart may have an actual pizza dough base, as well as the filo pastry base used here, and the topping ingredients can vary too, often including cheese and tomatoes. The tarts can be eaten hot or at room temperature.

ITALY   **SERVES 4**   **OVEN: 200°C/400°F/GAS 6**

8 large sheets filo pastry
75 g butter, melted

Fold each sheet in half to make two layers, and use two double sheets per tortino. Butter the insides. Place the first doubled filo sheet into a shallow 20 cm tart tin with a removeable base. Brush with melted butter, then top with another doubled sheet of filo and butter that. Do the same with three other tins and the remaining filo sheets.

450 g tomatoes, skinned, seeded, diced and well drained
2 x 5 ml spoons fresh oregano leaves
salt and freshly ground pepper

Divide between the tops of the *tortinos*, then bake in the preheated oven for 5–8 minutes. Remove from the oven. Season lightly.

4 x 15 ml spoons soured cream
320 g smoked salmon, thinly sliced

Divide between the tops of the *tortinos*, and then replace in the oven for 1 minute. Remove from the oven.

a few sprigs of fresh dill
extra virgin olive oil

Sprinkle the top of the *tortinos* with dill, and brush with a little olive oil. Serve immediately.

SALT COD FRITTERS
Little salt cod fritters are popular in some form or other throughout all the West Indian islands. In Jamaica they are known as 'stamp and go': this version, *acrats de morue*, is adopted from the fritters eaten in the French islands of Martinique and Guadaloupe.

CARIBBEAN   **MAKES ABOUT 24**

225 g boneless and skinless salt cod
salt and freshly ground pepper

Cut into 5 cm pieces, and place in a bowl. Cover with cold water and leave to soak for at least 24 hours, changing the water several times. Drain well in a sieve, then place in a pan. Cover with fresh water and simmer for about 15 minutes or until tender. Drain well, then purée in a blender (or pound in a mortar). Season.

60 g plain flour
100 ml milk
1 egg
½ x 5 ml spoon baking powder
¼ x 5 ml spoon ground allspice
1 garlic clove, peeled and minced

Add to the fish in the blender and blend again to a smooth paste. Transfer to a bowl.

3 spring onions, finely diced
1 fresh red chilli pepper, seeded and finely diced
1 x 15 ml spoon finely chopped fresh parsley or coriander

Stir well into the salt cod mixture. Season to taste.

vegetable oil

Pour into a frying pan to a depth of about 4 cm, and heat. Sauté 15 ml spoons of the salt cod mixture until golden on both sides, about 2–3 minutes. Drain very well on kitchen paper and serve hot.

Opposite: Smoked Salmon Tortino.

EMPANADILLAS

These little pasties are popular all over Spain, primarily as a *tapa*, and can be found too in various forms in South America. You can make small pies instead of turnovers, and shortcrust pastry is as effective and traditional as the choux-type pastry used here.

SPAIN   **MAKES ABOUT 20**   **OVEN: 180°C/350°F/GAS 4**

120 ml water 1½ x 15 ml spoons vegetable oil 20 g butter salt and freshly ground pepper	To make the pastry, combine in a pan, adding a pinch of salt, and simmer over a medium heat, stirring, until the butter melts. Remove from the heat.
150 g plain flour	Pour into the hot mixture and stir until completely blended.
1 egg, beaten	Pour half into the dough, and mix in well. Place the dough on a lightly floured board and, when cool enough to handle, knead until smooth and elastic, a few minutes. Cover and leave to stand for about 30 minutes at room temperature.
½ x 15 ml spoon olive oil 1 small onion, peeled and diced	Heat together in a sauté pan and sauté until the onion is transparent.

100 g tuna in oil, drained and flaked
about 2 x 15 ml spoons Tomato Sauce
   (see page 311)
½ red pepper, seeded and finely
   diced
2 x 15 ml spoons finely chopped parsley
	Add to the onion in the pan, with some salt and pepper to taste, and cook for 10 minutes, stirring occasionally. Leave to cool.

1 small egg, hard-boiled and finely diced	Roll the dough out thinly and cut into 7.5 cm circles. Place 2–3 x 5 ml spoons of the filling on each circle of pastry and fold one-half over to meet the other – or fold the edges up to make a tricorne shape. Use water to moisten the edges, then seal firmly by crimping or pressing with a fork. Place on a baking sheet and bake in the preheated oven for about 30 minutes or until golden brown. You could brush them first with the remaining beaten egg if you like. These little pasties are delicious, if not very traditional, served with a chilli pepper salsa – perhaps *piri-piri*, Portugal's best-loved sauce.

CRAB CAKES
Many different types of crab are native to the USA, but the Maryland blue crab, coming from the nutrient-rich waters of the Chesapeake Bay, the largest estuary in the USA, is perhaps the best known. This recipe is also from the east coast.

USA

SERVES 4

50 g celery, trimmed 50 g onion, peeled vegetable oil	Very finely dice the celery and onion, then sauté briefly in 1 x 15 ml spoon oil. Cool a little.
500 g fresh crab meat, white and brown	Make absolutely sure there are no bits of shell, then mix the crab meat with the onion and celery in a large bowl.
50 ml mayonnaise 2 x 15 ml spoons finely chopped fresh parsley 2 x 15 ml spoons melted butter a dash each of Worcestershire and Tabasco sauces salt and freshly ground pepper	Mix into the crab, seasoning to taste with salt and pepper.
fine white breadcrumbs	Mix enough into the crab mixture to hold it together. Form the mixture into thinnish cakes up to 6 cm in diameter, and shallow-fry in hot oil until browned on both sides. Drain very well on kitchen paper.
1 lemon, quartered	Use to garnish the crab cakes.

FISHCAKES WITH PARSLEY SAUCE
The traditional British fishcake is usually made from a mixture of mashed potato and flaked cooked fish, and served with a white sauce flecked with parsley. I have raised the profile of both cake and sauce slightly. (Photograph page 227)

GREAT BRITAIN

SERVES 4

225 g white fish fillet 225 g salmon fillet	Cut into 1 cm cubes and place in a bowl.
2 x 15 ml spoons finely chopped fresh parsley 1 x 15 ml spoon finely cut fresh chives 2 x 15 ml spoons White Wine Sauce (see page 314) salt and freshly ground pepper	Add to the fish in the bowl, seasoning to taste with salt and pepper. Mix to bind together.
250 g potatoes, peeled and boiled for a few minutes	Cool, then grate and squeeze lightly to get rid of excess moisture. Place on a plate and season well. Shape the fish mixture in your hands into eight balls. Roll these in the grated potato to coat the fish all over, then flatten into fishcake shapes.
1 x 15 ml spoon olive oil 15 g butter	Heat together in a non-stick frying pan and sauté the fishcakes gently on both sides until crisp and golden brown, about 6–7 minutes. Drain well on kitchen paper. Serve with a Parsley Sauce (see page 314).

TEMPURA
Tempura – battered and deep-fried fish and/or vegetables – is probably one of Japan's most famous dishes, but it is not part of the classic cuisine, the idea only having been introduced by Spanish and Portuguese traders and missionaries in the sixteenth century.

JAPAN

SERVES 4

250 ml *dashi* (see page 87)
50 ml *mirin* (Japanese sherry)
85 ml light soy sauce

To make the dipping sauce, mix together in a bowl. Divide between four saucers or small bowls.

200 g mixed small vegetables (shiitake mushrooms, carrots or aubergines, baby sweetcorn, slices of sweet potato, parsley sprigs etc.)

Prepare the vegetables, peeling and wiping clean if necessary, but leaving stalks on if appropriate.

4 large prawns
2 squid
4 fillets of white fish

Shell the prawns and devein them. Leave the tails on. Clean the squid, cut into small squares and score them. Make sure all bones and skin are removed from the fish fillets. Cut the fillets in half.

175 g plain flour mixed with 50 g cornflour
salt

Dust the vegetables and seafood with 2 x 15 ml spoons of the mixed flours and salt to taste. Place the rest of the flour in a bowl and make a well in the centre.

1 egg, beaten
200 ml iced water
25 g sesame seeds (optional)

Add to the well in the flour, along with a pinch of salt, and mix together to a thin batter.

fresh corn oil for deep-frying

Place in a suitable pan (or use a wok) and heat to around 160°C/325°F. Dip the vegetables, a few at a time, into the batter, holding by the stalk, or using a fork, skewer or chopsticks. Gently drop into the oil and pre-cook for about 1 minute, then remove and drain well on kitchen paper. This can be done in advance, and the final frying done just before serving.

¼ *daikon* (giant white radish), peeled and finely grated
3 x 5 ml spoons grated fresh root ginger

Mix together and arrange on individual plates. Have ready the little bowls of dipping sauce.

Re-fry the vegetables, as well as the seafood, in hot oil at about 170°C/340°F for a few minutes until crisp and golden. Drain well on kitchen paper.

Serve the tempura hot with the cold sauce and the gingered *daikon*. You could also deep-fry large won-ton 'skins' (see page 109) as 'platters' for the tempura.

Opposite: Tempura can be made with pieces of fish, or vegetables as here. Below: Fishcakes with Parsley Sauce (see page 225).

HERRINGS IN OATMEAL
Coating herrings in oatmeal is traditional in Scotland, and trout fillets are often cooked in the same way (try mackerel too). I've added a little extra, the apple which counters the oil in the fish. Instead of the vegetable oil you could use bacon fat.

SCOTLAND   **SERVES 4**

8 herring fillets

Check very carefully for any remaining small pin bones, and pick them out with tweezers.

120 g oatflakes
1 apple, peeled, cored and very
    finely grated
salt and freshly ground pepper

Sprinkle on to a plate and mix well, seasoning to taste with salt and pepper. Press the fillets into the oatflakes to coat both sides.

2 x 15 ml spoons vegetable oil

Heat in a large sauté pan and add the fillets. Sauté for a few minutes on each side. Drain well on kitchen paper.

2 lemons, cut in half

Serve each herring fillet with a half lemon to squeeze over.

EELS IN HERB SAUCE
The combination of eels and a tart green herb sauce is a speciality of Belgium, but eel dishes are popular in most places in Europe.

BELGIUM   **SERVES 4**

1 kg fresh eel, skinned

Cut into pieces 5–6 cm in length.

10 g each of nettles and salad burnet
    (or 20 g parsley or spinach)
5 g fresh root ginger, grated

For the herb infusion, pour boiling water over the greens and ginger in a jug or bowl and leave to infuse for 20 minutes. Strain through muslin or a fine sieve, and retain the liquid, discarding the greens.

50 g sorrel leaves
30 g watercress leaves
15 g butter

Sweat together gently for about 5 minutes.

120 g young spinach leaves, tough
    stalks removed
a few fresh tarragon leaves
1 x 15 ml spoon each of finely cut
    chervil and parsley

Add to the sorrel and watercress for a moment or so then turn into the liquidiser. Blend to a green purée. Add the herb infusion and boil to reduce to a third of its original volume.

salt and freshly ground pepper
40 ml olive oil

Season the eel pieces then sauté them in the oil until golden brown and cooked. Serve immediately on top of the sauce, or place the eel pieces *in* the sauce and cook for a few minutes more. Serve immediately.

GRAVLAX

Fish (which can include trout, mackerel and herring) are 'cooked' by salt, sugar and dill instead of by citrus juice as in the South American seviche. I learned how to marinate salmon in this way when I was working in the Grand Hotel in Stockholm, but this recipe is Norwegian. Sometimes a little aquavit is added to the marinade, and often the gravlax skin is fried until crisp and served on top of the succulent flesh.

NORWAY

SERVES AT LEAST 4

1.5 kg whole Norwegian (or Scottish) salmon

Get the fishmonger to clean the fish, remove the bones, and cut into fillets. The skin can remain. Carefully pick away any small pin bones, using tweezers. Place one fillet, skin down, on a large piece of clingfilm on top of a large piece of foil.

40 g coarse salt
25 g caster sugar

Mix together and scatter half over the flesh of the salmon.

at least 2 large bunches fresh dill

Arrange over the fillet, then scatter with the remaining salt and sugar. Place the second salmon fillet on top, skin side up. Wrap the clingfilm around both fillets, then enclose in the foil to make a parcel. Place in a deepish platter and leave to marinate in the fridge for at least 24 hours. Turn the foil parcel over occasionally, so that the copious juices moisten both fillets evenly.

To serve, remove the liquid and the dill, wipe, then cut as smoked salmon. An ideal topping for an open sandwich.

RAW BERMUDAN WAHOO WITH SASHIMI DRESSING

Wahoo is the fish used in this Japanese-inspired dish from Bermuda, but the very freshest salmon or turbot makes a good alternative.

BERMUDA

SERVES 4

25 ml sake (Japanese rice wine)
45 ml *mirin* (Japanese sherry)

For the sashimi dressing, heat gently together in a medium pan, then flame to burn off the alcohol.

1 x 2.5 cm piece of *kombu* (kelp seaweed), wiped with a damp sponge
1 x 15 ml spoon tamari sauce
225 ml dark soy sauce
5 g loose *bonito* flakes

Add to the sake mixture, bring to the boil, and simmer gently for 5 minutes. Remove from the heat and leave to stand in a cool place for a least 5–6 hours to infuse. Strain and reserve. (You will not need all of this dressing for the recipe, but it keeps well.)
Brush about 2 x 5 ml spoons dressing over each serving plate.

salt and freshly ground pepper

Season the plates with salt and pepper to taste.

350 g extremely fresh wahoo (salmon or turbot) fillet

Cut into very fine slices and arrange in a circle on each dressed plate. Generously brush with more of the dressing.

4 x 5 ml spoons finely sliced spring onions
2 x 5 ml spoons toasted sesame seeds

Sprinkle over the fish.

12 coriander leaves

Use as a garnish.

SASHIMI
The freshest raw fish, preferably newly killed, is cut carefully by highly skilled, especially trained chefs for *sashimi*, which is a major element of classical Japanese cuisine. The fish are used seasonally, and different types of fish are cut in different ways – in cubes, crossways into slices, and into very narrow strips.

JAPAN

SERVES 4

450 g the very freshest raw fish, cleaned and filleted

Choose from salmon, tuna, halibut, sea bream or bass, turbot, mackerel, etc. Chill to make the fish easier to slice.

½ *daikon* (giant white radish), peeled
½ cucumber, peeled
1 medium carrot, peeled

Shred with a mandoline or sharp knife, then chill in iced water.

4 x 15 ml spoons *shoyu* (Japanese soy sauce)
1 x 15 ml spoon *wasabi* (green horseradish paste)
freshly ground pepper

Put the soy sauce in a small dish. Mould the *wasabi* into a classic leaf shape and place on another dish.
   Cut the fish neatly into pieces, slivers or strips. Arrange decoratively on a platter or individual plates. Grind on some pepper. Drain the vegetable shreds well and arrange beside the fish. Offer the soy and *wasabi*. A little of the *wasabi* is stirred into the soy before being used as a dipping sauce.

SEVICHE
Variations of this dish are served throughout Latin America. A fish traditionally used is striped bass, but any other fish with firm and lean white flesh, except cod, can be substituted, red snapper or turbot, for example. Tuna or mackerel would also be successful prepared in this way.

SOUTH AMERICA

SERVES 4

450 g fish fillets, skinned and carefully pin-boned

Cut into small strips.

85 ml olive oil
1 garlic clove, peeled and halved

Heat together in a small pan for about 4 minutes, then discard the garlic. Let the oil cool.

juice of 2 limes
juice of 1 large lemon
1 fresh red chilli pepper, seeded and finely sliced
2 spring onions, peeled and finely sliced
4 black olives, pitted and halved
4 tomatoes, seeded and sliced (but keep and use the juices)
1 x 15 ml spoon fresh oregano

Combine in a bowl, add the cool garlic-flavoured oil, and mix well. Mix in the fish strips, and toss.

salt and freshly ground pepper

Season the fish, mix again, then leave in the fridge for at least 1 hour, and for up to 3 hours, until the fish has 'cooked' and turned opaque.

fresh parsley or coriander leaves
4 lemon or lime wedges

Arrange the fish and some of the marinade on small individual plates, or in small bowls, and garnish with the fresh herb leaves and lemon wedges.

Opposite: Above, Sashimi. Below, Seviche.

RED SNAPPER IN A TERRINE OF THREE SWEET PEPPERS

Red snapper belongs to a family of fish living in tropical or semi-tropical waters, and is sometimes found further north in American waters. This fresh and modern terrine is a favourite in my London club. (Photograph page 234)

USA **SERVES 12** **OVEN: 200°/400°F/GAS 6**

1 kg red snapper fillets, scaled, pinbones removed 400 ml Fish Stock (see page 315)	Place together in a saucepan and bring to the boil. Remove from the heat and remove the fillets from the stock. Pat the fillets dry with kitchen paper.
½ x 5 ml spoon saffron threads	Add to the stock and reserve.
200 g small fennel bulbs, leaves separated and quartered salt and freshly ground pepper	Blanch in the salted saffron stock for 8–10 minutes, then remove and cool. Reserve the stock to blanch the other vegetables in.
100 g red onions, peeled	Cut in half and peel off the layers from the root. Blanch in the fennel stock, about 5–8 minutes. Drain well.
200 g each of red, yellow and green peppers	Cut in quarters, remove white pith and seeds, and oven-roast as on page 52. Skin and slice evenly.
200 g green courgettes, topped and tailed	Cut in quarters lengthwise, slice the seeded middles off evenly, then blanch flesh in the fennel stock. Refresh in iced water and drain well.
butter	Use a little to lightly grease both sides of a piece of silicone paper cut to fit a Le Creuset terrine mould and allowing an overlap of paper about one long side height of the mould. Lay this flat on the work surface.
100 g spinach leaves, tough stalks removed	Blanch quickly in the fennel stock (10 seconds only), then place in iced water. Remove and pat dry on kitchen paper. Cover one side of the silicone paper with spinach leaves in one layer. Place the paper carefully in the terrine mould and smooth out with your fingers to the shape of the mould, allowing the overlap to hang down the outside of the mould. Refrigerate.

500 ml tomato juice
5 gelatine leaves, soaked in cold water to soften
1 x 5 ml spoon fresh lemon thyme leaves
a pinch of fresh oregano leaves
	Place the juice in a pan and warm gently through. Add the soaked and squeezed gelatine and herbs, and allow to cool to room temperature.
	    Spread a little of this in the base of the terrine mould, followed by a layer of pepper, onion, then courgette, fish fillets and fennel. Spread some juice between each layer, and season with salt and pepper. Continue layering in the same way until the ingredients are finished. Top with a final layer of juice, and fold over the overlap of spinach on the silicone paper.
	    Place a weight on top of the paper to press out all the air, and ensure the terrine layers stay together when cut. Leave to set in the fridge.

80 ml champagne vinegar 1 garlic clove, peeled and halved a pinch of powdered saffron finely grated zest of ¼ lemon	For the saffron vinaigrette, bring to the boil together in a pan, along with some salt and pepper to taste. Remove from the heat and allow to infuse for an hour. When cold, strain the liquid and discard the solids.
250 ml extra virgin olive oil	Whisk together with the flavoured vinegar, and keep at room temperature. To serve, carefully remove the terrine from the mould and remove the paper. Cut gently, using a very sharp knife, and serve a slice per person, garnished with the saffron vinaigrette.

HERRING SALAD
Early in my career I spent some time in Sweden, learning about herrings from the masters of the herring art. Lightly pickled herrings can be presented in a number of different sauces, and they feature in many meals, particularly the famous *smörgåsbord*. (Photograph page 234)

SWEDEN

SERVES 4

450 g sweet pickled herring fillets	Cut into small pieces and divide into three portions.
200 g natural yoghurt **100 ml soured cream**	Stir to mix, then divide into three portions.
1 x 15 ml spoon finely cut fresh dill	Stir into one portion of the yoghurt, and use to coat one portion of the herring fillets.
½ x 5 ml spoon powdered saffron **(or turmeric)**	Stir into the second portion of the yoghurt and use to coat a second portion of the herring fillets.
3 x 15 ml spoons beetroot juice	Stir into the remaining yoghurt, and use to coat the remaining herring fillets. Arrange a few pieces of each type of herring on individual plates.
fresh chives and parsley **shallot rings dipped in paprika**	Use to garnish the herring fillets. Plainly boiled new potatoes are a good accompaniment.

DANUBE SMOKED HERRING AND APPLE SALAD
Buckling are herring that have been lighted brined then hot-smoked, and are available in many Eastern and Northern European countries. The Dutch have a slightly different version, *bokking*, which consists of the entire fish; it is cold-smoked and must be gutted and beheaded before eating. (Photograph page 235)

YUGOSLAVIA

SERVES 4

2 smoked buckling, with roe	Split the fish open along the side, remove the roe with a small spoon, and place in a bowl. Discard the bones, and flake the flesh into large pieces. Set aside.
2 x 15 ml spoons grain mustard	Add to the roe in the bowl and mash together.
60 ml olive oil **2 x 15 ml spoons lemon juice** **salt and freshly ground pepper**	Slowly whisk the oil into the roe until it is amalgamated, then thin down with the lemon juice. Season to taste with salt and pepper.
225 g small new potatoes, cooked	Slice to 1 cm thick, then place in a bowl.
1 x 15 ml spoon finely cut dill **2 spring onions, sliced** **a pinch of cumin seeds**	Add half of the dill and onion to the potatoes, along with the cumin seeds. Season to taste with a little salt and pepper, and moisten with a little of the roe dressing.
1 dessert apple, cored and cut **into strips**	Mix with the flaked buckling, the remaining herb and spring onion, and enough dressing to bind it together.
a few salad leaves	Arrange on individual plates, and place some of the potato salad on top. Top this with a portion of buckling, and drizzle some dressing over.
1 small beetroot	Peel and cut into fine strips. Use these to garnish the salad.

PICKLED FISH
It was the peoples of South-East Asia, brought to work in South Africa by the Dutch, that introduced ways of preserving meat and fish. This fish dish, if kept cold, can last for several days. It is very similar to a fish of the Iberian Peninsula, *pescado en escabeche*, or marinated fish.

SOUTH AFRICA   **SERVES 4**

500 g fillets of white fish (cod, halibut, sole, plaice)
> Cut into small even pieces.

approx. 2 x 15 ml spoons plain flour
salt and freshly ground pepper
> Mix together, seasoning to taste, then use to coat the fish pieces lightly.

vegetable oil
> Heat about 1 x 15 ml spoon in a large pan and sauté as many pieces of fish as will fit into the pan to brown lightly on both sides. Drain well on kitchen paper. Clean out the pan, add fresh oil, and sauté the remaining pieces of fish, in batches, with new oil if necessary. Drain and leave to cool. Place in a china or glass shallow container.

2 large onions, peeled and sliced into rings
> Cook in 2 x 15 ml spoons oil until golden.

150 ml white wine vinegar
1 x 15 ml spoon clear honey
1 x 15 ml spoon curry powder
1 x 5 ml spoon black peppercorns
1 x 5 ml spoon turmeric
a pinch each of cayenne pepper and ground allspice
> Add to the onion, bring to the boil, then simmer gently for about 5 minutes to cook the curry powder thoroughly. Leave to cool, then pour over the fish. Cover with a lid and leave in the fridge for at least 48 hours, turning daily, and for up to 4 days.

4 fresh bay leaves
> Use as a garnish, and serve the fish cold with a salad, chutney and salted, grilled coconut shreds.

GARLIC PRAWNS
A simple way of cooking prawns, which would be ideal for a *tapa*. In Portugal, more chilli would be added; prawns are also cooked with curry powder, an echo of Goan influence. (Photograph page 239)

SPAIN   **SERVES 4**

16–20 raw jumbo prawns
salt
> Peel and devein the prawns, then wash briefly and dry well. Season with salt.

100 ml extra virgin olive oil
4 garlic cloves, peeled and thinly sliced
> Heat together in a large frying pan to soften the garlic, a few seconds only.

1 dried red chilli pepper, crumbled
> Add to the oil and garlic, along with the prawns, and stir-fry for about 2–5 minutes or until the prawns are cooked. Strain off the oil carefully, reserving the garlic with the prawns.

1 x 15 ml spoon chopped fresh parsley
> Sprinkle over the prawns and serve hot or cold.

Previous page: Above left, Herring Salad (see page 233). Below left, Red Snapper in a Terrine of Three Sweet Peppers (see page 232). Right, Danube Smoked Herring and Apple Salad (see page 233).

DEVILLED WHITEBAIT
Last century great shoals of whitebait, the tiny fry of the herring and sprat, used to be caught in the Thames and, fried and devilled, they were the speciality of many taverns at Greenwich and Blackwall. Serve as a starter, accompanied by wedges of lemon. (Photograph page 238)

ENGLAND   **SERVES 4**

450 g whitebait

Rinse carefully, then drain well and pat dry with a kitchen cloth.

120 g plain flour
1 x 5 ml spoon dry mustard powder
salt and freshly ground pepper

Mix together on a dish. Roll the whitebait, a few at a time, in the seasoned flour. Shake off the excess flour.

vegetable oil for deep-frying

Heat until hot, and deep-fry the whitebait in batches until crisp and golden, about 1–2 minutes. Remove and drain very well on kitchen paper.

cayenne pepper

Sprinkle to taste over the whitebait along with more salt to taste.

Crispy Seaweed (see page 70) or fresh
    parsley (optional)
1 lemon, quartered

Use as a garnish.

PRAWNS IN COCONUT MILK
Molee, mollee or *mouli* is a style of cooking from the south of India and Sri Lanka. The main ingredient, usually fish or shellfish, is cooked in coconut milk (a usage unknown in the north). The southern Indian version is very mild; the Sri Lankan version can be searingly hot.

INDIA   **SERVES 4**

675 g large raw prawns

Wash, shell and devein. (Locally, the shells are left on, as it is believed the prawns retain more flavour.)

1 x 15 ml spoon ghee or oil
2 onions, peeled and finely sliced
2 garlic cloves, peeled and crushed
1 x 5 ml spoon grated fresh root ginger
1 x 5 ml spoon black mustard seeds

Sauté together for a few minutes to soften the onion and garlic, but not to colour them. The seeds will pop.

2 fresh red or green chilli peppers,
    seeded and finely sliced
1 x 5 ml spoon turmeric
6 curry leaves

Add to the pan and sauté for a few minutes longer.

500 ml thick coconut milk
salt

Pour into the pan, adding salt to taste, and bring to simmering point. Simmer for 10 minutes, uncovered, and stirring every now and again. Add the prawns and cook for about 4 minutes or until they change colour and stiffen slightly. Remove the pan from the heat.

juice of 1 lemon or to taste
2 x 15 ml spoons finely chopped fresh
    coriander

Add, mix in well, and serve immediately, preferably with plain basmati rice or an Indian bread (see page 259).

Overleaf : Left, Devilled Whitebait. Right, Garlic Prawns.

SPICY PRAWNS WITH BLACK BEANS
The inspiration for this prawn dish is Chinese, using fermented black beans, soy beans which have been cooked, salted and fermented, causing them to turn almost black and soft. The couscous garnish is not traditional. Use rice instead if you like.

CHINA

SERVES 4

Brown Chicken Stock (see page 316)
a pinch of saffron strands

For the couscous, bring 200 ml stock to the boil in a pan, along with the saffron.

200 g couscous

Add to the hot liquid, stir, then cover and remove from the heat. Leave until the couscous absorbs the liquid.

50 g diced courgette
40 g diced red pepper
40 g diced black olives
vegetable oil

Sauté together gently for a few minutes, using about ½ x 15 ml spoon oil.

40 g pine kernels, toasted
1 x 15 ml spoon each of finely cut
    fresh coriander and chives
a dash of balsamic vinegar
salt and freshly ground pepper

Add and mix into the sautéed vegetables, along with the couscous and a little more chicken stock if needed. Season to taste with salt and pepper.

12 large raw tiger prawns, shelled and
    deveined

Cut in half along the length of the body. Stir-fry in about 1 x 15 ml spoon oil for a few minutes.

120 g Tomato Sauce (see page 311)
2 x 15 ml spoons fermented
    black beans
4 spring onions, finely chopped
2.5 cm piece of fresh root ginger,
    peeled and very finely chopped
1 fresh green chilli pepper, seeded and
    very finely chopped

Add to the prawns, and heat through, stirring constantly, for a few minutes. Season to taste with salt and pepper. Arrange the half prawns around the serving plates. Make a mound of couscous in the middle, using a suitable mould.

a handful of fresh coriander leaves

Use to garnish the prawns.

BOILED YABBIES
Crayfish are a seasonal treat wherever they are found – in Australia, France, Scandinavia. The Swedes cook them in water strongly flavoured with dill; the Finns eat them with dill, bread and butter, schnapps and beer; the French might serve them with a white wine sauce and asparagus. (Photograph page 243)

AUSTRALIA

SERVES 4

2 large carrots

Peel, cut with a cannelle knife, and slice into rings.

1 onion

Peel and cut into thin rings.

1 leek

Clean and cut into thin rings.

Fish Stock (see page 315)
salt

Bring a very large pot full of stock to the boil, and season it with salt. Add the carrot, leek and onion rings and cook for 4–5 minutes.

| 32–40 medium yabbies or crayfish | Put into the stock. |

| 2 large bunches fresh dill
a few julienne strips of lemon rind, blanched | Add half of the dill and the lemon rind to the pot when all the crayfish are in the stock, then cook for 6–8 minutes.
  Remove the cooked dill from the pot. Leave the crayfish in the liquid to cool, along with most of the remaining fresh dill, if you want to serve the fish cold. Or serve hot, in bowls with a little carrot, onion and leek, and sprigs of fresh dill. A good accompaniment is a lemon and dill mayonnaise. |

SOFTSHELL CRABS WITH COOKED TOMATO VINAIGRETTE

The softshell crab is a blue or shore crab, found on the east coast of the United States, which is caught when shedding its shell. The ideas here encompass what has become known as Californian cuisine, a mixture of influences, but resulting in delicious combinations which are uniquely fresh and light. (Photograph page 242)

USA   SERVES 4   OVEN: 180°C/350°F/GAS 4

| 4 softshell crabs | Wash and drain, then place in the top half of a steamer. |

| 2 spring onions, finely diced
½ celery stalk, finely diced
white of ½ small leek, finely diced
½ carrot, finely diced
olive oil | For the cooked tomato vinaigrette, sweat together, with ½ x 15 ml spoon olive oil over a very low heat until softened. |

| 2 medium tomatoes, skinned, seeded and diced
75 ml each of tomato juice and champagne vinegar
1 x 5 ml spoon each of balsamic vinegar and sherry vinegar | Add to the pan, still at a very low temperature, and mix well. |

| ½ x 15 ml spoon each of finely cut lemon thyme, tarragon and basil
salt and freshly ground pepper
cayenne pepper | Add to the pan, seasoning to taste with a pinch or so of salt, pepper and cayenne. Cook until the tomatoes have become paste-like, then place in the blender and whizz until smooth. Pour into a bowl and cool.
  When cool, slowly add 225 ml olive oil to the mixture, whisking it in until the consistency is like that of a vinaigrette. Pass through a fine sieve into a jug. |

| 4 plum tomatoes, skinned, seeded and diced
3 x 15 ml spoons finely cut chives
1 x 15 ml spoon finely cut basil, parsley or coriander | Mix into the strained and cooked vinaigrette. Leave to one side. |

| 1 sprig fresh parsley
1 lemongrass stalk
1 shallot, peeled and halved
1 fresh red chilli pepper, seeded and halved
1 x 5 ml spoon black peppercorns
2 x 15 ml spoons sherry vinegar
200 ml water | Place in the base of the steamer, and put the top half containing the crabs on top. Cover, bring to the boil, and steam for 3–5 minutes. Serve the crabs with the vinaigrette poured over them. |

POTTED CRAB WITH POACHED QUAIL'S EGGS
Potting of fish (and meat) is one of the oldest known methods of preservation, and there are many recipes in the British repertoire. Before Tudor times, the potting medium was suet; since then butter has made the ingredients airtight. In France *confits* are preserved in goose or duck fat. (Photograph page 243)

ENGLAND

SERVES 4

1 x 1.25 kg crab, cooked	Pick the meat from the crab, keeping the white separate from the brown.
225 g clarified butter	Heat 100 g in a small pan until melted.
a large pinch each of ground mace, grated nutmeg and cayenne pepper	Add to the butter, and cook gently for 1–2 minutes until fragrant. Mix into the white crab meat.
salt and freshly ground pepper lemon juice	Season to taste with salt, pepper and lemon juice then pour in most of the remaining melted butter. Spoon into four individual ramekins and press down firmly. Cover their tops with the remaining melted butter. Cover and chill to set, about 1 hour.
1 x 15 ml spoon mayonnaise	Mash with the brown crab meat, and season to taste with salt and pepper. Turn the potted crab out on to individual plates, and top with a spoonful of the brown meat.
4 quail's eggs, soft poached	Place on top of the brown crab meat and serve at room temperature with Melba toast.

SCALLOPS IN LIME JUICE
This dish, known as *opihis*, would originally have been made in the Hawaiian islands, with limpets. It is not dissimilar to Seviche (see page 230) in concept, and many such dishes involving salmon and other fish and shellfish are common throughout Polynesia.

HAWAII

SERVES 4

225 g scallops, weighed after shelling	Scallops in Hawaii are very small. If large, cut in quarters. Place in a bowl.
juice of 4 limes Tabasco sauce to taste salt and freshly ground white pepper	Pour into the bowl, adding a couple of dashes of Tabasco and salt and white pepper to taste. Leave for 5–6 hours in the fridge, stirring occasionally.
1 x 15 ml spoon soured cream 2 x 15 ml spoon coconut milk 2 spring onions, finely sliced ½ red pepper, seeded and finely diced ½ green pepper, seeded and finely diced	Stir into the lime-'cooked' scallops and serve as an appetiser.

Previous pages: Left, Softshell Crabs with Cooked Tomato Vinagrette (see page 241). Above right, Boiled Yabbies (see page 240). Below right, Potted Crab with Poached Quail's Eggs.

SANTIAGO SCALLOPS

The Santiago of the recipe title is not the South American one, but Santiago de Compostela in northern Spain, where the patron saint of Spain, St James the Apostle, is said to have been buried. These scallops are often served as a *tapa*.

SPAIN

SERVES 4

Ingredients	Method
12 large scallops	Clean the scallops, saving the corals if they have them. Cut the scallops in two horizontally.
1 medium onion, peeled and finely chopped 2 garlic cloves, peeled and crushed olive oil	Place in a sauté pan, along with 1 x 15 ml spoon oil, and sweat until the onion is transparent. Add the scallops, turn up the heat, and sauté for 1 minute, turning the scallops once. Remove from the heat and transfer the scallops to a bowl.
a few thyme leaves ½ red chilli pepper, seeded and finely sliced 2 x 15 ml spoons finely chopped parsley 120 g button mushrooms, sliced salt and freshly ground pepper	Add to the onions in the sauté pan and mix together, seasoning to taste with salt and pepper. You may need another 15 ml spoon of olive oil. Sauté for 5 minutes.
2 x 15 ml spoons brandy	Add to the frying pan, ignite and shake gently until the flames subside. Mix in the scallops (and corals) and transfer to a baking dish (or scallop shells).
175 ml dry white wine 85 ml Tomato Sauce (see page 311)	Pour into the frying pan and bring to the boil. Stir for about 5–10 minutes, then pour over the scallops in the dish.
4 x 15 ml spoons fresh white breadcrumbs	Sprinkle over the scallops and drip some oil over the crumbs. Grill under a preheated grill until the topping is golden, about 2–3 minutes. Serve immediately.

STEAMED SCALLOPS
An hors d'oeuvre recipe which is a basic of many a Chinese restaurant menu, but which clearly illustrates how essentially simple most Chinese recipes are – scallops are briefly steamed with a little chilli, ginger, garlic and soy sauce.

CHINA   **SERVES 4**

12 fresh scallops

Open, clean the scallops and loosen from their shells. Discard the flat shell, and return the scallops to the rounded bottom shells.

½ x 5 ml spoon finely sliced fresh red chilli pepper, seeded
2 cm piece of fresh root ginger, cut into very thin strips
2 x 5 ml spoons sesame oil
1 garlic clove, peeled and crushed
3 x 15 ml spoons dark soy sauce

Mix together in a bowl, and spoon a little of this sauce on top of each scallop in the shell. Steam the scallops in their shells in a steamer (in batches if necessary), for about 60 seconds, depending on size. Remove the shells carefully from the steamer to retain all the juices, and arrange on a serving plate.

2 x 5 ml spoons fresh coriander leaves

Place a coriander leaf on top of each scallop and a shred each of chilli and ginger. Place the bowl of sauce in the middle of the scallops; more sauce should be spooned on to the scallops before eating, and then the juices should be drunk from the shell afterwards.

MOULES MARINIERE
I love mussels and think they are not eaten enough in the UK and elsewhere. They are very versatile, and can be used in the traditional northern French way as here, or in a soup, or with pasta and on pizzas. The sauce can be thickened slightly by adding some *beurre manié* (softened butter mixed with plain flour).

FRANCE   **SERVES 4**

1.5 kg small to medium mussels
salt and freshly ground pepper

Wash and scrub very well, and pull the beards off. Place in clean water with a little salt for a couple of hours to help cleanse of sand. Discard any that are broken or that do not close when tapped sharply. Place in a large shallow pan, in one layer if possible.

300 ml Fish Stock (see page 315)
100 ml dry white wine
40 g shallots, peeled and finely chopped
1 garlic clove, peeled and crushed
3 celery stalks, finely diced

Add to the pan, cover and bring to the boil. Simmer until the mussels open, about 3–4 minutes. Discard any that are still closed. Strain off the liquor through muslin into a clean saucepan. Keep the mussels warm. Boil the liquor to reduce it by one-third.

50 g unsalted butter, diced
or 100 ml double cream

Stir into the liquid, the butter cube by cube, and season to taste with salt and pepper.

1 x 15 ml spoon lemon juice
1 x 15 ml spoon mixed chopped herbs (parsley, thyme, fennel etc.)

Add to the liquid and stir in well. Arrange the mussels in a large dish and pour the liquid over. Serve immediately with lots of crusty French bread.

Opposite: Steamed Scallops.

OYSTERS CASINO
Oysters occur all round the coasts of North America, particularly on the east coast, around the Chesapeake, and they are eaten and cooked in a variety of ways. They feature in a stew, in the Californian Hangtown Fry (floured and fried), and in the La Médiatrice and oysters Rockefeller of New Orleans.

USA

SERVES 4

24 large oysters

Remove from the shell, reserving their juices and the deeper half shell of each. Place the fish in the deep half shell, and arrange in baking tins or suitable dishes. They should not tip; if they do, prop them up using crumpled foil. (Or you could set them in beds of coarse salt.)
Preheat the grill to its highest.

2 rashers lean bacon

Fry over moderate heat in a heavy frying pan until crisp and brown and the fat has all been rendered. Transfer, using a slotted spoon, to kitchen paper to drain. Crumble and keep to one side.

25 g shallots, peeled and finely diced
1 celery stalk, peeled and finely diced
½ green pepper, seeded and finely diced

Add to the fat in the pan and fry gently for about 5 minutes, or until soft but not brown. Drain in a sieve then put in a bowl.

4 x 5 ml spoons lime or lemon juice
2 x 5 ml spoons Worcestershire sauce
6 drops Tabasco sauce

Add to the bowl along with the crumbled bacon, and toss together. Spoon over the top of each oyster.
 Grill the oysters about 7–8 cm from the heat, for 3–4 minutes, or until the edges curl slightly. Serve immediately, 6 shells per person.

1 lemon, quartered

Use as a garnish.

SYDNEY ROCK OYSTERS WITH BUCKWHEAT NOODLES
Oysters are prolific in Australia as well as in New Zealand, and here the garnishes – two vinaigrettes, one based on sake (rice wine) and soy sauce, the other on chilli and coriander – reveal influences from Japan to the north.

AUSTRALIA

SERVES 4

48 small oysters

Open and remove the oysters, reserving the juices and the deeper shells. Keep cool. Arrange the deeper shells on individual plates, 12 per plate.

20 ml each of light soy sauce and sake (Japanese rice wine)
80 ml grapeseed oil
a splash of rice vinegar
freshly ground pepper

For the sake and soy vinaigrette, mix together with the juices from the oysters, then add pepper to taste. Place in a small dish.

20 ml each of sake and rice vinegar
80 ml grapeseed oil
1 x 5 ml spoon each of finely chopped fresh coriander and fresh red chilli pepper
a pinch of grated fresh root ginger

For the chilli and coriander vinaigrette, mix together. Place in a small dish.

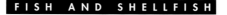

250 g buckwheat noodles (see page 106)	Cook in boiling salted water until al dente, then drain well and leave to cool. Divide between the oyster shells on the plates. Arrange an oyster on top of each little mound of noodles.
40 g pickled ginger, finely diced 40 g finely cut chives	Sprinkle over the oysters and serve them either with a dash of each vinaigrette on top, or with the vinaigrettes separately for guests to help themselves.

OYSTERS WITH SPICY TOMATO VINAIGRETTE

The waters around New Zealand are teeming with life, and oysters are very widely available, along with scallops, crayfish, whitebait, marlin, shark, and the rare shellfish toheroa. This recipe is typical of the fresh ideas that are now current in the country's cooking. (Photograph page 250)

NEW ZEALAND   **SERVES 4**

250 g ripe plum tomatoes	For the vinaigrette, skin, seed and dice roughly, then blend to a purée in the food processor.
60 ml olive oil 2 x 15 ml spoons balsamic vinegar Tabasco sauce salt and freshly ground pepper	Add to the processor with the motor still running, adding a couple of shakes of Tabasco and seasoning to taste with salt and pepper. Chill.
24 oysters	Open, prepare, and discard one shell from each oyster. Chill until ready to use. Spoon the vinaigrette over the oysters on individual plates.
1 plum tomato	Skin, seed and dice very finely.
4–6 young spinach leaves, washed and shredded 1 x 15 ml spoon shredded or slivered fresh horseradish (optional) 1 x 15 ml spoon finely cut fresh chives	Mix with the tomato dice and use to garnish the oysters.

Oysters with Spicy Tomato Vinaigrette

MAURITIAN SQUID CURRY
This curry, which I ate in Mauritius, an Indian Ocean island, is probably the best I have ever tasted. It combines Creole, Indian, Chinese and South-East Asian ingredients and ideas, along with many French accents, and is uniquely Mauritian. It was cooked by Chef Mesh.

MAURITIUS

SERVES 4

1 x 15 ml spoon coriander seeds
1 x 5 ml spoon cumin seeds

Dry-fry for about 3 minutes over a low heat. Place in a food processor.

3 x 15 ml spoons sliced shallot
2 garlic cloves, peeled
1 x 5 ml spoon diced fresh root
  ginger
1 lemongrass stalk, sliced
20 curry leaves
3 fresh red chilli peppers, seeded
2 x 5 ml spoons curry powder
1 x 5 ml spoon salt

Add to the food processor and blend to obtain a fine-textured paste.

Mauritian Squid Curry

2 x 15 ml spoons corn oil	Heat in a pan and sauté the curry paste until fragrant, about 5 minutes.
250 g tomatoes, skinned, seeded and quartered	Add to the pan and cook for 5–6 minutes.
250 ml thick coconut milk 250 ml Fish Stock (see page 315)	Add, stir well, and cook until the mixture begins to have an oily sheen. The flavour will improve if this is now left to stand and mature for a while.
500 g fresh small squid, cleaned and cut into squares or rings salt and freshly ground pepper	Add to the pan, bring to the boil, then turn the temperature down and simmer for about 5 minutes or until the squid is tender. Adjust the seasoning with salt and pepper.
4 x 15 ml spoons fresh coriander leaves	Sprinkle over the squid, and serve immediately, accompanied by plain boiled or steamed rice.

BREADS, CAKES AND PASTRIES

GRISSINI
The breadsticks seen on Italian restaurant tables, which are said to have originated in Turin, are easy to make at home. For added texture and flavour, you can mix 2 x 15 ml spoons black sesame seeds into half the mixture (see the photograph opposite).

ITALY   MAKES 40–50   OVEN: 180°C/350°F/GAS 4

250 ml lukewarm water
2½ x 5 ml spoons active dry yeast

Whisk together in a small bowl and leave to one side.

450 g plain flour
1 x 5 ml spoon salt

Sift together into a larger bowl. Make a well in the centre.

75 ml extra virgin oil

Mix into the flour along with the yeast liquid, and stir until the mixture comes together to form a dough. Turn out on to a lightly floured work surface and knead until smooth, adding more flour if necessary. Place in a lightly oiled bowl, cover and leave to rise in a warm place until doubled in size, about 40–60 minutes.

Knock the dough back, then knead again for a few minutes. Pat the dough into a 23 cm square then cut in half to form two rectangles. Cut each rectangle into strips 11.5 x 1 cm. (Keep the dough not being worked with under a damp cloth.) Roll and stretch each piece of dough in the palms of the hands to form a narrow stick about 30 cm long.

3 x 15 ml spoons cornmeal

Dust over baking trays, and arrange the breadsticks in the trays about 2.5 cm apart. Rest for 10 minutes, then place both trays in the preheated oven and bake for 20–30 minutes until the *grissini* are firm and crisp, switching the positions of the trays halfway through cooking. Leave to cool on a cooling rack.

PIZZA DOUGH
Virtually anything can be used as the topping for a pizza. But always remember to brush on some olive oil, then you need an aromatic, slightly liquid base such as tomato sauce or purée, or tapenade. A cheese or cheeses that can melt on top are good, then you can add salamis, vegetables, olives, herbs, eggs etc.

ITALY   MAKES 2 DEEP OR 4 LARGE PIZZA BASES   OVEN: 220°C/425°F/GAS 7

15 g fresh yeast
150 ml warm water
2 x 15 ml spoons runny honey

Dissolve the yeast in the warm water with the honey. Set aside in a warm place until the mixture starts to bubble, about 7–10 minutes.

200 g strong white bread flour
100 g wholewheat or rye flour
1 x 5 ml spoon salt
60 ml olive oil

Combine the flours, salt and 45 ml of the olive oil in a mixing bowl. Make a well in the centre, then add the yeast mixture. Stir until the ingredients come together roughly. Turn the dough on to a lightly floured board and knead until smooth, adding more flour as necessary. Clean the bowl, brush it with the remaining olive oil and return the kneaded dough to the bowl. Turn the dough over so the whole surface is covered with the oil. Cover and let the dough rise in a warm place until doubled in size, about 30 minutes.

Turn the dough out on to a floured board, knead, then leave to rest for another 15 minutes. Divide the dough into two or four, and shape into flat circles. Roll them, or stretch and pat them out to 20 cm flat rounds. Place these in oiled pans or on an oiled baking sheet.

extra virgin olive oil

Brush over the pizza bases, and top with the chosen topping. Bake in the preheated oven for about 7–8 minutes. Serve hot and sizzling.

FLOUR TORTILLAS
These pancakes are the basic bread of Mexico, and are used in any number of ways: see the Quesadilla recipe on page 133, and to make tacos (snacks). Genuine tortillas are made with *masa harina*, a special corn meal or flour, but this wheat flour version also works well. A special tortilla press is available.

MEXICO

MAKES 10

120 g light brown flour
3 x 15 ml spoons fine cornmeal
salt

Mix together in a bowl, adding salt to taste.

25 g lard

Cut into small pieces and mix into the flour with your fingers, pressing and rubbing until the mixture feels fine in texture. Make a well in the centre.

50–120 ml lukewarm water

Mix the water in gradually, adding only enough to form a soft dough. It should not be sticky. Cover with clingfilm and chill for 30 minutes.

Lightly flour a work surface, and heat a heavy frying pan or griddle. Divide the dough into ten portions, and roll each out to a circle of about 15 cm in diameter. Cover with a damp cloth.

Lightly grease the griddle and then fry each tortilla for about 1–2 minutes on each side, turning when the edges are dry looking and brown spots appear. Leave flat if for Quesadillas (see page 133), or fold if for tacos.

ZOPF
The traditional Swiss Sunday loaf, without which no Sunday breakfast would be complete. It is similar to the Jewish *chollah* in that it is made with milk, and also because it is plaited.

SWITZERLAND

MAKES 1 PLAITED LOAF   **OVEN: 190°C/375°F/GAS 5**

15 g fresh yeast
1 x 5 ml spoon clear honey
250 ml lukewarm milk

Cream the yeast and honey together in about 2 x 15 ml spoons of the warm milk. Leave for about 10 minutes to become frothy.

50 g butter, melted
1 x 5 ml spoon salt

Add along with the rest of the milk to the yeast mixture.

450 g strong white bread flour

Place in a bowl, and make a well in the centre. Gradually stir in the yeast mixture.

1 egg, beaten

Mix in, then knead the dough for about 5 minutes on a lightly floured surface. Cover with a cloth and leave to rise in a warm place for about 1½ hours.

Knock back the dough and divide into three equal pieces. Shape each piece into a long thin strip. Start to plait together from the centre. Turn the loaf around and over and plait from the other end. Cover with a cloth and leave to rise a second time for about 30 minutes. Before baking, put in a cool place for 10 minutes.

1 egg yolk

Brush over the bread and bake in the preheated oven for about 45 minutes. Leave to cool on a rack.

WHEATMEAL CROISSANTS

Croissants (which were actually 'invented' in Budapest), are usually made with puff pastry or a special leavened dough as here. The wheatmeal flour here is not at all traditional, but I think it makes the croissant a little healthier and different. Start at least 7 hours in advance of cooking.

FRANCE **MAKES 18** **OVEN: 220°C/425°F/GAS 7**

30 g caster sugar
2 x 5 ml spoons salt
300 ml lukewarm water

Dissolve the sugar and salt in one-third of the water in a jug.

20 g fresh yeast or 10 g dried
25 g dried milk powder (or 1 egg)

In a bowl, whisk into the remaining lukewarm water. Leave for about 10 minutes to become frothy.

250 g each of strong plain
   bread flour and wheatmeal flour

Place in a bowl (or in an electric mixer), and mix in first the sugar and salt liquid, then the yeast mixture. Beat until well blended and the dough comes away from the sides of the bowl. Do not overwork.

a little vegetable oil

Put the dough in a base of a large oiled bowl and cover with clingfilm. Leave to rise in a warm place for about 30–45 minutes, to double in size.
   Knock back the dough, and knead for a moment or two. Form in a large ball. Cut a cross in the top of the dough.

plain flour for dusting

On a lightly floured surface, roll out the ball of dough in four places, making a quarter turn each time so that there are four 'petals' around a central piece.

300 g butter, firm, but not too hard

Flatten out the butter to a tile shape, with square edges. Place in the centre of the dough, and fold the four 'petals' over it, completely enclosing the butter. Roll the dough away from you carefully into a rectangle about 40 x 70 cm. Fold dough into three, wrap in oiled polythene and chill for at least 45 minutes. Repeat this rolling, folding and chilling process twice more, rolling with the fold on the left each time. Dust the work surface lightly with flour each time.
   Roll the dough out to a 45 cm square. Trim the edges then cut into nine 15 cm squares. Cut these squares in half diagonally to make eighteen triangles. Arrange these on baking sheets, cover lightly with polythene and chill for a few minutes.
   When ready to shape and bake, have the triangles point away from you. Starting at the broad base, roll up each triangle loosely and finish with the point underneath. Squeeze the ends gently and curve the rolls into a crescent shape. Cover loosely and leave to rise in a very warm, draught-free place until doubled in size, about 1–2 hours.

1 egg yolk, beaten with 1 x 15 ml
   spoon milk

Brush very lightly over each croissant, then bake in the preheated oven for 15 minutes. Transfer to a cooling rack immediately, but they are good eaten warm.

NAAN

Naan is the Indian bread that is traditionally made in the tandoor (clay oven): it is made in a circular or teardrop shape. Stuff *Naan* by adding a filling to the dough before baking – meat for a *keema naan*, almonds for a *peshwari naan* – or top with Chicken Tikka (see page 192) and/or vegetables and yoghurt, rather like a pizza.

INDIA   **MAKES 4**

½ x 5 ml spoon dried yeast (or 2 x 5 ml spoons baking powder)
85 ml warm water

Mix together in a small bowl and leave for 10 minutes to become frothy.

350 g plain flour
½ x 5 ml spoon salt

Combine in a large bowl, and make a well in the centre.
   Add the frothy mixture to the well, and knead together thoroughly. Cover with a damp cloth and leave to rise for at least 8 hours (or overnight in the fridge).
   Divide the dough into four and roll into circles no thinner than 6 mm.

1 x 15 ml spoon melted butter
1 x 5 ml spoon sesame or wild onion seeds (or a mixture, optional)

Brush both sides of the naan with butter and sprinkle the top with the seeds if liked. Toast under a preheated grill, preferably on a piece of foil, for at least 3–5 minutes per side, until puffed and golden with patches of darker colour. Serve at once.

RYE BREAD

Rye breads, light and dark, are eaten all over Northern Europe, particularly in Poland, Russia and Scandinavia. Rye contains little gluten, so the loaves made with it can be dense, although it has great flavour. Rye breads make good bases for open sandwiches.

POLAND   **MAKES 2 LOAVES**   **OVEN: 200°C/400°F/GAS 6**

300 g rye flour
300 g white flour
1 x 15 ml spoon salt

Stir together in a bowl, and make a well in the centre.

25 g fresh yeast, or 12.5 g dried
1 x 5 ml spoon caster sugar
300 ml milk and water mixed, warmed to blood temperature

Cream together to a liquid, using a little of the milk and water. Leave for 10 minutes or so to become frothy, then add to the well in the flour.

1 x 15 ml spoon black treacle

Add to the well in the flour along with the remaining milk and water, and mix all together to a firm dough. Knead well on a lightly floured surface. Cover with a cloth and leave in a warm place to prove for 1½ hours.
   Knock back the dough and shape into two round leaves. Place on a baking sheet. Cover with a cloth and leave to prove again for 45 minutes in a warm place. Bake in the preheated oven for 35–40 minutes. Remove from the oven and leave to cool on a rack before slicing.

Opposite: Naan.

CREPES

Pancakes, crêpes or galettes feature in many cuisines, but particularly that of Brittany in northern France, where lacy galettes enfold a variety of fillings. They can be sweet or savoury, or made with wheat or buckwheat flour. Pancakes made with herbs are a major constituent of the Russian 'fish pie', Coulibiac.

FRANCE   **MAKES 14–15 x 18 cm CRÊPES**

100 g plain flour (or half plain, half buckwheat flour)
a pinch of salt

Sift together into a bowl, and make a well in the centre.

2 eggs, beaten
250 ml milk

Mix together, then add to the well in the flour and mix, gradually incorporating the flour from the sides. Whisk to a smooth batter.

unsalted butter

Melt 25 g and add to the batter. Leave to stand and rest for about 30 minutes.

30 g caster sugar (optional)
2 x 15 ml spoons finely cut fresh herbs (optional)

If a sweet crêpe is required, add the sugar to the batter. If a herb crêpe is required (see Coulibiac of Salmon on page 221), stir in the herbs.

Melt a knob of butter in an 18 cm pancake pan (or the size of pan you have or need), and add enough batter to cover the base of the pan thinly. Cook quickly on a medium heat until set on top and brown beneath. Turn and cook the other side. Continue, using more butter as needed, until the batter is used up. Keep warm in a cloth or wrap and chill or freeze. Serve plain with sugar and lemon juice or jam, or wrapped round any type of filling, depending on the type of crêpe made.

BLINIS

Like the British pancakes eaten on Shrove Tuesday, blinis were once principally associated with the carnival week before Lent. Traditionally these buckwheat pancakes are topped with soured cream and caviar, but try, too, smoked salmon and hard-boiled egg, or soured cream with finely cut celery.

RUSSIA   **MAKES ABOUT 24**

15 g fresh yeast
a pinch of caster sugar
250 ml lukewarm milk

Cream together in a small bowl, and leave in a warm place to become frothy.

120 g plain flour

Place in a bowl, make a well in the centre, and beat in the yeast mixture. Leave in a warm place to prove and expand, about 30–60 minutes.

3 egg yolks
150 g buckwheat flour

Mix into the flour mixture, then leave to prove again for another 30 minutes.

3 egg whites
a pinch of salt

Whisk together until stiff, then fold into the buckwheat batter.

butter

Heat a little in a frying pan or griddle. Drop 2 x 15 ml spoons of the batter separately into the pan at a time. Space them apart, and cook for 2–3 minutes until bubbles start to appear on the top and the underside is golden. Turn over to cook the other side, another 2 minutes or so. Place on a rack and cover with a cloth. Use as required.

COTTAGE CHEESE PANCAKES
The Hungarian cuisine makes great use of dairy products, particularly cottage and curd cheese and soured cream. Pancakes are also popular, and are wrapped around a variety of fillings, both savoury and sweet.

HUNGARY

MAKES ABOUT 36 x 5 cm PANCAKES

100 g curd cheese
225 g cottage cheese, beaten
   until smooth

With the back of a spoon, rub through a fine sieve into a bowl.

5 eggs, lightly beaten

Pour gradually into the bowl, beating constantly, until well amalgamated.

70 g plain flour

Add a 15 ml spoon at a time, folding in carefully.

150 g unsalted butter, melted
   and cooled
1 x 5 ml spoon pure vanilla extract
a pinch of salt

Stir in 120 g of the butter, along with the vanilla and salt.
   Warm a griddle over moderate heat and grease lightly with some of the remaining melted butter. Place about 2–3 x 15 ml spoons' worth of the batter on to the griddle; this will make a 5 cm pancake. Do the same to make other pancakes, allowing space between for them to spread. Fry for 2 minutes on each side, or until golden and crisp around the edges. Transfer the pancakes to a platter, and place inside a folded tea towel to keep them warm. Repeat with the remaining batter, greasing the griddle with butter each time, until all the pancakes are cooked. Serve warm with a good jam – perhaps sour cherry, peach or apricot – which is traditional in Hungary.

CORNBREAD
This cornbread is very typical of North America. To make the bread spicy you can add 2 fresh red chillies, seeded and finely chopped; or for colour and flavour, add 1–2 x 15 ml spoons chopped sun-dried tomatoes in oil. Herbs to taste, or alternative vegetables to sweetcorn can be added as well. (Photograph page 262)

USA

MAKES ABOUT 12   **OVEN: 200°C/400°F/GAS 6**

1 x 5 ml spoon melted butter

Use to grease cornbread moulds, patty tins or a Swiss roll tin measuring 25 x 38 cm.

150 g plain flour
150 g fine yellow cornmeal
1 x 15 ml spoon baking powder
1 x 5 ml spoon salt
1½ x 5 ml spoons caster sugar

Combine in a bowl, and make a well in the centre.

180 ml buttermilk
2 x 15 ml spoons melted butter
2 eggs, lightly beaten

Mix together well, then pour into the well in the dry ingredients. Stir together very briefly.

flavouring of choice (see above)
100 g sweetcorn kernels, blanched

Add to the mixture, then pour into the greased mould(s). Bake in the preheated oven for 10–15 minutes until the breads are firm to the touch. Serve warm. Cut the bread made in the Swiss roll tin into small pieces.

Cornbread (see page 261) and Polenta (see page 88).

BRIOCHE

The most familiar brioche shape is *brioche à tête* ('with a head') as below, but there are others – circles, plaits, tall cones, etc. Brioche dough can also be enriched with fruit stuffings, or by cubes of Gruyère cheese – or, as in the photograph, by cranberries: add 150 g to the dough, and use for turkey sandwiches, or with *foie gras*.

FRANCE **MAKES 1 LOAF OR 20 ROLLS** **OVEN: 200°C/400°F/GAS 6**

15 g fresh yeast
1 x 5 ml spoon clear honey
100 ml lukewarm water

Cream the yeast with the honey, then add the lukewarm water. Mix well, and leave for about 10 minutes to become frothy.

500 g strong plain flour

Add 100 g to the yeast mixture, and mix into a thin batter. Cover and set aside in a warm place for about 30 minutes. Place the remaining flour in a bowl and make a well in the centre.

Brioche made with cranberries

unsalted butter, softened
1 x 5 ml spoon salt
4 eggs, beaten

Cream 150 g of the butter until soft, then add it, salt and beaten eggs to the well in the flour along with the yeast mixture. Mix to form a dough. Knead on an unfloured surface for about 15 minutes until smooth, elastic and shiny, by slapping and stretching the dough on to and upwards from the surface. Chill for 30–40 minutes.

If making rolls, butter 20 small brioche moulds. Divide the dough into 50 g pieces. Divide each piece into two-thirds and one-third. Roll the bigger pieces into balls and place in the moulds. Using a floured wooden spoon handle, make an indentation in each roll and brush inside with water. Put the smaller pieces, also rolled into balls, into the holes.

If making one large loaf, use a 1 litre brioche mould, also buttered. Cut about one-sixth off the dough for the 'hat', and form as the rolls.

Cover loaf or rolls with a cloth and leave to rise in a warm place for about 30–40 minutes.

1 egg, beaten with a pinch of salt

Brush over the risen rolls, and bake in the preheated oven for about 15 minutes until golden brown. Cool.

Brush egg over the loaf, and bake it in the oven for 45–50 minutes, covering with foil if it is browning too quickly. Cool.

KULITSCH

This yeast-raised cake is traditionally served at Easter, along with *paskha*, a rich creamy cheese pudding (see page 293). The cake is usually made in tall tins which give it its unique shape; you could use deep round cake tins (20–23 cm) instead.

RUSSIA   **SERVES 8**   **OVEN: 180°C/350°F/GAS 4**

600 g plain flour	Sift 200 g flour into a bowl, then sift the rest into another.
40 g fresh yeast 175 ml warm milk	Dissolve the yeast in the milk and leave in a warm place for about 10 minutes. Add this mixture to the bowl holding the 200 g flour, and mix well. Cover and leave to rise until doubled in size, about 1 hour.
2 large eggs, separated a pinch of salt 100 g caster sugar 150 g unsalted butter, softened seeds of 1 cardamom pod, crushed	Mix the egg yolks, salt, sugar, butter and cardamom together until well blended, then fold into the risen dough. Whip the egg whites until stiff, and fold these in too, along with 225 g more of the flour. Mix by hand, adding more flour until the dough leaves the sides of the bowl. Cover and leave to rise again for about 2 hours.
butter and flour for the moulds	Grease two tall tins or large cake tins with butter, and then flour them. Tip out any excess flour.
80 g each of raisins and currants 80 g each of candied fruit and blanched almonds diced	Knock back the dough, and mix in the dried fruit and nuts. Divide between the two prepared moulds and leave to prove, about 1 hour. The dough should come near to the top of the tins before baking.
1 egg, beaten	Brush over the tops of the cakes and then bake in the preheated oven for about 45 minutes. An inserted skewer should come out clean, if the cake is ready. Turn out of the tin and leave to cool. Decorate if you like with more chopped fruit and nuts.

STOLLEN

Germany is famous for her breads and biscuits, and *Stollen* is a very ancient recipe, dating from at least the fourteenth century. The bread was symbolic of the Christ child, thus its alternative name of *Christstollen*, and its traditional appearance at Christmas. Sometimes *Stollen* contains marzipan.

GERMANY   **OVEN: 160°C/325°F/GAS 3**

30 g fresh yeast, or 1 x 15 ml spoon dried yeast 100–150 ml tepid milk	Dissolve the yeast in 2 x 15 ml spoons of the milk, and stand in a warm place for 10 minutes to become frothy.
70 g unsalted butter, very soft 40 g caster sugar	Cream together until pale.
1 egg, beaten	Add to the butter, and work in well.
300 g plain flour 5 g salt	Add to the butter and egg mixture, along with the yeast mixture and remaining milk. Beat very well with a wooden spoon until the dough looks smooth, about 15 minutes.

30 g each of candied orange and lemon peels 50 g blanched almonds, diced 60 g sultanas 2 x 5 ml spoons rum	Mix into the dough, then place in a bowl and leave to rise in a warm place for 45–60 minutes. During this time knead it every 15 minutes to give it smaller air bubbles. Roll the dough out to a 2 cm thick oval. Fold one end up three-quarters of the length of the dough. Place on a lightly floured baking sheets, and allow to rise for another 30 minutes. Chill for 20 minutes.
2 x 15 ml spoons melted butter	Brush half over the dough and then bake in the preheated oven for 30–40 minutes. Brush the remaining butter over the bread while still warm, then leave to cool.
icing sugar	Sprinkle generously over the bread before serving.

FRUIT AND NUT CAKE

This cake uses some of the magnificent fruits that are indigenous to Australia or that have been introduced, and is clearly based on the British fruit cake brought by British immigrants. Some other fruit cakes contain pineapple alone.

AUSTRALIA **MAKES 1 CAKE** **OVEN: 160°C/325°F/GAS 3**

unsalted butter	Use a little to grease a 30 x 6 cm terrine dish. Line the base and sides with non-stick baking paper.
125 g glacé pineapple 90 g glacé apricots 80 g glacé cherries 60 g glacé ginger	Cut into small pieces, and place in a large mixing bowl.
finely grated rind of 1 orange and 1 lemon 2 x 15 ml spoons port	Add to the fruit in the bowl. Leave to macerate for 12 hours.
160 g caster sugar 3 large eggs	Cream the sugar with 180 g of the butter until fluffy, then add the eggs, one by one, mixing in well.
300 g plain flour 1 x 5 ml spoon powdered cinnamon	Sift on to the butter and egg mixture, then stir in well. Add the fruit.
70 g shelled macadamia nuts 50 g shelled walnuts	Dice, then stir thoroughly into the cake mixture. Spoon into the prepared dish, then bake in the preheated oven for about 1½ hours. If a skewer comes out clean, the cake is ready. Cool in the dish.
25 ml dark rum	Make a slit down the middle of the cake and pour the rum into this. Serve in slices.

FLAPJACKS

These are the classic American breakfast pancakes, also known as griddle cakes. They are more like a crumpet or drop scone than an English pancake. Serve with maple syrup, bacon or sausages or fruit for breakfast, or as a snack or dessert with ice cream and your favourite topping.

USA

MAKES ABOUT 12

225 g plain flour
a pinch of salt
2 x 15 ml spoons caster sugar
2 x 5 ml spoons baking powder

Sift into a large mixing bowl. Make a well in the centre.

275 ml milk or buttermilk
2 eggs, beaten
3 x 15 ml spoons melted butter

Mix, then pour into the well in the flour. Stir together thoroughly, then set aside to rest.

butter

Melt 1 x 5 ml spoon in a griddle or heavy frying pan. Add 60 ml ladlefuls of the batter, as many as will fit on the griddle (usually about three or four), and cook until the top bubbles. Flip over with a spatula and brown the other side. Continue with melted butter and ladlefuls of the batter until the batter is used up. Keep the flapjacks warm or leave to cool.

BANANA BREAD

More a cake than a bread, this loaf is good served with afternoon tea or morning coffee. It is especially popular in Jamaica, where sultanas are often added to the mixture. Local macadamia nuts are used in a banana bread baked in Hawaii.

CARIBBEAN

MAKES 1 LOAF   **OVEN: 180°C/350°F/GAS 4**

100 g unsalted butter, softened

Use a little to grease a 23 cm loaf tin.

150 g caster sugar
3 eggs

Beat together in a bowl along with the remaining butter.

4 very ripe medium bananas, peeled

Mash well, then mix with the egg mixture.

225 g plain flour
2 x 5 ml spoons baking powder
1 x 5 ml spoon freshly grated
   nutmeg
a pinch of salt

Sift into the banana mixture and beat well.

80 g shelled walnuts (or pecans),
   diced
50 ml dark rum

Stir into the banana mixture. Pour into the prepared loaf tin and bake in the preheated oven until the loaf is done, about 1 hour. Insert a skewer into the centre of the bread; if it comes out clean, the bread is ready. Turn the bread out on to a rack and allow to cool before slicing.

Opposite: Flapjacks.

RUEBLITORTE

There is a fine tradition of baking in Switzerland, and this cake, made with grated carrots and ground almonds, is a speciality of Aargau in the north (which is known as 'carrot land'). It is traditionally decorated with tiny carrots made from marzipan.

SWITZERLAND **SERVES 10** **OVEN: 180°C/350°F/GAS 4**

2 lemons	Finely zest both lemons, and squeeze the juice from one.
6 eggs, separated 300 g caster sugar	Beat the egg yolks in a large bowl with half the caster sugar and the lemon juice and zest until pale and sticky.
300 g carrots, peeled and finely grated 300 g ground almonds	Fold carefully into the egg yolk mixture.
75 g cornflour a pinch of ground cinnamon 10 g baking powder	Sift together, and fold into the cake mixture lightly with a spatula. Whisk the egg whites until stiff, and fold in the rest of the sugar. Carefully fold this into the carrot mixture. Place in a prepared 25 cm cake tin and bake in the preheated oven for 1 hour. Test to see that it's cooked by feeling the centre: it should spring back when pressed. Turn out of the tin and place on a rack to cool.
200 g apricot jam (if you are icing the cake)	Place in a small pan and heat gently with a little water until runny. Sieve into a small container. Brush this glaze over the cake.
150 g fondant icing or icing sugar carrots made from marzipan	Ice the cake or simply dust with icing sugar. Decorate with the little carrots if desired.

MINCE PIES

At one time, many British pies, even the savoury ones, were very sweet as well as richly spiced. The classic mince pie served at Christmas is the direct descendant of this, made with spices, dried fruits, orange peel and sugar. The 'mincemeat' still contains suet, but lacks the meat.

GREAT BRITAIN **MAKES ABOUT 24** **OVEN: 200°C/400°F/GAS 6**

200 g plain flour
a little salt

For the pastry, sift together on to a work surface, then make a well in the centre.

130 g unsalted butter, softened
85 g icing sugar
finely grated zest of 1 lemon
1 egg, beaten

Add to the well in the flour, and work together before starting to gradually incorporate the flour. Work to a smooth dough. Rest in the fridge, covered with clingfilm for 20–30 minutes. Remove from the fridge, leave for a few minutes, then roll out on a lightly floured surface to about 3 mm thick. Using a 3 cm round cutter, stamp out 24 rounds. Line two 12 x 3 cm hole patty tins. Chill for another 30 minutes, then fill with baking beans and blind-bake in the preheated oven for 20 minutes. Cool.

400 g best mincemeat
brandy (optional)

Add a little brandy to the mincemeat if you like. Divide between the pastry-lined patty tins, filling to just over half their depth.

4 sheets filo pastry

Cut each sheet into strips, 6 x 5 cm. Ruffle one strip slightly, then place over the mincemeat as a lid. Do the same for the remaining pies. Bake in the preheated oven for about 15 minutes until light golden brown. Cool on a wire rack. Serve dusted with icing sugar or with brandy butter.

LAMINGTONS

The Victoria sponge is said to have originated in Australia, and covering it with chocolate, as here, would have kept it from drying out. This cake was named for a Baron Lamington, Governor of Queensland from 1895 until 1901, after he had returned to Britain.

AUSTRALIA **OVEN: 220°C/425°F/GAS 7**

6 eggs
350 g caster sugar

For the sponge, beat together in a large bowl until light and fluffy.

250 g self-raising flour
125 g plain flour
a good pinch of baking powder
225 ml warm water

Sift the dry ingredients together, then add to the egg mixture, alternating with the water. Mix until well blended. Pour the mixture into a greased Swiss roll tin and bake in the preheated oven for 15–20 minutes. Remove from the oven and leave to cool in the tin.

250 g icing sugar
125 g cocoa powder
500 ml water

For the chocolate sauce, sift the dry ingredients into a saucepan, then gradually mix in the water. Bring to the boil.

65 g dark chocolate, broken into
    pieces
20 ml brandy

Add the chocolate first, stirring constantly over a reduced heat, then the brandy. Stir well, then remove from the heat and cool. When sponge and sauce are cold, cut the sponge into 5 cm squares. Dip these into the chocolate sauce to coat.

desiccated coconut

Place on a plate, and use to coat the sauce-covered sponges thoroughly. Leave to set.

CHOCOLATE CHIP COOKIES

These crisp biscuit-cakes, with their surprise internal nuggets of chocolate, are also known as Toll House Cookies, having been invented by a restaurant of that name in Massachusetts. Use the best chocolate that you can find.

USA   MAKES ABOUT 20   OVEN: 190°C/375°F/GAS 5

175 g plain flour
½ x 5 ml spoon bicarbonate of soda
½ x 5 ml spoon salt

Sift together into a bowl.

120 g unsalted butter
120 g light brown sugar
50 g granulated sugar

Cream together in another bowl until light and fluffy.

1 egg, beaten
1 x 5 ml spoon pure vanilla extract

Mix into the butter mixture. Work the flour into the butter gradually, doing it in three batches.

175 g good chocolate chips
50 g shelled walnuts, diced

Stir into the mixture.

30 g cocoa powder (optional)

If you would like dark as well as light coloured biscuits, mix into half the mixture in another bowl.

Drop the mixture(s) in rounded 15 ml spoonfuls on to greased baking sheets, about six per sheet, allowing room for the cookies to expand during baking.

Bake in the preheated oven for 8–10 minutes or until the cookies are set and lightly browned. Remove from the oven, leave for a minute, then transfer to a cooling rack using a spatula.

SPECULAAS

Ginger spiced biscuits are plentiful in Europe at Christmas. *Lebkuchen*, honeyed ginger biscuits, are popular in Germany, and ginger is also the main flavouring of the Swedish *pepperkakor*, the *pain d'épices* of France, and the St Nicholas biscuits or *speculaas* of The Netherlands. The latter two are usually baked in the shape of a man with a beard, bishop's hat, mitre and flowing robes; special wooden moulds are used.

THE NETHERLANDS   MAKES 8–16 BISCUITS   OVEN: 150°C/400°F/GAS 2

100 g plain flour
1 x 5 ml spoon baking powder
a pinch of salt
½ x 5 ml spoon each of powdered
   cinnamon, ginger and freshly grated
   nutmeg
50 g soft brown sugar

Place in a bowl and mix.

50 g unsalted butter, softened
1 x 15 ml spoon milk

Add to the dry ingredients and work together to a smooth dough. Roll out on a floured surface to one large round and cut into 8 wedges, or cut into 12–16 rounds or ovals. Place on greased baking sheets and bake in the preheated oven for 20 minutes.

Opposite: Chocolate Chip Cookies.

CHOCOLATE BROWNIES

Brownies are an American phenomenon. Every cook across the continent has his or her own recipe, the authenticity of which is sworn to. Most contain chocolate, some classically fudge-like, some like marble cakes, and a few are paler, with a butterscotch flavour. This is my version, made without flour.

USA   MAKES ABOUT 16 BROWNIES   OVEN: 180°C/350°F/GAS 4

100 g unsweetened cooking chocolate, diced	Place in a bowl over a pan of hot water and melt. Cool a little.
50 g unsalted butter, diced	Add, and stir well, still over the hot water, until the butter has melted and blended with the chocolate. Remove from the pan of water.
2 eggs 175 g caster sugar 1 x 5 ml spoon pure vanilla extract	In a separate bowl, beat together until fluffy and light, and then blend into the chocolate and butter mixture.
a good pinch each of baking powder and salt	Fold into the mixture.
50 g shelled pecan nuts or walnuts, roughly diced	Mix in. Pour the batter into a 20 cm square baking tin lined with greaseproof paper and bake in the preheated oven for about 15 minutes. Allow to cool, then cut into squares.

BLUEBERRY MUFFINS

Because a muffin batter is heavier then that of a popover (another American bread), it needs leavening (the baking powder), but this means that it can also take 'weightier' additions – blueberries as here (blackberries or cranberries), or dried fruit, chopped onion or bacon bits.

USA   MAKES 24 SMALL MUFFINS   OVEN 200°C/400°F/GAS 6

100 g blueberries plain flour	Wash the berries then place in a sieve. Sprinkle a little flour over the berries, tapping the sieve to get rid of any excess.
50 g butter, melted	Use about 2 x 15 ml spoons to generously grease 24 muffin cups or patty tins.
10 g baking powder 1 x 5 ml spoon salt 70 g caster sugar	Sift together into a bowl along with 250 g plain flour.
2 eggs, beaten 200 ml milk freshly grated zest of ½ lemon a drop of pure vanilla extract	Mix into the flour, along with the remaining melted butter. Fold in the floured berries. Spoon into the buttered cups or tins, allowing the mixture to come two-thirds of the way up the sides. Bake in the preheated oven for 20–25 minutes until risen and light brown in colour. Remove from the oven and rest for a few minutes before removing from the moulds. Serve warm, in a napkin-lined basket, spreading them with butter if liked.

CRULLAS
A plaited doughnut which is an Aberdeenshire speciality, but which was thought to have been introduced by the Dutch to the area, the name coming from the Dutch word for curl. Dutch settlers introduced them to the USA, where they are known as crullers.

SCOTLAND **MAKES ABOUT 24**

50 g butter 50 g caster sugar	Cream together in a bowl until light.
1 egg, beaten with 100 ml milk or buttermilk	Beat into the creamed mixture.
250 g plain flour ½ x 15 ml spoon baking powder ½ x 5 ml spoon each of salt and freshly grated nutmeg	Sift together, then stir into the egg mixture to make a fairly stiff dough. Chill for half an hour. Turn on to a floured board and knead until smooth. Roll out to 5 mm thick, and cut into lengths of 13 cm, 1 cm wide. Cut these into three even lengths, but keeping one end attached. Plait these lengths and seal the end together with a little water.
vegetable oil for deep-frying	Heat to about 170°C/340°F, and deep-fry the plaited lengths until light brown, turning once. Drain very well on kitchen paper.
icing sugar	Sprinkle over the crullas and serve warm or cold.

GHORIBA
Almonds grow in profusion all over North Africa, and many of the desserts, pastries and biscuits of the region make use of them. The name *ghoriba* is derived from the Arabic *ghorayebah*, or lovers' pastries, and they can be made in a variety of shapes, and stuffed with dates or other fruits.

ALGERIA **MAKES 12–16** **OVEN: 180°C/350°F/GAS 4**

150 g icing sugar 1 medium egg	Beat together in a bowl until white.
250 g ground almonds finely grated zest of 1 lemon 1 x 5 ml spoon orange-flower water or pure vanilla extract ½ x 5 ml spoon powdered cinnamon	Mix together well in a separate bowl, then gradually stir into the egg mixture. Knead for a few minutes to make the dough pliable. If too sticky, add a little plain flour.
plain flour	Lightly dust the work surface with flour and roll the dough out to a long sausage. Cut into 12–16 pieces, and roll each of these into a ball. Flatten to discs of about 8 cm in diameter. Place, spaced apart, on greased baking trays.
icing sugar sesame seeds (optional)	Sprinkle over the top of the biscuits, and then bake in the preheated oven for 6–8 minutes or until golden. Remove from the oven, and leave to cool, then store in an airtight tin.

BRANDY SNAPS

The original British gingerbread was hard and crisp rather like these biscuits. They were traditionally sold at fairs, thus they are occasionally known as 'fairings'. The biscuit mixture can also be made into flat circles or baskets to accompany desserts such as ice cream.

ENGLAND   **MAKES ABOUT 20**   **OVEN: 180°C/350°F/GAS 4**

120 g unsalted butter
120 g golden syrup
120 g granulated sugar

Place together in a small pan and stir over a low heat until the sugar has completely dissolved. Cool slightly.

120 g plain flour
a pinch of salt
2 x 5 ml spoons ground ginger
1 x 15 ml spoon brandy

Mix together, then stir well into the syrup. Drop 5 ml spoonfuls of the mixture on to two well greased baking sheets, allowing a lot of room for them to spread. Bake in the preheated oven for 6–8 minutes. Remove the top baking sheet, leaving the other in the turned-off oven with the door slightly ajar. (They need to be kept warm or they will set hard too soon.) Quickly loosen one biscuit at a time, lift on a spatula and wrap round the handle of a wooden spoon. Leave until set into a cigar shape, a matter of moments. Repeat with the other biscuits, working swiftly, and repeat the whole process with the biscuits from the oven. Bake any remaining mixture in the same way. When completely cold, store the biscuits in an airtight tin.

350 ml double cream

Whip, then pipe or spoon into the brandy snaps just before serving.

BAKLAVA

These crisp, sweet and very sticky pastries are served all over the Middle East, particularly in Greece and Turkey. They are looked upon as festival food as well as something to accompany tea or coffee.

TURKEY   **OVEN: 180°C/350°F/GAS 4**

200 g caster sugar
50 g clear honey
150 ml water
juice of ½ lemon

For the syrup, mix together in a pan and heat gently until it thickens slightly.

1 x 15 ml spoon orange-flower water

Add to the syrup and simmer for a few minutes more. Leave to cool, then chill.

250 g unsalted butter, melted
500 g filo pastry

Brush butter over the base and sides of a deep, medium square or rectangular baking dish or tin. Arrange a quarter of the filo sheets in it, one by one, brushing the top of each with melted butter.

300 g shelled nuts (walnuts, almonds or pistachios, or a mixture), finely diced
2 x 15 ml spoons caster sugar
1 x 5 ml spoon ground cinnamon

Mix together and scatter a third over the top layer of filo. Top with another quarter of the filo sheets, each one again brushed with butter, and scatter again with half the remaining nuts. Do this once more, and then top the baklava with the last quarter of filo sheets. Trim or tuck in the edges, and brush the neat top sheet with melted butter. Score diagonally through the layers to make diamond shapes. Bake in the preheated oven for 30 minutes, then raise the temperature to 220°C/425°F/Gas 7 and bake for a further 15 minutes or until the top of the baklava is crisp and a rich gold. Remove from the oven.

Quickly pour the cold syrup all over the hot baklava, then leave to cool. Cut in previously marked diamonds to serve.

Opposite: Brandy Snaps.

DESSERTS AND FRUIT

APPLE AND BLACKBERRY CRUMBLE
A classic of English desserts, using the apples which crop in the autumn, at the same time as blackberries – or brambles – ripen in the hedgerows. Add some very finely chopped almonds – about 2 x 15 ml spoons – to the crumble topping if you like.

ENGLAND · **SERVES 4** · **OVEN: 180°C/350°F/GAS 4**

3 large dessert apples	Peel, core and finely dice.
30 g unsalted butter	Heat in a pan, add the apple dice and gently sauté.
150 g caster sugar a pinch of ground cinnamon	Add and continue stirring until the apples are still a little crisp. A bit more cinnamon or sugar can be added to taste.
80 g fresh blackberries	Add to the apples and stir very gently for a moment, then remove from the heat. Spoon into little individual ovenproof dishes, or one large dish.
50 g unsalted butter, diced 100 g plain flour 50 g caster sugar	Lightly rub the butter into the flour and sugar until crumbly. Sprinkle this crumble mix over the top of the dish(es) until the fruit is just covered. Place in the preheated oven and bake until the topping is a light golden brown.
Vanilla Sauce (optional, see page 314) raspberry coulis (optional, see page 300) icing sugar 4 sprigs fresh mint	Serve the crumble with vanilla sauce, and with raspberry coulis drizzled over the top. Sprinkle with icing sugar and garnish with fresh mint.

CARROT HALWA
An Indian sweet, Middle Eastern in concept and origins, which can be served hot as a dessert or cold as a 'fudge' or fudgy cake. This recipe can be made using pumpkin or courgette instead of the carrot, and other types of nuts can replace the pistachios.

INDIA · **SERVES 4**

500 g carrots	Trim, peel and finely grate. Place in a large heavy-bottomed pan.
750 ml milk 6 cardamom pods, lightly crushed	Add to the pan and bring to the boil. Turn the heat down to very low indeed, cover, and cook to reduce the milk. Stir every now and again to prevent sticking. It can take up to 2 hours for the mixture to become thick and dryish. Remove the cardamom.
50 g unsalted clarified butter or ghee	Heat in a large non-stick frying pan and add the dry carrot mixture. Stir and fry for about 10–15 minutes until the mixture changes colour, becoming a glossy dark orange.
100 g caster sugar 1 x 5 ml spoon ground cardamom 25 g shelled unsalted pistachios, roughly ground	Add to the mixture and fry for a few minutes more. Remove from the heat and serve hot, or pour into a suitable container and leave to cool and 'set'.

Apple and Blackberry Crumble

PAIN PATATE

This sweet potato pudding is a Creole dish from New Orleans. In Hawaii, chopped pineapple, orange juice and orange zest are added to the plain mixture of sweet potato and butter before baking.

USA

SERVES 4   **OVEN: 180°C/350°F/GAS 4**

4 large sweet potatoes	Scrub, then bake in the preheated oven for 1–1½ hours, or until tender. Cool a little, then peel. Rub the soft yellow flesh through a sieve into a bowl.
3 medium eggs, separated	Add the yolks to the potato flesh and mix well.
300 g caster sugar **50 g unsalted butter, melted** **salt and freshly ground pepper**	Beat into the potato, seasoning very minimally, to taste, with salt and pepper.
300 ml milk	Stir in gradually, followed by the egg whites, whipped to a froth. Fold together gently to a smooth, soft, batter consistency. Pour into a suitable buttered pie dish and bake in the preheated oven for 1 hour until well browned.

DESSERTS AND FRUIT

APPLE AND STRAWBERRY STRUDEL
The Turks may have introduced the idea of tissue-thin pastry to Hungary and Austria, but the Hungarians have made strudels uniquely their own. The filling is not traditional – but it is delicious!

HUNGARY　　　　　**SERVES 4**　　　　**OVEN: 200°C/400°F/GAS 6**

3 large strudel (filo) pastry sheets
165 g unsalted butter, melted

Lay the sheets of pastry out flat on the work surface. Brush with about 100 g of the butter, enough to completely cover the pastry. Stack on top of each other.

200 g soft white breadcrumbs

Pan-fry in most of the remaining melted butter, about 50 g, until coloured. Spread evenly over the pastry, leaving a 1 cm border around the outside edge.

4 large dessert apples

Peel, quarter and slice half of the apples. Roughly chop the remainder. Heat the remaining butter in a heavy-bottomed pan. Sweat the apples until slightly softened. Spread the apples over the breadcrumbs.

250 g strawberries

Arrange on top of the apples without crushing.

150 g flaked toasted hazelnuts
30 g brown sugar

Sprinkle over the top of the strawberries.
　　Fold the long edge of the filo in by 1 cm. Roll the strudel, starting from the short side nearest you. Lift carefully on to a lightly oiled baking sheet. Ensure that the 'fold' is underneath. Bake in the preheated oven until golden brown, basting occasionally with more melted butter, about 30–40 minutes.

800 g natural yoghurt
juice of 1 lemon
20 g caster sugar
a pinch of ground cinnamon

For the yoghurt sauce, blend the ingredients together, adding cinnamon to taste.
　　Slice the strudel and serve each portion with some of the sauce.

BREAD AND BUTTER PUDDING
When I first came to England, to London to work in The Dorchester, I was introduced to a cuisine that I thought was a little heavy. Bread and butter pudding attracted me particularly, so, after a few experiments, I came up with a lighter and therefore much healthier version.

ENGLAND　　　　　**SERVES 4**　　　　**OVEN: 160°C/325°F/GAS 3**

30 g unsalted butter

Use a little to grease a large ovenproof dish lightly.

3 small bread rolls, sliced

Use the rest of the butter to spread over the bread slices. Arrange the bread slices in the base of the dish.

250 ml each of milk and double cream
a little salt
1 vanilla pod, split

Place together in a pan and bring to the boil gently.

3 eggs
125 g caster or vanilla sugar

Beat together in a bowl until pale. Gradually add the milk and cream mixture to the eggs, stirring well to amalgamate. Strain into a clean pan.

10 g sultanas, soaked in water and drained

Add to the bread in the dish, along with the milk mixture. The bread will float to the top. Place the dish in a bain-marie on top of folded newspaper, and pour in enough hot water to come halfway up the sides of the dish. Bake carefully in the preheated oven for 45–50 minutes. When the pudding is ready, it should wobble very slightly in the middle. Remove from the oven and cool a little.

20 g apricot jam
icing sugar

Gently heat the jam, thinning with a little water if necessary. Lightly brush a thin coat of the warm glaze over the top of the pudding, then dust with icing

PASSION FRUIT SOUFFLE

This is one of the most popular desserts at my club, and thus should really be defined as English, although the passionfruit hail originally from South America and the concept is French. To make the juice, scoop seeds and flesh from about 12–14 fruit and place in a blender. Liquidise briefly to release the seeds from the juice, taking care not to break up the seeds, then strain.

ENGLAND   SERVES 4   OVEN: 180°C/350°F/GAS 4

melted butter and sugar for the dish

Butter a 1.5 litre glass, china or silver soufflé dish evenly and carefully. Brush it on in two even layers, chilling well in between. Dust with sugar. Have ready a water bath or bain-marie half full of boiling water.

3 egg yolks
210 g caster sugar
150 ml passionfruit juice

Beat the yolks with half the caster sugar and two-thirds of the passionfruit juice.

6 egg whites

Whisk the whites with the remaining caster sugar until thick and creamy, as for meringues. Very carefully fold the whites into the yolk mixture. Pour the mixture into the prepared dish and give it a fairly firm tap against the work surface to make it nice and smooth, with no air bubbles.

Poach in the steaming bain-marie on top of the stove for 8–10 minutes. Remove the soufflé dish from the bain-marie and bake in the preheated oven for 25–30 minutes.

seeds and flesh of 1 passionfruit
20 g caster sugar
juice of ½ lemon
2 x 15 ml spoons water

To make the passionfruit sauce, boil up with the remaining passionfruit juice.

1 x 5 ml spoon cornflour, slaked in a little water

Mix into the warm sauce and bring to the boil, stirring. Blend for 30 seconds. Serve lukewarm.

icing sugar

Dust over the top of the soufflé when it is ready, and serve immediately. Serve the sauce separately, perhaps with a little whipped cream or natural yoghurt as well.

CAPPUCCINO CREME BRULEE
A mixture of Italian and English concepts, this is another popular dessert at Mosimann's. It's a cupful of coffee-flavoured custard with a sweet coffee sabayon on top – the brûlée is sandwiched in between them!

ITALY

SERVES 4

600 ml double cream
50 g instant coffee
1 vanilla pod, cut in half
1 cinnamon stick

Place in a large saucepan, scraping in the seeds from the vanilla pod. Bring the mixture to the boil, then remove from the heat. Remove and rinse the vanilla pod; dry and reserve for another use. Remove the cinnamon stick.

6 medium egg yolks
85 g caster sugar

Make sure that the yolks are completely free of the whites. Whisk the yolks with the sugar until the sugar is completely dissolved. Slowly whisk the warm cream into the egg mixture until well blended. Return the mixture to a clean pot. Stirring constantly (otherwise the mixture will curdle), cook the mixture over very low heat until the custard thickens and will coat the back of a wooden spoon. Remove from the heat. Strain into a clean pot.
Divide the mixture between four ramekins or heatproof dessert cups: only fill them about two-thirds full. Chill quickly, preferably overnight.

65 g caster sugar
130 ml water

Melt together to make a stock syrup. Cool.

150 g caster sugar 130 ml Kahlua 6 medium egg yolks	For the sabayon, whisk together with the stock syrup in a bowl over simmering water until hot. Remove from the heat and keep whisking until it is light and fluffy. Keep warm.
60 g soft brown sugar	Sprinkle over the custard cream in the dessert cups. Put the cups on a tray and place the tray under a hot grill to caramelise. Pour the sabayon over the caramelised sugar to the top of the dessert cups.
ground cinnamon	Sprinkle over the top of the desserts using a stencil for decoration.

CREME CARAMEL
This is another classic of the French kitchen, but in ingredients (milk, sugar and eggs basically), and method of cooking, it is very like the baked custards of British tradition. Similar dishes actually recur in many European cuisines – in Spain, Portugal and Belgium.

FRANCE **SERVES 6** **OVEN: 150°C/300°F/GAS 2**

vegetable oil	Use a little to lightly grease six small moulds that can hold 100 ml liquid each. They must have a level bottom.
100 g caster sugar	Place in a small pan and heat gently to melt, stirring continuously with a wooden spoon.
1 x 15 ml spoon water	When the sugar has gone a light caramel colour, add and mix quickly, then pour into the six oiled moulds, to a depth of about 3 mm. Leave to cool. (Any leftover caramel can be boiled up with some water for a sauce.)
500 ml milk ¼ vanilla pod, chopped	Bring to the boil together in a medium pan.
100 g caster sugar 3 eggs 2 egg yolks	Beat together thoroughly in a large bowl. Gradually stir in the hot milk to make the custard base. Strain through a fine sieve and pour into the prepared moulds. Place the moulds into a water bath or bain-marie, containing enough hot water to come halfway up the sides of the moulds. Cook in the preheated oven for about 40 minutes or until set. Remove the moulds from the oven and the bain-marie, and leave to get cold. To serve, run the point of a knife round the mould, and then turn the crème caramels out on to serving plates.

ZABAGLIONE
A creamy dessert flavoured with the sweet wine of Sicily, Marsala. It should be eaten warm, freshly made in goblets or glasses, but it can also be served cold; carry on whipping over ice until cool.

ITALY **SERVES 4**

4 egg yolks 60 g caster sugar	Place in the top of a double boiler, or in a bowl that will fit over (not in) a pan of simmering water. Off the heat, beat with a wire whisk (or a hand-held electric mixer) until pale yellow and fluffy.
6 x 15 ml spoons Marsala (or, if difficult to find, a fruit eau-de-vie or a sweet white wine)	Whisk into the egg yolks and place the pan or bowl over the heat. If using the bowl, it must not touch the water. Continue whisking until the mixture triples in size and becomes very thick, light and hot. Serve immediately.

SALZBURGER NOCKERLN

A famous dessert said to have been invented by a chef of the Salzburg archbishop in the eighteenth century. These meringue dumplings are occasionally poached on top of the stove in the same way as Oeufs à la Neige. (See page 299)

AUSTRIA　　　　　**SERVES 4**　　　**OVEN: 220°C/425°F/GAS 7**

40 g unsalted butter	Use to grease an oval ovenproof dish 33 cm long lightly.
6 eggs, separated 75 g caster sugar	Whip the egg whites in a large bowl until stiff, gradually adding the sugar. Add the egg yolks at the side of the bowl, mixing them with a little of the whipped egg white.
25 g plain flour seeds from ½ vanilla pod	Sprinkle over the whipped egg white, then use a balloon whisk to distribute these and the yolks as evenly as possible, without deflating the whipped egg white. 　　Heat the dish so that the butter melts. Scoop up the mixture into 8 portions, and place in the hot dish. Transfer immediately to the preheated oven and bake for 5–8 minutes, until the dumplings become golden brown in colour.
icing sugar	Sift over the dumplings and serve immediately.

GULAB JAMUN

One of the most famous Indian desserts. A fragrant batter-dough is deep-fried slowly in ball shapes, then immersed in cold syrup. The syrup can be flavoured further – with lime juice and zest perhaps, or cardamom seeds.

INDIA　　　　　**SERVES 4**

25 g plain flour 120 g dried milk powder 25 g unsalted butter, softened 1 x 15 ml spoon ground almonds 1 x 5 ml spoon ground cardamom	Mix together, using a little water to form a stiff dough. Rest for a few minutes, then form into eight balls.
300 ml water 150 g caster sugar	Bring to the boil together, then simmer to make a thickened syrup.
1 x 5 ml spoon rose water	Add to the syrup.
vegetable oil or ghee for deep-frying	Heat in a suitable pan and deep-fry the balls over a low to medium heat until golden brown on the outside, about 5 minutes. Drain very well on kitchen paper, then immerse in the syrup. Leave to cool.
50 g unsalted shelled pistachio nuts, chopped	Sprinkle over the balls. Serve them warm or cold, drained from the syrup.

COCONUT CUSTARD
The Thais substitute coconut milk for cows' milk in this custard dish, *sankhaya*, introduced by the colonising Portuguese and Spanish – in whose cuisines even today flans or custards play a significant role. They also introduced custards to their colonies in South America and the Philippines.

THAILAND

SERVES 4

285 ml thick coconut milk
115 g light brown sugar
a pinch of salt

Stir together well to dissolve the sugar.

about 120 g fruit

Choose from a variety: mango, papaya, banana etc. Prepare as appropriate, and then cut into small pieces. Divide between four ramekin dishes (you could use four half baby green coconut shells!).

3 medium eggs, lightly beaten

Whisk into the coconut milk and strain into the ramekin dishes on top of the fruit. Place in a steamer basket over boiling water. Cover the tops of the dishes with foil, and cook for 25 minutes, or until the custards have just set.

1 x 15 ml spoon apricot glaze

Brush over the tops of the custards. Serve hot or cold.

APPLE AND APRICOT TART
The Dauphiné region stretches from the Alps to the Rhône Valley, and it is famous for its vineyards and its fruit trees, particularly peaches and apricots.

FRANCE

SERVES 8   **OVEN: 200°C/400°F/GAS 6**

sweet pastry (see page 288)

Roll the dough out and use to line a 25 cm tart tin with a removeable base. Chill. Line with foil, fill with baking beans, then bake blind in the preheated oven for about 10 minutes. Remove the beans and foil, and bake the flan case for another 6–10 minutes. Cool. Reduce the temperature of the oven to 180°C/350°F/Gas 4.

600 g crisp dessert apples

Peel, core and slice.

75 g unsalted butter
50 g caster sugar

Melt the butter in a large frying pan and add the apple slices. Sprinkle with the sugar and fry gently for a few moments.

2 x 15 ml spoons apple or apricot
    brandy (optional)

Pour over the fruit and flame, if using. Remove from the heat and leave to cool slightly. Arrange the apple slices neatly over the base of the pastry-lined tart tin.

4–6 fresh apricots

Wash, dry, then halve and stone. Arrange decoratively on top of the apple slices, cut side down.

2 eggs
75 g icing sugar
40 g ground almonds
250 ml double cream

Beat together in a bowl, then pour over the apple and apricots in the tart tin. Bake in the preheated oven for 20–25 minutes, until the cream topping has set. Serve warm.

CARAMELISED APPLE TART

France is famous for her fruit tarts and pies, and especially for a large number of apple tarts. This one comes from Normandy, the home of apples, apple cider, and apple brandy or Calvados. It uses an almond cream, a frangipane, as a base for the sliced apples. Pears could be used instead.

FRANCE **SERVES 4** **OVEN: 190°C/375°F/GAS 6**

4–5 dessert apples

Peel, core and halve the apples. Cut into very thin slices.

80 g unsalted butter, very soft
80 g caster sugar

To start the frangipane, whisk together until light and fluffy.

1 large egg, beaten
100 g ground almonds
30 g plain flour
1 x 15 ml spoon milk
a splash of Calvados

Fold into the butter and sugar.

4 thin rounds puff pastry, approx.
    15 cm in diameter

Chill well or freeze before use. Arrange on a lightly greased baking sheet, and spread each with the frangipane, leaving a narrow margin clear. (You may have some left over. Freeze for another use.) Smooth the surface. Arrange the apple slices around the pastry in a circle, starting at the edge and working towards the centre.

25 g unsalted butter, melted

Brush over the top of the tartlets. Bake in the preheated oven for about 30–35 minutes or until the pastry is light brown in colour.

icing sugar

Dust over the tops of the tartlets, then place under a hot grill to caramelise, a few moments only.

4 scoops Vanilla Ice Cream (see page 300)
4 sprigs fresh mint

Serve the tartlets at room temperature decorated with scoops of vanilla ice cream and the mint.

ENGADINE WALNUT TART

The Grisons or Graubünden area of eastern Switzerland is famous for its pastry cooks, and this nut tart – *Engadiner Nusstorte* – is typical of their wares. It is a closed tart, made with a rich pastry, and with a filling of walnuts (or hazelnuts), cream and honey.

SWITZERLAND   **SERVES 8**   **OVEN: 200°C/400°F/GAS 6**

350 g plain flour
125 g caster sugar
150 g unsalted butter, softened

For the shortbread pastry, place in a bowl, and rub together until the texture resembles fine crumbs.

1 egg
1 egg yolk
a tiny pinch of salt
finely grated zest of ¼ lemon

Add to the bowl, using only half of the egg yolk, and mix well. Press two thirds of this into the base and up the sides of a greased 20 cm flan ring. Prick the base with a fork. Chill.

225 g caster sugar
50 ml liquid glucose
2 x 15 ml spoons lemon juice

To start the filling, place in a medium pan, and melt slowly to a light caramel.

150 ml double cream

Pour carefully into the caramel, mix well and bring to the boil. Turn the heat down immediately.

50 g clear honey
300 g shelled walnuts, halved
200 g caster sugar
25 g unsalted butter

Mix into the cream to melt sugar and butter, and leave to cool until still just warm. Spoon into the lined flan ring, and smooth the top. Roll out the remaining shortbread pastry to a circle for the lid. Place on top of the filling and pinch the edges to seal. Brush the top with the remaining egg yolk. Bake in the preheated oven for 25 minutes. Leave to cool.

100 g dark Swiss chocolate

Melt over hot water, then drizzle over the top of the tart. Store for a day before serving.

LEMON AND MASCARPONE TART WITH BLUEBERRY SAUCE

This delicious tart is made with Florida lemons and Italian soft cheese, and sauced by native American blueberries. Use the sweet pastry here for other tart bases.

USA   **SERVES 8**   **OVEN: 200°C/400°F/GAS 6**

300 g blueberries (or blackberries)

For the sauce, purée in a liquidiser, then push through a fine sieve.

30 g icing sugar
juice of 1 lemon

Add to the berry liquid, and chill until ready to use.

185 g plain flour
60 g icing sugar
a pinch of salt

For the sweet pastry, mix together in a bowl, then make a well in the centre.

2 medium egg yolks 140 g unsalted butter, softened	Add to the well, and bring the mixture quickly but gently together. (If you over-work the dough, the pastry will be tough.) Wrap in clingfilm and chill for at least 2–3 hours. When chilled, grate the dough into a 25 cm tart tin with a removeable base, and gently press over the base and up the sides of the tin. Or you could roll the pastry between pieces of greaseproof paper or clingfilm, and fit into the tin. Chill for at least 20–30 minutes. Line with foil, fill with baking beans and bake in the preheated oven for 15 minutes. Remove the foil and beans. Reduce the oven temperature to 180°C/350°F/Gas 4.
6 medium eggs 4 medium egg yolks 350 g caster sugar	For the lemon filling, whisk together in a mixer or processor until light and fluffy. Make sure the sugar has dissolved.
90 g unsalted butter, softened 150 g mascarpone cheese, softened zest of 5 lemons	Add to the egg mixture, and continue whisking at top speed for a few minutes until thoroughly amalgamated. Reduce the speed of the mixer.
juice of 6 lemons	Add to the mixture and mix in well. Pour the lemon mixture into the tart shell and bake in the reduced temperature oven for 30–40 minutes, or until firm.
a little demerara sugar	Sprinkle over the surface of the tart and place under a hot grill to caramelise. To serve, cut in wedges, and decorate the plate with some of the berry sauce.

CHOCOLATE PECAN PIE
Pecan pie is a classic American recipe, coming from the South where pecan trees, native to America, grow both wild and cultivated in great profusion. I have added some chocolate to the sweet filling, another ingredient native to the Americas, although from even further south then the pecan.

USA **SERVES 8** **OVEN: 200°C/400°F/GAS 6**

sweet pastry (see page 288)	Roll out and use to line a 20 cm tart tin. Chill. Line with foil, fill with baking beans, then bake blind in the preheated oven for 10 minutes. Remove the beans and foil, and bake the flan case for another 6–10 minutes. Cool. Reduce the temperature of the oven to 180°C/350°F/Gas 4.
120 g plain chocolate, chopped into small pieces 50 g unsalted butter	Melt together gently over a pan of hot water.
4 eggs 230 ml dark corn syrup (or maple syrup) a few drops of pure vanilla extract	Whisk together, then mix well with the melted chocolate.
225 g shelled pecan nuts	Stir into the chocolate mixture, then pour into the cooled pastry case. Bake in the moderate oven for about 30 minutes until the tart has puffed slightly in the centre and is just set. Serve warm.

LINZER TORTE

Austria, and especially Vienna, is known the world over for the quality and diversity of her pâtisserie, which includes *Dobostorte*, *Gugelhopf* and *Sachertorte*. *Linzer Torte* is one of the most famous, a latticed shortcake with raspberry jam. It tastes best a few days after baking.

AUSTRIA   MAKES 1 x 16 cm TART   OVEN: 180°C/350°F/GAS 4

125 g plain flour 125 g unsalted butter, softened	For the torte base, place in a large bowl, and mix together lightly with the fingers until the texture is like fine crumbs.
125 g ground hazelnuts 100 g caster sugar 3 x 5 ml spoons cocoa powder 1 x 5 ml spoon ground cinnamon	Mix into the flour.
2 x 5 ml spoons Kirsch	Mix well into the dry mixture. Press most of this – a little more than three quarters – into the base and up the sides of a buttered and floured 16 cm tart tin. Chill. Wrap the remaining mixture in clingfilm and chill as well.
70 ml raspberry jam	Spread over the base of the chilled tart.
1 egg yolk	Roll the remaining tart base mixture out and cut into strips to make the traditional lattice pattern on top. Glaze the strips with the yolk. Bake in the preheated oven for 1 hour (less for individual tarts).
about 2 x 15 ml spoons apricot jam	Heat to melt, then, using a pastry brush, brush the liquid over the lattice of the tart to glaze it. Leave to cool.

CHOCOLATE PUDDING

One of the famous Austrian baked desserts, this is sometimes known as *Mohr im Hemd* (which translates as 'Othello in his Nightgown') because of the darkness of the pudding contrasting with the whiteness of the cream served with it.

AUSTRIA   SERVES 10   OVEN: 160–180°C/325–350°F/GAS 3–4

100 g dark plain chocolate, broken into pieces	Melt in a bowl over hot water.
6 eggs, separated seeds from ½ vanilla pod 80 g caster sugar	Add the egg yolks, vanilla seeds and half the sugar to the chocolate, and mix well, beating until the egg yolks become fluffy. 　　Beat the egg whites with the remaining sugar until stiff, then mix a quarter of them into the chocolate mixture.
100 g shelled almonds, finely chopped 50 g soft white breadcrumbs	Mix together and then fold carefully into the chocolate mixture, along with the remaining whisked egg white.
butter and caster sugar	Grease a 1.25 litre pudding mould with a little butter and dust with sugar, shaking out any excess. Pour in the pudding mixture and then place in a water bath or bain-marie. The water should reach almost up to the rim of the mould. Bake in the preheated oven for 35–40 minutes.
lightly whipped double cream	Serve with the hot pudding, poured down over the top of the whole pudding, or over each portion.

Opposite: Linzer Torte.

MOUSSE AU CHOCOLAT
Chocolate mousse is a classic French dessert, although there are a myriad different recipes. This one is a favourite of mine. You can add other flavourings such as Benedictine, Cointreau or Kirsch, or a little finely grated orange zest (good with chocolate).

FRANCE

SERVES 4

5 eggs, separated
caster (or vanilla) sugar

Whip the egg whites until stiff, gradually adding 50 g of the sugar.
Beat the egg yolks with 25 g of the sugar until the mixture is airy and the sugar has dissolved.

200 g dark plain chocolate, broken into pieces

Meanwhile, melt in a bowl over a pan of hot water.

4 x 15 ml spoons strong hot coffee (preferably mocha)

Stir into the chocolate. Stir the egg yolks into the chocolate mixture.

150 ml double cream, lightly whipped

Fold into the chocolate mixture, followed by the whipped egg whites. Pour into a serving bowl or bowls, cover with clingfilm, and chill for at the most 2 hours. Serve with a little more cream.

CHOCOLATE TRUFFLE DELICE
A popular dessert at Mosimann's, using some of Switzerland's wonderful chocolate. You can serve it with a chocolate sauce as here, or with Vanilla Ice Cream (see page 300) and a chocolate fan or other decoration as in the photograph on page 294. It is often made with a chocolate genoese sponge base.

SWITZERLAND

SERVES 8

75 ml water
50 ml liquid glucose
1½ gelatine leaves, soaked in water to soften, drained

Heat together in a pan for a few minutes to melt the gelatine.

250 g good dark chocolate, finely chopped

Place in a pan, and pour in the gelatine mixture to melt the chocolate. Mix until smooth, then cool to body temperature.

500 ml whipping cream, semi-whipped

Working quickly, fold into the chocolate mixture and mix well. Pour into a 20 cm round cake tin with a removeable base. Leave to set in a cool place.

cocoa powder

Dust over the top of the cake.

375 ml water
250 g good dark Swiss chocolate, finely chopped

For the chocolate sauce, bring the water to the boil, add the chocolate, then remove from the heat.

125 g cocoa powder
125 g caster sugar
125 ml water

Mix to a thick paste and combine with the melted chocolate. Return to the pan and bring back to the boil. Mix until smooth and creamy.
To serve, portion the cake, and serve with the chocolate sauce (or vanilla sauce), or vanilla ice cream.

CRANACHAN

A simple cream dessert which uses Scottish oatmeal, Scotch whisky (or rum), and some of the luscious Scottish raspberries which grow wild in many parts of the country, and are also cultivated.

SCOTLAND

SERVES 4

100 g medium oatmeal

Toast until golden in a dry pan. Cool.

300 ml double cream
caster sugar
malt whisky or rum (or pure vanilla extract)

Whip the cream until stiff, adding sugar and liquor or vanilla to taste. Stir in the toasted oatmeal, and divide between four shallow glasses. Chill.

175 g fresh raspberries
a little raspberry coulis (see page 300)

Prepare the raspberries, then moisten them with the coulis. Use to decorate the oatmeal cream. Or layer the cream, raspberries and coulis in the glasses.

PASKHA

A rich creamy cheese pudding that is made at Easter and is traditionally served with Kulitsch (see page 264). 'Paskha' means 'Easter' in Russian. The pudding is usually made in a tall, four-sided mould with a hole in the bottom; use a large clean flowerpot instead – the whey must drain out.

RUSSIA

SERVES 8

675 g curd or ricotta cheese

Hang in a muslin bag over a bowl in a cool place for about 12 hours so that excess whey can drip out. Or place in a colander and put a heavy weight on top. When the cheese is dry, rub it through a sieve into a bowl.

50 g each of blanched almonds, candied fruit and peel, and glacé cherries
75 g raisins

Keep a little of the almonds and cherries aside (for decoration), then chop all the fruit except for the raisins. Mix evenly into the smooth cheese.

100 g unsalted butter, softened
1 x 5 ml spoon pure vanilla extract

Mix into the cheese.

2 small eggs
100 g caster sugar

Beat together, then mix into the cheese. Beat until smooth.

50 ml double cream or soured cream

Stir into the cheese and again beat the mixture until smooth. Pour the mixture into the chosen, muslin-lined mould, fold the muslin over, and weight down. Stand in a dish so that any remaining whey can drain out, and chill for 12 hours.
　　Turn out of the mould, remove the muslin, and decorate with the reserved almonds and cherries.

Chocolate Truffle Délice (see page 292).

PAVLOVA
The pavlova, a soft-centred meringue 'nest', was made for the great ballet dancer, Anna Pavlova, when she visited Australia in the 1930s. The meringue nest can be filled with cream mixed with one of the traditional pavlova fruits, passionfruit, and decorated with the other, kiwi fruit, both of which grow extensively in Australia and New Zealand.

AUSTRALIA   **SERVES 4**   **OVEN: 150°C/300°F/GAS 2**

4 egg whites	Beat in a large bowl until foamy.
½ x 5 ml spoon salt	Add and continue to beat until the whites become stiff and form peaks.
225 g caster sugar	Beat in, a little at a time, until the pavlova mixture is glossy and all the sugar has been incorporated.

Pavlova

2 x 5 ml spoons cornflour **2 x 5 ml spoons white wine vinegar**	Blend together, then fold into the pavlova mixture. Spoon the mixture into small compact circles on an oiled sheet of silicone paper on a baking sheet. You need at least four. Use a wetted spoon to make the top of each pavlova slightly concave. Place in the preheated oven and immediately reduce the temperature to 120°C/250°F/Gas ½. Bake for about 45–60 minutes. Leave to cool in the oven. Keep in a dry atmosphere.
150 ml double cream, whipped	To serve, place a little cream into the concave pavlova tops.
appropriate national, or seasonal, fruit **e.g. strawberries, kiwi fruit, mango,** **raspberries and passionfruit**	Decorate the top of the pavlova with the prepared fruit.
raspberry coulis (see page 300), **a little pouring cream or natural yoghurt** **icing sugar**	Decorate the plates with a little coulis and some pouring cream or yoghurt, and sprinkle with icing sugar.

CHEESECAKE WITH BLACKBERRY COULIS
Cheesecakes originated in the Old World and were taken to the New by settlers from Germany, Hungary, England. These were baked cheesecakes; the use of gelatine has developed in the USA. (Photograph page 298)

USA

SERVES 4

35 g unsalted butter	Melt in a small pan.
90 g digestive or gingernut biscuits	Make into crumbs, and then mix with the melted butter. Press these crumbs all over the bases of four small ramekins in an even layer. Chill to set.
1 recipe blackberry coulis (see page 300)	Spoon 1 x 15 ml spoon into each ramekin.
175 g soft cream cheese 45 g caster sugar finely grated zest of ½ lemon	Beat together until soft and creamy.
1 egg yolk	Beat into the cheese mixture until light and fluffy.
150 ml double cream 1 x 5 ml spoon Kirsch	Beat together until the cream just holds soft peaks.
1 egg white	Whisk until stiff.
juice of 1 lemon 1 gelatine leaf, soaked in cold water to soften	Heat the lemon juice gently, add the soaked gelatine, and dissolve. Cool, then stir into the cheese mixture and beat well together. Fold in the whipped cream and then the whisked egg white. Pour the mixture into the prepared biscuit-lined dishes, smooth the tops, and chill until set, about 1–2 hours. Serve with the remaining blackberry coulis on the side.

BANANA FLAMBE
Bananas grow in the tropics all round the world, and feature in cuisines as diverse as Malay and South American. The principle of this recipe, too, has been adopted in many countries, but the lime and rum proclaim it as indisputably Caribbean. A recipe from Antigua bakes the bananas in the oven with some rum instead of sautéing them, then flames them at the end.

CARIBBEAN

SERVES 4

4 large, medium-ripe bananas	Just before you want to serve, peel and cut in half lengthways.
25 g butter	Melt in a frying pan large enough to hold the banana pieces. Sauté the banana on high heat until browned, turning once.
120 ml lime juice 50 g caster sugar 120 ml dark rum	Combine, using only half the rum. Pour the mixture over the bananas, and cook for a couple of minutes. Pour the remainder of the rum into the pan and set alight. Serve as soon as the flames have died down.

FRUIT SUSHI
This is not traditional, but a sweet adaptation of the sushi concept — a flavoured rice with a delicious topping. Use any fruit available. Choose from starfruit, mango, pawpaw, lychees or rambutan, kiwi, strawberries, peaches — the more colourful the better. Madori is a green melon liqueur, made in Japan.

JAPAN

SERVES 4

350 g Japanese rice, well rinsed 260 ml each of milk and water, mixed	Place in a pan, bring to the boil, then cover and simmer very slowly for 15 minutes. Remove from the heat and leave to stand for 15 minutes, still covered. The rice should have absorbed all the liquid. Drain well if necessary. Transfer to a large bowl.
45 ml thick coconut milk 1 x 15 ml spoon caster sugar 1 x 15 ml spoon Madori liqueur	Mix into the rice, and then leave to cool completely. The rice should be very flavourful. Mould into little sushi ovals and arrange on a platter or individual plates, about 5–6 per plate.
150 g assorted prepared fresh fruit in season	Cut, trim, slice etc as appropriate, and place on top of the rice ovals.
split almonds, pistachio nuts, lemon and orange rind julienne, mint leaves etc.	Use as decoration.
1 quantity raspberry or other fruit coulis (see page 300, optional)	Serve with the fruit sushi if liked.

PINEAPPLE WITH BLACK PEPPER
Pineapples are native to eastern South America and the West Indies, and the fruits were not known in the West until after Columbus discovered the New World. They feature in many ways in Caribbean cooking, in poultry dishes, in ice creams, mousses and other desserts, and in the famous West Indian rum cocktails such as daiquiri and piña colada.

CARIBBEAN

SERVES 4

100 g caster sugar	To start the sauce, melt in a pan and let it become slightly brown, a caramel.
50 ml each of fresh orange juice and dark rum 20 ml lime juice	Add, and gently simmer to reduce a little.
30 g unsalted butter, melted finely cut zest of ½ orange, blanched	Add to the sauce, and keep to one side.
1 pineapple, about 300 g	To prepare the pineapple, peel the fruit and cut into slices of about 1 cm thick. Remove the middle core.
freshly ground black pepper	Sprinkle over the pineapple slices.
40 g unsalted butter 25 ml dark rum	Heat the butter in a wide shallow pan, add the pineapple slices, and flame with the rum. Cook until tender. Add the sauce and heat gently. To serve, divide the pineapple slices between four plates.
4 oval scoops Vanilla Ice Cream (see page 300)	Arrange an oval of ice cream in the middle of each slice of pineapple. Pour the hot sauce over the ice cream and serve immediately.

RUMTOPF

A classic Rumtopf – or 'bachelor's jam', as it is sometimes known! – is started in the summer, and fruits are added to the jar as they come into season, along with more sugar and alcohol to cover. The covered jar is carefully kept until Christmas, and the fruit is served with ice creams or with cream. This fresh version can be eaten within a week.

AUSTRIA/GERMANY

SERVES 4

150 g caster sugar
150 ml water

In a small saucepan, bring the sugar and water to the boil, making sure that the sugar is dissolved. Remove from the heat and cool completely.

80 ml dark rum
150 g each of fresh strawberries and raspberries
200 g mixed summer berries (wild strawberries, blackberries, blueberries, blackcurrants, tayberries or loganberries)

Add to the cold syrup, and leave to marinate in the fridge, covered with clingfilm, for up to a week.

OEUFS A LA NEIGE

These famous French 'snow eggs' are made from a meringue mixture which is poached (although it can also be baked); because so little sugar is used, the meringue remains soft and airy rather then becoming light and brittle. The poaching milk is used for the sauce, here a dessert vanilla sauce or pouring custard; often the meringue eggs are offered floating on chilled custard, when they are known as *iles flottantes*, or 'floating islands'.

FRANCE

SERVES 4

3 egg whites

Place in a bowl and whisk until stiff.

75 g caster sugar

Add, a little at a time, still whisking.

a squeeze of lemon juice

Add, and continue to whisk until stiff.

300 ml milk
1 vanilla pod, split

Heat together in a large shallow pan, and allow to infuse for a few minutes. Spoon or pipe eight large meringue shapes – the *oeufs* or eggs – into the milk. Simmer very gently for about 4 minutes, turning once. Drain carefully on a clean teatowel. Arrange two eggs on each plate.

Vanilla Sauce (see page 314), made with the hot poaching milk

Pour this around the eggs on the plates.

50 g caster sugar
2 x 15 ml spoons water

To make a caramel, heat gently together, then simmer until dark golden in colour. Drizzle over each egg.

2 x 15 ml spoons split almonds, toasted
icing sugar

Sprinkle the warm almonds over the eggs, and a little icing sugar over the plate.

Opposite: Above, Oeufs à la Neige. Below left, Summer Pudding (see page 300). Below right, Cheesecake with Blackberry Coulis (see page 296).

SUMMER PUDDING
The concept of summer fruit encased in bread is part of the Great British pudding tradition, and, like other stars in the same firmament, the recipe evolved as a way of using up leftover bread. Now it is a very special treat for the few weeks that the fruit are in season. Use white or wholemeal bread. (Photograph page 298)

GREAT BRITAIN   **SERVES 4**

a little vegetable oil

Brush lightly over four dariole moulds or small pudding basins.

at least 4 large thin slices bread

Remove crusts, and cut the bread into triangles. Use about half to line the inside of the moulds neatly.

2 gelatine leaves, soaked in cold
   water to soften
50 ml water
juice of ½ lemon

Squeeze the gelatine dry, then dissolve in the water. Stir in the lemon juice, then divide this liquid between three small pans.

100 g each of ripe strawberries,
   raspberries and blackberries
   (or blueberries)

Add the three fruits separately to the three pans, and stew for moments only until the juices just start to run, and the fruits still hold their shape. Cool.
   Place alternative layers of individual fruits and some of the remaining bread in the four moulds, finishing with a layer of any fruit left, mixed, along with some of the juices. Top with the last pieces of bread, cover with a saucer, and weight down with something heavy. Allow to set in the fridge overnight so that the juices can soak through the bread.

200 g raspberries
2 x 15 ml spoons icing sugar
juice of ½ small lemon

For the raspberry coulis, press the raspberries through a non-metal sieve, and mix the pulp with the sugar and lemon juice.
   Unmould the puddings on to the centre of four serving plates and carefully pour the sauce over to cover the bread and make it uniformly red.

seasonal fruit
4 fresh mint sprigs
icing sugar

Decorate the puddings with the chosen seasonal fruit, and top with the mint. Sprinkle the plate with a little icing sugar.

VANILLA ICE CREAM
Ice creams are said to be the province of the Italians, and the Americans claim to have invented them, but this creamy, richly vanilla-flavoured cream seems quintessentially French to me. It is certainly an apt partner for many French fruit tarts (see page 286).

FRANCE   **SERVES 10**

4 egg yolks
90 g caster sugar

Whisk together well in a bowl.

250 ml milk
250 ml double cream

Heat together in a pan until hot, then gradually pour into the yolks, stirring continuously. Pour the mixture back into the cleaned saucepan.

½ vanilla pod, cut lengthwise

Add, and bring the mixture to just below boiling point, stirring continuously, until the mixture coats the back of the wooden spoon or spatula.
   Remove from the heat and allow to cool in a cold bain-marie, stirring occasionally. Strain through a fine sieve and freeze in an ice-cream machine, or in the freezer in a suitable container, stirring every so often to prevent ice crystals forming.

KHOSHAF

A dried fruit compote, but one which is uncooked. It is popular all over the Middle East, and is quite often made with only apricots and raisins. It's good with yoghurt or ice cream, and is delicious for breakfast.

MIDDLE EAST   **SERVES 4**

2 x 15 ml spoons clear honey
700 ml water
zest and juice of 1 lemon
zest of ½ orange
juice of 1½ oranges
1 x 15 ml spoon each of rose water
    and orange-flower water
1 x 10 cm cinnamon stick

Mix together in a saucepan, then bring to the boil. Simmer for 3–4 minutes, then allow to cool.

500 g mixed dried fruit

Choose from apple rings, apricots, pears, peaches, prunes and raisins or sultanas. Place in a bowl, cover with the strained syrup and leave to soak for at least 48 hours.

50 g each of shelled almonds, walnuts
    and pistachios, soaked overnight in
    cold water

Drain well, and mix into the fruit salad about an hour before serving.

KULFI

Although it seems unlikely, ice cream has been made in India for many centuries. Kulfi is very firm and sweet, and is made with reduced milk – milk that has been simmered for hours – rather than with cream. Traditionally, it is frozen in small conical moulds.

INDIA   **SERVES 4**

1.5 litres milk

Place in a large and heavy wide pan. Bring slowly up nearly to the boil, then reduce the heat and simmer quite vigorously (but without boiling over) until the milk has reduced by about one-third of its original volume, and has thickened. Stir constantly to prevent burning and sticking. This takes about 1–1½ hours.

6 cardamom pods, slightly crushed

Add halfway through the reduction.

3 x 15 ml spoons caster sugar
75 g unsalted shelled pistachio nuts,
    finely ground

Add gradually to the thickened hot milk (known as *khoa* or *khoya*) off the heat and stir to melt the sugar. Leave to cool.
  When cold, place in a suitable container and freeze, stirring every now and again to break down the ice crystals, or churn in an ice-cream machine.

ICED ORANGE SOUFFLE

This cold soufflé is a classic of French *haute cuisine*. You will need to prepare a 1.25 litre freezerproof soufflé dish by wrapping it around the outside with a collar of good silicone paper, doubled. This collar must rise 4–5 cm above the rim of the dish. Secure.

FRANCE   **SERVES 10**

8 egg yolks 125 g caster sugar	Cream together until light – by hand or by machine. Transfer to a bowl sitting over a pan of warm water (or a double boiler).
3 gelatine leaves, soaked in cold water to soften, or 15 g powdered gelatine	Add to the bowl, stir in, then start to warm the egg yolk mixture, stirring constantly with a wooden spoon, until the mixture thickens enough to lightly coat the back of the spoon. Remove from the heat.
300 ml fresh orange juice, strained 100 ml Cointreau	Stir carefully into the mixture, then cool quickly and chill for about 30 minutes until the mixture becomes syrupy.
4 egg whites 125 g caster sugar	Whisk the whites until stiff, gradually adding the sugar. Stir a little into the orange and egg yolk mixture, then fold the remainder in carefully, using a large metal spoon.
350 ml double cream 25 g caster sugar	Whip together until stiff, and then fold carefully into the soufflé mix, using a wooden spoon. Pour into the prepared soufflé dish, and place in the freezer. Leave for at least 4 hours. Do not remove the collar.
cocoa powder	Dust a little over the top of the frozen soufflé and serve, cutting with a knife, or portioning with a spoon. Orange segments marinated in Grand Marnier could be used as a decoration.

PINK GRAPEFRUIT SORBET

Florida, the 'sunshine state', which consists of a peninsula pointing south towards the Caribbean, has a flourishing citrus fruit industry, and oranges, lemons, limes and grapefruit are widely grown and used in the local cooking.

USA   **SERVES 4**

90 g caster sugar 1 x 15 ml spoon water	Boil together carefully until the sugar melts. Leave the syrup to get cold.
125 ml pink grapefruit juice (use 1–1½ fruits) juice of ½ lemon 100 ml medium dry white wine 35 ml Campari	Mix together then strain and mix with the sugar syrup.
1 egg white	Beat until half stiff, then stir in the grapefruit mixture. Freeze in an ice-cream machine, or in the freezer in a suitable container, stirring every so often to prevent ice crystals forming.

Opposite: Individual Iced Orange Soufflés. At my club, we encase them in chocolate and top them with spun sugar.

DIPS, SAUCES
RELISHES AND
STOCKS

GUACAMOLE
Avocado trees are so common in Mexico, growing wild and in cultivation, that this fresh green paste is eaten with almost every meal – as a sauce for *chilli con carne*, as a filling for tortillas, as a side salad or as a dip for tortilla chips, crisps, crudités etc.

MEXICO

SERVES 4

2 large ripe avocadoes

Halve and remove the stones. Scoop the flesh from the skins into a bowl, and mash with a fork.

2–3 x 15 ml spoons fresh lime (or lemon) juice

Work into the avocado quickly to prevent discoloration.

1 small onion, peeled and finely diced
1 large tomato, skinned, seeded and diced
2 x 15 ml spoons finely chopped fresh coriander
1–2 fresh green chillies, seeded and finely sliced (serrano or jalapeño for authenticity)
salt to taste

Fold evenly into the avocado purée, and use as quickly as possible. If keeping for a while, brush with lemon juice and cover tightly with clingfilm.

TAPENADE
An olive dip/spread typical of the south of France. The name comes from the Provençal word for caper, an important ingredient. Use as a dip for crudités, or spread on biscuits or crostini for canapés; it could also be served as a pâté, and as a topping or sauce for hard-boiled eggs.

FRANCE

MAKES ABOUT 400 g

250 g oil-cured black olives, stoned
1 medium garlic clove, peeled
1½ x 15 ml spoons drained large capers
50 g anchovy fillets in oil, drained
50 g tuna in oil, drained

Purée in a blender or, more traditionally, pound together in a mortar.

4 x 15 ml spoons olive oil

Add as if making mayonnaise, a little at a time, until smooth.

juice of 1 lemon
2 x 5 ml spoons brandy (optional)
½ x 5 ml spoon dry mustard powder

Add the lemon juice as well as the other ingredients if liked. Keep in the refrigerator.

PESTO
This basil and pine kernel sauce is a speciality of Genoa, and is used as a pasta or fish sauce, and can be stirred at the last minute into soups. Non-traditionally, it can be made with parsley instead of basil, and the pine kernels can be replaced by walnuts.

ITALY

SERVES 4

25 g basil leaves
2 x 15 ml spoons pine kernels
1 garlic clove, peeled and crushed

Place in a mortar or liquidiser, and purée to a fine paste.

25 g fresh Parmesan, finely grated
100 ml olive oil

Add gradually, mixing in by hand or machine, until the pesto is smooth and creamy.

VINEGARED CUCUMBER
Serve as an accompaniment to almost any Japanese fish or meat dish.

JAPAN

SERVES 4

4 Japanese cucumbers, or 2 western
  cucumbers

Peel both types, and seed the western cucumbers. Cut into very fine slices (use a mandoline or a very sharp knife). Spread out on a large board or work surface.

salt

Sprinkle moderately over the cucumber slices and then work together with your hands for about 1 minute. Place in a bowl.

125 ml rice wine vinegar
125 ml *dashi* (see page 87)
2 x 15 ml spoons light soy sauce
2 x 5 ml spoons soft brown sugar

For the sauce, combine in a small non-stick pan and bring to a simmer to melt the sugar. Cool quickly (over ice cubes if possible).
   Gently squeeze the cucumber to rid it of juices and salt. Pour the sauce over the squeezed cucumber, and transfer to small individual dishes. Serve at room temperature.

CUCUMBER RELISH
This relish is good with the Thai Fishcakes on page 219. Garlic pickled in vinegar is enjoyed in both Thailand and China as a side dish, and is commonly available in cans or jars.

THAILAND

SERVES 4

60 ml Thai coconut or rice vinegar
60 ml water
50 g granulated sugar

Bring to the boil together in a small pan, then stir until the sugar dissolves. Remove from the heat and leave to cool.

1 head pickled garlic, diced
1 cucumber, quartered lengthways and
  sliced
4 shallots, peeled and finely sliced
1 x 15 ml spoon diced fresh root ginger
2 fresh red chilli peppers, seeded and
  finely sliced

Place in a bowl, pour in the cooled vinegar dressing, and mix well.

TSUKEMONO
Salted pickles such as this are served with rice at the end of every Japanese meal. You can make a mixed pickle, and cabbage can also be used, although it takes longer to 'pickle', up to four days. You could add a little lemon juice to the *daikon* or turnip pickle, or a little sliced red chilli pepper.

JAPAN

SERVES 4

300 g *daikon* (giant white radish, or
  mooli), or 4 small turnips, or 4 small
  pickling cucumbers

Prepare the chosen vegetable as appropriate. Peel the *daikon* and turnips and cut into slices about 5 mm thick, and then quarter these slices. Wipe the cucumbers, trim the ends, but do not peel; quarter lengthways, then cut into slices about 5 mm thick. Place in a bowl.

2 x 5 ml spoons salt

Sprinkle over the chosen vegetables, and mix well. Place on top of the vegetable a suitable saucer or plate and weight down with a heavy weight. Leave for at least 1 hour, and up to 4 hours.
   Drain thoroughly, then divide between four small individual plates.

shoyu (Japanese soy sauce, optional)

Sprinkle over the pickle just before it is eaten.

SPICY SAMBAL
Serve with Indonesian or other South-East Asian dishes.

INDONESIA

SERVES 4

1 medium onion, peeled and finely chopped
2 x 15 ml spoons vegetable oil

Heat gently together in a pan, and then cook for a few minutes to soften the onion.

3 garlic cloves, peeled and crushed

Add to the onion, and cook for a few minutes longer.

1 dried red chilli pepper, crushed
1 tomato, skinned, seeded and diced
1 x 5 ml spoon soft brown sugar
2 x 5 ml spoons *kecap ikan* (fish sauce)
salt and freshly ground pepper

Add to the onion, and season to taste with salt and pepper. Stir well, and continue to cook for a further 10 minutes. Serve hot or cold.

HARISSA
Harissa is a fiery sauce which features in a number of North African cuisines. It flavours fish or vegetable stews and soup, and it can spike a stew of chicken or meat. In Morocco, it is used as a condiment for Couscous (see page 90). It keeps well, and larger quantities may easily be made.

NORTH AFRICA

SERVES 4

2 dried red chilli peppers

Put in a bowl of cold water and leave to soak for about 45 minutes. Cut open and remove seeds and stalks. Drain the flesh then put in a liquidiser (or, more traditionally, in a mortar).

1 garlic clove, peeled
1 x 5 ml spoon caraway (or cumin) seeds
1 x 5 ml spoon coarse salt
3–4 x 15 ml spoons olive oil (or water)

Add to the pepper and whizz or pound until smooth, adding only enough oil or water to make it fluid and paste-like.

CAPE APRICOT CHUTNEY
The spices in this apricot chutney are typical, showing a Cape Malay influence.

SOUTH AFRICA

MAKES ABOUT 1–1.5 kg

125 g dried apricots, cut into thin strips
250 g seedless raisins
1 litre white wine vinegar

Soak together overnight in a preserving pan.

250 g soft brown sugar
2 large onions, peeled and minced
2 x 15 ml spoons each of ground ginger and coriander
1 x 15 ml spoon salt
1 x 15 ml spoon mustard seeds
2 dried red chilli peppers, crumbled

Add to the pan, mix well, then bring slowly to the boil, stirring continuously with a wooden spoon. Simmer until the mixture is thick, about 2 hours.

Spoon into sterilised jars and seal immediately. Leave to cool, then store in a cool and dry place. Leave for about a month before eating.

PICKLED LEMONS OR LIMES
These add an extraordinary tang to meat, poultry or fish dishes in Algeria, as well as in Morocco and other North African countries. Only the peel is used.

ALGERIA

organic thin-skinned lemons or limes	Scrub the fruit well, then cut through from one end in a cross, as if to quarter them. Do not cut the whole way through, but leave the pieces attached.
coarse salt	Sprinkle generously inside each fruit, and then close up to a lemon shape again. Press into sterilised kilner or other preserving jars, and sprinkle with some more salt.
boiling water acidulated with lemon juice	Fill the jar(s) to the brim, and then seal tightly. Store in a dry place for about 3 weeks. To cook, discard the pulp, using the peel only. In Morocco, the pickling liquid is often used in salads instead of vinegar.

CRANBERRY AND ORANGE COMPOTE
Cranberries, blueberries and huckleberries are the American relations of the European bilberry (also known as blaeberry, whinberry and whortleberry) and the Scandinavian lingonberry. They are all northern hemisphere plants, sour-sweet to taste, and any one of them – except perhaps the sweeter cultivated blueberry – could substitute for the cranberry. This compote adds tang to any poultry or game bird dish, or indeed a Christmas or Thanksgiving turkey, or venison.

USA   **SERVES 10 AS A GARNISH**

3 oranges, zested then segmented	Blanch the zest in boiling water, then put to one side. Put the segments to one side as well.
120 g caster sugar	Place in a pan, and gently heat to caramelise – to melt and start to turn golden brown.
200 ml orange juice	Immediately add to the sugar pan, and stir to deglaze.
250 g fresh cranberries (or frozen)	Add to the sugar and juice along with the blanched orange zest, and cook gently for 10 minutes.
a pinch each of powdered cinnamon and cloves	Add and mix in to taste. Add the orange segments, and heat through just before serving. Serve hot (or cold), and store in the fridge.

BANANA CHUTNEY
A chutney inspired by the British tradition, but using the local bananas. Serve with plain fish or fishcakes.

BERMUDA

SERVES 4

450 g onions, peeled and chopped
8 bananas, peeled and sliced
225 g fresh dates, stoned and chopped
350 ml white wine vinegar

Place in a non-stick saucepan and bring to the boil, stirring. Reduce the heat, cover the pan, and simmer gently for 20 minutes.

2 x 5 ml spoons grated fresh root ginger
120 g raisins
1 x 5 ml spoon each of salt and curry powder
150 g brown sugar
450 ml water

Add to the pan, mix, then boil together, uncovered, until the mixture thickens. Cool, then pour into jars, and seal. Keep for a week or so before using.

FRESH GREEN CHUTNEYS
Green chutneys are very popular in India, and are eaten with almost every meal: they are good with fried foods, grilled fish or chicken, and as a dip for pakoras or bhajias. They must be eaten immediately they are made, however, as it is their freshness that is important and they will discolour. With each type, blend all the ingredients together to a very fine and smooth paste in a food processor.

INDIA

CORIANDER (AND MINT) WITH LEMON
2 x 300 ml cups packed with fresh coriander leaves (or half mint)
½–1 fresh green chilli pepper, seeded
4 x 15 ml spoons lemon juice
½ x 5 ml spoon salt

CORIANDER (AND MINT) WITH YOGHURT
1 x 300 ml cup packed with fresh coriander leaves (or half mint)
½–1 fresh green chilli pepper, seeded
1 garlic clove, peeled
4 x 15 ml spoons natural yoghurt
½ x 5 ml spoon salt

CORIANDER WITH COCONUT
1 x 300 ml cup packed with fresh coriander leaves
½–1 fresh green chilli pepper, seeded
2 x 15 ml spoons desiccated coconut (or fresh or creamed)
4 x 15 ml spoons lemon juice
½ x 5 ml spoon salt

PAPAYA JAM
Papaya (or pawpaws) and mangoes are *the* fruit of the Caribbean islands, and there unripe fruit are usually made into chutneys. This jam, using ripe fruit, is full of flavour and is very easy to make.

CARIBBEAN

MAKES ABOUT 1 kg

1 kg ripe papayas

Cut in half and remove the seeds. Spoon the soft ripe flesh out of the skins, and pass through a sieve or food mill.

juice of 6 limes

Mix into the pulp.

pectin-enriched sugar

Weigh the papaya pulp and mix in the same amount of sugar.
Place in a heavy-based saucepan and heat very gently to dissolve the sugar. Simmer for 10 minutes, then test for setting. Put 1 x 5 ml spoon of the hot mixture on to a chilled saucer and allow to cool (in the freezer, for speed, if you like). If, when cool, the mixture crinkles when pushed with a finger, then the jam is ready. If it is still runny, continue to boil.

40 ml dark rum

If the jam is ready, remove any scum using a metal spoon. Season the jam with the rum, stirring it in well. Pour into clear jars whilst hot. Seal firmly and store in a cool dark place.

ROUILLE This is a spicy version of mayonnaise, traditionally served with fish soups such as Bouillabaisse (see page 212) and other French *soupes de poissons*.

FRANCE   **MAKES ABOUT 50 ml**

1 fresh red chilli pepper, seeded   Finely chop and then place in a mortar.
2 garlic cloves, peeled

a pinch of salt   Add to the mortar, and pound together with the pestle until smooth.
1 egg yolk

150 ml olive oil   Blend in gradually, drop by drop at first, as for mayonnaise.

Tomates Concassées   If the *rouille* – which means 'rust' – is not red enough, add a little home-
** (see page 312, optional)**   made tomato paste.

TOMATO SAUCE A classic tomato sauce recipe which is useful in many ways – for topping pizzas, for saucing pasta and for accompanying many dishes.

ITALY   **SERVES 4**

2 x 15 ml spoons olive oil   Heat together in a large saucepan, and cook gently until the onion is soft.
1 small onion, peeled and finely chopped
2 garlic cloves, peeled and crushed

1 kg ripe red tomatoes, skinned,   Add, seasoning to taste with salt, pepper and sugar. Stir to mix in the
** seeded and chopped**   seasoning, then bring to a simmer. Purée in a blender, then push through a
1 x 15 ml spoon Tomates Concassées   food mill. Return to a clean pan and cook uncovered, stirring from time to
** (see page 312)**   time, until most of the liquid has evaporated, about 20 minutes.
4 basil leaves
1 x 5 ml spoon finely chopped fresh
** oregano**
salt and freshly ground pepper
caster sugar

TOMATES CONCASSEES
This tomato paste or purée is useful in many recipes, much more flavourful than commercial purées or pastes. It can be sieved to make a pulp, or left rough.

FRANCE

SERVES 4

1 kg ripe flavourful tomatoes

Remove stalks then blanch in boiling water for approximately 12 seconds. Remove from the water, slip skins off, and cut in half. Discard the seeds, and cut flesh into small dice.

1 shallot, peeled and finely chopped
2 whole garlic cloves, peeled
2 x 5 ml spoons olive oil

Heat together in a large pan and sweat until the shallot is tender. Do not colour.

1 x 5 ml spoon each of finely chopped
    fresh oregano and thyme
salt and freshly ground pepper

Add to the shallot along with the tomato dice, seasoning to taste with salt and pepper. Cover and simmer very, very carefully for about 15 minutes, or until the mixture is soft and paste-like, and all the liquid has evaporated. Remove and discard the garlic cloves, and season again if necessary. Pass through a sieve for a smoother result if liked. Store in the fridge.

SALSA VERDE 1
This sharp sauce/relish is served with Bollito Misto (see page 148). It is also good with fish, when lemon juice is used instead of the red wine vinegar.

ITALY

SERVES 8

4 x 15 ml spoons roughly chopped
    parsley
4 x 15 ml spoons drained capers
1 garlic clove, peeled
8 anchovy fillets
1 x 15 ml spoon red wine vinegar
salt and freshly ground pepper

Place in a blender and blend to a purée, seasoning to taste with salt and pepper. Remove to a bowl.

150 ml olive oil

Dribble in the oil, mixing well as if making a mayonnaise. Check flavour and add more seasoning or vinegar (or lemon juice) to taste. Store in the fridge.

SALSA VERDE 2
This is a classic example of the fresh sauces prepared in Mexico, and this or its counterpart, *salsa cruda*, appear at virtually every meal as a topping for tortillas or as a relish. The Mexican green tomato with which the sauce should be made is not a green unripe tomato, but a close relative of the physalis, or Cape gooseberry (which originated in Peru). They are available in cans, as *tomate verde* or *tomatillo*. You can use ordinary tomatoes but then the sauce is no longer *verde*, green!

MEXICO

SERVES 4

300 g Mexican green tomatoes,
    drained
75 g onions, peeled and diced
2 or more fresh green chilli peppers,
    seeded if liked
3 x 15 ml spoons fresh coriander
    leaves
1 garlic clove, peeled

Place in a blender and purée until smooth. Or use a mortar and pestle, which is more traditional.

salt

Season the sauce to taste, then serve it at room temperature.

WILD MUSHROOM SAUCE
This sauce is delicious with a number of dishes, but particularly as the flavouring of a risotto (see page 97). The intense flavours are due to the mushrooms themselves, but also to the reductions of the alcohol and stock.

ITALY **SERVES 4**

10 g butter 1 medium shallot, peeled and diced	Heat together in a frying pan and sweat for about 15 minutes until the shallot is transparent.
350 g mixed wild mushrooms, trimmed and finely sliced	Add to the shallot and cook gently until soft.
1 x 5 ml spoon plain flour	Dust over the mushrooms and stir in.
50 ml Madeira	Add to the pan and boil to reduce almost completely.
150 ml Brown Veal Stock (see page 316)	Add to the pan and boil to reduce almost completely.
100 ml double cream	Add to the pan, stir in, and simmer to reduce by half.
½ x 15 ml spoon lemon juice salt and freshly ground pepper	Stir in, and season to taste with salt and pepper.

PEANUT SATAY SAUCE
Similar sauces to this one, using locally grown peanuts, are common throughout South-East Asia. In Malaysia and Singapore, it is based on spiced coconut milk with ground peanuts; in Indonesia a sweeter sauce, made with *kecap manis*, a sweet soy sauce, is more popular.

SINGAPORE **SERVES 4**

60 ml corn oil 2 garlic cloves, peeled and crushed 1 small onion, peeled and finely chopped ½–1 x 5 ml spoon ground red chilli pepper ½ x 5 ml curry powder 1 x 15 ml spoon finely chopped lemongrass	Place together in a medium pan and cook gently for 2–3 minutes.
250 ml coconut milk 150 ml milk or water 1 x 4 cm cinnamon stick 2 bay leaves 2 x 5 ml spoons tamarind paste 1–3 x 15 ml spoons *nam pla* (fish sauce) (to taste) 3 x 15 ml spoons dark brown sugar 3 x 15 ml spoons lemon juice 250 g chunky peanut butter	Add to the pan and stir well together. Bring to the boil, then reduce the heat to a simmer. Cook slowly, stirring frequently, until the sauce thickens, about 30 minutes. Take care that the sauce does not stick to the bottom of the pan and burn. Remove whole spices and herbs, and serve hot with Singapore Satay (see page 196).

WHITE WINE SAUCE

This white wine sauce accompanies plainly cooked fish and chicken dishes well, but you must always use the appropriate stock. The sauce can also act as a 'binder' for the fishcakes on page 225, and as the base for the parsley sauce to accompany those same fishcakes: simply mix in 2–3 x 15 ml spoons finely chopped parsley. Liquidise with a stick blender to make it smooth.

ENGLAND   **SERVES 4**

400 ml stock (Fish, Chicken or Vegetable, as appropriate)
100 ml dry white wine
50 ml Noilly Prat
1 small shallot, peeled and finely diced

Combine in a shallow saucepan and reduce by half by fast boiling.

150 ml double cream

Add, and simmer gently to reduce the sauce to a coating consistency. Remove the pan from the heat. Strain the sauce through a fine sieve or muslin, and reheat gently.

salt and freshly ground pepper

Season to taste and serve.

VANILLA SAUCE

Custards are vital in the dessert cookery of many countries, but particularly those of France and Britain, forming the basis of mousses, ice creams, *crème caramel*, *crème brûlée* or burnt cream, and that most British of puddings, bread and butter pudding.

GREAT BRITAIN   **SERVES 4**

300 ml milk
1 vanilla pod, split

Heat gently together in a pan.

3 egg yolks
2 x 15 ml spoons caster sugar

Whisk together in a medium bowl until light, then pour in the hot milk, stirring continuously. Place into a double boiler or a basin over a pan of simmering water and cook until the mixture thickens enough to coat the back of a wooden spoon. Cool slightly.

150 ml thick natural yoghurt (or double cream)

Stir into the custard, then strain. Serve warm, or leave to go cold.

VEGETABLE STOCK

This stock is usually used for soups, sauces and vegetarian dishes.

MAKES 1 LITRE

40 g each of onions, leeks, tomatoes and cabbage
20 g each of celery and fennel

Wash and trim and peel as appropriate, then chop finely, keeping the vegetables separate.

30 g butter

Heat in a stockpot and sweat the onion and leek for 4–5 minutes. Add the remaining vegetables and sweat for a further 10 minutes.

1.5 litres water
1 bay leaf
½ clove

Add to the stockpot, bring to the boil, then reduce the heat and simmer, uncovered, for 20 minutes. Strain the stock through a cloth or fine sieve, allowing the liquid to drip slowly.

salt and freshly ground pepper

Season to taste.

FISH STOCK
To produce the best fish stock, use the bones of good fresh white fish such as sole or turbot, or plaice or halibut.

MAKES 1 LITRE

1 kg white fish bones and trimmings	Break up into small pieces, and then thoroughly wash.

20 g butter
50 g white vegetable dice
    (onion, celery and white of leek)
30 g mushrooms, chopped,
    or mushroom trimmings
	Heat the butter gently in a stockpot, then sweat the vegetable dice and mushroom for about 2 minutes.

200 ml dry white wine 1.25 litres water a few white peppercorns, crushed a few sprigs of dill, basil, fennel or parsley	Add to the pan, along with the fish bones and trimmings, and bring to the boil. Reduce the heat and simmer, uncovered, for about 20 minutes, occasionally skimming and removing the fat. Strain through a cloth or fine sieve, allowing the liquid to drip slowly.
salt and freshly ground pepper	Season to taste.

WHITE CHICKEN OR VEAL STOCK
Use a boiling fowl or raw chicken (or turkey) pieces, or veal bones, chopped into little pieces by your butcher. This is a lighter stock then the brown one described overleaf, but it can be reduced to intensify the flavours.

MAKES 1 LITRE

1 kg raw poultry pieces or a boiling fowl, or veal bones, finely chopped	Blanch the poultry or boiling fowl first in boiling water, then drain. Place the poultry or fowl or the veal bones in a stock pot.

2 litres cold water
50 g white bouquet garni (onion, white
    of leek, celery or celeriac, and
    herbs tied together)
	Add, and bring to the boil, then reduce the temperature. Simmer carefully, uncovered, for 2 hours, occasionally skimming and removing the fat.
	    Strain through a cloth or fine sieve, allowing the liquid to drip slowly.

salt and freshly ground pepper	Season to taste.

BROWN CHICKEN, VEAL OR GAME STOCK

This stock is more intense in taste than white stock. Use raw chicken (or turkey) pieces, or veal bones and trimmings (or raw game pieces), finely chopped by your butcher. If you like, you can add 300 ml wine to the first water or stock quantity (dry white for the veal, red for the game stock), and you could add 4–5 juniper berries to the game stock.

MAKES 1 LITRE   **OVEN: 180°C/350°F/GAS 4**

1 kg raw poultry or veal (or game) bones, cut in small pieces

Place in a roasting tray and brown in the oven on all sides for about 30–40 minutes. Strain off the fat.

50 g vegetable dice (onion, carrot, celeriac or celery and herbs)
100 g tomatoes, diced

Add to the roasting tray and continue to roast carefully for a further 4–5 minutes. Remove the tin from the oven and transfer its contents to a stockpot.

2.5 litres water (or appropriate white stock)

Add 500 ml to the stockpot, bring to the boil, then boil to reduce to a glaze Add the same amount of water again and reduce to a glaze. Add the remaining water and simmer carefully, uncovered, for 2 hours, occasionally skimming and removing the fat.
  Strain through a cloth or fine sieve, allowing the liquid to drip slowly.

salt and freshly ground pepper

Season to taste.

BEEF, LAMB OR VENISON STOCK

Use beef, lamb or venison bones to make the individual stocks. This makes a brown, well flavoured stock. If you want a lighter clearer stock, do not roast the bones first. Simply blanch them very briefly, then drain and bring to the boil in the measured water with a bouquet garni instead of the vegetables.

MAKES 1 LITRE   **OVEN: 240°C/475°F/GAS 9**

1 kg raw beef (lamb or venison) bones, chopped into small pieces

Place in a roasting tray, and brown on all sides for about 20 minutes. Drain of all fat and place the bones in a stockpot.

50 g vegetable dice, (onion, carrot, celeriac or celery, leek)

Add to the roasting tray and roast carefully for a further 4–5 minutes.

2 litres cold water

Use a little to deglaze the roasting tin, then add all the water to the stock pot. Bring to the boil and skim. Allow to simmer for about 2 hours, uncovered, occasionally skimming and removing the fat.
  Strain through a cloth or fine sieve, allowing the liquid to drip slowly.

salt and freshly ground pepper

Season to taste.

Picture acknowledgments
The Anthony Blake Photo Library: Anthony Blake pp10, 14, 15, 18, 24, 38, 136, 208, 252, 276; Heather Brown p26; Gerrit Buntrock p21; Bill Double p35; John Heseltine p40; John Sims pp11, 12; Nigel Lea-Jones p17; Guy Moberly pp25, 27, 30, 304 *Cephas*: Nigel Blythe pp2, 32, 34, 76, 104; Kate Couch p182; Sand Hambrook p29; John Heinrich p122; Pierre Hussenot p19; Mick Rock pp9, 23, 31 Nic Barlow p6; Anton Mosimann: pp3, 6, 7